A Modern Approach to Artificial Intelligence

A Modern Approach to Artificial Intelligence

Edited by **Akira Hanako**

CLANRYE
INTERNATIONAL

New Jersey

Published by Clanrye International,
55 Van Reypen Street,
Jersey City, NJ 07306, USA
www.clanryeinternational.com

A Modern Approach to Artificial Intelligence
Edited by Akira Hanako

International Standard Book Number: 978-1-63240-008-6 (Hardback)

Contents

Preface

In a world where there are technological marvels on a daily basis, the idea of Artificial Intelligence or AI is not that farfetched. Artificial Intelligence is a term that means exactly what it spells out, referring to human-like intelligence exhibited by machines or software. Machines are fast integrating themselves into our lives and often in indispensable ways. Something that shows such propensity for human-like thinking is capable of helping and enhancing our lives in a plethora of ways but one also faces the questions of human identity once machines begin to have intelligence equal to ours. Detractors will argue that once machines are given capabilities that might surpass those of humans, what it would do to the sense of identity possessed by him. Furthermore, philosophical questions aside, there would be economic, social and cultural ramifications as well. While true AI is still not a reality, with many machines still confined to routine tasks or game playing level intelligence, it has started expanding into various fields like robotics, human language recognition and expert systems. There are many industries, most notably the factory line companies which make extensive use of machines with the most rudimentary of AI. On the other hand there are many toys and even phone operating systems that endeavor to achieve a certain AI, though it still only in the lowest of levels.

An effort has been made in this book to explain the various fields that constitute that of AI and form a tentatively cohesive argument about it. I would like to thank all those whose researches have contributed to the production of this book.

Editor

Study on the Effectiveness of the Investment Strategy Based on a Classifier with Rules Adapted by Machine Learning

A. Wiliński, A. Bera, W. Nowicki, and P. Błaszyński

West Pomeranian University of Technology, Żołnierska 49, 71-210 Szczecin, Poland

Correspondence should be addressed to P. Błaszyński; pblaszynski@wi.zut.edu.pl

Academic Editors: J. Bajo and K. W. Chau

This paper examines two transactional strategies based on the classifier which opens positions using some rules and closes them using different rules. A rule set contains time-varying parameters that when matched allow making an investment decision. Researches contain the study of variability of these parameters and the relationship between learning period and testing (using the learned parameters). The strategies are evaluated based on the time series of cumulative profit achieved in the test periods. The study was conducted on the most popular currency pair EURUSD (Euro-Dollar) sampled with interval of 1 hour. An important contribution to the theory of algotrading resulting from presented research is specification of the parameter space (quite large, consisting of 11 parameters) that achieves very good results using cross validation.

1. Introduction

The aim of this work is to verify the hypothesis of patterns extraction possibility from time series, which could be classified as providing better statistic and more accurate prognosis. Another important objective is confirmation of assumption that financial markets time series have a "memory" of pattern efficiency in a time period following the time series that was used in learning period. This approach is consistent with the classic aim of machine learning shown by Murphy [1], especially to financial markets described by Satchwell [2]. Research intention was also to follow reproducibility principle of other researchers' studies, as well as by themselves, in other data environments, to make sense of the use of computational intelligence in its reasonable reproducibility [3, 4], in extracting of the regularity from chaos [5, 6].

An investment strategy with a relatively high complexity (measured by the number of factors included in the model) was built, derived from a strategies group called strategy of simple rules. In the literature those strategies are considered to be mainly strategies based on moving averages—their intersections and derivatives shown, for example, by Brock et al. [7], Cai et al. [8], and many other authors [9–11]. Of course, the world of algorithms as well as prediction methods using a completely different nature, such as regression [12], multiple regression [13, 14], Fourier and wavelet transforms, and many others [15, 16] is plenteous. These methods are used as a basis for comparison; however the main focus is on mentioned simple rules.

This paper proposes strategy, which differs by suggesting different behaviors than the ones proposed when using Bollinger's Band, which has its foundation in a band built in an unusual way. According to the strategy based on that band, generally it can be assumed that the trend is horizontal and it is recommended to open position to the center of the band, after its cross by the price from the inside. In proposed strategies, another band that is based on maxima of the maxima and minima of the minima of last several candles is used.

Considered strategies move away from the principle of opening positions to the center of the band. In one modification, hereinafter referred to as substrategy, position opens into the center of the band, whereas in another one, position opens on the outside. By treating the two considered substrategies as an entirety and as strategies that are mutually retrieving (although a more appropriate word would be complementary) it is assumed that, in the selected trading section, opening positions in opposite directions, of course

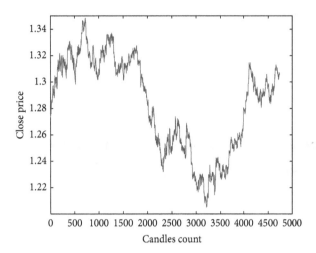

FIGURE 1: Time series EURUSD 1 h.

not at the same time, can be done intentionally and effectively. During the trading, nature of the market (trend, volatility) may change. The market may be in some periods horizontal, in other trended. It is appropriate to seek all opportunities for profit. A similar philosophy is applied by several Krutsinger correspondents [17], who belong to most prominent traders in USA, who advocate unfounded reversal of the direction of opening the positions in case of series of failures.

Returning to the issue of complexity of strategy, there are often opinions that the growing complexity of the prediction model is not indicated, because in learning section it leads to overfitting [1, 8, 14]. This results in a greater error in the test sections. The problem of selecting the proper ratio between learning and testing phase is still unsolved for the nonstationary time series [5, 18]. In this situation the right approach seems to be the use of the idea of computational intelligence [3, 6] which helps to compute adequate length of learning and testing period.

Therefore in this paper two rather complex strategies (described below) are used, achieving results that are assessed as rewarding. Attention is drawn to the fact that the satisfaction problem belongs to the other sciences and depends on the trader's individual perception of the relationship between profit and risk, greed and fear [19]. However, the issue of emotions in the trade is not considered here, but only noticed because there is the assumption that trading is done automatically.

The tests were deliberately performed in a fragment of the time series of a heavily diversified course, which contains both rising and downward trends as well as horizontal elements (Figure 1). This time series consists of 4734 1-hour candles, of the most important and the most fluent currency pair EURUSD from October 22, 2012.

A choice of parameters essential for defining the rules of opening and closing positions is crucial to the effectiveness of the strategy. Parametric space presented in this paper is a result of many trials prior to its final approval.

2. Characteristics of Investment Strategies

The objective of the two strategies considered is to make investment decisions about buying or selling—opening long or short position in the market studied—the currency pair EURUSD. The decision is based on the intersection of the current price and one of two barriers of additional indicator, called the ribbon. The band is made of two values calculated at the opening of each candle on the basis of historical data of the market. During the candle, values of the band do not change; therefore, barriers are creating step functions. In case when the current price exceeds any of the barrier values (goes out of the band), a decision to buy or sell is made—the type of decision depends on the variant of the considered strategy—decision for substrategy TewiMiC is different than in case of TewiMiD. Names of the strategies are derived from the name of the project, in which the research was carried out.

2.1. Definition of the Band. The values of barriers forming a band are calculated using the maximum and minimum values of the last candle (OHLC: Open, High, Low, Close prices). In the case of the upper band, it is the maximum of the maximal values of the n last candles, whereas in the case of the bottom band, it is the minimum of the minimal values of m last candles:

$$\text{topBorder} = \max\left(H_{i-n}, \ldots, H_{i-1}\right),$$
$$\text{bottomBorder} = \min\left(L_{i-m}, \ldots, L_{i-1}\right). \tag{1}$$

As mentioned earlier, strategy comes in two versions that differ in terms of opening the positions when crossing the band. These differences result from different investor assumption about currently prevailing market trend. In the first case it is believed that the trend has just started and positions need to be opened in accordance with it. In the second case, the play is against the trend. The two considered variants, TewiMiC and TewiMiD, are based on excesses of the lower limit of the band. TewiMiD implies existence of a downward trend, for which when crossing (down) the lower limit of the band, a short position (assuming the price drop) is opened. This is known in the literature and in trading as Sell Stop model.

TewiMiC assumes the opposite case; therefore it is needed to open a long position (assuming the price increase). This is Buy Limit model.

2.2. Strategy Parameters. Considered strategies are based on a objects classification (events that meet the conditions contained in the set of rules which depend on the value of certain parameters). Object—the event—is another candle. Rules are logical sentences like "if the price is greater than the upper barrier of the band" and the parameter is, for example, the upper barrier, which is a variable value.

These parameters will determine whether the strategy will earn or lose. Appropriate selection of parameter values is therefore a key optimization issue in the use of the strategy. Considered strategies have 11 parameters, which are subject of optimization.

$p1$ is the number of candles, based on which the calculation of the current value of the band barrier is made; for researched time series, value of $p1$ generally ranges from 10 to 30;

$p2$ is the number of steps forward, after which the position is closed in case when none other close conditions were met before; this value belongs to range from 3 to 40;

$p3$ is StopLoss condition; usually it remained in range from 0.002 to 0.017 expressed in values of EURUSD, which in researched period stayed in range from 1.2 to 1.4, as can be seen in Figure 1;

$p4$ is TakeProfit condition, generally ranged from 0.0015 to 0.009;

$p5$ is band buffer, offset from the barrier of the band defining the actual level of the expected crossing of the price, ranged from −0.002 to 0.003;

$p6$ is maximum number of open positions at the same time, ranged from 3 to 20;

$p7$ is the number of candles that determines average volume value; generally ranged from 2 to 10;

$p8$ is maximum value of the difference between the current value of the volume and the average value calculated on the basis of $p7$ candles back, ranged from 150 to 500;

$p9$ is the number of candles on the cumulative profit curve, based on which current drawdown is calculated, ranged from 5 to 25;

$p10$ is the highest acceptable drawdown on the cumulative yield curve; generally ranged from 0.0021 to 0.008;

$p11$ is acceptable amount of the cumulative loss for all currently open positions, ranged from 0.0005 to 0.003.

2.3. Conditions of Opening.

As mentioned before, the signal to open the position is the intersection of the current price of the observed value and some barrier (that results from the calculated band). Special parameter called the buffer ($p5$) has been added, causing the offset of barrier from its actual value. Thus, the condition for opening TewiMIC strategy is

$$if \left[(price < bottomBorder(p1) - buffor(p5)), \right.$$

$$\left. (current\ p6 < p6), (Vol - meanVol(p7) < p8) \right] \quad (2)$$

then open position long,

where price is current value for EURUSD, bottomBorder ($p1$) is value of lower band barrier for parameter $p1$, here minimum of last $p1$ minima, buffor ($p5$) is value of buffer that moves said barrier, current $p6$ is number of currently opened positions, Vol is current value of volume (in the candle),

meanVol ($p7$) is mean of volume of last $p7$ candles, and the opening condition for TewiMiD is as follows:

$$if \left[(price < bottomBorder(p1) - buffor(p5)), \right.$$

$$\left. (current\ p6 < p6), (Vol - meanVol(p7) > p8) \right] \quad (3)$$

then open position short.

As a result of these conditions, long positions, in substrategy TewiMIC, are opened when three conditions are met simultaneously: crossing the bottom barrier reduced by buffer by the current price, the number of open positions is less than the limit (which is the optimized parameter $p6$), and the difference between the current volume and the average of the volume of the last $p7$ candle is less than the parameter $p8$.

For TewiMiD strategy, analogously, with significant differences, short positions will be opened and it is advisable that current volume should be greater than the average. As the result of conducted research, authors concluded that volume (number of price changes in observed time frame—here during one hour) was the most important and most sensitive factor of decision model.

These conditions can be met in two cases during the period of the current considered candle. They can be met immediately at the opening of the candle; that is, the opening value of the current candle is smaller than the barrier bottomBorder reduced by parameter $p5$. That condition can be met within the candle, when the current value of the price breaks through the lower barrier.

The result of that is that we have two distinctly different opening conditions.

2.4. Conditions of Closing.

In both substrategies there are 7 cases of closing the open positions, which results in their complexity—both in terms of logic and calculation. This complexity, however, exhausts all the possible surprises and does not leave any opportunity for the unexpected market behavior. Of course, depending on the values of the parameters, frequency occurrences of closure cases can be very different.

Firstly the terms for closing the long positions that were opened by conditions for TewiMiC will be presented.

(1) Opened long position will be closed, if at the close of the candle ($i + p2$) the position remained open, where i is number of candle, which was opened.

(2) Position will be closed if at the opening of the next ($i + k$)th, the candle after ith candle, in which the position was opened, the following condition is met:

$$Price\ O(i + k) - Price(i) < -SL, \quad (4)$$

where Price $O(i + k)$ is the opening value for ($i + k$)th candle and SL is StopLoss (level of acceptable risk in one trade) in pips.

Then the profit (in this case loss) will be calculated as

$$Profit = Price\ O(i + k) - Price(i). \quad (5)$$

(3) Position will be closed if inside the next $(i + k)$th, the candle after ith candle, in which the position was opened, the following condition is met:

$$(\text{Price } O\,(i + k) - \text{Price}\,(i)) > -\text{SL},$$
$$(\text{LowPrice}\,(i + k) - \text{Price}\,(i)) < -\text{SL}. \tag{6}$$

Then the profit (in this case loss) will be calculated as

$$\text{Profit} = -\text{SL}, \tag{7}$$

where $\text{LowPrice}(i + k)$ is a minimum value of $(i + k)$th candle.

(4) Position will be closed if at the opening of the next $(i + k)$th, the candle after ith candle, in which the position was opened, the following condition is met:

$$\text{Price } O\,(i + k) - \text{Price}\,(i) > \text{TP}, \tag{8}$$

where TP is TakeProfit (maximum reward level in single trade) in pips.

Then the profit will be calculated as

$$\text{Profit} = \text{Price } O\,(i + k) - \text{Price}\,(i). \tag{9}$$

(5) Position will be closed if inside the next $(i + k)$th, the candle after ith candle, in which the position was opened, the following condition is met:

$$(\text{Price } O\,(i + k) - \text{Price}\,(i)) < \text{TP},$$
$$(\text{HighPrice}\,(i + k) - \text{Price}\,(i)) > \text{TP}. \tag{10}$$

Then the profit will be calculated as

$$\text{Profit} = \text{TP}, \tag{11}$$

where $\text{HighPrice}\,(i + k)$ is the maximum value for $(i + k)$ candle.

(6) Position will be closed if at the opening of the next $(i + k)$th, the candle after ith candle, in which the position was opened, the following condition is met:

$$\text{Price } O\,(i + k) > \text{topBorder}\,(i + k). \tag{12}$$

Then the profit will be calculated as

$$\text{Profit} = \text{Price } O\,(i + k) - \text{Price}\,(i). \tag{13}$$

(7) Position will be closed if inside the next $(i + k)$th— the candle after ith candle, in which the position was opened, following condition is met:

$$\text{Price}\,(i + k) > \text{topBorder}\,(i + k). \tag{14}$$

Then the profit will be calculated as

$$\text{Profit} = \text{topBorder}\,(i + k) - \text{Price}\,(i). \tag{15}$$

In substrategy TewiMiD conditions will look slightly different.

(1) Opened short position will be closed if at the close of the candle $(i + p2)$th the position remained open.

(2) Position will be closed if at the opening of the next $(i + k)$th, the candle after ith candle, in which the position was opened, the following condition is met:

$$\text{Price}\,(i) - \text{Price } O\,(i + k) < -\text{SL}. \tag{16}$$

Then the profit (in this case loss) will be calculated as

$$\text{Profit} = -\text{Price } O\,(i + k) + \text{Price}\,(i). \tag{17}$$

(3) Position will be closed if inside the next $(i + k)$th, the candle after ith candle, in which the position was opened, the following condition is met:

$$(-\text{Price } O\,(i + k) + \text{price}\,(i)) > -\text{SL},$$
$$(-\text{HighPrice}\,(i + k) + \text{Price}\,(i)) < -\text{SL}. \tag{18}$$

Then the profit (in this case loss) will be calculated as

$$\text{Profit} = -\text{SL}. \tag{19}$$

(4) Position will be closed if at the opening of the next $(i + k)$th, the candle after ith candle, in which the position was opened, the following condition is met:

$$\text{Price}\,(i) - \text{Price } O\,(i + k) > \text{TP}. \tag{20}$$

Then the profit will be calculated as

$$\text{Profit} = -\text{Price } O\,(i + k) + \text{Price}\,(i). \tag{21}$$

(5) Position will be closed if inside the next $(i + k)$th, the candle after ith candle, in which the position was opened, the following condition is met:

$$(-\text{Price } O\,(i + k) + \text{Price}\,(i)) < \text{TP},$$
$$(-\text{LowPrice}\,(i + k) + \text{Price}\,(i)) > \text{TP}. \tag{22}$$

Then the profit will be calculated as

$$\text{Profit} = \text{TP}. \tag{23}$$

(6) Position will be closed if at the opening of the next $(i + k)$th, the candle after ith candle, in which the position was opened, the following condition is met:

$$\text{Price } O\,(i + k) > \text{bottomBorder}\,(i + k). \tag{24}$$

Then the profit will be calculated as

$$\text{Profit} = -\text{Price } O\,(i + k) + \text{Price}\,(i). \tag{25}$$

(7) Position will be closed when inside the opening of the next $(i + k)$th, the candle after ith candle, in which the position was opened, the following condition is met:

$$\text{Price} (i + k) > \text{bottomBorder} (i + k). \quad (26)$$

Then the profit (in this case loss) will be calculated as

$$\text{Profit} = -\text{bottomBorder} (i + k) + \text{Price} (i). \quad (27)$$

Additional conditions that are checked with each closing are the rules containing parameters $p9$, $p10$, and $p11$. These parameters are found in the rules limiting the risk of an unacceptable failure. Moreover, the principle stating that in the case when the opening took place at the beginning of the candle, it is permissible to keep it open until following candle is opened was used. Because of that, it was possible to avoid ambiguity involving the unpredictable sequence of the SL and TP.

3. Strategy Analysis

In both strategies a fixed period of learning is assumed (in the presented solution, 1000 one-hour candles), followed by a testing period. Data from learning period were used to find a class of patterns which allowed achieving maximum for the selected criterion, in this study Calmar ratio (which is defined as a final profit to maximum drawdown ratio) was selected. The same patterns were then searched during the test period and the test results were computed for previously unused data space. Of course, these results do not have to already be positive and acceptable and could negatively surprise investors. During the test the maximum rate of net profit (with transaction costs) was considered as a measure of the effectiveness of the investment. The authors believe that these two criteria in evaluating the quality of simulation results are legitimate. In the first phase of the validation, the training period is indicated for moderate and prudent risk management. In the test phase (in terms of actual trading) investor is mainly interested in profit.

The main aim of the research was to obtain the most effective investment strategies by dynamic selection of test period duration. Later in this paper concepts of learning period, a fixed-length 1000 candles but with different start in time, were used. Immediately after period of learning there was a variable-length test period. The authors look for the best (by the criteria described above) length of the test period in their research. This most preferred length of the learning period can be understood in two ways. This length can be changed after each learning period adjusted by additional current information feedback about profits or losses in the test period. It may also be the average length of the test window established on the basis of several recent validations.

Given that the search space is relatively broad and unknown (it is difficult to estimate how specific combination of parameters would influence strategy's effectiveness) it is necessary to define its boundaries and then to find a combination of parameters that would maximize strategy's efficiency. In the first step of the process, a pseudorandom

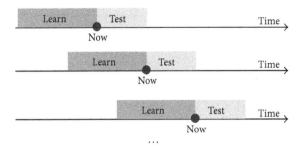

FIGURE 2: Methods of testing carried out to test the variable size window.

strategy is used to find the boundaries of the parameter space in which may exist the optimal solution. Calmar ratio value was used to assess the adequacy of randomly selected parameter combinations for a given period of learning. It would be possible to use an iterative method that would traverse the search space with certain step. However it would be extremely time consuming method given that the space is 11-dimensional. In the second stage PSO (Particle Swarm Optimization) [20] algorithm, which already has been proved useful in finding optimal strategy parameters [21] and allows to find a satisfying combination of parameters values in relatively short time even in broad search spaces, was used. Search space for PSO algorithm has been defined in previous step. The objective function was to maximizing the Calmar ratio, as it was in the first step. The above tactic was used for each stage of the learning period and then checked "sustainability" of designated sets of parameters for test periods of different lengths—the basic rate of 100 candles and the other in the range of 10–400. Figure 2 shows how the research was conducted. Having historical data for 1000 candles, optimal parameters, for said data, have been found using approach described above. After the parameters search, tests was performed on the current data. The strategy for the learned parameters should be used as long as it will bring satisfactory results on new data. When results were no longer good enough, the next parameters search were performed on next piece of historical data. Thus, the authors aim is to determine the point where those parameters should be recalculated. Additionally, the authors set out to test a new standard of quality prediction. Now, extending the period of testing can produce better results, but more slowly or with local drawdown in comparison to first period, when the classifier "remembers" the nature of the market. This new criteria is profit attributable to one candle of the testing period.

Figures 3(a) and 3(b) show the cumulative profit for the test period equal to 100 candles (hours) for the two examined strategies.

It may be noted that the two policies, for the test period of 100, allow for systematic profit in examined period with only small drawdowns. Profit for the strategy TewiMiC 0.355, for TewiMiD profit is several times smaller and amounts to 0.094. But second strategy has smaller drawdowns. In addition, it is confirmed with the higher Calmar ratio—12.79—where

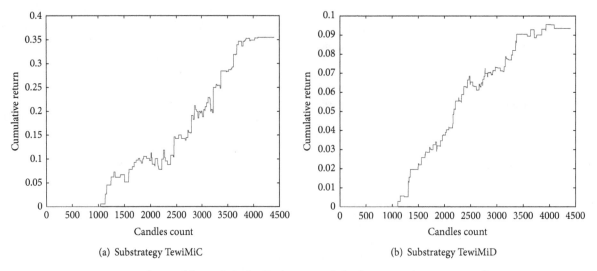

(a) Substrategy TewiMiC

(b) Substrategy TewiMiD

FIGURE 3: Charts of the profit for both strategies with fixed test period size—100 candles.

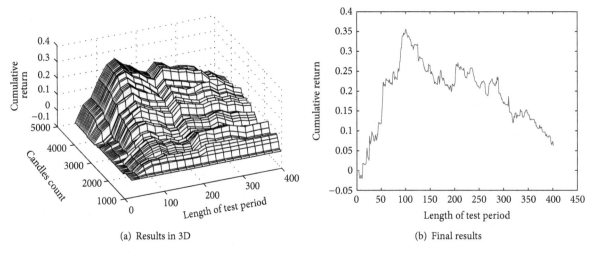

(a) Results in 3D

(b) Final results

FIGURE 4: Earnings accumulated over time, depending on the length of the test period for TewiMIC.

the result for first of these strategies is 10.22. According to the authors, results are excellent, achieved on testing sections, not on the learning periods. On learning periods, of course, significantly better results were achieved with classifier matching. It is also clear that asymmetry results for the two strategies arise from different approaches—the first one is focused on horizontal trend, the other on a downward trend. The results depend on the nature of the market, which is automatically founded by learning strategies. Perhaps at another period of time, for other data these results could be different. In addition to the basic performance of the length of the test period equal to 100, a number of studies were conducted on different lengths of the testing period. There may be more favorable length of test window than arbitrarily selected window length of 100 candles.

Results for TewiMiC. Figures 4 and 5 show the results of the strategy TewiMiC. First (Figure 4(a)) shows the effect of test duration on the profit curve in time. To show how long

in the test period optimal results are achieved we plotted 2D (twodimensional) chart of final profit for each of the examined sizes. Figure 4(b) shows that the number of candles for achieving high and satisfactory results are attributable to 80–120. The window size 100 reflects quite well expected test section.

Due to the different lengths of studied test periods, more reliable value used when making the decision is earnings per candle (that shows how much can strategy earn in one hour). This is shown in Figures 5(a) and 5(b). On this basis, Table 1, it can be concluded that the strategy is most effective for the testing period length between 60 and 110 hours. It can therefore be concluded that the average window of 100 candles well "remembers" the learned classifier parameters. Many times in the classification of patterns, it is important whether patterns are frequent. Part of the dilemma is solved by introducing earnings per candle but also in Table 1 a count of opened market positions in the testing periods is presented.

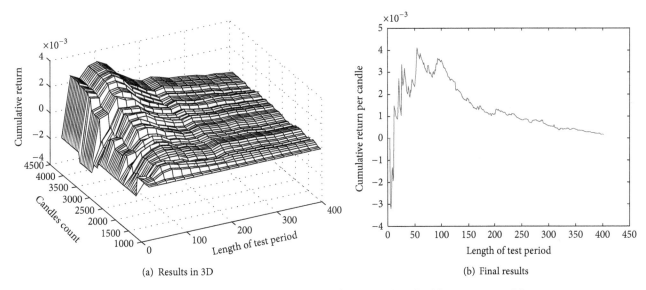

(a) Results in 3D

(b) Final results

FIGURE 5: Cumulative profit for one candle in time depending on the length of the testing period for TewiMiC.

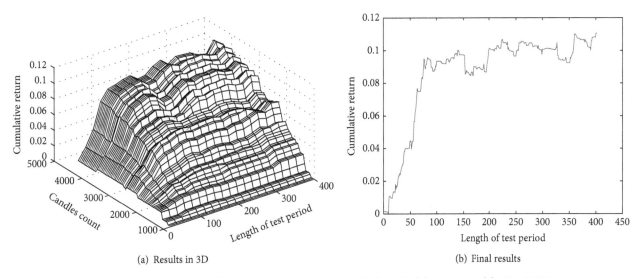

(a) Results in 3D

(b) Final results

FIGURE 6: Earnings accumulated over time, depending on the length of the test period for TewiMID.

Results for TewiMiD. Figures 6(a) and 6(b) show impact of the length of the test period on the profit curve. In case of TewiMiD strategy it is difficult to determine the optimal interval length of the testing period.

It is possible, however, due to graphs showing earnings per hour (candle) (Figures 7(a) and 7(b)), depending on the length of the period and Table 2 listing the final results of the two studies. Similarly to the first strategy, length of this period is between 60 and 90 candles.

Of course, the optimal convergence test window length, at least approximately, is a great convenience in design of automatic strategy for algotrading. It should be noted that the authors assume that it is possible to test each strategy separately and it is not required to synchronize.

4. Conclusion

Following a review of various lengths dependence validation periods shown in Figures 4(a) and 4(b) were obtained. It is fairly obvious that a good fit of the parameters of the test period will continue for some time after the end of the learning. This is due to the assumption that there are trends in the market in different direction. The nature of trends is well explored during the learning process. The authors have found that the use of optimization methods derived from the area of artificial intelligence, including the PSO [20], given good and quickly reached the optimum values of the rules of the classifier, and good results in the initial stages of the test period. Also PSO method proves its effectiveness in similar optimization problems [22, 23]. For longer test periods, it

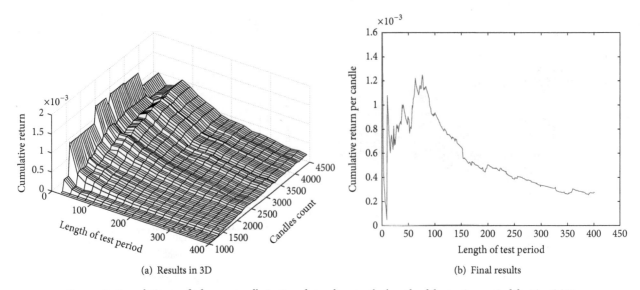

(a) Results in 3D

(b) Final results

FIGURE 7: Cumulative profit for one candle in time depending on the length of the testing period for TewiMiD.

TABLE 1: Final profits and Calmar ratio for the selected length of the test period for TewiMiC.

Size	Profit	Profit per candle	Calmar	Open positions	Percentage (%)
30	0.0812	0.0027	2.4182	93	10
40	0.0768	0.0019	1.4048	120	9.68
50	0.1176	0.0024	2.4069	134	8.65
60	0.2318	0.0039	5.3914	153	8.23
70	0.2211	0.0032	4.7859	176	8.11
80	0.2359	0.0029	5.1063	196	7.9
90	0.3005	0.0033	8.6589	221	7.92
100	0.3548	0.0035	10.221	245	7.9
110	0.3294	0.003	9.4905	262	7.68
120	0.3172	0.0026	8.6479	283	7.61
150	0.2648	0.0018	4.6295	345	7.42
200	0.2194	0.0011	2.8244	482	7.77
250	0.2091	0.0008	2.2352	574	7.41
300	0.1684	0.0006	1.5345	720	7.74
350	0.1399	0.0004	1.0402	804	7.41
400	0.073	0.0002	0.5074	914	7.37

can indeed get good results; however, the effectiveness of the strategy per hour decreases significantly. Obtained results allow concluding that the constant average length of the test window is more efficient and easier to manage than a strategy adaptively changing the length of the period. Strategies properties discovered during the learning period are effective for a short time—for test data period—good lengths for both strategies are about 50 to 120 hours at 1000 hours of learning time. In the real market it usually means from 2 to 5 days. It can be assumed that the re-learning of the parameters of the strategy should be carried out 1-2 times a week. This frequency is quite practical even for manual search of optimal parameters without fully automatic trading.

Presented trading strategies (substrategy TewiMiC and TewiMiD) are complementary, since each variant can develop a set of different parameters. Separate sets of parameters are adapted better to the nature of the market during optimization. It allows, for example, trading long positions in the markets with more frequent upward trends. It should be noted that a further optimizations discovered trends that are short-term and during one cycle of validation several changes in these trends can occur. These changes could be of different lengths. Then there is the situation that one of the variants of the strategy takes into account the length of trends for deviating significantly from trends indicated by the second variant. The two strategy variants are part of an investment strategy that allows you to combine the four options of trading strategies. You can join the strategies presented with the strategies associated with the opening of long positions based on condition (order) Buy Stop and short positions in accordance with the model Sell Limit. It is possible to add to the current strategies additional sub strategies associated

TABLE 2: Final profits and Calmar ratio for the selected length of the test period for TewiMiD.

Size	Profit	Profit per candle	Calmar	Open positions	Percentage (%)
30	0.0249	0.0008	4.2953	47	5.05
40	0.0401	0.001	8.012	60	4.84
50	0.0443	0.0009	8.868	66	4.26
60	0.0636	0.0011	13.25	83	4.46
70	0.0771	0.0011	16.0687	95	4.38
80	0.0914	0.0011	19.0396	118	4.76
90	0.0899	0.001	10.5222	130	4.66
100	0.0935	0.0009	12.7934	141	4.55
110	0.0921	0.0008	12.6559	150	4.4
120	0.0949	0.0008	13.0337	159	4.27
130	0.0955	0.0007	13.1243	178	4.42
200	0.1011	0.0005	9.464	263	4.24
250	0.0965	0.0004	9.0392	328	4.23
300	0.1008	0.0003	9.3983	410	4.41
350	0.0924	0.0003	7.2935	467	4.3
400	0.1105	0.0003	8.1655	558	4.5

with opening long positions (based on condition for Buy Stop order) and short positions (in accordance with the Sell Limit model). Interesting, according to the authors, may also be improving the combined strategies through the synthesis of recommendations. An example of such improvement may be combination of four variants, some of which (e.g., 3) indicate the need for the purchase, and some (such as 1) the need to conclude the sale of stock—then the number of transactions that were made results from accumulating all of the variants (in presented case—2 purchases). This implies a lower cost (e.g., 2 times smaller). Transaction costs for certain decisions tests can be omitted, and this reduction significantly affects the efficiency improvement investment strategy. The studies take into account the transaction costs for the pessimistic (above average costs in popular brokers). In practical terms, the strategy has big potential. With traditional software, trading programs (such as Metatrader) do not have the possibility of converting simple strategy parameters during operation. This implies the need for a hybrid solution, consisting, for example, of interprocess communication between the trading software and program developed in universal high-level language (e.g., Matlab, C#). Algotarding future will very likely be increasingly active domain for experts in algorithmization and programming and less and less for economists and econometricians.

Authors are aware of the fact that the parametric space is broad and choosing right ones is not a trivial task. It is not obvious that chosen and presented in this paper parameters are the best. There are no obvious sources that would suggest which parameters should be considered in investment strategies. To determine the parameters utilized in presented strategies an iterative computation has been used—after adding parameter the results were assessed and when they were acceptable the following parameter was added to the strategy. Even though selected parameters resulted in high efficiency, it does not mean that one should refrain from searching for better choice of parameters. Presented results can be considered as particularly good and are reproducible by scrupulous reader. Alternative strategies can be compared with presented ones using the same criteria (i.e., Calmar ratio). For many years the authors have been improving following strategy and its implementation in the real market. Current and future research aims to study the influence of the number of parameters—expanding or limiting the parameter space—and adding two additional substrategies based on the same band as aforementioned.

Conflict of Interests

The authors declare that there is no conflict of interests regarding the publication of this paper.

Acknowledgment

This work is done within the Project TEWI financed from the Innovative Economy Programme in years 2012 and 2013.

References

[1] K. P. Murphy, *Machine Learning: A Probabilistic Perspective*, Cambridge, Mass, USA, 2012.

[2] C. Satchwell, *Pattern Recognition and Trading Decisions*, Irwin Trader's Edge Series, McGraw-Hill, 2005.

[3] G. Polya, *How To Solve It*, Garden City, Egypt, 1957.

[4] D. L. Donoho, A. Maleki, M. Shahram, I. U. Rahman, and V. Stodden, "Reproducible research in computational harmonic analysis," *Computing in Science and Engineering*, vol. 11, no. 1, pp. 8–18, 2009.

[5] P. Ball, *Critical Mass: How One Thing Leads to Another*, Farrar Straus Giroux, 2006.

[6] W. Pedrycz, *Computational Intelligence: An Introduction*, Computer Engineering, Software Programming, CRC Press, 1998.

[7] W. Brock, J. Lakonishok, and B. LeBaron, "Simple technical trading rules and the stochastic properties of stock returns," *Journal of Finance*, vol. 47, no. 5, pp. 1731–1764, 1992.

[8] B. M. Cai, C. X. Cai, and K. Keasey, "Market efficiency and returns to simple technical trading rules: further evidence from U.S., U.K., Asian and Chinese stock markets," *Asia-Pacific Financial Markets*, vol. 12, no. 1, pp. 45–60, 2005.

[9] R. Gençay, "Linear, non-linear and essential foreign exchange rate prediction with simple technical trading rules," *Journal of International Economics*, vol. 47, no. 1, pp. 91–107, 1999.

[10] B. LeBaron, "Technical trading rules and regime shifts in foreign exchange," Tech. Rep., 1991.

[11] G. G. Tian, H. U. A. Guang Wan, and G. U. O. Mingyuan, "Market efficiency and the returns to simple technical trading rules: new evidence from U.S. Equity Market and Chinese Equity Markets," *Asia-Pacific Financial Markets*, vol. 9, no. 3-4, pp. 241–258, 2002.

[12] A. Muriel, "Short-term predictions in forex trading," *Physica A*, vol. 344, no. 1-2, pp. 190–193, 2004.

[13] A. Wilinski, "Prediction models of financial markets based on multiregression algorithms," *CSJ of Moldova*, vol. 19, no. 2, pp. 178–188, 2011.

[14] K. Fujimoto and S. Nakabayashi, "Applying GMDH algorithm to extract rules from examples," *Systems Analysis Modelling Simulation*, vol. 43, no. 10, pp. 1311–1319, 2003.

[15] R. Raghuraj and S. Lakshminarayanan, "Variable predictive models—a new multivariate classification approach for pattern recognition applications," *Pattern Recognition*, vol. 42, no. 1, pp. 7–16, 2009.

[16] P. Klesk and A. Wilinski, "Market trajectory recognition and trajectory prediction using Markov models," in *Artificial Intelligence and Soft Computing*, vol. 6113 of *Lecture Notes in Computer Science*, pp. 405–413, 2010.

[17] J. Krutsinger, *Trading Systems: Secrets of the Masters*, McGraw-Hill, 1997.

[18] A. G. Ivakhnenko, *An Inductive Sorting Method for the Forecast of Multidimensional Random Processes and Analog Events with the Method of Analog Forecast Complexing*, Pattern Recognition and Image Analysis, 1991.

[19] D. Kahneman, P. Slovic, and A. Tversky, *Judgment Under Uncertainty: Heuristics and Biases*, Cambridge University Press, 1982.

[20] J. Kennedy and R. Eberhart, "Particle swarm optimization," in *Proceedings of the IEEE International Conference on Neural Networks*, vol. 4, pp. 1942–1948, December 1995.

[21] F. Wang, P. Yu, and D. Cheung, "Complex stock trading strategy based on Particle Swarm Optimization," in *Proceedings of the IEEE Conference on Computational Intelligence for Financial Engineering Economics (CIFEr '12)*, pp. 1–6, 2012.

[22] K. W. Chau, "Application of a PSO-based neural network in analysis of outcomes of construction claims," *Automation in Construction*, vol. 16, no. 5, pp. 642–646, 2007.

[23] J. Zhang and K.-W. Chau, "Multilayer ensemble pruning via novel multi-sub-swarm particle swarm optimization," *Journal of Universal Computer Science*, vol. 15, no. 4, pp. 840–858, 2009.

BPN Based Likelihood Ratio Score Fusion for Audio-Visual Speaker Identification in Response to Noise

Md. Rabiul Islam[1] and Md. Abdus Sobhan[2]

[1] Department of Computer Science & Engineering, Rajshahi University of Engineering & Technology, Rajshahi 6204, Bangladesh
[2] School of Engineering & Computer Science, Independent University, Dhaka 1229, Bangladesh

Correspondence should be addressed to Md. Rabiul Islam; rabiul_cse@yahoo.com

Academic Editors: J. Molina, M. Monti, M. Ture, and J. M. Usher

This paper deals with a new and improved approach of Back-propagation learning neural network based likelihood ratio score fusion technique for audio-visual speaker Identification in various noisy environments. Different signal preprocessing and noise removing techniques have been used to process the speech utterance and LPC, LPCC, RCC, MFCC, ΔMFCC and ΔΔMFCC methods have been applied to extract the features from the audio signal. Active Shape Model has been used to extract the appearance and shape based facial features. To enhance the performance of the proposed system, appearance and shape based facial features are concatenated and Principal Component Analysis method has been used to reduce the dimension of the facial feature vector. The audio and visual feature vectors are then fed to Hidden Markov Model separately to find out the log-likelihood of each modality. The reliability of each modality has been calculated using reliability measurement method. Finally, these integrated likelihood ratios are fed to Back-propagation learning neural network algorithm to discover the final speaker identification result. For measuring the performance of the proposed system, three different databases, that is, NOIZEUS speech database, ORL face database and VALID audio-visual multimodal database have been used for audio-only, visual-only, and audio-visual speaker identification. To identify the accuracy of the proposed system with existing techniques under various noisy environment, different types of artificial noise have been added at various rates with audio and visual signal and performance being compared with different variations of audio and visual features.

1. Introduction

Biometric authentication [1] has grown in popularity as a way to provide personal identification. Person's identification is crucially significant in many applications and the hike in credit card fraud and identity thefts in recent years indicate that this is an issue of major concern in wider society. Individual passwords, pin identification, or even token based arrangement all have deficiencies that restrict their applicability in a widely networked society. Biometrics is used to identify the identity of an input sample when compared to a template, used in cases to identify specific people by certain characteristics. No single biometrics is expected to effectively satisfy the needs of all identification applications. A number of biometrics have been proposed, researched and evaluated for authentication applications. Each biometrics has its strengths and limitations, and accordingly, each biometrics appeals to a particular identification application [2]. Biometric characteristics can be divided in physiological and behavioral classes [3]. Physiological characteristics are related to the shape of the body and thus it varies from person to person. Fingerprints, face recognition, hand geometry, and iris recognition are some examples of this type of Biometrics. Behavioral characteristics are related to the behavior of a person. Some examples in this case are signature, keystroke dynamics, voice, and so on.

The Audio-Visual speaker identification system combines the speech and face biometric characteristics which mix the physiological and behavioral characteristics. There are different levels where the audio and visual features can be concatenated. Preclassification and post-classification are the two broad categories for information fusion in biometric

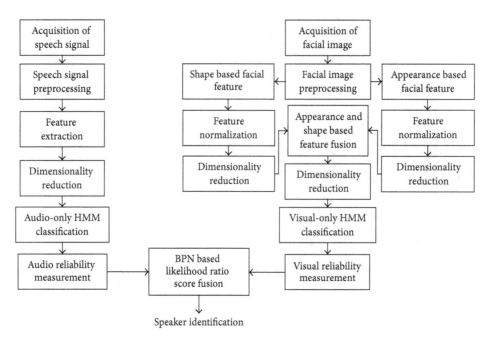

FIGURE 1: Paradigm of the proposed BPN based likelihood ratio score fusion for audio-visual speaker identification system.

system [4]. In preclassification, multimodal information is fused before going to the classifier decision. But, in postclassification, information is combined after the decision of multiple classifiers. In this proposed system, feature level fusion has been performed under preclassification approach. Appearance and shape based facial features are combined for visual identification result. Decision level fusion has been applied in the proposed system where audio and visual speaker identification decisions are concatenated to find out the final identification result. However, both feature level and decision level fusion are performed for the proposed system.

The rest of the paper is constructed as follows: Section 2 describes the literature review and the proposed system architecture, Section 3 focuses on the audio-only identification performance, visual-only identification has been elaborated in Section 4, Audio and visual reliability measurement techniques are focused on Section 5 and back-propagation learning neural network based likelihood ratio score fusion technique has been shown in Section 6. NOIZEUS speech database has been used to measure the performance of the Audio-Only speaker identification, visual-only performance has been populated using ORL database and overall system performance that is, back-propagation learning neural network score fusion based performance has been counted by applying VALID audio-visual multimodal database.

2. Literature Review and Proposed System Architecture

Since human speech is bimodal in nature [5, 6], visual speech information can play a vital role for the improvement of natural and robust human-computer interaction [7–11]. Most published works in the areas of speech recognition and

speaker recognition focus on speech under the noiseless environments and few published works focus on speech under noisy conditions [12–15]. Indeed, various important human-computer components, such as speaker identification, verification [16, 17], localization [18], speech event detection [19], speech signal separation [20], coding [21], video indexing and retrieval [22] and text-to-speech [23, 24] have been shown to benefit from the visual channel [25]. Adaptive weighting in decision fusion with acoustic and visual features from a given Audio-Visual speech datum, the recognized utterance class has been proposed [26]. The reliability of each audio and visual modality can be measured in various ways such as average absolute difference of loglikelihood [27], variance of loglikelihood [28], average difference of log-likelihood from the maximum [29], and inverse entropy of posterior probability [30]. Decision level information integration techniques have been developed where each biometric matcher individually decides on the best match based on the input presented to it. Methods like majority voting [31], behavior knowledge space [32], weighted voting based on the Dempster-Shafer theory of evidence [33], AND rule and OR rule [34], and so forth are some of the decision level fusion techniques proposed by different researchers.

The proposed architecture of the audio-visual speaker identification system is shown in Figure 1. Signal preprocessing and noise removing techniques have been applied after acquisition of the speech utterances. Then features are extracted using various standard speech feature extraction methods such as LPC, LPCC, RCC, MFCC, ΔMFCC, and $\Delta\Delta$MFCC. Principal Component Analysis (PCA) has been used to reduce the dimensionality of the extracted feature vector. Now the reduced feature vector is feed to Discrete Hidden Markov Model (DHMM) to get the log likelihood of each speech modality. Reliability measurement method has been used to measure the reliability for audio signal. For visual identification, captured faces are preprocessed using different noise removing techniques and Active Shape Model (ASM) is used to extract the appearance and shape based features. These two different types of features are fused after applying feature normalization and PCA based dimensionality reduction techniques. The concatenations of these features are important in the sense when the appearance based feature is captured with noise (i.e., light variations) then shape based features can retain the performance on a satisfied level. This is also true when the shape based feature is captured by noise highly. By combining this approach, the proposed system performs very well especially in various lighting environmental conditions. Finally, log likelihood of visual modality has been evaluated using DHMM classification and reliability has been measured using the same reliability measurement technique like audio modality. Integrated weights of audio and visual reliability measurement are fed to the Backpropagation learning neural network algorithm to calculate the final speaker identification result.

Rogozan and Deléglise [26] developed a technique for combining different likelihoods of multilevel biometric identification. In this proposed system, BPN algorithm has been used to combine the likelihood of audio and visual modality to enhance the performance of audio-visual speaker identification. This is the main contribution of the proposed system. Experimental results show the superiority of BPN based approach over the Rogozan and Deléglise [26] method in terms of audio-visual speaker identification system.

3. Audio-Only Speaker Identification

3.1. Speech Signal Preprocessing and Feature Extraction. Speech signal preprocessing plays an important role for the efficiency of speaker identification. After capturing the speech utterances, wiener filter has been used to remove the background noise from the original speech utterances [35]. The wiener filter is a noise removing filter based on Fourier iteration. Its main advantage is the short computational time it takes to find a solution [36].

Let $s(t)$ be the smear signal let and $r(t)$ be the known response that causes the convolution. Then $s(t)$ is related to $u(t)$ by

$$s(t) = \int_{-\infty}^{\infty} r(t - \tau) u(\tau) d\tau \qquad (1)$$

or

$$S(f) = R(f) U(f), \qquad (2)$$

where S, R, U are Fourier Transform of s, r, and u. Consider the following.

The second source of signal corruption is the unknown background noise $n(t)$. Therefore the measured signal $c(t)$ is a sum of $s(t)$ and $n(t)$

$$c(t) = s(t) + n(t). \qquad (3)$$

To deconvolve s to find u, simply divide $S(f)$ by $R(f)$ that is, $U(f) = S(f)/R(f)$ in the absence of noise n. To deconvolve c where n is present then one needs to find an optimum filter function $\phi(t)$ or $\phi(f)$ which filters out the noise and gives a signal $\tilde{u}$ by

$$\tilde{U}(f) = \frac{C(f)\phi(f)}{R(f)}, \qquad (4)$$

where $\tilde{u}$ is as close to the original signal as possible.

For $\tilde{u}$ to be similar to u, their differences square is as close to zero as possible; that is,

$$\int_{-\infty}^{\infty} |\tilde{u}(t) - u(t)|^2 dt \qquad (5)$$

or

$$\int_{-\infty}^{\infty} |\tilde{u}(f) - u(f)|^2 df \qquad (6)$$

is minimized.

Substituting the above three equations, the Fourier version becomes:

$$\int_{-\infty}^{\infty} |R(f)|^{-2} |S(f)|^2 |1 - \phi(f)|^2 + |N(f)|^2 |\phi(f)|^2 df \qquad (7)$$

after rearranging. The best filter is one where the above integral is a minimum at every value of f. This is, when

$$\phi(f) = \frac{|S(f)|^2}{|S(f)|^2 + |N(f)|^2}. \qquad (8)$$

Now, $|S(f)|^2 + |N(f)|^2 \approx |C(f)|^2$, where $|C(f)|^2$, $|S(f)|^2$, and $|N(f)|^2$ are the power spectrum of C, S, and N. Therefore,

$$\phi(f) \approx \frac{|S(f)|^2}{|C(f)|^2}. \qquad (9)$$

Figure 2(a) shows a sample signal with background noise and Figure 2(b) shows the signal after applying the wiener filter.

Speech end points detection and silence part removal algorithm have been used to detect the presence of speech and to remove pulse and silences in the speech utterance [37, 38] which is shown in Figure 3.

To detect word boundary, the frame energy is computed using the short-term log energy equation [39]

$$E_i = 10 \log \sum_{t=n_i}^{n_i+N-1} S^2(t). \qquad (10)$$

Preemphasis has been used to balance the spectrum of voiced sounds that have a steep roll-off in the high frequency region [38]. The transfer function of the FIR filter in the z-domain is [40]

$$H(Z) = 1 - \alpha \cdot z^{-1}, \quad 0 \le \alpha \le 1, \qquad (11)$$

where α is the preemphasis parameter.

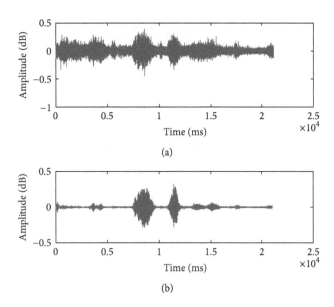

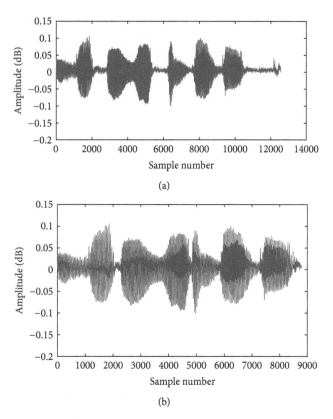

FIGURE 2: Effects of filtering technique (a) signal with noise (b) signal after applying Wiener filtering technique.

FIGURE 3: (a) Speech with silence parts (b) Results after applying silence parts removal algorithm.

Frame blocking has been performed with an overlapping of 25% to 75% of the frame size. Typically a frame length of 10–30 milliseconds has been used. The purpose of the overlapping analysis is that each speech sound of the input sequence would be approximately centered at some frame [41].

From different types of windowing techniques, a hamming window has been used for this system. The purpose of using windowing is to reduce the effect of the spectral artifacts that results from the framing process [42]. The hamming window can be defined as follows [43]:

$$
w(n) = \begin{cases} 0.54 - 0.46 \cos \dfrac{2\pi n}{N}, & -\left(\dfrac{N-1}{2}\right) \le n \le \left(\dfrac{N-1}{2}\right) \\ 0 & \text{Otherwise.} \end{cases}
$$
(12)

To extract the audio features, RCC, LPCC, MFCC, ΔMFCC, and $\Delta\Delta$MFCC based various standard speech feature extraction techniques [44, 45] have been used to enhance the efficiency of the system because the quality of the system depends on the proper feature extracted values.

3.2. Experimental Results according to NOIZEUS Speech Database. NOIZEUS speech corpus [46, 47] has been used to calculate the accuracy of the audio-only speaker identification system which contains 30 IEEE sentences (produced by three male and three female speakers) corrupted by eight different real-world noises at different SNRs. The noise was taken from the AURORA database and includes suburban train noise, babble, car, exhibition hall, restaurant, street, airport and train-station noise. The sentences were originally sampled at 25 kHz and downsampled to 8 kHz [48].

To measure the performance of the system according to NOIZEUS speech database, one clean speech utterance has been used for learning and four different noisy speeches

ranging from 0 dB to 20 dB with 5 dB interval are used for testing purpose. Tables 1, 2, 3, 4, 5, 6, 7, 8, and 9 show the results of audio-only speaker identification rate at different types of noisy environments with different SNRs.

Table 9 shows the overall average speaker identification rate for NOIZEUS speech corpus. From the table, it is easy to compare the performance among MFCC, ΔMFCC, $\Delta\Delta$MFCC, RCC and LPCC methods for DHMM based audio-only speaker identification system. It is shown that ΔMFCC has greater performance 48.85% than any other methods such as MFCC, $\Delta\Delta$MFCC, RCC and LPCC. It also shows that ΔMFCC feature can perform better than any other feature extraction method in all of eight different environmental conditions.

4. Visual-Only Speaker Identification

4.1. Facial Feature Extraction and Dimensionality Reduction. After acquisition of a face image, Stams [49] Active Shape Model (ASM) has been used to detect the facial features. Then the binary image has been taken. The Region Of Interest (ROI) has been chosen according to the ROI selection algorithm [50, 51]. Lastly the background noise has been eliminated [52] and finally appearance based facial feature has been found. The procedure of the facial image pre-processing parts is shown in Figure 4 where Figures 4(d) and 4(e) shows the shape based and appearance based facial feature respectively.

TABLE 1: Airport Noise Average Identification Rate (%) for NOIZEUS Speech Corpus.

SNR	Method				
---	MFCC	ΔMFCC	ΔΔMFCC	RCC	LPCC
15 dB	60.67	63.33	53.67	53.67	56.67
10 dB	53.33	58.67	43.33	43.67	53.33
5 dB	50.00	53.33	30.00	33.33	43.33
0 dB	17.67	17.67	10.67	12.33	15.00
Average	45.42	48.25	34.42	35.75	42.08

TABLE 2: Babble Noise Average Identification Rate (%) for NOIZEUS Speech Corpus.

SNR	Method				
---	MFCC	ΔMFCC	ΔΔMFCC	RCC	LPCC
15 dB	62.67	65.33	53.67	56.67	60.00
10 dB	56.33	60.33	43.33	43.67	56.67
5 dB	43.33	53.33	33.33	43.33	50.00
0 dB	17.67	18.00	11.33	13.33	12.00
Average	45.00	49.25	35.42	39.25	44.67

TABLE 3: Car Noise Average Identification Rate (%) for NOIZEUS Speech Corpus.

SNR	Method				
---	MFCC	ΔMFCC	ΔΔMFCC	RCC	LPCC
15 dB	56.67	60.33	43.33	50.00	53.33
10 dB	56.67	56.67	33.33	40.67	53.33
5 dB	46.33	46.67	30.00	40.33	42.33
0 dB	15.33	17.33	10.00	12.33	15.00
Average	43.75	45.25	29.17	35.83	41.00

TABLE 4: Exhibition Hall Noise Average Identification Rate (%) for NOIZEUS Speech Corpus.

SNR	Method				
---	MFCC	ΔMFCC	ΔΔMFCC	RCC	LPCC
15 dB	65.67	67.33	50.00	53.33	60.33
10 dB	60.00	63.33	43.33	46.67	56.33
5 dB	53.67	56.67	33.33	43.33	50.00
0 dB	18.33	18.33	10.33	13.33	16.33
Average	49.42	51.42	34.25	39.17	45.75

TABLE 5: Restaurant Noise Average Identification Rate (%) for NOIZEUS Speech Corpus.

SNR	Method				
---	MFCC	ΔMFCC	ΔΔMFCC	RCC	LPCC
15 dB	60.00	63.33	43.33	53.33	56.67
10 dB	56.67	60.00	40.00	46.67	53.33
5 dB	53.33	56.67	33.33	40.00	46.67
0 dB	17.33	18.67	13.67	15.00	15.67
Average	46.83	49.67	32.58	38.75	43.09

TABLE 6: Street Noise Average Identification Rate (%) for NOIZEUS Speech Corpus.

SNR	Method				
---	MFCC	ΔMFCC	ΔΔMFCC	RCC	LPCC
15 dB	63.33	67.67	53.67	56.67	60.00
10 dB	53.33	60.00	46.67	43.33	50.00
5 dB	50.00	50.00	30.00	43.33	43.67
0 dB	17.33	18.67	11.33	13.67	16.00
Average	46.00	49.09	35.42	39.25	42.42

TABLE 7: Train Noise Average Identification Rate (%) for NOIZEUS Speech Corpus.

SNR	Method				
---	MFCC	ΔMFCC	ΔΔMFCC	RCC	LPCC
15 dB	63.33	67.67	50.00	53.33	58.33
10 dB	60.00	63.33	43.33	46.67	53.33
5 dB	46.67	50.00	30.00	43.33	43.67
0 dB	18.33	18.67	12.33	13.67	15.33
Average	47.08	49.92	33.92	39.25	42.67

TABLE 8: Train Station Noise Average Identification Rate (%) for NOIZEUS Speech Corpus.

SNR	Method				
---	MFCC	ΔMFCC	ΔΔMFCC	RCC	LPCC
15 dB	63.67	63.33	48.33	50.00	58.33
10 dB	60.67	56.67	43.33	46.67	53.33
5 dB	56.00	53.33	33.33	46.67	46.67
0 dB	16.67	18.33	12.67	13.33	18.00
Average	49.25	47.92	34.42	39.17	44.08

To improve the performance of the face recognition system and since we want to compare the proposed technique with the appearance and shape based feature fusion method, we have to combine the appearance and shape based features. The concatenation procedure of two different features is shown in Figure 5. Initially raw 5000 dimension appearance based features and 176 dimension shape based features are extracted. The Principal Component Analysis method [53, 54] has been used to reduce the dimension of appearance and shape based features into 192 and 14, respectively. Two different features are added and produced 206 dimension features. Finally, PCA has been used again to resize from 206 dimensional to 130 dimensional appearance-shape based facial feature vector.

4.2. Experimental Results according to ORL Facial Database. Olivetti Research Laboratory (ORL) face database [55] produced by AT&T Laboratories has been used for measuring the performance of the proposed system. The database contains 10 different images of 40 distinct subjects. For some of the subjects, the images were taken at different times, varying lighting slightly, facial expressions (open/closed eyes, smiling/nonsmiling), and facial details (glasses/no-glasses).

TABLE 9: Overall Average Speaker Identification Rate (%) for NOIZEUS Speech Corpus.

Various Noises	Method				
	MFCC	ΔMFCC	ΔΔMFCC	RCC	LPCC
Airport Noise	45.42	48.25	34.42	35.75	42.08
Babble Noise	45.00	49.25	35.42	39.25	44.67
Car Noise	43.75	45.25	29.17	35.83	41.00
Exhibition Hall Noise	49.42	51.42	34.25	39.17	45.75
Restaurant Noise	46.83	49.67	32.58	38.75	43.09
Street Noise	46.00	49.09	35.42	39.25	42.42
Train Noise	47.08	49.92	33.92	39.25	42.67
Train Station Noise	49.25	47.92	34.42	39.17	44.08
Average Identification Rate (%)	46.59	48.85	33.70	38.30	43.22

All the images are taken against a dark homogeneous background and the subjects are in upright, frontal position (with tolerance for some side movement). The size of each face image is 92×112 and 8-bit grey levels. Experiment results are evaluated according to various dimensions such as optimum value selection of the number of hidden states of DHMM, response of the system based on noisy facial images and the system accuracy based on appearance, shape and combined appearance and shape based facial features.

4.2.1. System Response for Noisy Facial Images. The facial identification performance has been tested with the variations of different noises. Filtering is used for modifying or enhancing an image. To emphasize certain features or remove other features from an image, different filtering techniques are used. Filtering is a neighbourhood operation in which the value of any given pixel in the output image is determined by applying some algorithm to the values of the pixels in the neighbourhood of the corresponding input pixel. A pixel's neighbourhood is some set of pixels defined by their locations relative to that pixel. To remove the noise from the facial images, wiener filtering technique has been used. Wiener filtering technique has been used to remove or reduce white Gaussian noise from the facial image. Wiener filter can be used adaptively to an image where the variance is large, wiener filter performs little smoothing and where the variance is small, wiener filter performs more smoothing. Wiener filtering technique performs selective operation compared with other filters, preserving edges and other high-frequency parts of an image.

For measuring the accuracy of the face system, noise has been added in various rates for appearance based, shape based and appearance-shape based feature fusion technique with PCA based dimensionality reduction where Euclidian distance has been used as a classifier. Table 10 shows the response of applying Wiener filtering technique.

4.2.2. Performance Measurements between Single and Multiple Feature Fusion Based Techniques. Facial identification performance has been measured according to individual feature based technique such as appearance based feature, shape based feature and appearance-shape based feature fusion based technique. Receiver Operating Characteristics (ROC) curve is generated for the above mentioned techniques where a tradeoff is made between security and user friendness. The performance graph is shown in Figure 6. From the graph, it is shown that the appearance-shape based feature fusion can achieve compared with highest accuracy individual appearance based and shape based technique. For example, at a FRR = 30%, the appearance based, shape based and appearance-shape feature fusion FAR are 42%, 30%, and 28% respectively.

5. Audio and Visual Reliability Measurements

Since DHMM learning and testing models have been adopted for the audio and visual system, an ergodic discrete HMM (DHMM), θ_k [56], has been built in DHMM training phase for each face k. The model parameters (A, B, and θ) have been estimated to optimize the likelihood of the training set observation vector for the kth face by using the Baum-Welch algorithm. The Baum-Welch reestimation formula has been considered as follows [57, 58]:

$$\overline{\Pi}_i = \gamma_1(i), \qquad \overline{a}_{ij} = \frac{\sum_{t=1}^{T-1} \xi_t(i,j)}{\sum_{t=1}^{T-1} \gamma_t(i)},$$

$$\overline{b}_j(\vec{k}) = \frac{\sum_{t=1(s,t,\vec{o}_t=\vec{v}_k)}^{T} \gamma_t(j)}{\sum_{t=1}^{T} \gamma_t(j)}. \tag{13}$$

In the DHMM testing phase, for each unknown face to be recognized which includes

(i) measurement of the observation sequence, $O = \{o_1, o_2, \ldots, o_n\}$, via a feature analysis of the corresponding face,

(ii) transformation of the continuous values of O into integer values,

(iii) calculation of model likelihood for all possible models, $P(O \mid \theta_k)$, $1 \le k \le K$,

(iv) declaration of the face as k^* person whose model likelihood is highest—that is,

$$k^* = \arg\max_{1 \le k \le K} [P(O \mid \theta_k)]. \tag{14}$$

In this work, the probability computation step has been performed using Baum's Forward-Backward algorithm [58, 59]. By applying HMM as a learning phase, the log likelihood of each appearance and shape based feature of each person face have been captured. After getting the log likelihood of each modality separately, their outputs are combined by a weighted sum rule to produce the final decision. In this work, match score level is used to combine the appearance and shape based outputs. For a given appearance-shape test datum of O_A and O_S, the final recognition C^* is given by [60]

$$C^* = \arg\max_i \left\{ \gamma \log P\left(\frac{O_A}{\lambda_A^i}\right) + (1-\gamma) \log P\left(\frac{O_S}{\lambda_S^i}\right) \right\}, \tag{15}$$

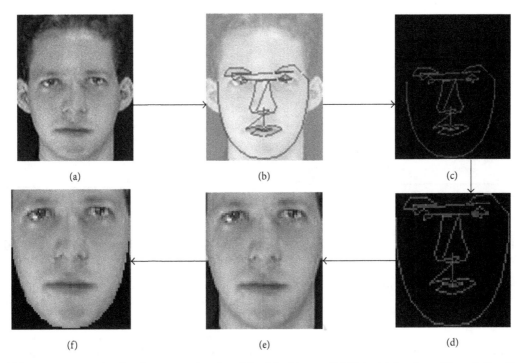

FIGURE 4: Facial image preprocessing for the proposed system (a) original image: (b) Output taken from Stams Active Shape Model (c) extracted facial edges (d) shape based features (e) region Of interest (ROI) selection with background noise, and (f) appearance based facial features.

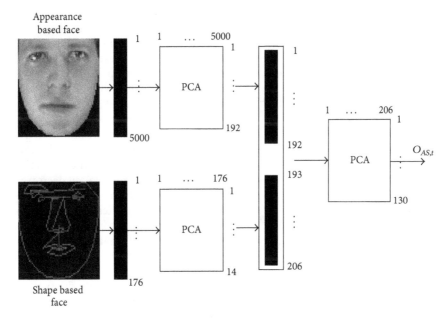

FIGURE 5: Process of appearance and shape based feature fusion.

where λ_A^i and λ_S^i are the appearance and the shape HMMs for the ith utterance class, respectively, and $\log P(O_A/\lambda_A^i)$ and $\log P(O_S/\lambda_S^i)$ are their log-likelihood against the ith class.

Among various types of score fusion techniques, baseline reliability ratio-based integration has been used to combine the appearance and shape recognition results. The reliability

of each modality can be measured from the outputs of the corresponding HMMs. The reliability of each modality can be calculated by the most appropriate method which is the best in performance [61],

$$S_m = \frac{1}{N-1} \sum_{i=1}^{N} \left(\max_j \log P\left(\frac{O}{\lambda^j}\right) - \log P\left(\frac{O}{\lambda^i}\right) \right) . 0 \quad (16)$$

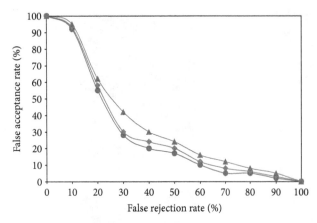

FIGURE 6: Performance comparison among individual modality and multimodal feature fusion techniques.

TABLE 10: Results after Applying Wiener Filter.

Noise addition rate (in Variance)	Recognition rate based on PCA		
	Appearance based feature	Shape based feature	Appearance-shape based feature fusion
0.01	89%	91%	93%
0.05	88%	88%	90%
0.08	82%	85%	87%
0.1	80%	81%	82%
0.4	75%	77%	80%

Which means the average difference between the maximum log-likelihood and the other ones and N is the number of classes being considered to measure the reliability of each modality, $m \in \{A, S\}$.

Then the integrated weight of appearance based reliability measure γ_A can be calculated by [62]

$$\gamma_A = \frac{S_A}{S_A + S_S}, \qquad (17)$$

where S_A and S_S are the reliability measures of the outputs of the appearance and shape HMMs, respectively.

The integrated weight of shape modality measure can be found as

$$\gamma_S = (1 - \gamma_A). \qquad (18)$$

6. BPN Based Likelihood Ratio Score Fusion

A Back-propagation learning feed-forward neural network [63] with tan-sigmoid transfer functions has been used in both the hidden layer and the output layer which is shown in Figure 7. Three-layer Back-propagation learning neural network algorithm has been used to classify the visual speech features [64].

If the input vector is $I = [p_1, p_2, \ldots, p_n]$, then the output of hidden layer has been calculated as follows:

$$n = IW + b,$$

$$a = f(n) = \frac{2}{\left(1 + e^{(-2*n)}\right)^{-1}}, \qquad (19)$$

where, W is weight vector and b is bias input. The error is calculated as the difference between the target output and the network actual output. The goal is to minimize the average of the sum of these errors. Consider the following:

$$\mathrm{mse} = \frac{1}{M} \sum_{k=1}^{M} e(k)^2 = \frac{1}{M} \sum (t(k) - a(k))^2. \qquad (20)$$

Here, mse means mean square error, $t(k)$ represents the target output, and $a(k)$ represents the network output. The weights and bias values are updated based on the goal average error value.

In the proposed audio-visual system, the final weights and bias values are calculated in the training stage. In test phase, the output of the network has been calculated for the new input and compared with the target output to select the class of the input. The numbers of input layers, hidden layers and output layers nodes are 2, 100, and 8, respectively. The overall procedure for the proposed system with likelihood ratio based score fusion with Back-propagation learning neural network is shown in Figure 8.

The major drawbacks of Back-propagation learning neural network algorithm are the training time and local minima. Convergence time of the Back-propagation algorithm is inversely proportional to the error tolerance rate. In learning, effective use of error rate can decrease the convergence time. At first, select the final error rate. Then converge the weights such that all the patterns overcome some of the percentage error of the total system (the error must be higher than the final error rates). Finally, converge the system to the next lower error rate until crossing the final targeted error. For example, if the error rate of the system is 0.001, first the converged error rate for all of the patterns is 0.009, then 0.005, 0.003, and finally 0.001. This process is known as SET-BPL [65].

100 speech utterances are trained in Back-propagation learning neural network and the effects of applying SET-BPL of the proposed system areshown in Figure 9. Sometimes local minima problem occurs in a Back-propagation learning neural network algorithm. As a result, some precautions such as addition of internal nodes and lowering the gain term have been considered to set the learning parameters. The addition of internal nodes and lowering the gain term can increase the convergence time. To overcome these learning difficulties, a momentum term has been used to speed up the convergence process for this proposed speaker identification system.

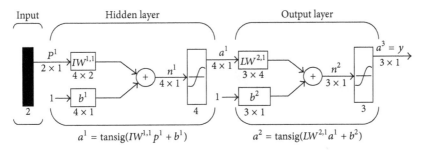

FIGURE 7: Architecture of Back-propagation neural network.

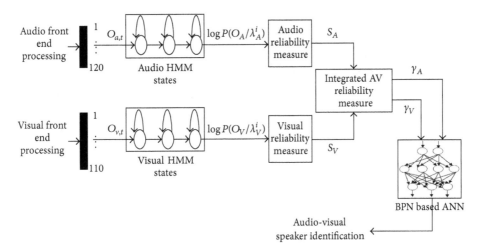

FIGURE 8: BPN based score fusion technique for proposed audio-visual speaker identification system.

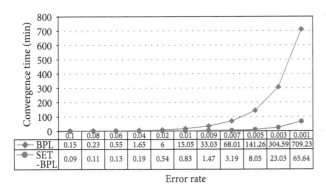

FIGURE 9: Effects of applying SET-BPL process of the proposed system.

	0.1	0.08	0.06	0.04	0.02	0.01	0.009	0.007	0.005	0.003	0.001
BPL	0.15	0.23	0.55	1.65	6	15.05	33.03	68.01	141.26	304.59	709.23
SET-BPL	0.09	0.11	0.13	0.19	0.54	0.83	1.47	3.19	8.05	23.03	65.64

6.1. Experimental Evaluation according to VALID Audio-Video Database.

VALID audio-visual multimodal database [66] has been used to measure and compare the accuracy between the proposed and existing system. For visual features, database contains 106 subjects each with four office lighting conditions, gathered periodically over one month giving some temporal variation and one studio session with controlled lighting. The 576×720 stills were extracted from the video segments. Three sets of these are offered, the 1st, 10th, and 50th frames for each of the 106×5 sessions. The five sessions were recorded over a period of one month, allowing for variation in the voice, clothing, facial hair, hairstyle and cosmetic appearance of the subjects and also variation of the visual background, illumination, and acoustic noise. The first session was recorded under controlled acoustic/illumination conditions, that is, controlled environment. The database is designed to be realistic and challenging; hence the other four sessions were recorded in noisy real-world scenarios with no control on illumination or acoustic noise that is, uncontrolled environment. Some processed facial images of VALID database are shown in Figure 10.

For the speech wave, the database contains 106 subjects with one studio and four office conditions recordings for each person corresponding to the facial images where the following two different speech utterances are found:

Uttered sentence 1:

"Joe Took Father's Green Shoe bench Out,"

Uttered sentence 2: "5 0 6 9 2 8 1 3 7 4."

From the above two sentences, second sentence has been used for learning and testing operations. Out of five facial images and speeches, the neutral face and corresponding speech utterance have been used for learning and other four official noisy images and speeches have used for testing.

6.2. Performance Analysis between Existing and Proposed Method.

To evaluate the performance of BPN based likelihood ratio based score fusion technique, different variations

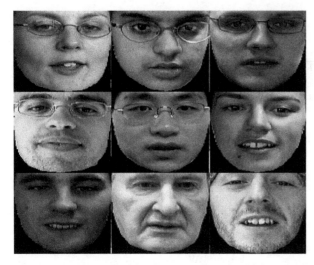

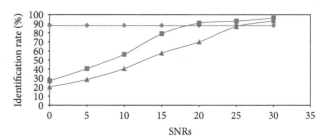

FIGURE 10: Some processed facial images of VALID database for the proposed system.

FIGURE 12: Shape based facial feature and MFCC based audio features for score fusion technique.

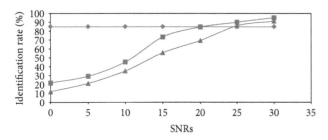

- Appearance based feature
- Appearance and MFCC based feature with Rogozan and Deleglise method
- Appearance and MFCC based feature with BPN

FIGURE 11: Results of score fusion for appearance based facial feature with MFCC based feature of audio feature.

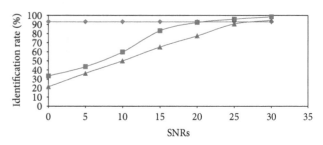

- Appearance and shape based feature
- Appearance, shape, MFCC, and LPCC based feature
- Appearance, shape, and MFCC based feature

FIGURE 13: Result of the combinations of audio features with combined appearance and shape based facial feature for score fusion technique.

of audio and visual features are combined and results are taken according to various SNRs of audio signal which are shown in the following subsections.

6.2.1. Experiment of Appearance Based Facial Feature with Audio Feature. Appearance based facial features are concatenated with MFCC based audio feature to populate the performance of the proposed score fusion based speaker identification. Results are shown in Figure 11 where the highest speaker identification rate has been found to be 95% at SNR of 30 dB for proposed BPN score fusion approach compared with existing Rogozan and Deléglise method of 91.33%.

6.2.2. Experiment of Shape Based Facial Feature with Audio Feature. Figure 12 shows the results of shape based facial feature and MFCC based audio feature. At SNR of 30 dB, the speaker identification rate of Rogozan and Deléglise method and proposed BPN score fusion approach has been achieved with 93.33% and 96.33%, respectively.

6.2.3. Experiment of Combined Appearance-Shape Based Facial Feature with Audio Feature. Results of appearance and shape based facial features with MFCC based audio feature for score fusion technique are shown in Figure 13. The highest speaker identification rate of 98.67% has been found at SNR of 30 dB with proposed BPN score fusion approach where existing Rogozan and Deléglise method achieves 95% at the same SNR.

Form the above experimental results, it has been shown that Back-propagation learning network based score fusion approach gives greater performance than any combination of audio and visual features compared with existing Rogozan and Deléglise method of score fusion. Here, it has also been focused on that combined appearance and shape based facial feature achieves higher accuracies than any individual facial feature based technique which is shown in Table 11.

7. Conclusions and Observations

In this work, proposed system performance has been evaluated in various levels with various dimensions. Two different types of facial features are combined with audio feature with various artificial noise addition rates. NOIZEUS speech database has been used to evaluate the performance of

TABLE 11: Performance Comparison of Various Combination of Facial Features with Audio Feature for Proposed BPN Approach.

SNRs	Type		
	Appearance and ΔMFCC based feature with BPN approach (in %)	Shape and ΔMFCC based feature with BPN approach (in %)	Appearance, shape and ΔMFCC based feature with BPN approach (in %)
0 dB	21.67	26.67	33.33
5 dB	29.33	40.25	43.67
10 dB	45.33	56.25	59.67
15 dB	73.25	79.00	83.25
20 dB	84.67	90.67	92.33
25 dB	90.00	93.00	96.00
30 dB	95.00	96.33	98.67

the Audio-Only speaker identification system whereas ORL facial database has been used for visual-only identification system. Finally, overall performance that is, audio-visual speaker identification has been measured according to VALID audio-visual database. Noise removing techniques have used to reduce or eliminate the noises from speech utterances and facial images. Experimental results and performance analysis shows the versatility of the proposed BPN score fusion approach over the existing Rogozan and Déléglise method for audio-visual speaker identification system which can be effectively used in various real life access control and authentication purposes.

Conflict of Interests

The authors declare that there is no conflict of interests regarding the publication of this paper.

References

[1] J. D. Woodward, "Biometrics: Privacy's foe or Privacy's friend?" *Proceedings of the IEEE*, vol. 85, no. 9, pp. 1480–1492, 1997.

[2] A. K. Jain, R. Bolle, and S. Pankanti, "Introduction to biometrics," in *Biometrics, Personal Identification in Networked Society*, A. K. Jain, R. Bolle, and S. Pankanti, Eds., pp. 1–41, Kluwer Academic Publishers, Dordrecht, The Netherlands, 1999.

[3] D. Bhattacharyya, R. Rahul, A. A. Farkhod, and C. Minkyu, "Biometric authentication: a review," *International Journal of U- and E- Service, Science and Technology*, vol. 2, no. 3, 2009.

[4] C. Sanderson and K. K. Paliwal, "Information fusion and person verification using speech and face information," Research Paper IDIAP-RR 02-33, IDIAP, 2002.

[5] D. G. Stork and M. E. Hennecke, *Speechreading by Humans and Machines*, Springer, Berlin, Germany, 1996.

[6] R. Campbell, B. Dodd, and D. Burnham, *Hearing by Eye II*, Psychology Press, Hove, UK, 1998.

[7] S. Dupont and J. Luettin, "Audio-visual speech modeling for continuous speech recognition," *IEEE Transactions on Multimedia*, vol. 2, no. 3, pp. 141–151, 2000.

[8] G. Potamianos, J. Luettin, and C. Neti, "Hierarchical discriminant features for audio-visual LVCSR," in *Proceedings of the IEEE Interntional Conference on Acoustics, Speech, and Signal Processing*, pp. 165–168, May 2001.

[9] G. Potamianos and C. Neti, "Automatic speechreading of impaired speech," in *Proceedings of the Conference on Audio-Visual Speech Processing*, pp. 177–182, 2001.

[10] F. J. Huang and T. Chen, "Consideration of lombard effect for speechreading," in *Proceedings of the IEEE 4th Workshop on Multimedia Signal Processing*, pp. 613–618, October 2001.

[11] G. Potamianos, C. Neti, G. Gravier, A. Garg, and A. W. Senior, "Recent advances in the automatic recognition of audiovisual speech," *Proceedings of the IEEE*, vol. 91, no. 9, pp. 1306–1325, 2003.

[12] D. A. Reynolds, "Experimental evaluation of features for robust speaker identification," *IEEE Transactions on Speech and Audio Processing*, vol. 2, no. 4, pp. 639–643, 1994.

[13] S. Sharma, D. Ellis, S. Kajarekar, P. Jain, and H. Hermansky, "Feature extraction using non-linear transformation for robust speech recognition on the aurora database," in *Proceedings of the IEEE Interntional Conference on Acoustics, Speech, and Signal Processing (ICASSP '00)*, pp. 1117–1120, June 2000.

[14] D. Wu, A. C. Morris, and J. Koreman, "MLP internal representation as discriminant features for improved speaker recognition," in *Proceedings of the International Conference on Non-Linear Speech Processing (NOLISP '05)*, pp. 25–33, Barcelona, Spain, 2005.

[15] Y. Konig, L. Heck, M. Weintraub, and K. Sonmez, "Nonlinear discriminant feature extraction for robust text-independent speaker recognition," in *Proceedings of the RLA2C, ESCA Workshop on Speaker Recognition and Its Commercial and Forensic Applications*, pp. 72–75, 1998.

[16] C. C. Chibelushi, F. Deravi, and J. S. D. Mason, "A review of speech-based bimodal recognition," *IEEE Transactions on Multimedia*, vol. 4, no. 1, pp. 23–37, 2002.

[17] X. Zhang, C. C. Broun, R. M. Mersereau, and M. A. Clements, "Automatic speechreading with applications to human-computer interfaces," *EURASIP Journal on Applied Signal Processing*, vol. 2002, no. 11, pp. 1228–1247, 2002.

[18] D. N. Zotkin, R. Duraiswami, and L. S. Davis, "Joint audio-visual tracking using particle filters," *EURASIP Journal on Applied Signal Processing*, vol. 2002, no. 11, pp. 1154–1164, 2002.

[19] P. de Cuetos, C. Neti, and A. W. Senior, "Audio-visual intent-to-speak detection for human-computer interaction," in *Proceedings of the IEEE Interntional Conference on Acoustics, Speech, and Signal Processing*, pp. 2373–2376, June 2000.

[20] D. Sodoyer, J.-L. Schwartz, L. Girin, J. Klinkisch, and C. Jutten, "Separation of audio-visual speech sources: a new

approach exploiting the audio-visual coherence of speech stimuli," *EURASIP Journal on Applied Signal Processing*, vol. 2002, no. 11, pp. 1165–1173, 2002.

[21] E. Foucher, L. Girin, and G. Feng, "Audiovisual speech coder: using vector quantization to exploit the audio/video correlation," in *Proceedings of the Conference on Audio-Visual Speech Processing*, pp. 67–71, Terrigal, Australia, 1998.

[22] J. Huang, Z. Liu, Y. Wang, Y. Chen, and E. Wong, "Integration of multimodal features for video scene classification based on HMM," in *Proceedings of the Workshop on Multimedia Signal Processing*, pp. 53–58, Copenhagen, Denmark, 1999.

[23] M. M. Cohen and D. W. Massaro, "What can visual speech synthesis tell visual speech recognition?" in *Proceedings of the Asilomar Conference on Signals, Systems, and Computers*, Pacific Grove, Calif, USA, 1994.

[24] E. Cosatto and H. P. Graf, "Photo-realistic talking-heads from image samples," *IEEE Transactions on Multimedia*, vol. 2, no. 3, pp. 152–163, 2000.

[25] G. Potamianos, C. Neti, and S. Deligne, "Joint audio-visual speech processing for recognition and enhancement," in *Proceedings of the Auditory-Visual Speech Processing Tutorial and Research Workshop (AVSP '03)*, pp. 95–104, St. Jorioz, France, 2003.

[26] A. Rogozan and P. Deléglise, "Adaptive fusion of acoustic and visual sources for automatic speech recognition," *Speech Communication*, vol. 26, no. 1-2, pp. 149–161, 1998.

[27] A. Adjoudani and C. Benoit, "On the integration of auditory and visual parameters in an HMM-based ASR," in *Humans and Machines: Models, Systems, and Applications*, D. G. Stork and M. E. Hennecke, Eds., pp. 461–472, Springer, Berlin, Germany.

[28] T. W. Lewis and D. M. W. Powers, "Sensor fusion weighting measures in audio-visual speech recognition," in *Proceedings of the Conference on Australasian Computer Science*, pp. 305–314, Dunedine, New Zealand, 2004.

[29] G. Potamianos and C. Neti, "Stream confidence estimation for audio-visual speech recognition," in *Proceedings of the International Conference on Spoken Language Processing*, pp. 746–749, Beijing, China, 2000.

[30] I. Matthews, J. A. Bangham, and S. Cox, "Audiovisual speech recognition using multiscale nonlinear image decomposition," in *Proceedings of the International Conference on Spoken Language Processing (ICSLP '96)*, pp. 38–41, October 1996.

[31] L. Lam and C. Y. Suen, "Application of majority voting to pattern recognition: an analysis of its behavior and performance," *IEEE Transactions on Systems, Man, and Cybernetics A*, vol. 27, no. 5, pp. 553–568, 1997.

[32] L. Lam and C. Y. Suen, "Optimal combinations of pattern classifiers," *Pattern Recognition Letters*, vol. 16, no. 9, pp. 945–954, 1995.

[33] L. Xu, A. Krzyzak, and C. Y. Suen, "Methods of combining multiple classifiers and their applications to handwriting recognition," *IEEE Transactions on Systems, Man and Cybernetics*, vol. 22, no. 3, pp. 418–435, 1992.

[34] J. Daugman, "Biometric decision landscapes," Tech. Rep. TR482, University of Cambridge Computer Laboratory, 2000.

[35] S. Doclo and M. Moonen, "On the output SNR of the speech-distortion weighted multichannel Wiener filter," *IEEE Signal Processing Letters*, vol. 12, no. 12, pp. 809–811, 2005.

[36] R. Wang and W. Filtering, "PHYS, 3301, scientific computing," Project Report for NOISE Group, May 2000.

[37] K. Kitayama, M. Goto, K. Itou, and T. Kobayashi, "Speech starter: noise-robust endpoint detection by using filled pauses," in *Proceedings of the 8th European Conference on Speech Communication and Technology (Eurospeech '03)*, pp. 1237–1240, Geneva, Switzerland, September 2003.

[38] Q. Li, J. Zheng, A. Tsai, and Q. Zhou, "Robust endpoint detection and energy normalization for real-time speech and speaker recognition," *IEEE Transactions on Speech and Audio Processing*, vol. 10, no. 3, pp. 146–157, 2002.

[39] N. Wiener and R. E. A. C. Paley, *Fourier Transforms in the Complex Domains*, American Mathematical Society, Providence, RI, USA, 1934.

[40] J. W. Picone, "Signal modeling techniques in speech recognition," *Proceedings of the IEEE*, vol. 81, no. 9, pp. 1215–1247, 1993.

[41] L. P. Cordella, P. Foggia, C. Sansone, and M. Vento, "A real-time text-independent speaker identification system," in *Proceedings of the 12th International Conference on Image Analysis and Processing*, pp. 632–637, IEEE Computer Society Press, 2003.

[42] F. J. Harris, "On the use of windows for harmonic analysis with the discrete Fourier transform," *Proceedings of the IEEE*, vol. 66, no. 1, pp. 51–83, 1978.

[43] J. Proakis and D. Manolakis, *Digital Signl Processing, Principles, Algorithms and Applications*, Macmillan, New York, NY, USA, 2nd edition, 1992.

[44] S. B. Davis and P. Mermelstein, "Comparison of parametric representations for monosyllabic word recognition in continuously spoken sentences," *IEEE Transactions on Acoustics, Speech, and Signal Processing*, vol. 28, no. 4, pp. 357–366, 1980.

[45] T. F. Li and S.-C. Chang, "Speech recognition of mandarin syllables using both linear predict coding cepstra and Mel frequency cepstra," in *Proceedings of the 19th Conference on Computational Linguistics and Speech Processing*, pp. 379–390, 2007.

[46] Y. Hu and P. C. Loizou, "Subjective comparison of speech enhancement algorithms," in *Proceedings of the IEEE International Conference on Acoustics, Speech and Signal Processing (ICASSP '06)*, pp. I153–I156, Toulouse, France, May 2006.

[47] Y. Hu and P. C. Loizou, "Evaluation of objective measures for speech enhancement," in *Proceedings of the 9th International Conference on Spoken Language Processing (INTERSPEECH '06)*, pp. 1447–1450, September 2006.

[48] Y. Hu and P. C. Loizou, "Evaluation of objective quality measures for speech enhancement," *IEEE Transactions on Audio, Speech and Language Processing*, vol. 16, no. 1, pp. 229–238, 2008.

[49] S. Milborrow, *Locating facial features with active shape models [Masters dissertation]*, Faculty of Engineering, University of Cape Town, Cape Town, South Africa, 2007.

[50] R. Herpers, G. Verghese, K. Derpains, and R. McCready, "Detection and tracking of face in real environments," in *Proceedings of the International IEEE Workshop Recognition, Analysis and Tracking of Face and Gesture in Real- Time Systems*, pp. 96–104, Corfu, Greece, 1999.

[51] J. Daugman, "Face detection: a survey," *Computer Vision and Image Understanding*, vol. 83, no. 3, pp. 236–274, 2001.

[52] R. C. Gonzalez and R. E. Woods, *Digital Image Processing*, Addison-Wesley, 2002.

[53] M. Turk and A. Pentland, "Eigenfaces for recognition," *Journal of Cognitive Neuroscience*, vol. 3, no. 1, pp. 71–86, 1991.

[54] T. Matthew and A. Pentland, *Face Recognition Using Eigenfaces*, Vision and Modeling Group, The Media Laboratory, Massachusetts Institute of Technology, 1991.

[55] F. S. Samaria and A. C. Harter, "Parameterisation of a stochastic model for human face identification," in *Proceedings of the 2nd IEEE Workshop on Applications of Computer Vision*, pp. 138–142, Orlando, Fla, USA, December 1994.

[56] R. O. Duda, P. E. Hart, and D. G. Strok, *Pattern Classification*, A Wiley-Interscience Publication, John Wiley & Sons, 2nd edition, 2001.

[57] V. Sarma and D. Venugopal, "Studies on pattern recognition approach to voiced-unvoiced-silence classification," in *Proceedings of the IEEE International Conference on Acoustics, Speech, and Signal Processing (ICASSP '78)*, vol. 3, pp. 1–4, 1978.

[58] L. R. Rabiner, "Tutorial on hidden Markov models and selected applications in speech recognition," *Proceedings of the IEEE*, vol. 77, no. 2, pp. 257–286, 1989.

[59] P. A. Devijver, "Baum's forward-backward algorithm revisited," *Pattern Recognition Letters*, vol. 3, no. 6, pp. 369–373, 1985.

[60] A. Rogozan and P. Deléglise, "Adaptive fusion of acoustic and visual sources for automatic speech recognition," *Speech Communication*, vol. 26, no. 1-2, pp. 149–161, 1998.

[61] J. S. Lee and C. H. Park, "Adaptive decision fusion for audio-visual speech recognition," in *Speech Recognition, Technologies and Applications*, F. Mihelic and J. Zibert, Eds., p. 550, 2008.

[62] A. Adjoudant and C. Benoit, "On the integratio of auditory and visual parameters in an HMM-based ASR," in *Humans and Machines: Models, Systems, and Speech Recognition, Technologies and Applications*, D. G. Strok and M. E. Hennecke, Eds., pp. 461–472, Springer, Berlin, Germany, 1996.

[63] J. A. Freeman and D. M. Skapura, *Neural Networks, Algorithms, Applications and Programming Techniques*, Addison-Wesley, 1991.

[64] W. C. Yau, D. K. Kumar, and S. P. Arjunan, "Visual recognition of speech consonants using facial movement features," *Integrated Computer-Aided Engineering*, vol. 14, no. 1, pp. 49–61, 2007.

[65] M. R. Islam and M. A. Sobhan, "Improving the convergence of backpropagation learning Neural Networks Based Bangla Speaker Identification System for various weight update frequencies, momentum term and error rate," in *Proceedings of the International Conference on Computer Processing of Bangla (ICCPB '06)*, pp. 27–34, Independent University, 2006.

[66] A. F. Niall, A. O. Brian, and B. R. Richard, "VALID: a new practical audio-visual database, and comparative results," in *Audio- and Video-Based Biometric Person Authentication*, vol. 3546 of *Lecture Notes in Computer Science*, pp. 201–243, 2005.

Weighed Nonlinear Hybrid Neural Networks in Underground Rescue Mission

Hongxing Yao,[1,2] **Mary Opokua Ansong,**[1,3] **and Jun Steed Huang**[4]

[1] *Institute of System Engineering, Faculty of Science, Jiangsu University, 301 Xuefu, Zhenjiang 212013, China*
[2] *College of Finance and Economics, Jiangsu University, 301 Xuefu, Zhenjiang 212013, China*
[3] *Department of Computer Science, School of Applied Science, Kumasi Polytechnic, P.O. Box 854, Kumasi, Ghana*
[4] *Computer Science and Technology, School of Computer Science & Telecommunication, Jiangsu University, 301 Xuefu, Zhenjiang 212013, China*

Correspondence should be addressed to Hongxing Yao; hxyao@ujs.edu.cn

Academic Editors: O. Castillo, K. W. Chau, D. Chen, and P. Kokol

In our previous work, a novel model called compact radial basis function (CRBF) in a routing topology control has been modelled. The computational burden of Zhang and Gaussian transfer functions was modified by removing the power parameters on the models. The results showed outstanding performance over the Zhang and Gaussian models. This study researched on several hybrids forms of the model where cosine ($_{\cos}$) and sine ($_{\sin}$) nonlinear weights were imposed on the two transfer functions such that $Y(\text{out}) = \text{logsig}(R) + [\exp(-\text{abs}(R))] * (\pm \cos \text{ or } \pm \sin(R))$. The purpose was to identify the best hybrid that optimized all of its parameters with a minimum error. The results of the nonlinear weighted hybrids were compared with a hybrid of Gaussian model. Simulation revealed that the negative nonlinear weights hybrids optimized all the parameters and it is substantially superior to the previous approaches presented in the literature, with minimized errors of 0.0098, 0.0121, 0.0135, and 0.0129 for the negative cosine (HSCR-BF$_{-\cos}$), positive cosine (HSCR-BF$_{+\cos}$), negative sine (HSCR-BF$_{-\sin}$), and positive sine (HSCR-BF$_{+\sin}$) hybrids, respectively, while sigmoid and Gaussian radial basis functions (HSGR-BF$_{+\cos}$) were 0.0117. The proposed hybrid could serve as an alternative approach to underground rescue operation.

1. Introduction

1.1. Background. In our earlier work we demonstrated how a routing path was generated and how the compact radial basis function could be improved by reducing the computational burden of Gaussian by removing the power parameter from the model. We had discussed the robustness and fault tolerant nature of the compact radial basis function for an emergency underground rescue operation and had discussed the performance of the sigmoid basis function and the compact radial basis function of which the latter optimised its parameters better than that of the former [1]. In this paper we look at the hybrid form of this novel algorithm, by introducing nonlinear weights of positive and negative cosine and sine.

1.2. Sigmoid Basis Function (SBF) and Radial Basis Function (RBF). Sigmoid basis function (SBF) and radial basis function (RBF) are the most commonly used algorithms in neural training. The output of the network is a linear combination of radial basis function of the inputs and neural parameters. Radial basis function networks have many uses, including function approximation, time series prediction [2, 3] classification, and system control. The structure supports the academic school of connectionist and the idea was first formulated in 1988 by Broomhead and Lowe [4]. The SBF, a mathematical function having an "S" shape (sigmoid curve), and is related to brain reasoning and the structure favors the computational believers. The sigmoid function refers to the special case of the logistic function. Another example is the Gompertz curve which is used in modeling systems that saturate at large values of input, for example, the ogee curve used in spillway of dams. A wide variety of sigmoid functions have been used as activation functions of neurons, including the logistic and hyperbolic tangent weight functions. Sigmoid curves are also common in statistics such as integrals and logistic distribution, normal distribution, and Student's probability density functions. In our opinion, SBF offers nonlinear effects for large input value and RBF provide nonlinear effect at small input value. A nonlinear hybrid of cosine and sine will result in more nonlinear blending across the entire region.

1.3. Wireless Sensor Networks (WSN). Wireless sensor networks (WSN) gather and process data from the environment and make possible applications in the areas of environment monitoring, logistics support, health care, and emergency response systems as well as military operations. Transmitting data wirelessly impacts significant benefits to those investigating buildings, allowing them to deploy sensors which monitor from a remote location. Multihop transmission in wireless sensor networks conforms to the underground tunnel structure and provides more scalability for communication system construction in rescue situations. A significant discovery in the field of complex networks has shown that a large number of complex networks including the internet are scale-free and their connectivity distribution is described by the power-law of the form $\rho(k) \sim k^{-\phi}$, to allow few nodes of very large degree to exist making it difficult for random attack. A scale-free wireless network topology was therefore used.

This paper proposes a nonlinear Hybrid Neural Networks using radial and sigmoid transfer functions in underground communication, based on particle swarm optimisation. An alternative to this model is without hybrid, either RBF or SBF. The SBF is known to be fast, while RBF is accurate [5] and therefore blending the two will provide both speed and accuracy. In addition the two models have been examined in our previous work [1]. To this end, we model the incident location as a pure random event and calculate the probability that communication chain through particular rock layers to the ground is not broken and allows neural network to memorize the complicated relationship, such that when real accident happens, the neural network resident in the robot is used to predict the probability based on the rock layer it sees instantly. If the result is positive, the robot waits to receive the rescue signal; otherwise it moves deeper to the next layer and repeats the procedure.

Section 2 explains the preliminaries to the study and generates the routing path that has the highest survival probability for the neural training. Section 3 discusses related work to the study. Section 4 discusses the network optimization model based on the nonlinear weight on the compact radial basis function. Section 5 highlights the method used and Section 6 shows the simulation results of the various hybrids and compare with the Gaussian model whiles Section 7 gives a summary of the findings and future work.

2. Preliminaries

2.1. Sensor Deployment. Some assumptions, such as 20% of software failure, 2 safe exits assumed to be available after accidents and additional errors committed after the accidents,

and the failure rate of radio frequency identification (RFID), were made in various sections. These assumptions are already included in the model and they are there to ensure that the system remains reliable.

Topological deployment of sensor nodes affects the performance of the routing protocol [6, 7]. The ratio of communication range to sensing range as well as the distance between sensor nodes can affect the network topology.

Let Ω be the sensor sequence for the deployment of total sensors $T = xyz = L, R, C$, such that

$$
\Omega = \begin{cases}
\text{For } t = t + 1 \\
\text{node } (t, 2) = \left(\dfrac{\left\| -(R+1) * \left(1 + (-1)^{\text{tog}J}\right) \right\|}{2} + j \right) \\
\text{node } (t, 3) = \left(\dfrac{\left\| -(C+1) * \left(1 + (-1)^{\text{tog}K}\right) \right\|}{2} + k \right)
\end{cases}
$$

for, $i = 1 : L$, $j = 1 : R$, $k = 1 : C$ and node $(t, 1) = i$.
(1)

$\text{tog}^J = \text{ceil}(t/C/R)$ and $\text{tog}^K = \text{ceil}(t/C)$ check source and destination node, respectively.

$\Omega(i, j, k) = \{1, 1, 1\}, \{1, 2, 1\}, \ldots, \{i\text{th}, j\text{th}, k\text{th}\}$ for [level 1, row 1, column 1], [level 1, row 2, column 1], [...], and [ith level, jth row, and kth column], respectively. Therefore $T = T \times T$ matrix, in an underground mine with dimensions of $L = 3$, $R = 2$, and $C = 1$ for depth (level), row (length), and width (column), respectively, with "pm" a sensor apart, implies that a minimum of 6 sensors will have to be deployed.

2.2. Communication. The Through-The-Earth (TTE) Communication system transmits voice and data through solid earth, rock, and concrete and is suitable for challenging underground environments such as mines, tunnels, and subways. There were stationary sensor nodes monitoring carbon monoxide, temperature, and so forth, as well as mobile sensors (humans and vehicles) distributed uniformly. Both stationary and mobile sensor nodes were connected to either the Access Point (AP) and/or Access Point Heads (AP Heads) based on transmission range requirements [6]. The AP Heads serve as cluster leaders and are located in areas where the rock is relatively soft or signal penetration is better to ensure that nodes are able to transmit the information they receive from APs and sensor nodes. The APs are connected to other APs or Through-The-Earth (TTE) which is dropped through a drilled hole down 300 meters apart based on the rock type. The depth and rock type determine the required number of TTEs needed. Next the data-mule is discharged to carry items such as food, water, and equipments to the miners underground and return with underground information to rescue team.

2.3. Signal/Transmission Reach. Major challenges of sensor networks include battery constraints, energy efficiency, network lifetime, harsh underground characteristics, better transmission range, and topology design, among others. Several routing approaches for safety evacuation have been

TABLE 1: Common rocks found in typical mines in relation to hardness or softness.

Nonlinear mapping	Mica	Coal	Granite	Feldspar	Quartz	Mineral
Softness	0.70	0.80	0.83	0.86	0.875	0.90
Hardness	2	3	5	6	7	9
Distance	750 m	470 m	390 m	315 m	278	78 m

proposed [8–14]. These were developed depending on specific emergency situations and management requirements. Transmitting data wirelessly impacts significant benefits to those investigating buildings, allowing them to deploy sensors and monitor from a remote location [15, 16]. To effectively gain the needed results, researchers have come out with a number of techniques to address the problem of topology control (TC). These include localization of nodes and time; error and path loss; transmission range and total load each node experiences; as well as energy conservation which is very crucial in optimizing efficiency and minimizing cost in wireless sensor networks [17–19]. Minimizing transmission range of wireless sensor networks is vital to the efficient routing of the network because the amount of communication energy that each sensor consumes is highly related to its transmission range [6]. The nodes signal reach $N\delta$ was defined as the integration of the change of the minimum and maximum signal reach, taking into consideration the number of cases (τ) of the rock structure β, β is the rock hardness, $N\delta$ is the signal reach for a node, and $N\delta_{min}$, $N\delta_{max}$ are minimum and maximum signal reach, respectively. The node signal reach is calculated as

$$N\delta = N\delta_{min} + \|N\delta_{min} - N\delta_{max}\| \, {}^{*}\text{random}\left('\beta', \text{rock}, 1, 1\right),$$

$$N\delta_{min} = \min\left(L, \min\left(\text{Row}, \text{Col}\right)\right),$$

$$N\delta_{max} = \max\left(L, \max\left(\text{Row}, \text{Col}\right)\right),$$
$$(2)$$

and where β is a geometric figure in the range of 0.7 to 0.9. For a connection to be made the absolute difference between i, j should be less than the node signal reach-$N\delta$. The connection matrix was given as

$$\varphi k\left(i, j\right) = \begin{cases} 1 & \text{if } \|i - j\| \leq N\delta \\ 0 & \text{otherwise.} \end{cases} \quad (3)$$

The relationship between rock hardness and the signal reach is a complicated nonlinear function, which is related to the skin depth of the rock with alternating currents concentrated in the outer region of a conductor (skin depth) by opposing internal magnetic fields as follows:

$$\text{Skin depth} = \sqrt{\frac{2}{\left(\rho * \omega * \sigma\right)}}. \quad (4)$$

ρ is material conductivity, ω is frequency, and σ is magnetic permeability.

The signal (B-field) is attenuated by cube of distance (d) : $B = (k)d^3$.

Signal reach (distance) is equal to 3^{*} skin depth.

Table 1 identifies 6 common rocks found in mines in relation to hardness or softness of each rock.

A routing path was modeled using a number of $T \times T$ size matrices namely the connection matrix (φk), routing matrix (φr), explosion matrix (φx), failed matrix (φf), hope matrix (φh), optimized matrix (φo), and the exit matrix (φe). The hardware survival rate vector (φh), the survival rate vector (φv) of each miner, and the final average survival rate vector (R) were also generated. A sensor node is named by its 3D integer (x, y, z) coordinates, where $1 \leq x \leq R, 1 \leq y \leq C$, $1 \leq z \leq L$ for $T = R * C * L$ being total number of nodes. If the node (a, b, c) is connected with node (d, e, f) then the element on $((a - 1) * C * L + (b - 1) * L + c)$th row and $((d - 1) * C * L + (e - 1) * L + f)$th column is 1; otherwise 0 and routing are limited to total number of multiple points connections that can be made. In arriving at the final optimized vector for transmission, each matrix was generated τ times.

The $\varphi r \subset \varphi k$; $M_\rho \leq \alpha$, M_ρ is even, M_ρ representing the maximum point-to-multipoint connection, and M_ρ is even allowing bidirectional communication, with i, j checking source and destination nodes, respectively:

$$\varphi r = \begin{cases} 1 & \text{if } \|i - j\| \geq \left(\dfrac{M_\rho}{2}\right), \\ 0 & \text{otherwise;} \end{cases} \quad (5)$$

$$\text{for } i, j = 1 : T.$$

2.4. Hardware, Software, and Network Fault Tolerant Considerations. Network security is a critical issue in wireless sensor networks as it significantly affects the efficiency of the communication and many key management schemes had been proposed to mitigate this constraint [18, 20]. In an event of accidents (ψ) occurring, the routing path would be affected by $(1 - \psi)$, where ψ is any random value within β, which would cause explosion on $R\varphi$ matrix and result in φx such that the resulting matrix would be the failed matrix (φf):

$$\varphi x = \left(1 - \psi\right) \varphi r,$$

$$\varphi f\left(i, j\right) = \begin{cases} 1 & \text{if } \{\varphi x\left(i, j\right) < \lambda L\} \\ 0 & \text{if } \{\varphi x\left(i, j\right) \geq \lambda L\} \end{cases} \quad (6)$$

$\varphi f(i, j) = 0$ if $\{\varphi x(i, j) \geq \lambda H\}$ else $\varphi f = \varphi x(i, j)/\lambda H$ for (λL or λH) representing the lower and higher accident impact thresholds, respectively.

A new set of routing paths (φh) and exit matrices (φe) for transmission was calculated as

$$\varphi h = \varphi f * \varphi r,$$

$$\varphi e = Ne - \psi. \quad (7)$$

The mathematical objective here is to find an optimized routing matrix (φo) that has the maximum survivability. The survivability is defined as the entropy of a number of parallel connections between every node to all the sink(s). The exit matrix (φe) described the success rate from each node to the sink(s), φe assumes that the number of exits (Ne) is available with an error margin (ψ). In most practical applications, more than one sink is used, and sink node is either through the fiber or Through-The-Earth (TTE) link. It is important to note that, in real rescue situations, the software (relational database management system (RDBMS)) and hardware including radio frequency identification (RFID) may fail as a result of the effect from the explosion and attack. The matrix (φs) was used to describe software survival rate including bugs or attacks:

$$\varphi s = 1 - \left(\left(\frac{1}{T + \text{random}} \right) (\text{``Geometric''}, \text{fail}, T, T) \right). \quad (8)$$

To obtain the final survival vector (φR) it was assumed that each miner will have an RFID; a vector φI was used to describe its failure rate, including risks of running out of battery, a vector φH for the hardware failure rate, for T = total number of nodes:

$$\varphi I = 1 - \left(\left(\frac{1}{T + r} \right) * (\text{``Geometric''}, \text{fail}, 1, T) \right). \quad (9)$$

r is a random number generated from the vector T and r : $0 \rightarrow \infty$, $T + \text{random} : T \rightarrow \infty$, $(1/(T + r)) : 1/T \rightarrow 0$; $1 - (1/(T + r)) : 1 - 1/T \rightarrow 1$ is the minimum; therefore for $T = N$ nodes, we have $1 - 1/N = (N - 1)/N \rightarrow 1$ for $(N - 1)/N \rightarrow$ node is dead and $1 \rightarrow$ node is alive:

$$\varphi H = \min\left(1, \varphi I\left[X\Psi\right]\right); \quad \text{for } [X\Psi] = \frac{\varphi e}{M_p}. \quad (10)$$

The survival rate of each miner was (φv). All these assumptions happen in real life and must be considered. The final survival rate vector (φR) was calculated:

$$\varphi v = \varphi s * \varphi e, \quad (11)$$

$$\varphi R = \varphi v * \varphi s, \quad (12)$$

$$R = \varphi R. \quad (13)$$

3. Related Work

3.1. Artificial Neural Networks (ANN).

Having found the optimum set of routing table that has the highest survival probability of communicating with and rescuing miners, it is important to train the neurons such that the initial error will be minimized and more importantly have a reliable system [21]. The topology of a neural network can be recurrent (with feedback contained in the network from the output back to the input), the feedforward (where data flow from the input to the output units). The data processing can extend over several layers of units, but no feedback connections are present. Many researchers have come out with neural network predictive models in both sigmoid and radial basis functions [22, 23]

with applications such as nonlinear transformation [23], extreme learning machine, predicting accuracy in gene classification [24], crisp distributed support vectors regression (CDSVR) model was monthly streamflow prediction was proposed by Valdez et al. [25] and other applications include fuzzy inference systems (FIS) which have been successfully applied in fields such as automatic control, data classification, decision analysis, and expert systems [26] among others. Artificial neural networks (ANN) are learning algorithm used to minimize the error between the neural network output and desired output. This is important where relationships exist between weights within the hidden and output layers, and among weights of more hidden layers. In addition other parameters including mean iteration, standard variation, standard deviation and convergent time (in sections) were evaluated. The architecture of the learning algorithm and the activation functions were included in neural networks. Neurons are trained to process store, recognize, and retrieve patterns or database entries to solve combinatorial optimization problems. Assuming that the input layer has 4 neurons, output layer 3 neurons, and the hidden layer 6 neurons, we can evolve other parameters in the feedforward network to evolve the weight. So the particles would be in a group of weights and there would be $4 * 6 + 6 * 3 = 42$ weights. This implies that the particle consists of 42 real numbers. The range of weight can be set to $[-100, 100]$ or a fitting range. After encoding the particles, the fitness function was then determined. The goodness of the fit was diagnosed using mean squared error (MSE) as against mean cubic error (MCE) and the mean absolute error (MAE). The mean cubic error will allow for fast convergence and that will gross over accuracy making the process unstable, while the mean absolute error is stable but converges slowly. A midway between the two is the MSE and is given as

$$\text{MSE} = \frac{1}{ns} \sum_{j=1}^{n} \sum_{i=1}^{s} \left(Y_{j,i} - y_{j,i}\right)^2, \quad (14)$$

where n is number of samples, s is the number of neurons at output layer, $Y_{i,j}$ is the ideal value of ith sample at jth output, and $Y_{i,j}$ is the actual value of ith sample at jth output.

3.2. The Gaussian and Zhang Models.

The standard or direct approach to interpolation at locations $\{x_1, ..., x_N\} \subset R^d$ without the first term, using Gaussian kernel is given as

$$\phi(r) = e^{-(\varepsilon r)^2}. \quad (15)$$

Zhang has [27] tried to modify the Gaussian model as follows: a function $\psi : [0, \infty) \rightarrow \mathbb{R}$ such that $k(x, x') = \varphi(\|x - x'\|)$, where, $x, x' \in \chi$ and $x \cdot x'$ denotes the Euclidean norm with $k(x, x') = \exp(-\|x - x'\|^2/\delta^2)$ as an example of the RBF kernels. The global support for RBF radials or kernels has resulted in dense Gram matrices that can affect large datasets and therefore construct the following two equations: $k_{C,v}(x, x') = \phi_{C,v}(\|x - x'\|)k(x, x')$ and $\phi_{C,v}(\|x - x'\|) = [(1 - \|x - x'\|/C)(\cdot)_+]^v$, where $C > 0$, $v \geq (d + 1)/2$, and $(\cdot)_+$ is the positive part. The function $\phi_C(\cdot)$ is a sparsifying operator, which thresholds all the entries satisfying $(\|x - x'\|) \geq C$ to zeros in the Gram matrix. The new kernel resulting from this construction preserves positive definiteness. This means that given any pair of inputs x and x' where $x = x'$ the shrinkage (the smaller C) is imposed on the function value $k(x, x')$; the result is that the Gram matrices K and K_{Cv} can be either very similar or quite different, depending on the choice of C. However Zhang also ended up with an extra power parameter.

4. The Proposed Hybrid

The previous work looked at the Gaussian model and paralyzed the computational power parameter. The result was compact radial basis function (CRBF). This was used to run both SBF and RBF and the results compared. The scalability and processing efficiency were also analyzed.

The novelty of this algorithm, the weighed nonlinear hybrid, was to find several hybrids and the best for rescue operations. The cosine and sine functions were used to reduce high level nonlinear and increase small level nonlinear. Both the previous and the current algorithm used the same preliminary considerations, but the results is slightly different because data are random.

The sigmoid basis function was given as

$$\log \text{sig}(R), \quad R = W \cdot P + B,$$
$$\log \text{sig}(W \cdot P + B) = \frac{1}{1 + e^{-(W \cdot P + B)}}. \tag{16}$$

Neuron function S (sigmoid) is log sig, W is weight matrix, P is input vector, and B is threshold. We therefore proposed a compact radial basis function based on the Gaussian radial basis function and Helens' [28] definition expressed as

$$[\exp(-\|R\|)], \quad R = W \cdot P + B,$$
$$(\exp(-\text{abs}((W \cdot P + B)))), \tag{17}$$
$$\phi(\text{out}) = [\exp(-\|R\|)].$$

W is weight matrix, P is input vector, and B is threshold. The focus was to improve on the radial basis function for the mine application.

An optimized vector R was generated as the optimum set of transmission routing table that has the highest survival probability for data transmission (13):

$$PN = \sum_{i=1}^{N} R_i S_i + \sum_{i=1}^{2} S_i + \sum_{i=1}^{2} S_i S_i + 1 \tag{18}$$
$$\text{for } 1 \leq i \leq S; \quad 1 \leq k \leq R.$$

R, S_1, S_2 are number of neurons at input, hidden, and output layers, respectively.

PN is the position of the nth particle:

$$W_i = S_i R, W_2 = S_i R, \ldots, W_m = S_m R,$$
$$P_i = [R(i - j) + K] = W_i(i, k). \tag{19}$$

There are two thresholds $(S_1 \Rightarrow B_1)$:

Hidden: $B_1(i, j) = P(RS_1 + S_1 S_2) \Rightarrow S_1$

Output: $B_2(i, j) = P(RS_1 + S_1 S_2) \Rightarrow S_2$.

From (16), (17), and (18) the nonlinear weight of $[\pm \cos(R)]$ or $[\pm \sin(R)]$ was imposed on the CRBF before being combined with the SBF as (HSCR-BF$_{-\cos}$, HSCR-BF$_{+\cos}$, HSCR-BF$_{-\sin}$, HSCR-BF$_{+\sin}$). The cosine weight was used to keep high level nonlinear for small input value and reduce the nonlinear for large input values, while sine weight was used to keep high level nonlinear for large input value and reduce the nonlinear for small input values:

HSCR-BF$_{-\cos}$:

$$Y(\text{out}) = \log \text{sig}(R) + [\exp(-\|R\|)] \cdot {}^*[-\cos(R)]$$

HSCR-BF$_{+\cos}$:

$$Y(\text{out}) = \log \text{sig}(R) + [\exp(-\|R\|)] \cdot {}^*[+\cos(R)]$$

HSCR-BF$_{-\sin}$:

$$Y(\text{out}) = \log \text{sig}(R) + [\exp(-\|R\|)] \cdot {}^*[-\sin(R)]$$

HSCR-BF$_{+\sin}$:

$$Y(\text{out}) = \log \text{sig}(R) + [\exp(-\|R\|)] \cdot {}^*[+\sin(R)]. \tag{20}$$

The nonlinear weight of $[+\cos(R)]$ was imposed on the GRBF before being combined with the SBF:

HSGR-YBF$_{+\cos}$:

$$Y(\text{out}) = \log \text{sig}(R) + [\exp(-\|R\|^2)] \cdot {}^*[+\cos(R)]. \tag{21}$$

5. Particle Swarm Optimization

Particle swarm optimization (PSO), an evolutionary algorithm, is a population based stochastic optimization technique. The idea was conceived by an American researcher and social psychologist James Kennedy in the 1950s. The theory is inspired by social behavior of bird flocking or fish schooling. The method falls within the category of swarm intelligence methods for solving global optimization problems. Literature has shown that the PSO is an effective alternative to established evolutionary algorithms (GA). It is also established that PSO is easily applicable to real world complex problems with discrete, continuous, and nonlinear design parameters and retains the conceptual simplicity of GA [29, 30]. Each particle within the swarm is given an initial random position and an initial speed of propagation. The position of the particle represents a solution to the problem as described in a matrix τ, where M and N represent the number of particles in the simulation and the number of dimensions of the problem, respectively [31, 32]. A random position representing a possible solution to the problem, with an initial associated velocity representing a function of the distance from the particle's current position to the previous position of good fitness value, was given. A velocity matrix V_{el} with the same dimensions as matrix τ_x described this:

$$\tau_x = \begin{pmatrix} \tau^{11}, \tau^{12}, \ldots, \tau^{1N} \\ \tau^{21}, \tau^{22}, \ldots, \tau^{2N} \\ \vdots \\ \tau^{m1}, \tau^{m2}, \ldots, \tau^{MN} \end{pmatrix},$$

$$\hspace{4cm}(22)$$

$$V_{el} = \begin{pmatrix} v^{11}, v^{12}, \ldots, v^{1N} \\ v^{21}, v^{22}, \ldots, v^{2N} \\ \vdots \\ v^{m1}, v^{m2}, \ldots, v^{MN} \end{pmatrix}.$$

The best feasible alternative is the genetic algorithm. However this is generally slow as compared to the PSO and therefore computationally expensive, hence the PSO.

While moving in the search space, particles commit to memorize the position of the best solution they have found. At each iteration of the algorithm, each particle moves with a speed that is a weighed sum of three components: the old speed, a speed component that drives the particles towards the location in the search space, where it previously found the best solution so far, and a speed component that drives the particle towards the location in the search space where the neighbor particles found the best solution so far [7]. The personal best position can be represented by an $N \times N$ matrix ρ_{best} and the global best position is an N-dimensional vector G_{best}:

$$\rho_{best} = \begin{pmatrix} \rho^{11}, \rho^{12}, \ldots, \rho^{1N} \\ \rho^{21}, \rho^{22}, \ldots, \rho^{2N} \\ \vdots \\ \rho^{m1}, \rho^{m2}, \ldots, \rho^{MN} \end{pmatrix},$$

$$\hspace{4cm}(23)$$

$$G_{best} = \left(g_{best}^{1}, g_{best}^{12}, \ldots, g_{best}^{N} \right).$$

All particles move towards the personal and the global best, with τ, ρ_{best}, V_{el}, and g_{best} containing all the required information by the particle swarm algorithm. These matrices are updated on each successive iterations:

$$V_{mn} = V_{mn} + \gamma_{c1}\eta_{r1}\left(\rho_{best_{mn}} - X_{mm} \right)$$

$$+ \gamma_{c2}\eta_{r2}\left(g_{best_n} - X_{mn} \right) \hspace{1cm}(24)$$

$$X_{mn} = V_{mn}.$$

γ_{c1} and γ_{c2} are constants set to 1.3 and 2, respectively, and η_{r1} η_{r2} are random numbers.

5.1. Adaptive Mutation according to Threshold. Particle swarm optimization has been effective in training neural networks such as a Parallel Particle Swarm optimization (PPSO) method with dynamic parameter adaptation used to optimize complex mathematical functions and improved evolutionary method in fuzzy logic [30, 31, 33]. To prevent particles from not converging or converging at local minimum, an

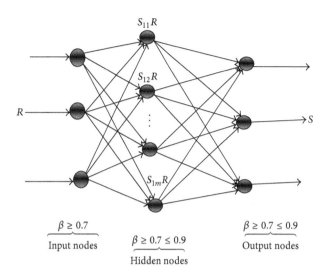

FIGURE 1: The structure AMPSO for CRBF, GRBF, and SBF transfer functions.

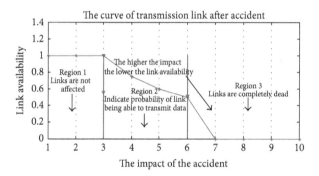

FIGURE 2: Impact of explosion/accident on transmission link.

adaptive mutation according to threshold was introduced. An alternative to this is the use of the nonadaptive mutation, and this could converge to the local minimum or fail to converge at all. The advantage of the nonadaptation is simple and fast but may not provide the needed results.

Particles positions were updated with new value only when the new value is greater than the previous value; 20% of particles of those obtaining lower values were made to mutate for faster convergence and the structure of adaptive mutation PSO (AMPSO) with threshold can be found in [1]. The input layer takes the final survival vector (13), with a number of hidden layers and an output layer. The feedforward neural network was used. The structure of Adaptive Mutation PSO (AMPSO) with threshold Neural Network was used, Figure 1, [32].

6. Results and Discussion

6.1. Generating the Routing Path. Elements 0, 1, and 2 in φx imply that the link(s) were not affected and elements 3, 4, 5, and 6, represent a probability for the links being able to transmit data, while figures from 7 means the link is totally dead. Region 1 that indicates that links are not affected, region

TABLE 2: Optimum set of routing table redundancy with the highest survival probability (6 cases).

Vectors for each case							Rock hardness cases
R1	0.5409	0.4281	0.8834	0.585	0.8134	0.5163	0.7
R2	0.4526	0.5841	0.4547	0.8997	0.8436	0.2696	0.8
R3	0.2931	0.5899	0.5903	0.8309	0.6971	0.2898	0.83
R4	0.4851	0.6085	0.6913	0.4002	0.5026	0	0.86
R5	0.4917	0.5857	0.7805	0.6037	0.5182	0.6472	0.875
R6	0.2902	0.7253	0.458	0.5762	0.1397	0	0.9

2 gives the probability of link available, and the last region indicates the link is completely down (Figure 2).

The matrices $\varphi i, \varphi k, \varphi r, \varphi x, \varphi h$ for $\tau = n$, with dimensions of $L = 3$, $R = 2$, and $C = 1$ for depth (level), row (length), and width (column), respectively, were generated as follows:

$$S_{eq} = \begin{pmatrix} 1 & 1 & 1 \\ 1 & 2 & 1 \\ 2 & 2 & 1 \\ 2 & 1 & 1 \\ 3 & 1 & 1 \\ 3 & 2 & 1 \end{pmatrix}, \quad i\varphi = \begin{bmatrix} 0 & 0 & 0 & 0 & 0 & 0 \\ 0 & 0 & 0 & 0 & 0 & 0 \\ 0 & 0 & 0 & 0 & 0 & 0 \\ 0 & 0 & 0 & 0 & 0 & 0 \\ 0 & 0 & 0 & 0 & 0 & 0 \\ 0 & 0 & 0 & 0 & 0 & 0 \end{bmatrix},$$

$$\varphi k = \begin{pmatrix} 1 & 1 & 1 & 1 & 0 & 0 \\ 1 & 1 & 1 & 0 & 0 & 0 \\ 0 & 1 & 1 & 1 & 0 & 0 \\ 0 & 0 & 1 & 1 & 1 & 0 \\ 0 & 0 & 0 & 1 & 1 & 1 \\ 0 & 0 & 0 & 1 & 1 & 1 \end{pmatrix}$$

1 = signal points,

$$\varphi r = \begin{pmatrix} 1 & 1 & 1 & 0 & 0 & 0 \\ 1 & 1 & 1 & 0 & 0 & 0 \\ 0 & 1 & 1 & 1 & 0 & 0 \\ 0 & 0 & 1 & 1 & 1 & 0 \\ 0 & 0 & 0 & 1 & 1 & 1 \\ 0 & 0 & 0 & 1 & 1 & 1 \end{pmatrix} \quad (25)$$

1 = transmission path,

$$\varphi x = \begin{pmatrix} 0 & 1 & 2 & 2 & 0 & 0 \\ 1 & 5 & 1 & 2 & 0 & 0 \\ 0 & 8 & 1 & 5 & 9 & 1 \\ 1 & 1 & 5 & 1 & 1 & 17 \\ 1 & 1 & 4 & 11 & 0 & 2 \\ 4 & 4 & 19 & 5 & 3 & 0 \end{pmatrix}$$

explosion sizes,

$$\varphi f = \begin{pmatrix} 1 & 1 & 1 & 1 & 1 & 1 \\ 1 & .6 & 1 & 1 & 1 & 1 \\ 1 & 0 & 1 & .6 & 0 & 1 \\ 1 & 1 & .6 & 1 & 1 & 0 \\ 1 & 1 & .75 & 0 & 1 & 1 \\ .75 & .75 & 0 & .6 & 1 & 1 \end{pmatrix},$$

$$\varphi h = \begin{pmatrix} 1 & 1 & 1 & 0 & 0 & 0 \\ 1 & .6 & 1 & 0 & 0 & 0 \\ 0 & 0 & 1 & .6 & 0 & 0 \\ 0 & 0 & .6 & 1 & 1 & 0 \\ 0 & 0 & 0 & 0 & 1 & 1 \\ 0 & 0 & 0 & .6 & 1 & 1 \end{pmatrix},$$

$$\varphi o = \begin{pmatrix} .8 & .8 & .8 & 0 & 0 & 0 \\ .8 & .48 & .8 & 0 & 0 & 0 \\ 0 & 0 & .8 & .48 & 0 & 0 \\ 0 & 0 & .48 & .8 & .8 & 0 \\ 0 & 0 & 0 & 0 & .8 & .8 \\ 0 & 0 & 0 & .48 & .8 & .8 \end{pmatrix},$$

$$\varphi e = \begin{pmatrix} 1.44 & 1.44 & 1.44 & 0 & 0 & 0 \\ 1.44 & .864 & 1.44 & 0 & 0 & 0 \\ 0 & 0 & 1.44 & .864 & 0 & 0 \\ 0 & 0 & .864 & 1.44 & 1.44 & 0 \\ 0 & 0 & 0 & 0 & 1.44 & 1.44 \\ 0 & 0 & 0 & .864 & 1.44 & 1.44 \end{pmatrix} \quad (26)$$

1 or fractional figures are transmission path.

Element "0" on φf depicts a connection lost, while "1" means that the connection will never go down and represent the connection to the fixed sink node(s) along the edge or the emergency connection to the mobile data mule(s):

$$\varphi s = \begin{pmatrix} .8333 & .8889 & .9091 & .8333 & .8571 & .8333 \\ .8889 & .8333 & .8750 & .8571 & .8750 & .8333 \\ .8571 & .9167 & .8750 & .9091 & .8889 & .8333 \\ .8750 & .8571 & .8571 & .8571 & .8571 & .8333 \\ .8333 & .8333 & .8571 & .8333 & .8889 & .9000 \\ .9167 & .8333 & .9091 & .8333 & .8889 & .8571 \end{pmatrix}. \quad (27)$$

The survival rate of RFID, hardware, and each miner vectors was displayed as

$$\varphi I = .8571 \quad .8750 \quad .8571 \quad .8889 \quad .8571 \quad .8333,$$
$$\varphi H = .6236 \quad .4976 \quad 1 \quad .6851 \quad .9286 \quad .6086, \quad (28)$$
$$\varphi v = .5409 \quad .4281 \quad .8834 \quad .5850 \quad .8134 \quad .5163.$$

Optimization was done numerically using Matlab simulation tool to find the optimum set of routing tables through particle swarm search for rescue operation as discussed in the preliminaries. From (13) the final survival vector for dimensions of $L = 3$, $R = 2$, and $C = 1$ will be an average of the 6 vectors as in Table 2. Total cases $Rn = \tau = T \times T$ (which

TABLE 3: Scalability of model to survival probability range, robot location and rock type.

Location	Mica	Coal	Granite	Feldspar	Quartz	Mineral
Compact radial basis function with negative nonlinear weight (HSCR-BF$_{-\cos}$)						
(10, 6, 5)	0.8769–1.0000	0.9070–0.9927	0.8402–0.9943	0.8023–0.9778	0.7386–0.9376	0.7345–0.8740
(10, 5, 4)	0.9024–0.9696	0.9032–0.9505	0.8836–0.9430	0.8633–0.9527	0.7944–0.9465	0.7263–0.8720
(6, 5, 4)	0.8906–0.9877	0.8827–0.9845	0.8384–0.9675	0.8627–0.9820	0.7911–0.9142	0.6392–0.7840
(3, 1, 10)	0.7302–0.8481	0.6588–0.7816	0.6341–0.7473	0.6503–0.7249	0.5930–0.7156	0.4445–0.5621
Gaussian radial basis function with positive nonlinear weight (HSGR-BF$_{+\cos}$)						
(10, 6, 5)	0.8732–0.9963	0.8526–0.9987	0.8492–0.9950	0.7867–0.9568	0.7404–0.9025	0.6606–0.8315
(10, 5, 4)	0.8843–0.9593	0.8843–0.9853	0.8444–0.9753	0.7746–0.9828	0.7304–0.9595	0.6678–0.8817
(6, 5, 4)	0.8785–0.9983	0.8902–0.9996	0.8200–0.9997	0.7927–0.9446	0.7065–0.8565	0.6572–0.8063
(3, 1, 10)	0.7608–0.8552	0.6600–0.8325	0.6090–0.7371	0.5482–0.6249	0.5026–0.6056	0.4856–0.5453

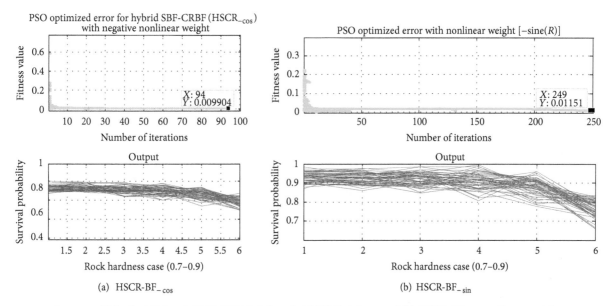

FIGURE 3: Hybrid of SBF and CRBF (HSCR-BF) with (a) HSCR-BF$_{-\cos}$ and (b) HSCR-BF$_{-\sin}$ nonlinear weight.

represent the total nodes deployed) for this scenario. Rock softness or hardness takes the values of β and each matrix is generated τ time/cases and the final routing vector will be an average of the n vectors φR = Average ($R1 : R6$) [Table 2] which becomes the input for the PSO training.

The final survival rate is R = (0.5409 0.4281 0.8834 0.585 0.8130 0.5163) from (13).

6.2. The Final Survival Vector.

The R = (0.5409 0.4281 0.8834 0.585 0.8130 0.5163) from (13) is the maximum survival probability for a total of 6 nodes deployed. It describes the success rate from each node to the sink(s). In most practical applications, more than one sink is used, and sink node is either through the fiber or TTE connection. The size of the vector depends on the dimensions of the field. The elements R = (0.5409 0.4281 0.8834 0.585 0.8130 0.5163) represent the probability of 54%, 43%, 88%, 59%, 81%, and 52% success of each node transmitting data to and from its source or destination. It assists decision makers as to whether to send data through one or more nodes or send each

message twice. The total nodes used for the simulation were 300 with underground mine dimensions of $L = 10$, $R = 6$ and $C = 5$ for depth (level), row (length), and width (column), respectively, with "pm" a sensor apart, pm = 100, $M_\rho = 4$, and $Ne = 2$. The PSO training used swarm size of 20, maximum position was set to 100, max velocity = 1, and maximum number of iteration = 250. The thresholds λL and λH were 3 and 6, respectively, $\tau = 6$ cases (each case represent, a rock hardness case and also represent, the total neurons used); thus each matrix and vectors were run 6 times before neural training. The survival probability (bottom) indicates that the model survived between 90 and 100%, where rock cases were relatively soft (≥ 0.7). The survival probability declines as the rock becomes harder and approaches 0.8. At the hardest rock of 0.9, the survival probability fell between 72 and 84% for the entire hybrids. In view of this the AP heads had to be deployed at a location where the rock is relatively soft for maximum signal strength. Each computer simulation incorporated all the 6 different cases of rock hardness/softness to produce the matrices. Detailed location analysis or the scalability of the model in relation to survival

TABLE 4: Hybrid of SBF and CRBF with negative nonlinear weight on CRBF (HSCR-BF$_{-\cos}$).

Runs	Mean iteration	Std variation	Std deviation	Convergent time	Final error
Total	231.020	343.498	0.382	916.50	0.0985
AVG	23.102	34.350	0.038	91.65	0.0098
Min/Max	29.540	45.314	0.024	80.000	0.0043

TABLE 5: Hybrid of SBF and CRBF with nonlinear weight on CRBF (HSCR-BF$_{-\sin}$).

Runs	Mean iteration	Std variation	Std deviation	Convergent time	Final error
Total	307.320	488.381	0.376	1143.00	0.135
AVG	30.732	48.838	0.038	114.30	0.013
Min/Max	30.740	56.926	0.007	61.500	0.021

probability range, robot location, and different rock types is recorded in Table 3. Figures 4–6 represent different scenarios of SBF and CRBF hybrids with the $[\pm \cos(R)]$ and $[\pm \sin(R)]$ nonlinear weights, while Figure 7 represents the SBF and Gaussian hybrids for $[+\cos(R)]$ nonlinear weight. The top half of each figure indicates the optimized error or the final error after the neural training and the bottom half reveals model survival probability.

Figure 3 discusses the SBF and CRBF hybrids (HSCR-BF) with nonlinear weight. Training in negative nonlinear weights (HSCR-BF$_{-\cos}$, HSCR-BF$_{-\sin}$) responded well. The HSCR-BF$_{-\cos}$ had a steady and compact routing path which was consistent through all rock layers, with initial survival probability between 87.7% and 100% in soft layers declining to 73.5%–87.4% at harder rock layers. The HSCR-BF$_{-\sin}$ performed quite well but was more dispersed (87.9% to 98.5 at the soft rock and 66.5% to 81.8% at the hard rock).

In addition, the various parameters, mean iteration, standard variance, standard deviation, and the convergent time, of HSCR-BF$_{-\cos}$ were optimised. This is demonstrated by finding the relationship between the maximum and the minimum values of the parameters and comparing with the average figures and the closer the difference is to the average the more consistent the data are in the dataset (Table 4); thus HSCR-BF$_{-\cos}$ provided the best results among the proposed hybrids. The HSCR-BF$_{-\sin}$ on the RBF yielded strength in mean iteration and standard variance with error of 0.013 (Table 5).

In Figure 4 training with nonlinear weight of positive cosine and sine of HSCR-BF (HSCR-BF$_{+\cos}$ and HSCR-BF$_{+\sin}$) had some similarities. The two models streamed well at the initial stages from 89.6% to 99.2% and 90.8% to 99.0% at soft layers of the rock, respectively. However at the last stages the probability of transmitting effectively became marginal, from 79.5% to 85.2% and 82.1% to 85.4%, respectively. Much as this hybrid could perform well in areas where routing conditions are much better in less dense rescue situations, this could hamper rescue mission in both cases due to battery drain or collision from traffic conjunction. The data for mean iteration and convergent time for HSCR-BF$_{+\cos}$ (Table 6) and mean Iteration, standard variance, the final

error HSCR-BF$_{+\sin}$ (Table 7) were consistent with the negative sine having better results than the positive cosine.

The survival probability of the positive nonlinear weight Gaussian hybrids (HSGR-BF$_{+\cos}$) in Figure 5 is more compact both at the initial (i.e., 87.3–99.6%) and later (66.1%–83.2%) stages declining to harder rock layers with an error of 0.01173 (Table 8).

At the initial stage particles are sensitive to inputs as they moved quickly in the search space towards the target and while particles peaked closer to the target it became less sensitive to the input and began to align (Figure 6). At the later stage more RBF are used to keep the error at minimum for accuracy. It was also noticed that instead of accelerating higher, and becoming more sensitive to the inputs, while particles were far from the target, the hybrids with $^*[-\sin(R)]$ and $^*[+\sin(R)]$ were less sensitive to the inputs as $^*[-\sin(R)]$ descended from $[x = -1, y = 0.5785]$ to $[x = 1, y = 0.4215]$, while $^*[+\sin(R)]$ descended from $[x = -3, y = 0.0404]$ to $[x = -1, y = -0.04062]$ before becoming conscious of the inputs. In addition the hybrids with the $^*[+\cos(R)]$ lagged slightly between $[x = -4, y = 0.006014]$ and $[x = -2, y = 0.06288]$ before becoming sensitive to inputs. However they all lined up for accuracy in terms of the minimised error.

The nonlinearity of the hybrids is presented (Figure 7); the negative cosine/sine weight is used to reduce nonlinear for small input values and this lies between $-1 < x < +1$, and the positive cosine/sine weight is used to keep high nonlinear for large inputs for the remaining region.

6.3. CPU Time Efficiency. The relationship between various hybrids with respect to the central processing time (CPU) was profiled for different runs (Table 9) and expressed in a sixth-order polynomial given as $Y_r = \beta_7 X_1^6 + \beta_6 X_1^5 + \beta_5 X_1^4 + \beta_4 X_1^3 + \beta_3 X_1^2 + \beta_2 X_1 + \beta_0$, where X_1 is time (seconds) and β is the coefficient of the polynomial (Figure 8). The proposed hybrid has better usage of CPU time with $R^2 = 0.9160$, followed by HSCR-BF$_{-\sin}$ and HSCR-BF$_{+\cos}$ with R^2 of 0.7551 and 0.7244, respectively (Table 10). Applying the proposed algorithm into Gaussian, the CPU usage had R^2 of 0.7345

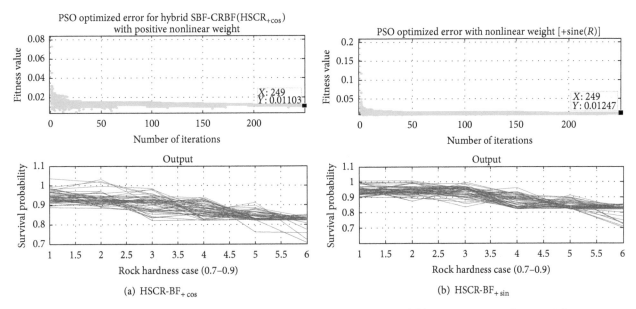

FIGURE 4: Hybrid of SBF and CRBF (HSCR-BF) with (a) HSCR-BF$_{+\cos}$ and (b) HSCR-BF$_{+\sin}$ nonlinear weight.

TABLE 6: Hybrid of SBF and CRBF with nonlinear weight on CRBF (HSCR-BF$_{+\cos}$).

Runs	Mean iteration	Std variation	Std deviation	Convergent time	Final error
Total	350.780	522.257	0.311	1156.50	0.121
AVG	35.078	52.226	0.031	115.65	0.012
Max/Min	54.840	63.413	0.009	93.500	0.006

and indeed marginally outperformed HSCR-BF$_{+\cos}$. Detailed work on SBF, CRBF, and GRBF, with regard to scalability, memory usage, and the central processing time, has been carried by the authors [1].

7. Conclusion

In summary, we made the following contributions. First we used the mix of SBF and CRBF to present several hybrids with different nonlinear weights of cosine and sine functions on compact radial basis function. Next we showed the performance of the proposed nonlinear weight hybrids; HSCR-BF$_{-\cos}$, HSCR-BF$_{+\cos}$, HSCR-BF$_{-\sin}$, and HSCR-BF$_{+\sin}$ optimised all the parameters with minimised error of 0.0098, 0.012, 0.013, and 0.013, respectively, compared to 0.0117 for Gaussian HSCR-BF$_{+\cos}$. The analyzed CPU usage with corresponding R^2 values of 0.9160, 0.75, 0.72440, 0.6731 and 0.7345 for HSCR-BF$_{-\cos}$, HSCR-BF$_{+\cos}$, HSCR-BF$_{-\sin}$, HSCR-BF$_{+\sin}$, and HSCR-BF$_{+\cos}$, respectively, demonstrated that the algorithm is scalable. There exist some evacuation models, that is, Goh and Mandic [11] which offered a choice for travelers and several schemes for the decision makers may not be applicable in emergency underground mine situations. *The proposed nonlinear hybrid algorithm with particle swarm optimisation has better capability of approximation to underlying functions with a fast learning speed and high robustness and* *is competitive and more computationally efficient to Gaussian with the same nonlinear weight. The algorithm is new and that makes it difficult to identify limitations and we intend to* investigate other hybrids and compare with genetic algorithm (GA) in the future.

Nomenclature

$N\delta_{\min}, N\delta_{\max}$:   Minimum and maximum signal reach

HSCR-BF/HSGR-BF: Hybrid of SBF with CRBF/Hybrid of SBF with GRBF

HSCR-BF$_{-\cos}$:   Hybrid of SBF and CRBF −cos nonlinear weight

HSCR-BF$_{+\cos}$:   Hybrid of SBF and CRBF +cos nonlinear weight

HSCR-BF$_{-\sin}$:   Hybrid of SBF and CRBF −sine nonlinear weight

HSCR-BF$_{+\sin}$:   Hybrid of SBF and CRBF +sine nonlinear weight

HSGR-BF$_{+\cos}$:   Hybrid of SBF and GRBF +cos nonlinear weight.

Conflict of Interests

The authors declare that there is no conflict of interests regarding the publication of this paper.

TABLE 7: Hybrid of SBF and CRBF with nonlinear weight on CRBF (HSCR-BF$_{+\sin}$).

Runs	Mean iteration	Std variation	Std deviation	Convergent time	Final error
Total	260.360	407.109	0.3457	998.00	0.129
AVG	26.036	40.711	0.0346	99.80	0.013
Min/Max	27.840	56.040	0.008	106.500	0.014

TABLE 8: Hybrid of SBF and GRBF with nonlinear weight on GRBF (HSGR-BF$_{+\cos}$).

Runs	Mean iteration	Std variation	Std deviation	Convergent time	Final error
Total	219.840	349.010	0.439	1121.00	0.1173
AVG	21.984	34.901	0.044	112.10	0.0117
Min/Max	27.000	46.580	0.008	80.000	0.0165

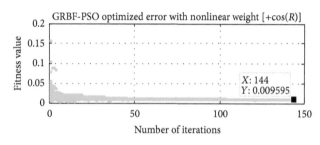

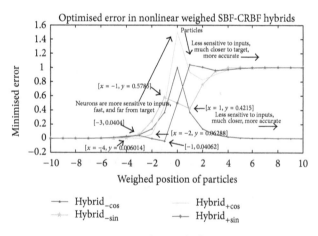

FIGURE 5: Hybrid of SBF and GRBF with nonlinear weight on GRBF (HSCR-BF$_{+\cos}$).

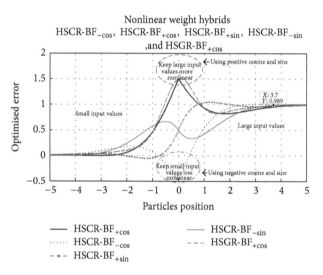

FIGURE 7: Nonlinear weighed curves for optimized error without Gaussian negative cosine curve.

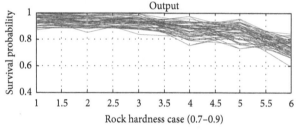

FIGURE 6: Particles weighed position.

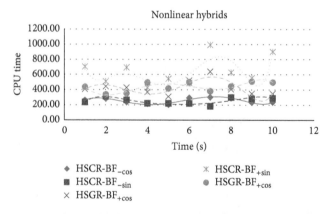

FIGURE 8: The trend of hybrids CPU time curves using sixth-Order Polynomial.

Acknowledgments

The authors would like to appreciate the immense contribution of the mining companies where the study was undertaken. The authors are grateful to these individuals for their immeasurable contributions to this work: Fred Attakuma, Patrick Addai, Isaac Owusu Kwankye, Thomas Kwaw Annan, Willet Agongo, Nathaniel Quansah, Francis Owusu Mensah, Clement Owusu-Asamoah, Joseph Adu-Mensah, Shadrack Aidoo, Martin Anokye, F. T. Oduro, Ernest Ekow

TABLE 9: CPU time usage efficiency for the hybrids.

Runs	HSCR-BF$_{-\cos}$	HSCR-BF$_{-\sin}$	HSCR-BF$_{+\cos}$	HSCR-BF$_{+\sin}$	HSGR-BF$_{+\cos}$
Total	2558.89	2543.50	4223.44	6439.62	4381.33
Average	255.89	254.35	422.34	643.96	438.13

TABLE 10: Analysis of CPU time on the various hybrids.

	β_6	β_5	β_4	β_3	β_2	β_1	β_0	R^2
HSCR-BF$_{-\cos}$	$0.0159x$	$-0.2575x$	$-0.759x$	$33.494x$	$-199.01x$	$403.45x$	25.322	0.9160
HSCR-BF$_{+\cos}$	$0.0903x$	$-2.3158x$	$19.932x$	$-58.027x$	$-31.337x$	$328.08x$	147.47	0.7244
HSCR-BF$_{-\sin}$	$-0.033x$	$1.1354x$	$-15.811x$	$113.68x$	$-433.7x$	$780.08x$	-207.94	0.7551
HSCR-BF$_{+\sin}$	$0.2571x$	$-14.263x$	$171.73x$	$-1006.9x$	$2993x$	$-4237.4x$	2787.9	0.6731
HSGR-BF$_{+\cos}$	$-0.0437x$	$1.0911x$	$-8.2923x$	$6.6218x$	$159.34x$	$-539.39x$	819.1	0.7345

Abano, E. Omari-Siaw, and Qiang Jia. This work was supported by the National Natural Science Foundation of China (no. 71271103) and by the Six Talents Peak Foundation of Jiangsu Province.

References

[1] M. O. Ansong, H. X. Yao, and J. S. Huang, "Radial and sigmoid basis functions neural networks in wireless sensor routing topology control in underground mine rescue operation based on particle swarm optimization," *International Journal of Distributed Sensor Networks-Hindawi*, vol. 2013, Article ID 376931, 14 pages, 2013.

[2] R. Neruda and P. Kudová, "Learning methods for radial basis function networks," *Future Generation Computer Systems*, vol. 21, no. 7, pp. 1131–1142, 2005.

[3] C. T. Cheng, J. Y. Lin, and Y. G. C. Sun, "Long-term prediction of discharges in Manwan hydropower using adaptive-network-based fuzzy inference systems models," in *Advances in Natural Computation*, vol. 3498 of *Lecture Notes in Computer Science*, pp. 1152–1161, 2005.

[4] D. Broomhead and D. Lowe, "Multivariate functional interpolation and adaptive networks," *Complex System*, vol. 2, pp. 321–355, 1988.

[5] Y. Chen, C. Chuah, and Q. Zhao, "Network configuration for optimal utilization efficiency of wireless sensor networks," *Ad Hoc Networks*, vol. 6, no. 1, pp. 92–107, 2008.

[6] P. S. Rajpal, K. S. Shishodia, and G. S. Sekhon, "An artificial neural network for modeling reliability, availability and maintainability of a repairable system," *Reliability Engineering and System Safety*, vol. 91, no. 7, pp. 809–819, 2006.

[7] W. Jang, W. M. Healy, and S. J. Mirosław, "Wireless sensor networks as part of a web-based building environmental monitoring system," *Automation in Construction*, vol. 17, no. 6, pp. 729–736, 2008.

[8] M. S. Pan, C. H. Tsai, and Y. C. Tseng, "Emergegncy guiding and monitoring application in indoor 3D environment by Wireless Sensor Network," *Internation Journal Os Sensor Newourk*, vol. 1, pp. 2–10, 2006.

[9] S. Zarifzadeh, A. Nayyeri, and N. Yazdani, "Efficient construction of network topology to conserve energy in wireless ad hoc networks," *Computer Communications*, vol. 31, no. 1, pp. 160–173, 2008.

[10] R. Riaz, A. Naureen, A. Akram, A. H. Akbar, K. Kim, and H. Farooq Ahmed, "A unified security framework with three key management schemes for wireless sensor networks," *Computer Communications*, vol. 31, no. 18, pp. 4269–4280, 2008.

[11] S. L. Goh and D. P. Mandic, "An augmented CRTRL for complex-valued recurrent neural networks," *Neural Networks*, vol. 20, no. 10, pp. 1061–1066, 2007.

[12] L. A. B. Munoz and J. J. V. Ramosy, "Similarity-based heterogeneous neural networks," *Engineering Letters*, vol. 14, no. 2, pp. 103–116, 2007.

[13] R. Taormina, K. Chau, and R. Sethi, "Artificial neural network simulation of hourly groundwater levels in a coastal aquifer system of the Venice lagoon," *Engineering Applications of Artificial Intelligence*, vol. 25, no. 8, pp. 1670–1676, 2012.

[14] K. Leblebicioglu and U. Halici, "Infinite dimensional radial basis function neural networks for nonlinear transformations on function spaces," *Nonlinear Analysis: Theory, Methods and Applications*, vol. 30, no. 3, pp. 1649–1654, 1997.

[15] F. Fernández-Navarro, C. Hervás-Martínez, J. Sanchez-Monedero, and P. A. Gutiérrez, "MELM-GRBF: a modified version of the extreme learning machine for generalized radial basis function neural networks," *Neurocomputing*, vol. 74, no. 16, pp. 2502–2510, 2011.

[16] C. L. Wu, K. W. Chau, and Y. S. Li, "Predicting monthly streamflow using data-driven models coupled with data-preprocessing techniques," *Water Resources Research*, vol. 45, no. 8, Article ID W08432, 2009.

[17] C. E. A. Cheng, "Long-term prediction of discharges in Manwan Reservoir using artificial neural network models," in *Advances in Neural Networks—ISNN 2005*, vol. 3498 of *Lecture Notes in Computer Science*, pp. 1040–1045, 2005.

[18] H. H. Zhang, M. Genton, and P. Liu, "Compactly supported radial basis function kernels," 2004.

[19] J. Kennedy and R. Eberhart, "Particle swarm optimization," in *Proceedings of the 1995 IEEE International Conference on Neural Networks*, pp. 1942–1945, December 1995.

[20] J. Eberhart, R. Eberhart, and Y. Shi, "Particle swarm optimization: developments, applications and resources," *IEEE*, vol. 1, pp. 81–86, 2001.

[21] R. Malhotra and A. Negi, "Reliability modeling using Particle Swarm optimisation," *International Journal of System Assurance Engineering and Management*, vol. 4, no. 3, pp. 275–283, 2013.

[22] D. Gies and Y. Rahmat-Samii, "Particle swarm optimization for reconfigurable phase-differentiated array design," *Microwave and Optical Technology Letters*, vol. 38, no. 3, pp. 168–175, 2003.

[23] F. Valdez, P. Melin, and C. Oscar, "An improved evolutionary method with fuzzy logic for combining Particle Swarm optimization and genetic algorithms," *Applied Soft Computing Journal*, vol. 11, no. 2, pp. 2625–2632, 2011.

[24] J. Zhang and K. Chau, "Multilayer ensemble pruning via novel multi-sub-swarm particle swarm optimization," *Journal of Universal Computer Science*, vol. 15, no. 4, pp. 840–858, 2009.

[25] F. Valdez, P. Melin, and O. Castillo, "Parallel Particle Swarm optimization with parameters adaptation using fuzzy logic," in *Proceedings of the 11th Mexican International Conference on Artificial Intelligence (MICAI '12)*, vol. 2, pp. 374–385, San Luis Potosi, Mexico, October 2012.

[26] J. Peng and C. P. Y. Pan, "Particle swarm optimization RBF for gas emission prediction," *Journal of Safety Science and Technology*, vol. 7, pp. 77–85, 2011.

[27] G. Ren, Z. Huang, Y. Cheng, X. Zhao, and Y. Zhang, "An integrated model for evacuation routing and traffic signal optimization with background demand uncertainty," *Journal of Advanced Transportation*, vol. 47, pp. 4–27, 2013.

[28] X. Feng, Z. Xiao, and X. Cui, "Improved RSSI algorithm for wireless sensor networks in 3D," *Journal of Computational Information Systems*, vol. 7, no. 16, pp. 5866–5873, 2011.

[29] F. Valdez and P. Melin, "Neural network optimization with a hybrid evolutionary method that combines particle swarm and genetic algorithms with fuzzy rules," in *Proceedings of the Annual Meeting of the North American Fuzzy Information Processing Society (NAFIPS '08)*, New York, NY, USA, May 2008.

[30] F. Fernandez-Navarro, C. Hervas-Martınez, P. A. Gutierrez, J. M. Pena-Barragan, and F. Lopez-Granados, "Parameter estimation of q-Gaussian. Radial Basis Functions Neural Networks with a Hybrid Algorithm for binary classification," *Neurocomputing*, vol. 75, pp. 123–134, 2012.

[31] H. Soh, S. Lim, T. Zhang et al., "Weighted complex network analysis of travel routes on the Singapore public transportation system," *Physica A*, vol. 389, no. 24, pp. 5852–5863, 2010.

[32] C. K. S. Kumar, R. Sukumar, and M. Nageswari, "Sensors lifetime enhancement techniques in wireless sensor networks—a critical review," *International Journal of Computer Science and Information Technology & Security*, vol. 3, pp. 159–164, 2013.

[33] S. Li and F. Qin, "A dynamic neural network approach for solving nonlinear inequalities defined on a graph and its application to distributed, routing-free, range-free localization of WSNs," *Neurocomputing*, vol. 117, pp. 72–80, 2013.

4

A Novel Web Classification Algorithm Using Fuzzy Weighted Association Rules

Binu Thomas[1] and G. Raju[2]

[1] Department of BCA, Marian College, Kuttikkanam, Kerala, India
[2] Department of Information Technology, Kannur University, Kannur, Kerala, India

Correspondence should be addressed to Binu Thomas; binumarian@gmail.com

Academic Editors: J. García, J. A. Hernandez, and L. Mikhailov

In associative classification method, the rules generated from association rule mining are converted into classification rules. The concept of association rule mining can be extended in web mining environment to find associations between web pages visited together by the internet users in their browsing sessions. The weighted fuzzy association rule mining techniques are capable of finding natural associations between items by considering the significance of their presence in a transaction. The significance of an item in a transaction is usually referred as the weight of an item in the transaction and finding associations between such weighted items is called fuzzy weighted association rule mining. In this paper, we are presenting a novel web classification algorithm using the principles of fuzzy association rule mining to classify the web pages into different web categories, depending on the manner in which they appear in user sessions. The results are finally represented in the form of classification rules and these rules are compared with the result generated using famous Boolean Apriori association rule mining algorithm.

1. Introduction

Classification is a Data Mining function that assigns items in a collection to target categories or classes. The goal of classification is to accurately predict the target class for each case in the data. For example, a classification model could be used to identify loan applicants in a bank as low, medium, or high credit risks. A classification task begins with a data set in which the class assignments are known. A classification model that predicts credit risk could be developed based on observed data for many loan applicants over a period of time. In addition to the historical credit rating, the data might track employment history, home ownership or rental, years of residence, number and type of investments, and so on. Credit rating would be the target, the other attributes would be the predictors, and the data for each customer would constitute a case. Classification techniques include decision trees, association rules, fuzzy systems, and neural networks. Classification has many applications in customer segmentation, business modeling, marketing, credit analysis, web mining and biomedical, and drug response modeling.

Classification models include decision trees, Bayesian models, association rules, and neural nets. Although association rules have been predominantly used for data exploration and description, the interest in using them for prediction has rapidly increased in the Data Mining community. When classification models are constructed from rules, often they are represented as a decision list (a list of rules where the order of rules corresponds to the significance of the rules). Classification rules are of the form $P \rightarrow c$, where P is a pattern in the training data and c is a predefined class label (target) [1]. Association rule based classification is introduced by Liu et al. [2]. Association rule mining algorithm like Apriori can be used for generating rules and a second algorithm is used for building the classifier. The rules generated by association rules are called classification association rules (CARs), as they have a predefined class label or target. From the generated CARs, a subset is selected based on the heuristic criterion that the subset of rules can classify the training set accurately.

Servers register a Web log entry for every single access they get, in which important pieces of information about accessing are recorded, including the URL requested, the IP address from which the request originated, and a time-stamp. Applying Data Mining techniques on this web log data can reveal many interesting knowledge about the web users [3]. These web log data shows information accessed by the users and give their surfing pattern. When Data Mining techniques are implemented on these logs to extract hidden patterns between the URLs requested by the users [4], it is commonly known as Web Usage Mining. In recent years there has been an increasing interest and a growing body of work in Web usage mining [5] as an underlying approach in capturing and modeling Web user behavioral patterns and for deriving e-business intelligence. Web usage mining techniques rely on offline pattern discovery from user transactions. These techniques can be used to improve Web personalization based on historic browsing patters. Association rule mining can bring out precise information about user's navigational behavior. When we apply the association rule mining techniques with web log file, the result will be of the form $X \rightarrow Y$ where X and Y are URLs [6]. It means if a user accesses URL X then he would be accessing URL Y most likely. The user's navigational pattern information can be used in predictive prefetching of pages and web personalization. Development of such recommendation systems has become an active research area. Some recent studies have considered the use of association rule mining [7] in recommender systems [8, 9].

In this work, the association rule mining techniques are used for web classification based on the navigational patterns. A novel web classification algorithm is presented here, which is developed on the foundations of fuzzy association rule mining techniques. The concepts of weighted fuzzy transactions and fuzzy support and confidence framework are used to derive this algorithm. This associative classification algorithm finds longest possible access sequence patterns which lead to a web category. Here, each web category is considered as a class label. These identified classification rules can be later used for web personalization and predictive prefetching. The Boolean Apriori algorithm also used in the same framework to find access sequences which lead to a particular web category as the consequent. The results are compared and it is found that the new algorithm identifies more natural patterns.

2. Background and Related Work

In Data Mining area, general classification algorithms were designed to deal with transaction-like data. Such data has a different format from the sequential data, where the concept of an attribute has to be carefully considered. The association-rule representation is an extensively studied topic in Data Mining. Association rules were proposed to capture the co-occurrence of buying different items in a supermarket shopping. It is natural to use association rule generation to relate pages that are most often referenced together in a single server session [6]. In the association rule mining literature, weights of items are treated as insignificant until recently and a common weight of one (1) is assigned as a common

practice. Some of the very recent approaches generalize this and give item weights to reflect their significance to the user. In weighted association rule mining, the weights may be as a result of particular promotions for the items or their profitability, and so forth, [10]. Fuzzy weighted support, confidence, and transactions are also defined in a fuzzy association rule framework [11, 12]. The concepts and methods used in weighted association rule mining can be extended to web mining [13].

Muyeba et al. [12] presented a novel approach for effectively mining weighted fuzzy association rules [14]. The authors address the issue of weight of each item according to its significance with respect to some user defined criteria. Most works on weighted association rule mining do not address the downward closure property while some make assumptions to validate the property. This paper generalizes the weighted association rule mining problem with binary and fuzzy attributes with weighted settings. This methodology follows an Apriori approach but employs T-tree data structure to improve efficiency of counting item sets. The authors' approach avoids preprocessing and postprocessing as opposed to most weighted association rule mining algorithms, thus eliminating the extra steps during rules generation. The paper also presents experimental results on both synthetic and real-data sets and a discussion on evaluating the proposed approach.

In Boolean Apriori algorithm, all the products are treated uniformly, and all the rules are mined based on the occurrences of the products. However, in the social science research, the analysts may want to mine the rules based on the importance of the products, items or attributes. For example, total income attribute is more interesting than the height of a person in a household. Based on this generalized idea [15, 16], the items are given weights to reflect the importance to the users. The downward closure property of the support measure in the mining of association rules no longer exists in this approach. Here, they make use of a metric, called support bounds, in the mining of weighted fuzzy association rules. Furthermore, the authors introduce a simple sample method and the data maintenance method, based on the statistical approach, to mine the rules.

Mobasher et al. [4] proposed an effective and scalable technique for Web personalization based on association rule discovery from usage data. Here, the association rules are used for the development of a recommender system. In this work they proposed a scalable framework for recommender systems using association rule mining from click stream data. The recommendation algorithm utilizes a special data structure to produce recommendations efficiently in real-time, without the need to generate all association rules from frequent item sets. This method can overcome some of the limitations of low coverage resulting from high support thresholds or larger user histories and reduced accuracy due to the sparse nature of the data.

Suneetha and Krishnamoorti [17] suggested an improved version of Apriori algorithm to extracts interesting correlations, frequent patterns, and associations among web pages visited by users in their browsing sessions. In order to reduce repetitive disk read, a novel method of top down approach is proposed in this paper. The improved version of Apriori algorithm greatly reduces the data base scans and avoids generation of unnecessary patterns which reduces data base scan, time and space consumption. Kumar and Rukmani [18] used Apriori algorithm for web usage mining and in particular focuses on discovering the web usage patterns of websites from the server log files. In this work the memory usage and time usage of Apriori algorithm are compared with frequent pattern growth algorithm.

Ramli generates the university E Learning (UUM Educare) portal usage patterns using basic association rules algorithm called Apriori algorithm [19]. Server log files are used with Apriori algorithm to produce the final results. Here, web usage mining, approach has been combined with the basic association rule, Apriori algorithm to optimize the content of the university E Learning portal. The authors have identified several Web access pattern by applying the well known Apriori algorithm to the access log file data of this educational portal. This includes descriptive statistic and association Rules for the portal including support and confidence to represent the Web usage and user behavior for UUM Educare. The results and findings for this experimental analysis can be used by the Web administration and content developers in order to plan the upgrading and enhancement to the portal presentation.

Mei-Ling Shyu and Shu-Ching Chen proposed a new approach for mining user access patterns. The approach aims at predicting Web page requests on the website in order to reduce the access time and to assist the users in browsing within the website [20]. To capture the user access behavior on the website, an alternative structure of the Web is constructed from user access sequences obtained from the server logs, as opposed to static structural hyperlinks. Their approach consists of two major steps. First, the shortest path algorithm in graph theory is applied to find the distances between Web pages. In order to capture user access behavior on the Web, the distances are derived from user access sequences, as opposed to static structural hyperlinks. They refer to these distances as minimum reaching distance (MRD) information. The association rule mining (ARM) technique is then applied to form a set of predictive rules which are further refined and pruned by using the MRD information. In this paper, finally they propose a new method for mining user access patterns that allows the prediction of multiple nonconsecutive Web pages, that is, any pages within the website.

Srivastava et al. [21], proposed a data mining technique for finding frequently used web pages. These pages may be kept in a server's cache to speed up web access. Existing techniques of selecting pages to be cached do not capture a user's surfing patterns correctly. Here, they use a weighted association rule (WAR) mining technique that finds pages of the user's current interest and cache them to give faster net access [5]. This approach captures both user's habit and interest as compared to other approaches where emphasis is only on habit. If user A logs on to Internet every day for reading news and checking emails. He visits googlenews.com and gmail.com in any order. In this case, association rule would give rules (User A, googlenews.com) → (User A,

gmail.com) and gmail can be pre-fetched to the cache to reduce the access time.

Among these classification methods in Data Mining, Association rule mining is simple and effective in classification. In fact rules generated from association rule mining can be easily converted to classification rules so it becomes a natural choice for classification in Data Mining. This technique is known as associative classification [1]. In the research work [22], the author focused on the construction of classification models based on association rules. In order to mine only rules that can be used for classification, the well-known association rule mining Apriori algorithm is modified to handle user-defined input constraints. Using this characterization, a classification system is implemented based on association rules. In this work, the performance of this classification method is compared with the performance of several model construction methods, including CBA (classification based on association). This classification algorithm mines for the best possible rules above a user-defined minimum confidence and within a desired range for the number of rules.

3. Finding Weighted Associations from Web Logs

We model the pieces of Web logs as sequences of events to find the associations between web pages on the basis of sequential patterns over a period of time. Each sequence is represented as an ordered list of discrete symbols and each symbol represents one of several possible categories of web pages requested by the user. Let E be a set of events. A Web log piece or (Web) access sequence $S = e_1, e_2, \ldots, e_n$ $(e_i \in E)$ for $(1 \leq i \leq n)$ is a sequence of events, while n is called the length of the access sequence. An access sequence with length n is also called an n-sequence. In an access sequence S, repetition is allowed. Duplicate references to a page in a web access sequence imply back traversals, refreshes or reloads [6, 23]. For example, 1, 1, 2 and 1, 2 are two different access sequences, in which 1 and 2 are two events. Figure 1 shows a sample of such sequence. The Data we used for the experiment comes from Internet Information server (IIS) logs for msbc.com and news related portions of msn.com for one entire day. Each sequence in the data set corresponds to page views of a user during that day. There are 1 million records and we selected 64,000 samples. Each event in the sequence corresponds to a request for a page. Requests are recorded only at the level of page category. There are 16 categories of pages and these categories are given numeric codes from 1 to 16. The pages are included into one of these categories based on their content. These categories are front page(1), news(2), technology(3), local(4), opinion(5), on air(6), miscellaneous(7), weather(8), health(9), living(10), business(11), sports(12), summary(13), bbs(14), and travel(15), msn news(16). Although other information pertaining to the web access is available, we model only the categories of page requests.

When we try to find the hidden patterns in web access sequence using the Boolean association, we can consider

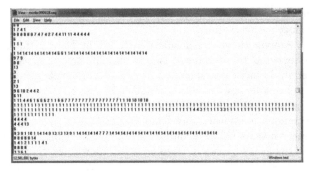

FIGURE 1: Web access sequences where numeric symbols are used to represent web pages.

only the presence or absence of pages in an access sequence. We do not give importance for the number of occurrences of a category of web pages in a sequence. If a particular category of web page is appearing together continuously then such occurrences also have to be processed with more significance. Instead of Apriori algorithm, if we use weighted fuzzy association rule mining algorithms, we will be able model the web sequences which reveal more natural patterns by considering all the above mentioned facts.

From Figure 1 it is clear that the weight of a category of web page in a browsing session of a user can be directly associated with the number of times the user visits that particular category of pages in his session. Again if the user is continuously visiting the same category of pages then more weight has to be given for such continuous accessing of same category of pages. Considering the above facts we define the following concepts for the development of the new web classification algorithm.

3.1. Definition 1. Fuzzy Weight of Web Page. The fuzzy weight of a web page is defined by considering the number of co-occurrences of a web category. The following expression is used for weight calculation:

$$\mu_i = \frac{n_i * \prod_{j=1}^{m} k_j}{n},$$ (1)

where μ_i is the fuzzy weight of the ith category web pages in a session. Here, we assume that there are m subgroups in a sequence which contains the ith category web pages. Then k_j is the number of successive ith category web pages appearing in the kth group and n_i is the total number of ith pages appearing in the session under consideration. Finally n is the total number of pages in the browsing session. The weight thus generated will be more than *one* in some cases and the values are normalized by dividing each weight with the maximum weight in a session. A portion of the values are given in Table 1.

3.2. Definition 2. Web Class of a Session. The class of a web sequence is defined as the web category in a sequence with maximum weight. It is assumed that in a web access sequence, the remaining page visits are leading to this web category with maximum weight. In an association rule framework,

the page category with maximum weight can be considered as the consequent and the remaining pages as the antecedents. A web class WC_i for an access sequence S_i is defined as

$$WC_i = Max\left(S_i\left(\mu\right)\right).$$ (2)

So, this concept work like a data mining classification problem where the available sequence patterns are classified into groups leading to a particular class and this information can be later used to predict the user behavior in browsing sessions. Using the above mentioned equation, all the web pages in the access patterns are converted into their corresponding weights. In this new approach, the web pages visited in a session are given weights, after considering the number of visits in that session and the extend of continuous visits of the same category of pages. The weights obtained in each session are normalized so that all the weights appear within the range of 0 and 1. Since we have sixteen categories of web pages, a new database table is created with sixteen attributes such that each attribute corresponds to a web category. All the sequences are converted into this fixed database table format with matching weights for each category. All the weights are normalized as shown in Table 1 so that they appear within a range of zero and one.

4. The Fuzzy Web Classification Algorithm (FWCA)

With the concept of web page weight and web access class, now the new algorithm for web classification can be derived. The algorithm has the following steps.

Step 1. Convert all the web pages in access sequences to corresponding fuzzy weights in a fixed database table format.

Step 2. Sort each web sequence in the descending order of weights and select the web page with maximum weight as the class (consequent) of a sequence.

Step 3. For each access sequence, the remaining pages (other than the consequent) are included into a classification rule sequence as long as the product of the weights is greater than a given support threshold.

Step 4. Select only those rules having the confidence value (associated with the number of times such rule sequences exist in the entire set of web access sequences) greater than the user specified threshold. The confidence for the jth rule for the ith web category C_{ji} is defined as

$$C_{ji} = \frac{s_{ji} * n_{ji}}{n_i},$$ (3)

where s_{ji} is support of jth rule for ith web category n_{ji} is number of jth rules identified for the ith web category n_i is total number of rules with i as the web class.

In Algorithm 1, we have the detailed pseudo code for the algorithm. In the algorithm, $W[n][p]$ is the weights of p page categories for the n browsing sessions. Weight is calculated

TABLE 1: Web groups and corresponding weights in browsing sessions.

Seq no.	Web categories and corresponding weights															
	1	2	3	4	5	6	7	8	9	10	11	12	13	14	15	16
1	0.00	0.03	0.00	0.05	0.00	1.00	0.00	0.00	0.01	0.00	0.00	0.00	0.00	0.00	0.03	0.02
2	1.00	0.00	0.00	0.22	0.06	0.56	0.00	0.34	0.00	0.00	0.00	0.30	0.00	0.06	0.00	0.00
3	0.81	0.00	0.00	0.03	0.00	1.00	0.00	0.00	0.05	0.00	0.00	0.02	0.00	0.63	0.00	0.21
4	0.00	0.00	1.00	0.00	0.00	0.60	0.90	0.16	0.00	0.00	0.00	0.00	0.00	0.00	0.00	0.00
5	0.00	0.00	0.08	1.00	0.08	0.08	0.00	0.00	0.08	0.23	0.00	0.00	0.00	0.26	0.00	0.00
6	0.71	0.00	0.00	1.00	0.00	0.00	0.00	0.00	0.00	0.00	0.14	0.00	0.04	0.02	0.00	0.00
7	1.00	0.00	0.00	0.00	0.00	0.03	0.00	0.00	0.00	0.00	0.00	0.04	0.00	0.00	0.00	0.00
8	1.00	0.00	0.00	0.00	0.00	0.00	0.00	0.00	0.00	0.36	0.00	0.00	0.00	0.00	0.00	0.00
9	0.00	0.00	0.22	0.00	0.00	0.00	0.00	1.00	0.00	0.00	0.00	0.00	0.24	0.00	0.00	0.21
10	0.34	0.00	0.00	0.05	0.00	1.00	0.00	0.00	0.00	0.00	0.30	0.00	0.00	0.48	0.00	0.00
11	0.00	1.00	0.00	0.00	0.00	0.27	0.00	0.00	0.00	0.46	0.00	0.00	0.00	0.00	0.47	0.00
12	0.00	0.00	0.00	1.00	0.00	0.00	0.35	0.00	0.50	0.00	0.00	0.50	0.00	0.00	0.00	0.00
13	0.22	0.00	1.00	0.00	0.00	0.00	0.00	0.00	0.00	0.00	0.28	0.00	0.00	0.54	0.00	0.00
14	0.00	0.00	0.25	0.00	0.00	0.00	0.74	0.00	1.00	0.00	0.00	0.00	0.00	0.00	0.85	0.00
15	0.00	0.00	1.00	0.00	0.00	0.00	0.00	0.55	0.00	0.00	0.32	0.06	0.00	0.00	0.00	0.00
16	0.05	0.08	0.00	0.00	0.00	0.00	0.00	0.00	0.05	0.00	0.00	1.00	0.00	0.31	0.00	0.00
17	0.00	0.00	0.13	0.00	1.00	0.00	0.00	0.40	0.00	0.00	0.00	0.00	0.00	0.10	0.00	0.00
18	0.05	0.00	0.00	0.04	0.21	0.00	0.00	0.00	0.15	0.00	0.00	0.00	1.00	0.00	0.03	0.00
19	0.00	0.15	0.00	0.00	0.23	0.14	0.00	0.00	5.14	0.00	0.06	0.00	0.00	0.00	0.00	0.03
20	0.00	0.50	0.00	0.00	0.00	0.50	0.00	0.00	1.00	0.00	0.00	0.00	0.02	0.00	0.00	0.00
21	0.02	0.00	0.00	0.00	0.05	0.00	0.03	0.00	0.00	0.00	0.32	1.00	0.00	0.00	0.12	0.00

using expression 1. $Sort(W[i][p])$ is used to sort the ith access sequence on the basis of the weights of web pages. The function $addwebtype(Wm)$ is used to get the web page category whose weight is the maximum in an access sequence. Finally $Seq[n]$ stores the rules generated. The algorithm find all fuzzy weighted classification rules from the web access sequence for a user specified support (∞) and confidence (β) threshold values.

In the algorithm, the weights of each category of web pages are calculated and stored in the two dimensional array w for all available sequences. In the next steps the weights are sorted in the decreasing order for every sequence. So in each sequence, the web category with maximum weight will be placed first and it is considered as the consequent of that sequence. The then highest weight category will be placed in the second position and so on. In each sequence the web categories are arranged in the decreasing order of their importance. The web page categories are included in to the rules (as antecedents in the association rule) in the order they are arranged.

We have a variable support and its initial value is the weight of the consequent. When one web category is included in to the rule its weight is multiplied with the support value. When the support becomes smaller than the given threshold alpha (∞) the rule generation for that user session is stopped. The next user session sequence is considered for the same process and this is done for all the available user session sequences and finally there will be "n" rules. In the next step, the global *confidence* of rules is checked.

Since the web categories are included into the rules as antecedents in the descending order of their weights, only the most significant web categories in a user session will be included into the rule generated for that session. Once all rules are generated, their global confidence count is found (the number of times the same antecedent-consequent sequence appears in the entire sessions). All the rules with confidences lesser than the user specified threshold *beta* are removed from the set of rules. By applying the weighted association rule mining approach to the web mining problem we could identify fifty five rules from one 64000 sessions these rules are given in (Table 2).

5. Finding Web Page Associations Using Apriori Algorithm

To find the Boolean associations between the co-occurrences of the web pages, first we converted the entire web sequences into true or false values. Since there are sixteen categories of web pages, here also we designed a database with sixteen fields. The presence and absence of a web page in a sequence is represented with true or false values in the corresponding record representing the web sequence. In this approach, we are considering only the presence of a web page in the sequence and we do not give any significance for the number of occurrences of the page in the sequence. With this preprocessing, the web sequence database is converted in to a true Boolean database with only true or false values indicating the presence and absence of web pages in the user sessions. Table 3 shows a portion of such Boolean database generated.

To apply the Apriori algorithm to the new dataset we used the IBM SPSS Modeler 14.1 data mining software. The Table 4

```
Algorithm FWCA (n, p)
{
// n is the number of access sequence
// p is the number of web categories
// W[n, p] is the weights of web pages for n sessions
// seq[n, p] is the rules generated
for i = 1 to n
  {
    for j = 1 to p
    {
      w[i, j] = weight(i, p)
    }
  }
Sort (w[n, p])
rule = 1
for i = 1 to n
  {
    k = 2
    Support = (Max(W[i, 1 … p]))
    while support≥ ∞
      {
        wm = (Max(W[i, k … p]))
        Seq[rule, k] = Addwebtype(wm)
        Support = support * wm
        Delete(wm)
        k = k + 1
      }
    Rule = rule + 1
  }
for i = 1 to rule
  {
    if confidence(seq[i, p]) > β
    print(seq[i, p])
  }
}
```

ALGORITHM 1: The new algorithm used for web classification.

represents the rules identified using Apriori algorithm. By applying Apriori algorithm, 45 rules were identified with a support value of 5 and confidence of 20. Among the rules, only seven are having more than one antecedent.

By comparing the rules generated from both the methods, it is clear that the fuzzy weighted approach for associative classification using the new proposed algorithm is far superior to Boolean Apriori Algorithm. This is in terms of the coverage of the rules and inclusion of web categories into the classification rules. In the case of Apriori algorithm we got only two antecedents in five cases and only one in all the remaining cases but in the case of weighted approach many rules are having more than three web categories as antecedents.

6. Discussions

Web server log files contains repository of web browsing information by the internet users. Mining on this data collection can bring out valuable information about the web access patterns of users. When we apply classification and

TABLE 2: The association rules generated using the FWCA method.

No.	Rules	Support	Confidence
	Rules 1–29		
1	2, 10, 4, 6, 7 → 1	4.88	0.762
2	11, 12 → 1	0.38	0.62
3	3, 7, 2, 15, 6 → 1	0.31	0.554
4	3, 11 → 1	0.17	0.409
5	6, 14 → 1	0.14	0.378
6	7, 6, 1 → 1	0.3	0.548
7	3, 4 → 2	0.09	0.296
8	6, 3, 12 → 2	0.02	0.125
9	3, 10, 1, 11 → 2	0.01	0.12
10	14, 1 → 2	0.01	0.119
11	7, 1, 6 → 3	0.04	0.198
12	1 → 3	0.02	0.139
13	12, 1, 11 → 3	0.01	0.1
14	4 → 3	0.01	0.98
15	11, 2 → 3	0.01	0.92
16	9 → 3	0.02	0.89
17	10, 3, 5, 6, 9 → 4	0.35	5.93
18	3, 9, 7, 12 → 4	0.07	0.26
19	7, 9, 1, 2 → 4	0.04	0.189
20	11, 2, 7, 8, 9 → 4	0.02	0.13
21	1 → 5	0.16	0.82
22	2, 6, 11, 1, 4 → 5	0.04	0.7
23	9 → 5	0.01	0.51
24	1 → 6	0.06	0.241
25	7, 3 → 6	0.05	0.233
26	15 → 6	0.05	0.23
27	2, 1, 10 → 6	0.03	0.176
28	9 → 6	0.02	0.152
29	12 → 6	0.01	0.106
	Rules 30–55		
30	1 → 7	0.04	0.202
31	3, 4, 6, 9 → 7	0.01	0.1
32	10, 2, 6, 1, 4 → 7	0.01	0.19
33	7, 6 → 8	0.02	0.132
34	2 → 8	0.01	0.12
35	9 → 8	0.01	0.118
36	1, 7 → 8	0.01	0.114
37	4, 7 → 8	0.01	0.103
38	3, 11 → 9	0.02	0.131
39	6, 7 → 9	0.02	0.13
40	4, 1, 3 → 9	0.01	0.12
41	12 → 9	0.01	0.114
42	6, 7, 2, 12, 1 → 10	0.02	0.135
43	1, 4, 15 → 10	0.02	0.127
44	2, 4, 7, 12, 1 → 10	0.01	0.105
45	1, 5 → 11	0.04	0.061
46	4, 9, 2 → 11	0.01	0.032
47	1 → 12	0.07	0.26
48	2, 1, 6, 15 → 12	0.01	0.114
49	2, 3, 4 → 12	0.01	0.106

TABLE 2: Continued.

No.	Rules	Support	Confidence
50	7, 14, 4 → 13	0.44	0.66
51	9 → 13	0.03	0.173
52	2, 1 → 14	0.38	0.616
53	13, 8 → 14	0.05	0.223
54	1, 10, 2, 12 → 14	0.02	0.131
55	6, 7, 2, 5, 10 → 15	0.01	0.137

TABLE 3: Boolean values representing presence of web categories in sessions.

1	2	3	4	5	6	7	8	9	10	11	12	13	14	15	16
F	T	T	T	F	F	F	F	F	F	F	F	F	F	F	F
F	F	F	F	F	T	T	T	F	F	F	F	F	F	F	F
F	F	T	T	T	T	F	F	T	T	F	F	F	F	F	F
T	F	F	F	F	T	F	F	F	F	T	F	F	T	F	F
T	F	F	F	F	T	F	F	F	T	F	F	F	F	F	T
F	F	F	F	F	F	F	T	F	F	F	F	F	F	T	F
F	F	F	F	F	T	F	F	F	F	F	T	T	F	F	F
F	F	F	F	F	F	F	F	T	F	F	T	F	F	F	F
F	F	T	F	F	F	F	F	T	T	F	F	F	F	F	F
F	F	F	F	F	F	F	F	T	F	F	F	F	F	F	F
F	F	T	F	F	F	F	F	F	F	F	F	F	F	F	F
F	F	F	F	T	F	F	F	F	T	F	F	T	F	F	F
F	F	F	F	F	F	F	F	F	F	F	F	T	F	F	F

prediction techniques in web usage mining environment, the access patterns web users can be predicted. The data used in this work contains *sixteen* web categories and 64,000 samples of web access sequences involving these web categories. Some of the web categories are highly popular among web users that these web categories appear in several access patterns. The importance of web categories is evident from the graphical representations (Figures 2 and 3) which are directly linked with the number of occurrences of web categories in access sequences.

Figure 2 shows the number of sequences in which the web categories appear. The Figure 3 is the total occurrences web categories in different sequences (a web category may appear many times in a sequence). From the figures it is clear that some of the web categories are more important in comparison with others. The concept of importance of web categories in access sequences is modeled using the concept of fuzzy weight of web categories (Table 1).

In this paper, the associations are found between the web categories using conventional Boolean Apriori algorithm and the FWCA. By using the new algorithm, *fifty-five* rules are identified and *forty-five* rules are identified using Apriori algorithm. It is found that the rules generated using the FWCA algorithm have more coverage (classification rules are identified for more web categories) and it identified classification rules leading to *fifteen* web categories. A comparison between the two techniques in terms of the number of rules identified from each web category is given in Figure 4.

TABLE 4: The rules identified using apriori algorithm.

No.	Rules	Support	Confidence
	Using Boolean Apriori algorithm		
1	11 → 1	5.97	57.39
2	10 → 1	5.00	53.21
3	7 → 1	8.01	46.56
4	2 → 1	17.76	42.99
5	12 → 1	11.18	39.35
6	14 → 1	11.96	34.09
7	4 → 1	12.43	33.05
8	3 → 1	12.38	27.48
9	6 → 1	21.84	18.88
10	15 → 1	21.84	18.88
11	10 → 2	5.00	34.53
12	11 → 2	5.97	30.88
13	7 → 2	8.01	24.28
14	6 → 2	32.19	23.72
15	4 → 2	12.43	22.23
16	12 → 2	11.18	21.04
17	3 → 2	12.38	20.23
18	14 → 2	11.96	16.14
19	1 → 3	7.64	18.96
20	12 → 3	5.00	18.36
21	7 → 4	8.01	33.40
22	3, 6 → 4	7.64	22.02
23	9 → 4	9.10	21.29
24	11 → 4	5.97	19.32
25	10 → 4	5.00	17.89
26	2 → 4	17.76	15.56
27	1, 7 → 6	8.01	40.31
28	15 → 6	5.00	27.53
29	1, 2 → 6	7.64	20.69
30	11 → 6	5.97	19.29
31	4 → 6	12.43	17.30
32	9 → 6	9.10	16.89
33	4 → 7	12.43	21.53
34	1, 2 → 7	7.64	16.94
35	6, 7 → 9	8.01	16.47
36	3 → 9	12.43	15.59
37	2, 7 → 10	7.64	15.83
38	12 → 11	7.64	18.07
39	2 → 12	7.64	20.30
40	15 → 12	5.97	19.09
41	10 → 12	5.00	18.03
42	14 → 13	11.96	15.25
43	13 → 14	7.78	23.44
44	2 → 14	7.64	16.48
45	11 → 14	5.97	15.93

The classification rules generated using the techniques show the associations between the web categories. The number of web categories involved in each rule shows the ability of the rule generation technique to find more inclusive rules

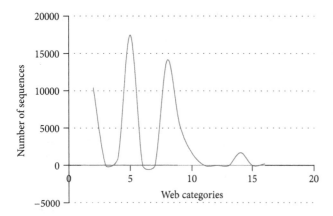

FIGURE 2: The web categories and the number of sequences they appear.

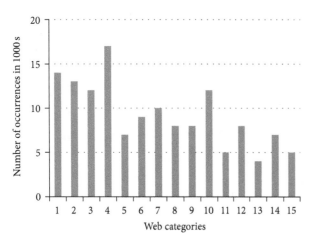

FIGURE 3: The total number of occurrences of web categories in all the sequences.

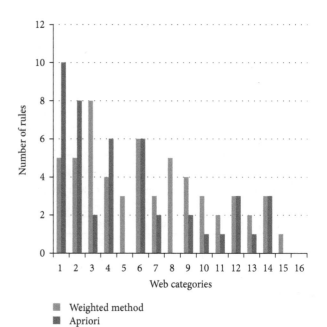

Weighted method
Apriori

FIGURE 4: The number of rules identified from each web category using the two methods.

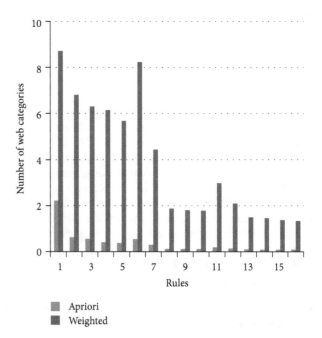

Apriori
Weighted

FIGURE 5: Average numbers of web categories (antecedents) involved in rules.

from the available web access sequences. The average number of web categories (antecedents) involved in each class of rules using the two rule generation techniques are given in Figure 5. It is evident from the figure that the FWCA is more inclusive (more web categories are included as antecedents in rules) while identifying the classification rules.

From the sample data, the number of access sequences in which the web categories appear similar to the antecedents of the web classification rules are also found. This is similar to the support threshold in association rule mining. Even though the rules generated using the fuzzy weighted algorithm have more antecedents, those rule patterns appear more in the access sequences than the Boolean rules (Figure 6). It shows that the new fuzzy based algorithm is more capable of identifying natural associations between web categories.

Finally the fuzzy weighted rules out perform the Boolean rules in terms of the number of access patterns which actually satisfy the rules. This is equivalent to the confidence measure of association rule mining technique. Actual validity and authority of the rules are analyzed by finding the number of occasions in which the access sequences from the sample

data perfectly satisfy the classification rules. The advantage of fuzzy weighted rules over Boolean rules in terms of number of cases from the sample data, satisfying the rules is demonstrated in Figure 7 The graph shows the number of cases satisfying the *forty-five* Boolean rules and *fifty-five* fuzzy weighted rules.

From the above discussion, it follows that the FWCA algorithm presented here to classify the access sequences has

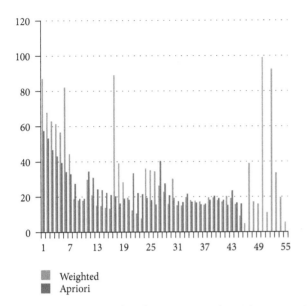

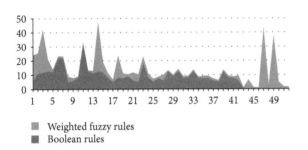

FIGURE 6: The rules (x axis) and support count (y axis): a comparison.

FIGURE 7: Number of cases (y axis in 100 s) satisfying the *forty six* Boolean rules and *fifty-five* fuzzy weighted rules (x axis).

(iv) The number of sequences in which the antecedents of a rule appear together from the sample sequences (the support count) is more in the case of FWCA. It shows that the rules generated by the algorithm are exactly revealing the access patterns of users.

(v) The number of sequences which actually satisfy the rules (Confidence measure) from the sample is also more for FWCA. It proves that that the rules generated by the algorithm are correct, that is, the antecedent sequences identified by the rules are leading to the web category of the rule.

The main advantage of this algorithm is that it can identify the longest possible frequent patterns in a single step by using the concepts of fuzzy weighted association, while the Apriori algorithm requires many passes over the data to generate the rules.

7. Summary

The concept of a market basket can be extended as the pages visited by a user in one session in web mining. Association rule mining techniques are used here to find associations between web pages visited by users. Here the problem is redefined like which pages are most frequently visited simultaneously by web users? The Boolean Apriori algorithm for association rule mining is used to find the association between the web pages visited together by users. But by using Apriori algorithm, only the presence and absence of web pages in a browsing session is considered. But, we also have to consider other important factors like the number visits of a web category, the time spent on a web page, and so forth, This paper discussed about a novel web classification algorithm using the principles of fuzzy association rule mining to classify the web pages into different classes in a single step, depending on the manner in which they appear in user sessions. In this approach, page visits in a browsing sessions are converted into fuzzy weighted values and association rules are generated from this. These fuzzy rules are used to classify access patterns in the form of classification rules.

noticeable advantage over the Boolean Apriori method. The benefits of this method are listed as follows.

(i) In a web access sequence the importance of web categories vary according to the user preferences. By using FWCA, we can assign more weight-age for frequently visited pages by uses. This consideration will help in evolving rule which represent natural access habits.

(ii) In the experiment, There are *sixteen* categories of web pages. A classification rule generation system for this sample data is efficient if it can identify rules which lead to most these web categories. FWCA identified rules which lead to *fifteen* web categories. Apriori algorithm identified rules for only *eleven* web categories.

(iii) These web classification rules can be used for prediction and selective prefetching of web pages. The rules will become useful if more number of web categories are involved in the rules. Using FWCA, more web categories are included as antecedents in the rules. It helps in identifying wide range of associations between web categories.

References

[1] J. Han, M. Kamber, and J. Pei, *Data Mining: Concepts and Techniques*, Morgan Kaufmann, 2006.

[2] B. Liu, W. Hsu, and Y. Ma, "Integrating classification and association rule mining," in *Proceedings of the Knowledge Discovery and Data Mining (KDD '98)*, pp. 80–86, AAAI, 1999.

[3] W. Jicheng, H. Yuan, W. Gangshan, and Z. Fuyan, "Web mining: knowledge discovery on the web," in *Proceedings of the IEEE International Conference on Systems, Man, and Cybernetics 'Human Communication and Cybernetics'*, vol. 2, pp. 137–141, October 1999.

[4] B. Mobasher, R. Cooley, and J. Srivastava, "Automatic personalization based on web usage mining," *Communications of the ACM*, vol. 43, no. 8, pp. 142–151, 2000.

[5] A. Srivastava, A. Bhosale, and S. Sural, "Speeding up web access using weighted association rules," *Pattern Recognition and Machine Intelligence Lecture Notes in Computer Science*, vol. 3776, pp. 660–665, 2005.

[6] J. Srivastava, R. Cooley, and P.-N. Tan, "Web usage mining: discovery and applications of usage patterns from Web data," *ACM SIGKDD Explorations Newsletter*, vol. 1, no. 2, pp. 12–23, 2000.

[7] R. Agrawal and R. Srikant, "Fast algorithms for mining association rules," in *Proceedings of the 20th International Conference on Very Large Data Bases (VLDB '94)*, pp. 487–499, Morgan Kaufmann, 1994.

[8] R. Kosala and H. Blockeel, "Web mining research: a survey," *ACM SIGKDD Explorations Newsletter*, vol. 2, no. 1, pp. 1–15, 2000.

[9] A. Abraham, "Business intelligence from web usage mining," *Journal of Information & Knowledge Management*, vol. 2, no. 4, pp. 375–390, 2003.

[10] W. Wang, J. Yang, and S. Philip, "Efficient mining of weighted association rules (WAR)," in *Proceedings of the 6th ACM SIGKDD International Conference on Knowledge Discovery and Data Mining (KDD '00)*, pp. 270–274, August 2000.

[11] M. S. Khan, M. Muyeba, C. Tjortjis, and F. Coenen, "An effective fuzzy healthy association rule mining algorithm (FHARM)," *databases*, vol. 4, no. 5, article 14, 2006.

[12] M. Muyeba, M. S. Khan, and F. Coenen, "Effective mining of weighted fuzzy association rules," *Computer*, vol. 90, 9 pages, 2010.

[13] S. K. Pal, V. Talwar, and P. Mitra, "Web mining in soft computing framework: relevance, state of the art and future directions," *IEEE Transactions on Neural Networks*, vol. 13, no. 5, pp. 1163–1177, 2002.

[14] M. Muyeba, M. S. Khan, and F. Coenen, "Fuzzy weighted association rule mining with weighted support and confidence framework," *New Frontiers in Applied Data Mining Lecture Notes in Computer Science*, vol. 5433, pp. 312–320, 2009.

[15] F. Karel, *Quantitative association rules mining—department of cybernetics [Ph.D. thesis]*, 2012, http://cyber.felk.cvut.cz/phd/completed/KAREL-phd%2012_2009.pdf.

[16] W. Wang, J. Yang, and S. Philip, "WAR: weighted association rules for item intensities," *Knowledge and Information Systems*, vol. 6, no. 2, pp. 203–229, 2004.

[17] K. R. Suneetha and R. Krishnamoorti, "Web log mining using improved version of apriori algorithm," *International Journal of Computer Applications*, vol. 29, no. 6, pp. 23–27, 2011.

[18] B. S. Kumar and K. V. Rukmani, "Implementation of web usage mining using Apriori and FP Growth algorithms," *International Journal of Advanced Networking and Applications*, vol. 400, pp. 400–404, 2010.

[19] A. A. Bin Ramli, "Web usage mining using apriori algorithm: UUM learning care portal case," in *Proceedings of the International Conference on Knowledge Management*, pp. 212–220, 2001.

[20] C. Haruechaiyasak, M.-L. Shyu, S.-C. Chen, and X. Li, "Web document classification based on fuzzy association," in *Proceedings of the 26th Annual International Computer Software and Applications Conference*, pp. 487–492, August 2002.

[21] A. Srivastava, A. Bhosale, and S. Sural, "Speeding up web access using weighted association rules," in *Pattern Recognition and Machine Intelligence*, pp. 660–665, Springer, Berlin, Germany, 2005.

[22] S. K. Palanisamy, *Association rule based classification [Ph.D. thesis]*, Worcester Polytechnic Institute, 2006.

[23] J. Pei, J. Han, B. Mortazavi, and H. Zhu:, "Mining access patterns efficiently from web logs," in *Proceedings of the 4th PAKDD*, pp. 396–407, Kyoto, Japan, 2000.

5

Health Monitoring for Elderly: An Application Using Case-Based Reasoning and Cluster Analysis

Mobyen Uddin Ahmed, Hadi Banaee, and Amy Loutfi

Center for Applied Autonomous Sensor Systems, Örebro University, 701 82 Örebro, Sweden

Correspondence should be addressed to Mobyen Uddin Ahmed; mobyen.ahmed@oru.se

Academic Editors: T.-C. Chen, G. L. Foresti, Z. Liu, and R. Rada

This paper presents a framework to process and analyze data from a pulse oximeter which remotely measures pulse rate and blood oxygen saturation from a set of individuals. Using case-based reasoning (CBR) as the backbone to the framework, records are analyzed and categorized according to their similarity. Record collection has been performed using a personalized health profiling approach in which participants wore a pulse oximeter sensor for a fixed period of time and performed specific activities for predetermined intervals. Using a variety of feature extraction methods in time, frequency, and time-frequency domains, as well as data processing techniques, the data is fed into a CBR system which retrieves most similar cases and generates an alarm according to the case outcomes. The system has been compared with an expert's classification, and a 90% match is achieved between the expert's and CBR classification. Again, considering the clustered measurements, the CBR approach classifies 93% correctly both for the pulse rate and oxygen saturation. Along with the proposed methodology, this paper provides a basis for which the system can be used in the analysis of continuous health monitoring and can be used as a suitable method in home/remote monitoring systems.

1. Introduction

Today, the possibility to remotely monitor physiological health parameters provides a new approach for disease prevention and early detection [1, 2]. Furthermore, such health monitoring systems could be useful for the elderly in independent and assisted living [3]. In developing health monitoring systems, several intelligent data processing methods have been proposed in the literature, for instance, neural network (NN) [4] and support vector machine (SVM) [5]. These methods are often black box methods and make it difficult for experts to gain further insight into the structure presented in the data.

In this paper, a clinical decision support system (CDSS) has been proposed where case-based reasoning (CBR) approach [6] is applied to analyze and process the data coming from a pulse oximeter that contain measurements of both pulse rate and blood oxygen saturation. A case-based reasoning (CBR) [6–17] approach can work in a way close to human reasoning, for example, it solves a new problem applying previous experiences, which is more common for doctors,

clinicians, or engineers. In the proposed system, CBR is the part of a large framework where first the data is preprocessed and features are extracted to find significant parameters of interest using time, frequency, and time-frequency domain features. In addition, to use the features directly, the CBR system can also produce similar matches based on input from a clustering approach that increases the retrieval process by looking only within the most similar group of cases. The method presented here is verified using data collected from a group of individuals who followed a controlled sequence of activities called a health profile. In the health profile, users are requested to perform specific activities for a predefined time intervals for example, deep breathing, walking, and so forth. Using the health profiling, ground truth data could be obtained, and a further verification has been done by three human experts who provided general classification of whether the data from a specific user seemed normal.

Previous work related to the proposed approach ranges from processing of data from physiological sensors that have typically relied on time domain features [2, 18, 19] to classifiers which may utilize known information from

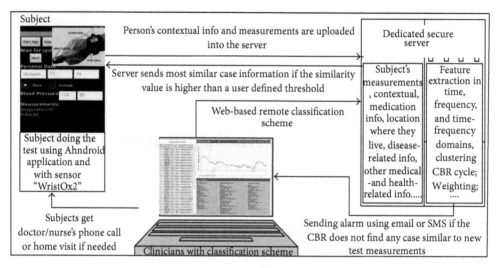

FIGURE 1: The steps and the data flow of the CDSS.

disease databases or consider only the physiological parameters [1, 20]. A notable example [21] in which the authors presented a health condition monitoring system using electrocardiogram (ECG), heart rate (HR), oxygen saturation, impedance pneumography, and activity patterns is included . The sensors were mounted in the patient's garments, and the service is applied in rehabilitation of cardiac ambulatory stable cardiorespiratory patients. Studies that consider only continuous biomedical data (i.e. pulse rate) and respective signal processing methods can be found in [22, 23]. All these works have demonstrated that the recent advancement in sensor technology could provide continuous detection of, for example, pulse, blood oximetry, and level of physical activity. Furthermore, through appropriate sensor data processing, it is also possible to detect changes and provide alerts and warnings to users [23]. However, in most of these studies, the main goal is to classify data into different labeled classes, or find similar cases by determining features. In this work, classification of data in a meaningful way, that is, retrieving the effective solution for similar measurements, and enabling diagnosis of anomaly cases are currently missing in this area. A further potential development which has been addressed in the current paper is to take into account personalization of the data processing which could be achieved by considering user conditions and tailoring the system towards specific groups of individuals, for example, elderly.

2. Overview of the Proposed Clinical Decision Support System (CDSS)

The case-based remote classification scheme, that is, the CDSS proposed here, consists of three modules, and the steps of the approach are illustrated in Figure 1. The *client side module* contains an Android application which is deployed in a smart phone using 2.3.3 programming environment. The Android application consists of a personalized health profiling approach and a Bluetooth communication protocol.

The personalized health profiling approach is a four-session approach in 9-minute duration, and the sessions are *baseline*, *deep breath*, *activity*, and *relax*. The details of the personalized health profiling approach can be found in [3]. The "WristOx2" sensor is connected as shown in Figure 1 and sends data through the Bluetooth communication. The details of Bluetooth communication and information about "WristOx2" sensor can be found in [24].

After each test, the measurements are stored into the smart phone in ".txt" format and finally uploaded to the server. When the *server side application module* receives the data file, the file is parsed, the features are extracted and a new problem case is formulated, and the CBR cycle is initiated as presented in Figure 2. Here, k-means clustering is used to group the cases offline. The new case is then entered into CBR cycle and in the retrieval step, the similarity value is calculated among the stored clustered cases.

The server retrieves the most similar cases depending on user defined similarity threshold and finally sends the most similar case information to the subject. At the same time, the server also sends an SMS and email notification to clinicians and generates an alert if the stored cases are not similar to the new case. Here, the system also considers user defined similarity threshold. Also, a web-enabled case-based CDSS is proposed here. Here, clinicians can see details about contextual information and measurements about a subject enabling remote monitoring of the subject. In the web-enabled CDSS, the system provides a number of functionalities, such as (1) *features level analysis*, (2) *CBR classification with clustered measurements*, and (3) *CBR classification with expert opinion*. In *features level analysis*, user can consider extracted features in different individual domains or their combination, that is, time, frequency, and time-frequency domains. In *CBR classification with clustered measurements*, users have the opportunity to see similar measurements individually, that is, similar pulse rate or similar oxygen saturation signals. Here, the signals are clustered separately using unsupervised clustering algorithm (i.e. k-means). Moreover, the CDSS can

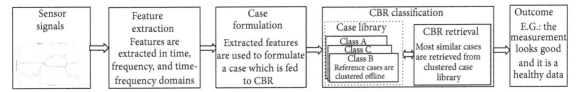

FIGURE 2: Different steps in the server system.

TABLE 1: A summary table with several criteria about the data collection.

Criteria	Values
Number of the subjects	15
Number of the measurements	29
Age range	65 to 83 years
Weight range	60 to 97 Kg
Height range	160 to 181 cm
Number of the male subjects	7
Number of the female Subjects	8
Speed on treadmill	3.0 to 5.0 km/h
Blood pressure range before	Systolic 132 to 201 diastolic 74 to 116
Blood pressure range after	Systolic 117 to 234 diastolic 63 to 119
Have diseases	6 subjects
Pulse rate	55 to 146 beats per minute
Oxygen saturation	82 to 100%

be also used while there is no expert classification available, that is, if the CBR system failed to retrieve any similar cases with a higher similarity value as a threshold.

3. Study Design and Data Analysis

Data were collected from 15 elderly persons using a 9-minute personalized health profiling approach with 4 sessions (i.e., baseline, deep breath, activity, and relax) discussed in [3]. The summary of the data observation is illustrated in Table 1. As it can be seen from Table 1, 29 measurements were collected from 15 subjects (7 were male and 8 were female) between the age of 65 and 83 years. Among the 15 subjects, 6 of them were diagnosed previously of having 1 or 2 kinds of different diseases and of which they were at the time of the experiment undergoing treatment. The others were comparatively healthy. However, some of them were having high blood pressure during the data collection.

During the test, the subjects used a treadmill in which the minimum speed was 3 km per hour and the maximum speed was 5 km per hour. The speed was considered according to the subject's capability of walking. The pulse rate among the subjects was 55 beats per minute as the minimum and 146 beats per minute as the maximum and oxygen saturation between 82% and 100% was observed. The sensor reading was closely monitored during data collection to ensure that the connection was not loose. The preprocessing done directly after data collection removed any erroneous data values caused by a loose collection, and one measurement was found

with a huge amount of sensor error in data reading and therefore it was not considered.

The collective 29 measurements of (a) pulse rate and (b) oxygen saturation are plotted in Figure 3, where the baseline, deep breath, activity, and relax are the 4 sessions. As it can be seen from Figure 3(a), the pulse rate varies between 65 and 95 in baseline and deep breath; however, the pulse rate increases when subjects are doing the activity task and decreases while they are resting (relax). Similarly, the oxygen saturation during the activity drops for some of the subjects as shown in Figure 3(b). Here, the changes of pulse rate and oxygen saturation are highly individual due to health factors, metabolic activity, and so forth. Thus, interpreting/analysing the measurements and understanding the large variations in the measurements from diverse subjects require knowledge and experience which is often very difficult to model even for an expert of the domain.

4. Features Extraction and Case Formulation

The collected measurements from the pulse oximeter are processed to extract features in time domain, frequency domain, and time-frequency domain. The numbers of features are considered based on previous study [4, 5, 25–27] and expert opinion. In the *time domain*, statistical features like maximum, minimum, arithmetic mean, and standard deviation of data are considered.

Frequency domain is also considered for the feature extraction as it has been observed in the previous works [25, 26] that the distinction between healthy and diseased people's data is visible in the frequency domain. In order to obtain the frequency domain features, a power spectral density (PSD) was calculated as shown in Figure 4. The PSD is the squared amplitude of the discrete Fourier transform (DFT) which is achieved by using fast Fourier transform (FFT) algorithm on the process measurements. In DFT, an input function is required which should be discrete, and this is done by sampling the pulse rate or oxygen saturation over a period of time. N length of time-series sequence is transformed into another sequence of N complex numbers by the function presented in (1), where T is the sampling frequency

$$Y\left[\frac{n}{NT}\right] = \frac{1}{N} \sum_{k=0}^{N-1} y[kT] e^{-i2\pi nkT/NT}. \tag{1}$$

Here, the measurements are processed through a scaling procedure to sample the measurements in 1 Hz frequency range. From the power spectral density low-frequency power, high-frequency power, low-frequency power to high-frequency power ratio, low-frequency peak power spectral

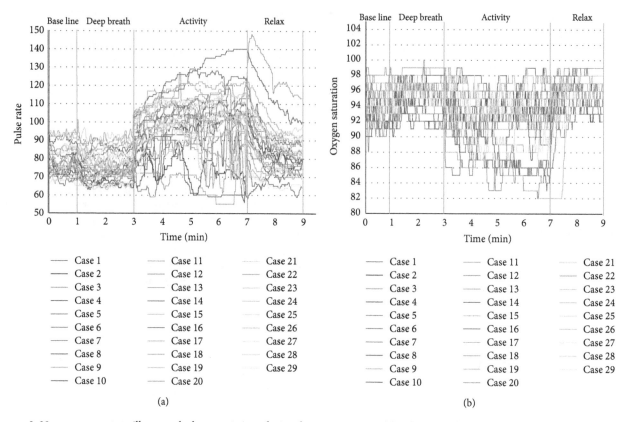

FIGURE 3: 29 measurements to illustrate the large variations during the 4 steps. y-axis: (a) pulse rate in beats per minute, (b) oxygen saturation in percentage and x-axis: time in minutes (total 9 minutes).

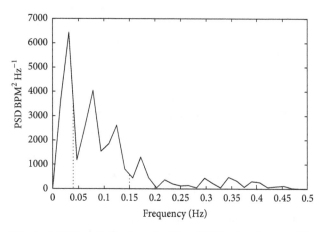

FIGURE 4: PSD plot of pulse rate, LF and HF region is marked by dotted line.

density, and high-frequency peak power spectral density were calculated [25]. Frequencies between 0.04 Hz and 0.15 were considered as low-frequency, and frequencies between 0.15 and 0.4 were considered as high-frequency as shown in Figure 4 [25]. The power in high- and low-frequency regions was calculated by numerical integration of the power spectral density of the corresponding frequency range. The unit of the power spectrum density and power for the pulse rate was BPM2 (beats per minute) Hz-1 and BPM2,

respectively. Similarly, the frequency domain features for the oxygen saturation were calculated, with the unit of the power spectrum density and the power of (%) 2 Hz-1 and (%) 2, respectively.

In *time-frequency domain* features, a discrete wavelet transform (DWT) is performed since it can keep the information of both time and frequency. Statistical features maximum, minimum, arithmetic mean, and standard deviations were calculated from the approximation coefficient of wavelet decomposition of level 1 [27]. The function "Daubechies 2" was used as the mother wavelet. The continuous wavelet transform linked to mother wavelet $\psi(t)$ can be defined by

$$W(a, b) = \int_{-\infty}^{\infty} y(t)\, \psi_{ab}(t)\, dt, \qquad (2)$$

where $y(t)$ is any square integral function and a, b are scaling and translation parameters, respectively. Evaluating the continuous wavelet at dyadic interval of the signal can be expressed by

$$y(t) = \sum_{k=-\infty}^{\infty} \sum_{j=-\infty}^{\infty} d_j(k)\, 2^{j/2} \psi\left(2^j t - k\right), \qquad (3)$$

where d_j is the discrete wavelet coefficient of the signal $y(t)$. Symmetric padding was used to make the data samples power of two to implement discrete wavelet transform [27].

In CBR, generally a case can be comprised using problem and solution part, in which the problem contains a vector of

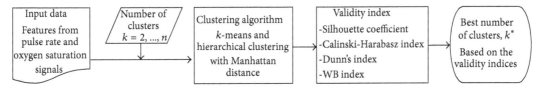

FIGURE 5: Schema diagram of clustering validity process.

features to describe a problem, and the solution part contains classification. To formulate a case, all features from the three domains in four sessions plus the subjects' contextual information (age, weight, gender, and blood pressure) were taken. Blood pressure was measured twice, once before and once after the end of taking measurements from pulse oximeter. As a result, each case contains total 59 ($4 \times 13 + 7$) features in problem description part of the cases. The list of the features with detail information is presented in our previous article [3]. As the solution of a case, this part of the cases contains expert classification where the classification is done considering three different classes. The three classes are (a) Class A, the measurement *looks good and it is a healthy data*, (b) Class B, the measurement *looks ok and it is a normal data*, and (c) Class C, the measurement *looks different and needs to look more in detail*.

5. Cluster Analysis in the System

In order to group the measurements, clustering methods have been applied. This group information helps CBR to do a fast retrieval; that is, it looks only most similar group of cases. Moreover, clinicians could get benefit in situations when CBR fails to retrieve any similar case for a given high threshold similarity value. To find a set of unlabeled similar groups of time-series, several clustering methods have been reported in the literature. Depending on problem and application, different kinds of clustering algorithms are applied [28]. The two most common algorithms of time-series clustering are hierarchical clustering and k-means in which the similarity function is effective on result [29].

Figure 5 illustrates the schema diagram for the process of finding the best number of clusters and the best algorithm for clustering data. In this process, two clustering algorithms, hierarchical and k-means, are applied on the feature vector of data. In *hierarchical algorithm*, in each step, pairwise distance of vectors (clusters) is computed and then the similar vector (clusters) are merged into a new cluster until all data goes to a single cluster [30]. To find the similarity between clusters, single linkage distance is used [29]. In k-means algorithm, k vectors are selected as initial centers of clusters. Then other vectors are assigned to these k centers based on the defined similarity function. (In this work we used Manhattan distance.) Then the center of each cluster is updated to the average of its members. These steps are repeated until the center of clusters is fixed [29].

In the step of Figure 5, to find the best clustering algorithm and also the best number of clusters, for each result of clustering step, some general methods and indices are applied

to measure the quality of clustering algorithms and validation of obtained clusters. Here, we used four validity indices. Silhouette coefficient (SC) [31] and Dunn's index (DI) [32] are the popular validity indices that show the compactness of data within the clusters and separation between clusters. Calinski-Harabasz index (CH) [32] is a sum of square-based index that evaluates the quality of partitioning [31]. In these three methods, the maximum of the index value determines the optimum clustering. WB index [33] is a new validity index that emphasizes the effect of sum of squares within cluster with multiplying the number of clusters. This method determines the optimum number of clusters by minimal value of index. By comparing the results of validity indices, this process will be able to recognize the best clustering algorithm and cluster numbers (k^*).

6. Case-Based Classification

The function of the case-based classification is to retrieve the most similar cases. Weighting of features is an important task for retrieving similar cases. To determine the degree of importance of each feature, expert knowledge is needed. As another alternative, feature weighting could be done automatically using some artificial intelligence techniques. In our previous research [7], the automatic weighting is investigated by learning from the case base; that is, it distinguishes individual features in terms of discriminating powers on the discretized universes of features. However, it does not show a better result than the expert's weighting. Moreover, in order to perform automatic weighting of features, the algorithm needs a high volume of cases with their corresponding classification. Therefore, in some medical domains, automatic weighting is not preferable. In this work, weights of the features are defined by a domain expert. These weights are then used to retrieve similar cases; the detail of features weighting is presented in our previous paper [3]. Similarity of a feature value between two cases (i.e., a target case and one case from library) is measured using the normalized Manhattan distance between the feature values of the two cases. Nonnumeric features such as gender are converted to a numeric value by substituting the contextual value with a numeric one (1 for male, 0 for female). The Manhattan distance function to calculate the similarity of a feature between two cases is shown in (4), where T_i and S_i are the ith feature values of target and source case, respectively,

$$\text{sim}(T_i, S_i) = 1 - \frac{|T_i - S_i|}{\max\{T_i, \text{Max}(i)\} - \min\{T_i, \text{Min}(i)\}}.$$

(4)

Here, $\text{Max}(i)$ and $\text{Min}(i)$ represent the *maximum* and *minimum* values of the feature i obtained from the whole case library. Then "max" and "min" functions compare the values between the new case feature T_i and *maximum* and *minimum* values obtained from the case library. The function returns 1 if the values are the same and returns 0 if the values are dissimilar. This is known as a local similarity function

$$\text{sim}\,(T, S) = \frac{\sum_i^n w_i \times \text{sim}\,(T_i, S_i)}{\sum_i^n w_i}. \tag{5}$$

The similarity between the two cases is then measured using the weighted average of all the features that are to be considered. The function for calculating similarity between two cases T and S with n features is presented in (5), where w_i is the weight of the feature i defined by an expert of the domain. Note that, in the weight vector w_i is also considered the weight of three domains (i.e., time, frequency, and time-frequency features) and the weight of four sessions (i.e., *baseline, deep breath, activity* and *relax*). In CDSS, the CBR system retrieves both of the cases of pulse rate and oxygen saturation in parallel since there is no domain knowledge defined to combine them. However, a weighting approach is added in the CDSS to find an overall classification. Here, according to expert, the measurement of the pulse rate is more important than the oxygen saturation. The weighted average function presented in (6) to calculate a complete similarity value, that is, to find an overall classification by the CBR retrieval, is used:

$$\text{Sim}_{\text{case}}\,(\text{Pulse}, \text{Oxy}) = \frac{W_P \times \text{Sim}_{\text{pulse}} + W_O \times \text{Sim}_{\text{oxy}}}{W_P + W_O}, \tag{6}$$

where $\text{Sim}_{\text{case}}(\text{Pulse}, \text{Oxy})$ calculated the complete similarity value considering the individual similarity value of pulse rate as $\text{Sim}_{\text{pulse}}$ and the similarity value of oxygen saturation as Sim_{oxy}. W_p and W_O are the weight given by the expert.

7. Experimental Works

The experimental work is conducted as: (1) *proof-of-concept prototype*, (2) *classification accuracy of CBR with controlled measurements*, (3) classification accuracy of CBR with clustered measurements, and (4) *classification accuracy of CBR considering expert classification*.

7.1. The Proof-of-Concept Prototype. The web-based CDSS has been built using PHP and JavaScript programming language, and case libraries are developed in MySQL database. The main goal of this experiment is to see whether the several functions implemented in the web-based system are working properly or not. The DSS using case-based retrieval is verified by implementation as a prototype in which all the implemented methods are compared according to their outcome, that is, in terms of the technical point of view. According to Watson [17], these trials have been conducted through the following 4 tests: (1) *retrieval accuracy*, (2) *retrieval consistency*, (3) *case duplication*, and (4) *global test*. For the test *retrieval accuracy*, a "leave-one-out" retrieval technique is used; that is, one case is taken from the case library as a query case, and then the system retrieves the most similar cases. Among the retrieved cases, the query case is also retrieved as the top similar case with the similarity value 1.0; that is, the similarity value of two same cases is computed as 100%. To test the *retrieval consistency*, the same query is used to perform more than one similar search, and if it has been found that the same stored cases have been retrieved with the same similarity, then the implemented retrieval function is considered to have consistency. It is also observed that no cases are identical during retrieval except the query case, when it matches itself; thus, *case duplication* is also checked. Regarding the global test, the classification accuracy of the CBR system is performed and discussed in the next section.

7.2. Classification Accuracy of CBR with Controlled Measurements. For these experiments, the proposed system uses the sessions from health profiling. That is, each case is then further divided into 4 categories according to the sessions that are, *baseline, deep breath, activity,* and *relax*. The reason behind this is that the measurements are very much controlled; subjects are following the tasks according to the condition of health profiling. Moreover, there is always a question about the gold standard of expert. The main goal of this experiment is to see how accurately the CBR approach can classify the signals. Two case libraries are used with 15 subjects; one is for only pulse rate (29 signals) and an other one is for oxygen saturation (29 signals). Each case library contains 116 cases (29 measurements × 4 sessions) with 4 classes in total, and each case contains 13 features extracted (both from time domain, frequency domain, and time-frequency domain) from the signals. For CBR classification, a "leave-one-out" retrieval technique (i.e., 1 out of 29 cases) is applied and the top most retrieved similar case ($k = 1$) is considered. If the considered case is retrieved from the same class, then we count 1 as correct classification, and percentage of each class is calculated after querying all 29 cases. The results for percentage of correct classification considering pulse rate case library are shown in Table 2.

Table 2 illustrates the results for the pulse rate cases; the first three columns present the classification accuracy considering only each of individual domain features. That is, when it is only time domain, all the other features in frequency and time-frequency domains are weighted as "0." It can be observed, CBR approach has achieved the highest percentage of classification accuracy while considering the frequency domain features. The average value of the classification accuracy for the frequency domain features is 85.3%, for the time domain features it is 44%, and for the time-frequency domain features it is 48.3%. However, when the features are combined, the highest accuracy has been increased on average to ≈5% which is presented in the last column of Table 2. The combination has been performed using a weight vector in which both the time and time-frequency domains features get 10% each, and frequency domain features get 80%. Average classification accuracy is around 90% while it combines all the domain features.

TABLE 2: Percentage of correct classifications of each class considering pulse rate case library.

Sessions	Using only time domain features (TmF)	Using only frequency domain features (FrqF)	Using only time-frequency domain features (TmFrqF)	Using a combination of features TmF = 10%, TmFrqF = 10%, and FrqF = 80%
Baseline	51.7%	96.5%	62.0%	96.5%
Deep breath	27.6%	79.3%	34.5%	83.0%
Activity	45.0%	96.5%	45.0%	100.0%
Relax	51.7%	69.0%	51.7%	80.0%
Average	44.0%	85.3%	48.3%	89.8%

TmF: time domain features, FrqF: frequency domain features, and TmFrqF: time-frequency domain features.

TABLE 3: Percentage of correct classifications of each class considering oxygen saturation case library.

Sessions	Using only time domain features (TmF)	Using only frequency domain features (FrqF)	Using only time-frequency domain features (TmFrqF)	Using a combination of features TmF = 10%, TmFrqF = 10%, and FrqF = 80%
Baseline	31.0%	100.0%	27.5%	100.0%
Deep breath	24.1%	65.5%	34.5%	72.0%
Activity	62.0%	100%	51.1%	100.0%
Relax	27.6%	38.0%	24.7%	48.0%
Average	36.2%	76.0%	34.5%	80.0%

TmF: time domain features, FrqF: frequency domain features, and TmFrqF: time-frequency domain features.

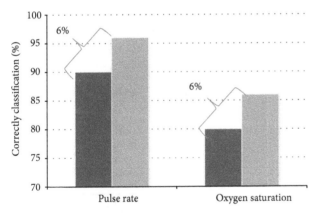

FIGURE 6: The classification accuracy increased 6% while considering top 2 retrieved similar cases, that is, $k = 2$.

Average classification accuracy ($k = 1$)
Average classification accuracy ($k = 2$)

TABLE 4: Confusion matrix for pulse rate (a) and oxygen saturation (b) considering $k = 2$, using CBR with extracted features.

(a)

	Baseline	Deep breath	Activity	Relax
Baseline	**29**	0	0	0
Deep breath	0	**28**	0	1
Activity	0	0	**29**	0
Relax	1	3	0	**25**
Accuracy in percentage	100%	96.5%	100%	86.2%

(b)

	Baseline	Deep breath	Activity	Relax
Baseline	**29**	0	0	0
Deep breath	0	**25**	0	4
Activity	0	0	**29**	0
Relax	0	12	0	**17**
Accuracy in percentage	100%	86.2%	100%	59%

Similarly, Table 3 presents the classification results based on the oxygen saturation case library.

Table 3 presents results for the oxygen saturation; it shows the highest percentage of correct classification using the frequency domain features. The result has increased 4% on an average while it combines the three domain features. The average value of the correct classification is 80% with combination of features and 76% without combination, that is, only considering the frequency domain.

Figure 6 presents the average value of correctly classified cases both for the pulse rate and oxygen saturation data. It shows the comparison result in the classification accuracy values while considering the top most similar retrieved case, that is, $k = 1$ and top 2 most similar retrieved cases, that is, $k = 2$. It can be seen from Figure 6 that the overall accuracy is increased by 6% while considering $k = 2$ and the classification accuracy for the pulse rate is 96% and for the oxygen saturation is 86%. The confusion matrices both for (Table 4(a)) the pulse rate and (Table 4(b)) oxygen saturation while considering top 2 cases are presented in Table 4.

The distribution of the classification using CBR can be seen both from the (a) pulse rate and (b) oxygen saturation in Table 4; the *baseline* and *activity* classes are classified 100%

correctly. However, the classification in *deep breath* and *relax* are missing. For example, in *deep breath* for the pulse data (Table 4(a)), one case is misclassified as *relax,* and in *relax* 4 cases are misclassified, 3 as *deep breath* and 1 as *baseline.* Similarly, Table 4(b), 4 *deep breath* cases are misclassified as *relax,* and 12 of *relax* class cases are misclassified as *deep breath.*

7.3. Classification Accuracy of CBR with Clustered Measurements. This experimental work has been conducted in twofold: (a) *evaluating the clustering* algorithms and (b) *classification accuracy* using CBR. Here, the entire measurement is considered and clustered using well-known clustering algorithm; that is, the measurements include all the sessions, baseline, deep breath, activity, and relax. However, the measurements of pulse rate and oxygen saturation are still separated and clustered separately.

(a) *Evaluating the Clustering Algorithms.* The main aim for this experimental work is to identify the clustering method and number of clusters. Here, all the extracted features (i.e., features in time, frequency, and time-frequency domains) form 29 measurements are considered.

Two well-known clustering algorithms, k-means and single linkage hierarchical clustering, are applied [29, 30], and up to 5 clusters are generated by each algorithm. In order to make meaningful clusters and also find the best clustering method, four validation indices, Silhouette coefficient (SC) [31], Dunn's index (DI) [34], Calinski-Harabasz index (CH) [32], and WB index (WB) [33], are compared. As it can be seen from Figure 7, for pulse rate (a) and oxygen saturation (b), k-means clustering is better than single linkage hierarchical clustering. Also the best number of clusters is 3 for both. In SC, DI, and CH the maximum value shows the best clustering and the best number of clusters (star points), and in WB the minimum value is the best. According to the above evaluation, k-means clustering algorithm with 3 clusters achieved the highest evaluation value. Therefore, here the clustered cases with k-means are considered. The distributions of cases in 3 clusters (i.e., Classes A, B, and C) for pulse rate are presented in Table 5(a), and Classes A$'$, B$'$, and C$'$ for the oxygen saturation are presented in Table 5(b).

(b) *Classification Accuracy of CBR.* The main goal is to see how close the CBR system can classify compared to the clustering method. The class information is added into the case solution part, and the "leave-one-out" retrieval technique is applied. Here, the top 2 most similar cases ($k = 2$) are considered; that is, if both the query case and one of the retrieved cases belong to a similar class, then the number of correctly classified cases is counted as 1.

Finally, a percentage of the correctly classified cases are calculated on a total of 29 cases, and the results are presented in Table 6. From Table 6, when $k = 1$, CBR performs ≈80% correctly for the pulse rate and ≈90% for the oxygen saturation as close to the clustering algorithm (i.e., k-means). However, the percentage of correctly classified cases is improved while $k = 2$ and the achieved value is ≈93% for both the pluse rate and oxygen saturation. For the pulse rate (a) and oxygen saturation (b) the confusion matrices of

TABLE 5: Case distribution in 3 clusters both for pulse rate (a) and oxygen saturation (b).

(a)

Criteria	Class A	Class B	Class C
Case_ids	1, 3, 5, 7, 14, 15, 16, 17, 19, 25, 26	2, 4, 11, 12, 18, 20, 22, 28, 30	8, 9, 10, 13, 21, 23, 24, 27, 29
Total number of cases	11	9	9

(b)

Criteria	Class A$'$	Class B$'$	Class C$'$
Case_ids	1, 3, 7, 8, 10, 12, 17, 22, 24, 28, 30	2, 5, 13, 14, 15	4, 9, 11, 16, 18, 19, 20, 21, 23, 25, 26, 27, 29
Total number of cases	11	5	13

TABLE 6: Classification accuracy in CBR considering clustering.

29 measurements	Percentage of correctly classified cases ($K = 1$)	Percentage of correctly classified cases ($K = 2$)
Pulse rate	79.30%	93.10%
Oxygen saturation	89.65%	93.10%
Average	84.5%	93.1%

TABLE 7: Confusion matrix for pulse rate (a) and oxygen saturation (b) considering $k = 2$.

(a)

	Class A	Class B	Class C	Total
Class A	**11**	0	0	11
Class B	0	**9**	0	9
Class C	1	1	**7**	9
Accuracy in percentage	100%	100%	78%	29

(b)

	Class A$'$	Class B$'$	Class C$'$	Total
Class A$'$	**11**	0	0	11
Class B$'$	0	**3**	2	5
Class C$'$	0	0	**13**	13
Accuracy in percentage	100%	60.0%	100%	29

correctly classified cases using CBR ($k = 2$) compare to the clustered cases are presented in Table 7.

7.4. Classification Accuracy of CBR Considering Expert Classification. The main goal of this experimental work is to investigate the classification performance of the CBR approach compared to an expert of the domain. Here, the word "expert" means a panel which consists of three researchers working mostly with biomedical sensor signals. The panel has examined and analyzed the cases and performed an overall classification; that is, all the 29 test data (both pulse and oxygen saturation measurements) from 15 subjects were classified by the panel into three classes. The three classes are

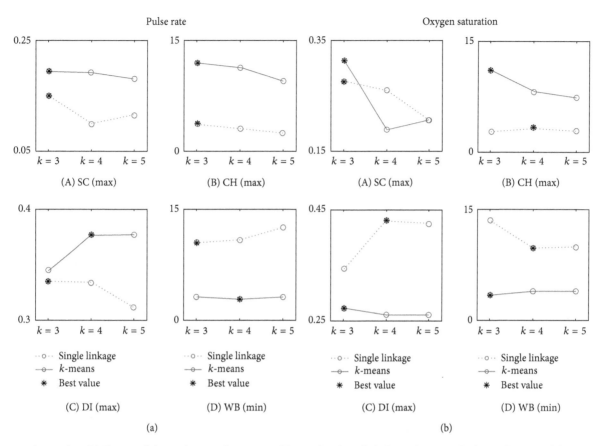

FIGURE 7: The results of different validity indices on k-means and hierarchical single linkage clustering for $k = 3$, $k = 4$, and $k = 5$ in pulse rate (a) and oxygen saturation (b). (A) Silhouette coefficient (SC), (B) Calinski-Harabasz index (CH), (C) Dunn's index (DI), and (D) WB index (WB).

(i) Class A, the measurement *looks good and it is a healthy data*, (ii) Class B, the measurement *looks ok and it is a normal data,* and (iii) Class C, the measurement *looks different and needs to look more in detail*. A majority voting approach is considered to perform the final classification on cases. For example, for a case "Case_id_7.1," a set of classification is achieved from the panel; that is, Case_id_7.1 = (Class B, Class B, and Class A) and Class B is taken for final classification of the case. Note that the panels agree with each other in 72.4% of the cases (21 cases out of 29).

Similar to the previous experiments, the "leave-one-out" retrieval technique is applied for CBR, and a percentage of correctly classification cases are calculated. Note that the final similarity value is calculated by the weighted average of individual similarity value of pulse rate and oxygen saturation where pulse rate receives a higher importance than the oxygen. Moreover, the experiment has been conducted considering both $k = 1$ and $K = 2$ as discussed earlier. The performance of the CBR system in terms of classification accuracy is illustrated in Table 8.

It can be observed from Table 8 that the CBR approach can classify with 92% accuracy for Class A, 37.5% for Class B, and 75% for Class C while considering the singular top most similar retrieved case (i.e. $k = 1$). The performance of the CBR classification increased while considering two

TABLE 8: Classification accuracy in CBR considering expert overall classification.

	Total number of cases	Percentage of correctly classified cases ($K = 1$)	Percentage of correctly classified cases ($K = 2$)
Class A	13	92.3%	100.0%
Class B	8	37.5%	62.5%
Class C	8	75.0%	75.0%
Total	29	72.3%	83.0%

top similar classes; that is, Class A achieved 100%, Class B achieved 62.5%, and Class C remains the same. So, in total, the accuracy of the CBR system was 72.3% for $k = 1$ and 83% for $k = 2$. The confusion matrix of correctly classified cases using CBR and $k = 2$ while comparing to the expert classes is presented in Table 9.

According to Table 9, 3 classes out of 8 cases in Class B were misclassified as Class A, and 2 classes out of 8 cases in Class C were misclassified as Class A, and Class B respectively. According to the class definition defined by the expert, Class A and Class B, represent as healthy or normal conditions of the subjects, and Class C is the opposite. So, in order to perform a sensitivity and specificity analysis, 29 cases were

TABLE 9: Confusion matrix considering $k = 2$ in CBR.

	Class A	Class B	Class C	Total
Class A	**13**	0	0	13
Class B	3	**5**	0	8
Class C	1	1	**6**	8
Accuracy in percentage	100%	62.5%	75%	29

TABLE 10: Statistical analysis of the CBR classification considering $k = 1$.

Criteria/indices	Values
Total cases	29
Not healthy (Class C) group (P)	8
Healthy (Class A + Class B) group (N)	21
True positive (TP)	6
False positive (FP)	1
True negative (TN)	20
False negative (FN)	2
Sensitivity = TP/(TP + FN)	≈0.75
Specificity = TN/(FP + TN)	≈0.95
Accuracy = (TP + TN)/(P + N)	≈0.90

further divided into 2 groups: *healthy* = (Class A + Class B) and *not healthy* = Class C. Therefore, the *healthy* group consists of 21 cases, and *not healthy* group consists of 8 cases. Note that this time we only consider $K = 1$ in CBR retrieval, and the results are presented in Table 10.

As can be observed from Table 10, in *healthy* group, 20 cases are correctly classified that represent true negative (TN), and 1 is misclassified that represent false positive (FP). Similarly, in *not healthy* group, 6 cases are correctly classified that represent true positive (TP), and 2 are misclassified that represent false negative (FN). So, the sensitivity, specificity, and overall accuracy achieved by the CBR approach are 75%, 95%, and 90%, respectively, while considering only one top similar retrieved case (i.e. $k = 1$).

8. Summary and Discussion

This paper proposed a case-based clinical decision support system to monitor individuals' health condition remotely. Here, a pulse oximeter is used together with a personalized health profile protocol. The pulse oximeter is low-cost and easy to use sensor in any environment. The protocol helps to establish individual health profile.

The system has been designed in three-tier client server architecture. The measurements are collected through an Android application, and a case library has been implemented in a remote server. The development of the server side consists of the feature extraction part to find key parameters of interest using time, frequency, and time-frequency domains. Besides, this paper introduces a time-series similarity measure and a clustering approach to group the cases offline which makes the retrieval process faster by looking only within the most similar group of cases. This will be helpful for large datasets, and our future target

is to test the system in a large-scale environment. A web-enabled CDSS with advanced signal analysis capability could be accessed via specific clients, for example, physician at a health clinic in order to monitor health. In the web-enabled CDSS, the system provides a number of functionalities, such as (1) features level analysis, (2) CBR classification with clustered measurements and (3) CBR classification with expert opinion.

The proposed CDSS has been evaluated considering *controlled measurements*, using *clustered measurements*, and considering *expert classification*. As can be observed from Figure 6, for the pulse rate, the classification accuracy of the CBR approach is 96%, and for the oxygen saturation it is 86% considering the controlled measurements. Here, the evaluation shows better performance when the three domains features are combined rather than single domain features. According to the confusion matrices presented in Table 4, the cases in *baseline* and *activity* conditions are well classified than the other two conditions, that is, *deep breath* and *relax*. The cases belong to these conditions are classified as each other and could be explained by the fact that the two conditions *deep breath* and *relax are rather similar* [35]. Note that the classification performance for CBR has been achieved by considering the 2 top most similar retrieved cases (i.e., $K = 2$) since the similarity value of these two cases is often very close to each other (e.g., 96.34 and 96.10). From these experiments, it can be observed that using different test data sets, methods and considering expert classification, the system can perform its classification task and generate alarms in an anomalous situation. The results show that the approach could be applicable to use in a clinical remote health monitoring. Nevertheless, the performance of the system could be experimented considering a large case library with reference cases. To show the superiority of the proposed approach, a comparison with the other approaches such as neural networks or support vector machine could be obtained, and this is now ongoing. Moreover, the system should be verified in real clinical environment for day-to-day usage.

References

[1] S. Youm, G. Lee, S. Park, and W. Zhu, "Development of remote healthcare system for measuring and promoting healthy lifestyle," *Expert Systems with Applications*, vol. 38, no. 3, pp. 2828–2834, 2011.

[2] J. Gong, S. Lu, R. Wang, and L. Cui, "PDhms: pulse diagnosis via wearable healthcare sensor network," in *Proceedings of the IEEE International Conference on Communications (ICC '11)*, pp. 1–5, 2011.

[3] M. U. Ahmed, A. M. Islam, and A. Loutfi, "A case-based patient identification system using pulse oximeter and a personalized health profile," in *Proceedings of the Health Sciences at 20th International Conference on Case-Based Reasoning (ICCBR '12)*, B. Isabelle, M. Stefania, and M. Cindy, Eds., Springer, Lyon, France, September 2012.

[4] Z. Jin, J. Oresko, S. Huang, and A. C. Cheng, "HeartToGo: a personalized medicine technology for cardiovascular disease prevention and detection," in *Proceedings of the IEEE/NIH Life*

Science Systems and Applications Workshop (LiSSA '09), pp. 80–83, April 2009.

[5] N. Krupa, M. A. MA, E. Zahedi, S. Ahmed, and F. M. Hassan, "Antepartum fetal heart rate feature extraction and classification using empirical mode decomposition and support vector machine," *BioMedical Engineering Online*, vol. 10, article 6, 2011.

[6] A. Aamodt and E. Plaza, "Case-based reasoning: foundational issues, methodological variations, and system approaches," *AI Communications*, vol. 7, no. 1, pp. 39–59, 1994.

[7] S. Begum, M. U. Ahmed, P. Funk, N. Xiong, and B. Von Schéele, "A case-based decision support system for individual stress diagnosis using fuzzy similarity matching," *Computational Intelligence*, vol. 25, no. 3, pp. 180–195, 2009.

[8] J. M. Corchado, J. Bajo, and A. Abraham, "GerAmi: improving healthcare delivery in geriatric residences," *IEEE Intelligent Systems*, vol. 23, no. 2, pp. 19–25, 2008.

[9] M. U. Ahmed, S. Begum, P. Funk, N. Xiong, and B. von Schéele, "A three phase computer assisted biofeedback training system using case-based reasoning," in *Proceedings of the 9th European Conference on Case-based Reasoning*, Trier, Germany, 2008.

[10] S. Montani, L. Portinale, G. Leonardi, R. Bellazzi, and R. Bellazzi, "Case-based retrieval to support the treatment of end stage renal failure patients," *Artificial Intelligence in Medicine*, vol. 37, no. 1, pp. 31–42, 2006.

[11] I. Bichindaritz, "Prototypical case mining from biomedical literature for bootstrapping a case base," *Applied Intelligence*, vol. 28, no. 3, pp. 222–237, 2008.

[12] M. U. Ahmed, S. Begum, P. Funk, N. Xiong, and B. von Schéele, "Case-based reasoning for diagnosis of stress using enhanced cosine and fuzzy similarity," *International Journal of Transactions on Case-Based Reasoning on Multimedia Data*, vol. 1, no. 1, pp. 3–19, 2008.

[13] M. U. Ahmed, S. Begum, P. Funk, N. Xiong, and B. von Schéele, "A multi-module case based biofeedback system for stress treatment," *International Journal of Artificial Intelligence in Medicine*, vol. 51, no. 2, pp. 107–115, 2010.

[14] M. U. Ahmed and P. Funk, "A computer aided system for post-operative pain treatment combining knowledge discovery and case-based reasoning," in *Case-Based Reasoning Research and Development*, vol. 7466 of *Lecture Notes in Computer Science*, pp. 3–16, 2012.

[15] S. Begum, M. U. Ahmed, P. Funk, N. Xiong, and M. Folke, "Case-based reasoning systems in the health sciences: a survey of recent trends and developments," *IEEE Transactions on Systems, Man and Cybernetics C*, vol. 41, no. 4, pp. 421–434, 2011.

[16] S. Begum, M. U. Ahmed, and P. Funk, "Case-based systems in health sciences: a case study in the field of stress management," *WSEAS Transactions on Systems*, vol. 8, no. 3, pp. 344–354, 2009.

[17] I. Watson, *Applying Case-Based Reasoning: Techniques For Enterprise Systems*, Morgan Kaufmann Publishers, San Fransisco, Calif, USA, 1997.

[18] M. Stacey and C. McGregor, "Temporal abstraction in intelligent clinical data analysis: a survey," *Artificial Intelligence in Medicine*, vol. 39, no. 1, pp. 1–24, 2007.

[19] I. Yoo, P. Alafaireet, M. Marinov et al., "Data mining in healthcare and biomedicine: a survey of the literature," *Journal of Medical Systems*, vol. 36, no. 4, pp. 2431–2448, 2011.

[20] S. Jeong, C. H. Youn, E. B. Shim, M. Kim, Y. M. Cho, and L. Peng, "An integrated healthcare system for personalized chronic disease care in home-hospital environments," *IEEE Transactions on Information Technology in Biomedicine*, vol. 16, no. 4, pp. 572–585, 2012.

[21] G. K. Pang, "Health monitoring of elderly in independent and assisted living," in *Proceedings of the International Conference on Biomedical Engineering (ICoBE '12)*, pp. 553–556, February 2012.

[22] R. M. Rahman and F. R. M. Hasan, "Using and comparing different decision tree classification techniques for mining ICDDR,B Hospital Surveillance data," *Expert Systems with Applications*, vol. 38, no. 9, pp. 11421–11436, 2011.

[23] C. M. Chen, "Web-based remote human pulse monitoring system with intelligent data analysis for home health care," *Expert Systems with Applications*, vol. 38, no. 3, pp. 2011–2019, 2011.

[24] G. Koshmak, *An Android Based Monitoring and Alarm System for Patients with Chronic Obtrusive Disease [M.S. thesis]*, Department of Technology at Örebro University.

[25] K. Dingli, T. Assimakopoulos, P. K. Wraith, I. Fietze, C. Witt, and N. J. Douglas, "Spectral oscillations of RR intervals in sleep apnoea/hypopnoea syndrome patients," *European Respiratory Journal*, vol. 22, no. 6, pp. 943–950, 2003.

[26] C. Zamarrón, F. Gude, J. Barcala, J. R. Rodriguez, and P. V. Romero, "Utility of oxygen saturation and heart rate spectral analysis obtained from pulse oximetric recordings in the diagnosis of sleep apnea syndrome," *Chest*, vol. 123, no. 5, pp. 1567–1576, 2003.

[27] D. Cvetkovic, E. D. Übeyli, and I. Cosic, "Wavelet transform feature extraction from human PPG, ECG, and EEG signal responses to ELF PEMF exposures: a pilot study," *Digital Signal Processing*, vol. 18, no. 5, pp. 861–874, 2008.

[28] R. Xu and D. Wunsch, "Survey of clustering algorithms," *IEEE Transactions on Neural Networks*, vol. 16, no. 3, pp. 645–678, 2005.

[29] T. W. Liao, "Clustering of time series data: survey," *Pattern Recognition*, vol. 38, pp. 1857–1874, 2005.

[30] C. A. Ratanamahatana, J. Lin, D. Gunopulos, E. J. Keogh, M. Vlachos, and G. Das, "Mining time series data," in *Data Mining and Knowledge Discovery Handbook*, pp. 1049–1077, 2010.

[31] L. Vendramin, R. J. G. B. Campello, and E. R. Hruschka, "On the comparison of relative clustering validity criteria," in *Proceedings of the 9th SIAM International Conference on Data Mining (SDM '09)*, pp. 729–740, May 2009.

[32] Y. Liu, Z. Li, H. Xiong, X. Gao, and J. Wu, "Understanding of internal clustering validation measures," in *Proceedings of the 10th IEEE International Conference on Data Mining (ICDM '10)*, pp. 911–916, December 2010.

[33] Q. Zhao, M. Xu, and P. Fränti, "Sum-of-squares based cluster validity index and significance analysis," in *Adaptive and Natural Computing Algorithms*, vol. 5495 of *Lecture Notes in Computer Science*, pp. 313–322, 2009.

[34] K. R. Žalik and B. Žalik, "Validity index for clusters of different sizes and densities," *Pattern Recognition Letters*, vol. 32, no. 2, pp. 221–234, 2011.

[35] M. U. Ahmed and A. Loutfi, "Physical activity classification for elderly based on pulse rate," in *Proceedings of the 10th International Conference on Wearable Micro and Nano Technologies for Personalized Health Tallinn*, June 2013.

6

Yield Prediction for Tomato Greenhouse Using EFuNN

Kefaya Qaddoum, E. L. Hines, and D. D. Iliescu

School of Engineering, University of Warwick, Coventry CV4 7AL, UK

Correspondence should be addressed to E. L. Hines; e.l.hines@warwick.ac.uk

Academic Editors: C. Kotropoulos, H. Ling, and L. S. Wang

In the area of greenhouse operation, yield prediction still relies heavily on human expertise. This paper proposes an automatic tomato yield predictor to assist the human operators in anticipating more effectively weekly fluctuations and avoid problems of both overdemand and overproduction if the yield cannot be predicted accurately. The parameters used by the predictor consist of environmental variables inside the greenhouse, namely, temperature, CO_2, vapour pressure deficit (VPD), and radiation, as well as past yield. Greenhouse environment data and crop records from a large scale commercial operation, Wight Salads Group (WSG) in the Isle of Wight, United Kingdom, collected during the period 2004 to 2008, were used to model tomato yield using an Intelligent System called "Evolving Fuzzy Neural Network" (EFuNN). Our results show that the EFuNN model predicted weekly fluctuations of the yield with an average accuracy of 90%. The contribution suggests that the multiple EFUNNs can be mapped to respective task-oriented rule-sets giving rise to adaptive knowledge bases that could assist growers in the control of tomato supplies and more generally could inform the decision making concerning overall crop management practices.

1. Introduction

Greenhouse production systems require implementing computer-based climate control systems, including carbon dioxide (CO_2) supplementation. The sort of systems we are concerned with here are normally in use all year-round so as to maximize product and thus are typically applied in scenarios where the greenhouse crops have a long growing cycle. The technological advances and the sophistication of greenhouse crop production control systems do not mean that greenhouse operation does not rely on human expertise to decide on the optimum values for yield weekly amount. Practiced greenhouse tomato growers and researchers evaluate plant responses and growth mode by observations of the plant morphology. Tomato growers use this information in decision making depending on climate conditions and crop management practices to shift the plant growth toward a "balanced" growth mode, or to be able to accurately predict regular crops amounts each year.

One of the dynamic and complex systems is tomato crop growth, and few models have studied it previously. Two of the dynamic growth models are TOMGRO [1, 2] and TOMSIM [3, 4]. Both models depend on physiological processes, and they model biomass dividing, crop growth, and yield as a function of several climate and physiological parameters. Their use is limited, especially for practical application by growers, by their complexity, and by the difficulty in obtaining the initial condition parameters required for implementation [3]. Moreover, critical measurements are required for calibration and validation for each application.

Tompousse [5] predicts yields in terms of the weight of harvested fruits. Their model was developed in France for heated greenhouses and required that the linear relationships of both flowering rate and fruit growth period were in an appropriately warm environment; when the system was implemented in unheated plastic greenhouses, in Portugal, for example, the model performed poorly and was only tested for short production cycles of less than 15 weeks.

Adams [6] proposed a greenhouse tomato model and implemented it in the form of a graphical simulation tool (HIPPO). A key objective of the model was to explain the weekly fluctuations of greenhouse tomato yields as characterized by fruit size and harvest rates. This model required hourly climate data in order to determine the rates of growth of leaf truss and flower production.

Although the seasonal fluctuations of yield in greenhouse crops is generally understood to be influenced by the periodic variation of solar radiation and air temperature, greenhouse growers are also interested in the short- and long-term fluctuations of yield. There are a number of useful tools that can help growers when they are making short- and long-term decisions. For example, there are crop models that predict yield rates and produce quality in defining climate control strategies, in synchronizing crop production with market demands, in handling the labour force, in emerging marketing strategies, and in maintaining a consistent year-round produce quality.

As we will show, EFuNN offers the advantage that it is able to model nonlinear system relationships and has been shown in other applications to be very robust when applied to data which is relatively imprecise, incomplete, and uncertain. EFuNN has been successfully applied in applications such as forecasting, control, optimization, and pattern recognition [7]. Intelligence is added to the process by computing the degree of uncertainty and computing with linguistic terms (fuzzy variables). More accuracy is obtained compared to mechanistic models.

Numerous studies have applied either neural networks (NNs) or fuzzy logic in greenhouse production systems. However, most of them have focused on modeling the air temperature in greenhouse environments [8–11] or optimal control of CO_2 with NN. Recent techniques have included modeling the greenhouse environment with hierarchical fuzzy modeling [12] or controlling the environment with optimized fuzzy control [13, 14]. Other studies concerning plant modeling have been reported: [15] implemented a hybrid neurofuzzy approach in terms of the system identification and modeling of the total dry weight yield of tomato and lettuce [16] and developed a fuzzy model to predict net photosynthesis of tomato crop canopies, and the results obtained correlated well with the results. TOMGRO [1] was used to model the prediction processes.

The objective of this study is to investigate how an IS technique such as EFuNN performs when applied to current crop and climate records from greenhouse growers, weekly prediction of greenhouse tomato yield from environmental and crop-related variables. Yield was characterized by yield per unit area ($Yield$, kg/m^2).

The rest of this paper is organized as follows. In Section 2, we discuss the methodology introduction and materials and methods. Section 3 is results, and finally Section 4 presents the conclusions.

2. Background to Rule Extraction

A wide variety of methods are now available, recently reviewed in [1, 17, 18]. Reference [17] revisits the Andrews classification of rule extraction methods and emphasizes distinction between decompositional and pedagogical approaches. Rule extraction methods usually start by finding a minimal network, in terms of number of hidden units and overall connectivity. The next simplification, the key feature of the method, is to cluster the hidden unit activations, then extract combinations of inputs, which will activate each hidden unit, singly or together, and thus the output generates rules as the general form of rules shown as follows:

$$\text{If } (x1 \leq t1) \text{ AND} \cdots \text{AND } (xp \geq tp) \text{ Then } Ci. \quad (1)$$

Taha and Ghosh [19] suggest binary inputs generating a truth table from the inputs and simplifying the resultant Boolean function. The growth of computational time with number of attributes makes minimizing the size of the neural network essential and some methods evolve minimal topologies. The pedagogical approaches treat the neural network as a black box [20] and use the neural network only to generate test data for the rule generation algorithm.

2.1. Taxonomy of Rule Extraction Algorithms. It is now becoming apparent that algorithms can be designed which extract understandable representations from trained neural networks, enabling them to be used for decision-making. In this section, we use a taxonomy presented in [21] which uses three criteria for classification of rule extraction algorithms: scope of use, type of dependency with the method of solution of the type "black box," and format of the extracted rules. The algorithms can be a regression or classification algorithms. There are some algorithms that can be applied to both cases, such as the G-REX [21]. On the second criterion, an algorithm is considered independent if it is totally independent of the model type black box used (such as ANN and Support Vector Machines). The algorithms that use information of the black-box methods are called dependent methods. Regarding the format of the extracted rules, the methods can be classified into descriptive and predictive. The predictive algorithms perform extraction of rules that allow the expert to make an easy prediction for each possible observation from input space. If this analysis cannot be made directly, the algorithms are known only as descriptive.

3. Materials and Methods

3.1. EFuNN Evolving Fuzzy Neural Networks and the EFuNN Algorithm

3.1.1. Fuzzy Background. Fuzzy inference systems (FISs) are very useful for inference and handling uncertainty. The basic models presented are [14]. Some important issues that must be considered when building an FIS are identification of structure and estimation of parameters. Efficient structure identification optimizes the number of fuzzy rules and yields better convergence [22]. Different membership functions (MFs) can be attached to the neurons (triangular, Gaussian, etc.). The number of rules and the membership functions were estimated by the designers in early implementations of FIS [14]. A more efficient structure is then employed to optimize the number of rules in adaptive techniques which are appropriate for learning parameters that change slowly; handle complex systems with speedily changing characteristics, considering the fact that it takes a long time after every important change in the system to relearn model parameters [23, 24].

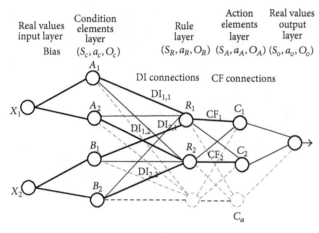

FIGURE 1: FuNN architecture.

References [14, 25] describe some techniques to learn fuzzy structure and parameters. In recent years, several evolving neurofuzzy systems (ENFSs) have been simulated, and these systems use online learning algorithms that can extract knowledge from data and perform a high-level adaptation of the network structure, as well as learning of parameters.

3.1.2. The General Fuzzy Neural Network (FuNN) Architecture. The fuzzy neural network (FuNN) (Figure 1) is connectionist feed-forward architecture with five layers of neurons and four layers of connections [26]. The first layer of neurons receives input information. The second layer calculates the fuzzy membership degrees of the input values which belong to predefined fuzzy membership functions, for example, small, medium, and large. The third layer of neurons represents associations between the input and the output variables, fuzzy If-Then rules. The fourth layer calculates the degrees to which output membership functions are matched by the input data, and the fifth layer does defuzzification and calculates values for the output variables. An FuNN has both the features of a neural network and a fuzzy inference machine. Several training algorithms have been developed for FuNN [26]: a modified back-propagation algorithm; a genetic algorithm; structural learning with forgetting; training and zeroing; combined modes. Several algorithms for rule extraction from FuNN have also been developed and applied. Each of them represents each rule node of a trained FuNN as an If-Then fuzzy rule.

3.2. EFUNN Architecture. EFuNNs are FuNN structures that evolve according to the Evolving Connectionist Systems (ECOS) principles. That is, all nodes in an EFuNN are generated through learning. The nodes representing membership functions can be modified during learning. As in FuNN, each input variable is represented here by a group of spatially arranged neurons to represent different fuzzy domain areas of this variable. Different membership functions can be attached to these neurons (triangular, Gaussian, etc.). New neurons evolve in this layer if for a given input vector the corresponding variable value does not belong to any of

the existing membership functions to a membership degree greater than a membership threshold, and this means that new fuzzy label neuron or an input variable neuron can be created during the adaptation phase of an EFuNN.

3.3. Yield Records and Climate Data. Crop records and climate data from a tomato greenhouse operation in *WSG* (*Wight Salads Group*) *in the Isle of Wight, United Kingdom*, were used to design and train evolving fuzzy neural networks for yield prediction. We used fuzzy inference system for implementing input parameter characterization. The data includes six datasets from two production cycles (S1: 2004 to 2007 and S2: 2008) and one greenhouse section (New Site). The total number of records is 1286, and each record included 14 parameters characterizing the weekly greenhouse environment and the crop features.

The environmental parameters which are to be controlled are the vapor pressure deficit (VPD) and the differential temperature between the daytime to nighttime ($T_d - T_n$). The setpoints for each environmental treatment were VPD = 2.0 kPa, 0.6 kPa, and uncontrolled; T_d/T_n = 26°C/18°C, 20°C/20°C, and 22°C/18°C, respectively, for each compartment. The date when they were planted and the period over which the crops were allowed to grow in the case of both datasets are summarized in Table 1.

The tomatoes were grown in greenhouses on a high-wire system with hydroponic, CO_2 supplementation, and computer climate/irrigation control. The greenhouses were equipped with hot-water heating pipes and roof vents for passive cooling.

The crop records consisted of 12 plant samples per greenhouse section that were randomly selected and continuously measured during the production cycle. The crop record data were collected by direct observation and by manually measuring or counting each of the morphological features. This system included an electronic sensor unit which measured the air temperature, humidity, and CO_2 concentration in each of the greenhouse sections. Outside weather conditions were determined via a weather station. Daytime, nighttime, and 24 h averages of daily climate data from outside and inside of the greenhouse section were also obtained by the grower; weekly averages were computed to match the weekly crop records.

3.4. Modeling the Parameters. Yield (Y_a, kg m^{-2} week^{-1}) is of interest to greenhouse growers as a means via which they can develop short-term crop management strategies; it is also useful for labour management strategies. Greenhouse tomato cumulative yield can be described, either as fresh weight (Cockshull, 1988) or as dry mass [27]. Both of these studies were performed in northern latitudes, without CO_2 enrichment, for short production periods (<100 days), and the plants were cultivated in soil, not hydroponically. These are not currently standard cultivation methods because most of the greenhouse growers make use of high-technology production facilities.

Yield development is influenced mainly by fruit temperature. This parameter is inversely related to fruit development

TABLE 1: Summary of datasets. Crop records include samples per week in New House Sites.

Season (years)	Greenhouse	Transplanted on WOY[a] and date	Crop duration[b] (weeks)	Cultivar
		Commercial DS		
1	New h21	(26) June 24, 2004	42	Campari
(2004-2005)	New h22	(28) July 8, 2004	47	Campari
2	New h21	(31) July 28, 2005	43	Campari
(2004–2007)	New h22	(25) June 16, 2005	44	Campari
	New h22	(33) Aug. 11, 2006	36	Cherry
	New h22	(41) Oct. 6, 2007	39	Cherry

[a, b]WOY: week of the year number.

```
for each evolving layer neuron h do
    Create a new rule r
    for each input neuron i do
        Find the condition neuron c with the largest
        weight W_{c,h}
        Add an antecedent to r of the form "i is c
        W_{c,h}" where W_{c,t} is the confidence factor for
        that antecedent
    end for
    for each output neuron o do
        Find the action neuron a with the largest weight
        W_{h,a}
        Add a consequent to r of the form "o is a
        W_{h,a}" where W_{h,a} is the confidence factor for
        that consequent
    end for
end for
```

ALGORITHM 1: EFuNN algorithm steps.

rate and shows a linear relationship with air temperature [28, 29]. This relationship is shown in Algorithm 1 for all the datasets, which show the relation between yield and air temperature (Ti_n 24).

3.4.1. Data Processing.
The steps of the preprocessing include making average through a certain amount of the certain point of some data records. We preprocessed 5 environmental variables (CO_2, temperature, vapor pressure deficit (VPD), yield, and radiation) for different tomato cultivars, from different greenhouses in WSG area, which were not ready for processing but had to be pre-processed. For instance, some values in some tomato records were missing and we had to replace them with 0, being not ready to be fed to an artificial neural network for processing. Thus, three preprocessing steps were taken.

(1) Edit each data file and group same tomato cultivar and type in one file with all environmental variables of that cultivar gathered from different greenhouses.

(2) For each cultivar, store values in a Microsoft Excel spreadsheet. Next, in the spreadsheet, 0 replaced null values. For some VPD and radiation missing values are averaged.

(3) The Excel spreadsheet content was converted to.dat file input to be fed into Matlab and EFUNN application.

3.5. Neural Network Model.
Computational NNs have proven to be a powerful tool to solve several types of problems in various real life fields where approximation of nonlinear functions, classification, identification, and pattern recognition are required. NNs are mathematical representations of biological neurons in the way that they process information as parallel computing units. In general, there are two types of neural network architecture: (1) static (feedforward), in which no feedback or time delays exist, and (2) dynamic neural networks, whose outputs depend on the current or previous inputs, outputs, or states of the network (Demuth et al. [30]).

We consider a neural network that consists of an input layer with $n\flat 1$ nodes, a hidden layer with h units, and an output layer with l units as follows:

$$y_i = g\left(\sum_{j=1}^{h} wijf\left(\sum_{k=1}^{n+1} vjkXk\right)\right), \quad i = 1, 2, \ldots, l, \quad (2)$$

where xk indicates the kth input value, yi the ith output value, vjk a weight connecting the kth input node with

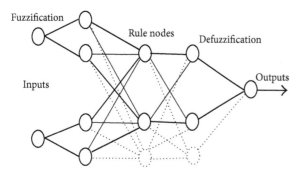

FIGURE 2: Simple EFuNN structure.

the *j*th hidden unit, and *wij* a weight between the *j*th hidden unit and the *i*th output unit. We start learning with one hidden layer, which would be updating the weights and thresholds to minimize the objective function by any optimization algorithm then terminate the network training with this number of hidden units when a local minimum of the objective function has been reached. If the desired accuracy is not reached, increase the number of hidden units with random weights and thresholds and repeat updating; otherwise, finish training and stop.

3.6. The EFuNN Algorithm. EFuNN consists of a five-layer structure, which begins with the input layer representing input variables, and each input variable is a presentation of group of arranged neurons representing a fuzzy quantization of this variable, which is then presented to the second layer of nodes. Different membership functions (MFs) can be attached to these neurons (triangular, Gaussian, etc.), where continuing modifications of nodes with a membership functions can be applied during learning.

Through node creation and consecutive aggregation, an EFuNN system can adjust over time to changes in the data stream and at the same time preserve its generalization capabilities. If EFuNNs use linear equations to calculate the activation of the rule nodes (instead of using Gaussian functions and exponential functions), the EFuNN learning procedure is faster. EFuNN also produces a better online generalization, which is a result of more accurate node allocation during the learning process. As Algorithm 1 shows, EFuNN allows for continuous training on new data, further testing, and also training of the EFuNN on the test data in an online mode, leading to a significant improvement of the accuracy.

The third layer contains rule nodes that evolve through hybrid-supervised learning. These rule nodes present prototypes of input-output data associations, where each rule node is defined by two vectors of connection weights *W1(r)* and *W2(r)*; also, *W2* is adjusted through learning depending on output error, and *W1* is modified based on similarity measure within input space in the local area.

The fourth layer of neurons represents fuzzy quantification of the output variables, similar to the input fuzzy neurons representation. The fifth layer represents the real values for the output variables. In the case of a "one-of-*n*" mode, EFuNN

transmits the maximum activation of the rule to the next level. In the case of a "many-of-*n*" mode, the activation values of *m* ($m > 1$) rule nodes that are above an activation threshold are transmitted further in the connectionist structure.

In this paper, EFuNN's: Figure 2 shows the evolving algorithm is based on the principle that rule nodes only exist if they are needed. As each training example is presented, the activation values of the nodes, the rule and action layers, and the error over the action nodes are examined; if the maximum rule node activation is below a set threshold, then a rule node is added. If the action node error is above a threshold value, a rule node is added. Finally, if the radius of the updated node is larger than a radius threshold, then the updating process is undone and a rule node is added.

EFuNN has several parameters to be optimized and they are

(1) number of input and output;

(2) learning rate for *W1* and *W2*;

(3) pruning control;

(4) aggregation control;

(5) number of membership functions;

(6) shape of membership functions;

(7) initial sensitivity threshold;

(8) maximum radius;

(9) *M*-of-*n* value.

3.7. Input/Output Parameters. The architecture and training mode of EFuNN depends on the input and output parameters as determined by the problem being solved. The tomato crop data includes biological entities that show nonlinear dynamic behaviour and whose response depends not only on several environmental factors but also on the current and previous crop conditions. Greenhouse tomatoes have long production cycles, and the total yield is determined by these parameters. The effects of several environmental factors (light, CO_2, air humidity, and air temperature) have both short- and long-term impacts on tomato plants. Air temperature directly affects fruit growth, and according to [28], it is the influential parameter on the growth process Figure 3.

Greenhouse tomatoes have a variable fruit growth period, ranging from 40 to 67 days. This deviation results from the changing 24-hour average air temperature in the greenhouse. Here the objective was to design an EFuNN that is simple enough and accurate enough to predict the variables of interest, since for many practical problems variables have

$$D_n = \frac{(1/2)\left(\sum_{i=1}^{c}|I_i - W_{i,n}|\right)}{\sum_{i=1}^{c}W_{i,n}} \quad (3)$$

different levels of importance and make different contributions to the output. Also, it is necessary to find an optimal normalization and assign proper importance factors to the variables, reduce the size of input vectors, and keep only the most important variables. This dynamic network architecture was chosen because of its memory association and learning

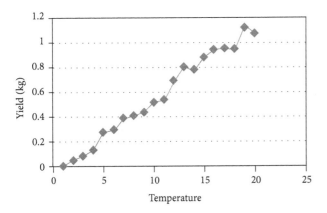

FIGURE 3: 24 h average air temperature relationship with yield grown in tomatoes greenhouse.

capability with sequential and time-varying patterns, which is most likely the biological situation for tomato plants.

4. Experiments Setup: Training and Performance Evaluation

The training process implies iterative adjustment of the biases of the network by minimizing a performance function when presenting input and target vectors to the network. The mean square error (MSE), selected as the performance function (Table 2), was calculated as the difference between the target output and the network output.

The supervised learning in EFuNN is built on the previously explained principles, so that when a new data example is presented, the EFuNN creates a new rule node to memorize the two input and output fuzzy vectors and/or adjusts the winning rule node. After a certain number of examples are applied, some neurons and connections may be pruned or aggregated and only the best are chosen. Different pruning rules can be applied in order to realize the most successful pruning of unnecessary nodes and connections. Although there are several options for growing the EFuNN, we restricted the learning algorithm to the 1-of-n algorithm.

Using Gaussian functions and exponential functions, the EFuNN learning procedure produces a better online generalization, which is a result of more accurate node allocation during the learning process. EFuNN allowed continuous training on new data; we did further testing and also training of the EFuNN on the test data in an online mode, which led to a significant improvement in accuracy. A significant advantage of EFuNNs is the local learning which allowed a fast adaptive learning where only few connections and nodes are changed or created after the entry of each new data item. This is in contrast to the global learning algorithms where, for each input vector, all connection weights changed.

Tomato plants were included in the training, testing, and validation process. The initial datasets were randomly divided so that 60% (771) of the records were assigned to the training set, 20% (257) to the validation set, and 20% (257) to the test set. The generalization in each of the networks was improved by implementing the early stopping method through the validation set. After training each of the networks to a satisfactory performance, the independent validation set was used to evaluate the prediction performance and to present the results.

We initialized $x(t)$, $x(t-1)$, $x(t-2)$, $x(t-n)$ in order to predict the $x(t+1)$, and the training was replicated three times using three different samples of training data and different combinations of network parameters. We used four Gaussian MFs for each input variable, as well as the following evolving parameters: number of membership functions = 3; sensitivity threshold $Sthr$ = 0.99; learning rate = 0.25; error threshold $Errthr$ = 0.001; learning rates for first and second layer = 0.05. EFuNN uses a one-pass training approach. The network parameters were determined using a trial and error approach. The training was repeated three times after reinitializing the network and the worst errors were reported in Figure 5. Online learning in EFuNN resulted in creating 2122 rule nodes as depicted in Figure 6. We illustrate the EFuNN training results, and the training performance is summarized in Table 3.

An investigation of the extracted rule set shown in Figure 4 from run 2 indicates that different compartments from the mentioned environmental variables affected yield prediction. Rules can be obtained from three different kinds of sources: human experts, numerical data, and neural networks. All the obtained rules can be used in rule selection method to obtain a smaller linguistic rule-based system with a higher performance. We explain the fuzzy arithmetic-based [31] approach to linguistic rule extraction from trained EFuNN for modeling problems using some computer simulations. Assume that our training output was five rules; for the nonlinear function realized by the trained neural network, we assume that the five terms (rules) are given for each of the two input variables. We also assume that the same five terms are given for the output variable.

TABLE 2: Test results and performance comparison of demand forecasting.

	EFuNN	ANN (Multilayer perceptron)
Learning epochs	1	2500
Training error (RMSE)	0.0013	0.116
Testing error (RMSE)	0.0092	0.118
Computational load (in billion flops)	0.536	87.2

TABLE 3: Results from 4 runs of the EFuNN.

RMS (training)	No. of rule nodes	Accuracy (%)
0.0045	77	82.95
0.0023	48	86.00
0.0029	75	84.91
0.0028	81	80.79

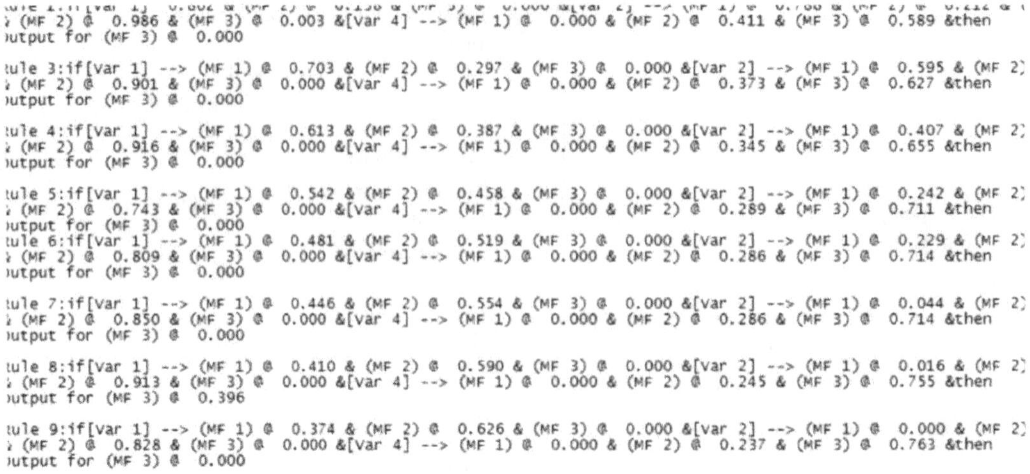

```
ule 1.1|[var 1]  @  0.802 @  (MF 2) @  0.198 @ (MF 3) @ 0.000 &[var 2] --> (MF 1) @ 0.788 @ (MF 2) @ 0.212 @ (
, (MF 2) @  0.986 & (MF 3) @  0.003 &[var 4] --> (MF 1) @  0.000 & (MF 2) @  0.411 & (MF 3) @  0.589 &then
)utput for (MF 3) @  0.000

tule 3:if[var 1] --> (MF 1) @  0.703 & (MF 2) @  0.297 & (MF 3) @  0.000 &[var 2] --> (MF 1) @  0.595 & (MF 2)
, (MF 2) @  0.901 & (MF 3) @  0.000 &[var 4] --> (MF 1) @  0.000 & (MF 2) @  0.373 & (MF 3) @  0.627 &then
)utput for (MF 3) @  0.000

tule 4:if[var 1] --> (MF 1) @  0.613 & (MF 2) @  0.387 & (MF 3) @  0.000 &[var 2] --> (MF 1) @  0.407 & (MF 2)
, (MF 2) @  0.916 & (MF 3) @  0.000 &[var 4] --> (MF 1) @  0.000 & (MF 2) @  0.345 & (MF 3) @  0.655 &then
)utput for (MF 3) @  0.000

tule 5:if[var 1] --> (MF 1) @  0.542 & (MF 2) @  0.458 & (MF 3) @  0.000 &[var 2] --> (MF 1) @  0.242 & (MF 2)
, (MF 2) @  0.743 & (MF 3) @  0.000 &[var 4] --> (MF 1) @  0.000 & (MF 2) @  0.289 & (MF 3) @  0.711 &then
)utput for (MF 3) @  0.000
tule 6:if[var 1] --> (MF 1) @  0.481 & (MF 2) @  0.519 & (MF 3) @  0.000 &[var 2] --> (MF 1) @  0.229 & (MF 2)
, (MF 2) @  0.809 & (MF 3) @  0.000 &[var 4] --> (MF 1) @  0.000 & (MF 2) @  0.286 & (MF 3) @  0.714 &then
)utput for (MF 3) @  0.000

tule 7:if[var 1] --> (MF 1) @  0.446 & (MF 2) @  0.554 & (MF 3) @  0.000 &[var 2] --> (MF 1) @  0.044 & (MF 2)
, (MF 2) @  0.850 & (MF 3) @  0.000 &[var 4] --> (MF 1) @  0.000 & (MF 2) @  0.286 & (MF 3) @  0.714 &then
)utput for (MF 3) @  0.000

tule 8:if[var 1] --> (MF 1) @  0.410 & (MF 2) @  0.590 & (MF 3) @  0.000 &[var 2] --> (MF 1) @  0.016 & (MF 2)
, (MF 2) @  0.913 & (MF 3) @  0.000 &[var 4] --> (MF 1) @  0.000 & (MF 2) @  0.245 & (MF 3) @  0.755 &then
)utput for (MF 3) @  0.396

tule 9:if[var 1] --> (MF 1) @  0.374 & (MF 2) @  0.626 & (MF 3) @  0.000 &[var 2] --> (MF 1) @  0.000 & (MF 2)
, (MF 2) @  0.828 & (MF 3) @  0.000 &[var 4] --> (MF 1) @  0.000 & (MF 2) @  0.237 & (MF 3) @  0.763 &then
)utput for (MF 3) @  0.000
```

FIGURE 4: Some rules extracted from EFuNN simulation.

The number of combinations of terms is 25. Each combination is presented to the trained neural network as a linguistic input vector $Aq = \{Aqi, \ldots, Aq2\}$. The corresponding fuzzy output Oq is calculated by fuzzy arithmetic. This calculation is numerically performed for the h-level sets of Aq for $h = 0.1, 0.2, \ldots, 1.0$. The fuzzy output Oq is compared with each of the five linguistic terms. The linguistic term with the minimum difference from the fuzzy output Oq is chosen as the consequent part Bq of the linguistic rule Rq with the antecedent part Aq. For example, let us consider the following linguistic rule.

Rule Rq: If $X1$ is medium and $X2$ is small Then y is Bq.

To determine the consequent part Bq, the antecedent part of the linguistic rule Rq is presented to the trained neural network as the linguistic input vector. The corresponding fuzzy output, Oq is calculated.

As a result, the rules shown in Table 3 will be shrinked into the range of [5–10] rules, which make it more efficient for operators to work with.

The results obtained from this study indicated that the EFuNN had successfully learnt the input variables and was then able to use these variables as a means of identifying the estimated yield amount.

From the results obtained from testing the EFuNN and its relative performance against Multilayer Perceptron, it is evident that the EFuNN models this task far better than any of the other models. In addition, the rules extracted from the EFuNN reflect the nature of the training data set and confirm the original hypothesis that more rules would need to be evolved to get better predictions. Accounting for the poor performance of the Multilayer Perceptron could be explained by examining the nature of this connectionist model. Having a fixed number of hidden nodes limits the number of hyperplanes these models can use to separate the complex feature space. Selection of the optimal number of hidden nodes becomes a case of trial and error. If these are too large, then the ability for the Multilayer Perceptron to generalize for new instances of records is reduced due to the possibility of overlearning the training examples. This work has sought

TABLE 4: Accuracy results for different algorithms.

Classifier	C-week	Week + 1	Week + 2
MLP	81.108	81.309	78.531
RBF	77.44	80.371	78.885
EFuNN	79.557	86.257	83.992

to describe a problematic area within horticulture produce management, that of predicting yields in greenhouses. The EFuNN has clearly stood out as an appropriate mechanism for this problem and has performed comparably well against other methods. But the most beneficial aspect of EFuNN architecture is the rule extraction ability. By extracting the rules from the EFuNN, we can analyse why the EFuNN made it more clear and identified deficiencies in its ability to generalize to new unseen data instances.

In terms of the size of the architecture for the Multilayer Perceptron, this was extremely large. This was because of the length of the input vector. Input vectors of this size require a significant amount of presentations of the training data for the Multilayer Perceptron to successfully learn the mapping between the input vectors and the output vectors. In addition, the small numbers of hidden nodes contained in the Multilayer Perceptron were unable to represent the mapping between the inputs and outputs. Raising the number of hidden nodes increased the ability for the Multilayer Perceptron to learn but created a structure that was an order of magnitude larger and thus took even longer to train. In conclusion it can be seen from the results of this experiment that the advantages of the EFuNN are twofold. One, the time taken to train the EFuNN was far less than Multilayer Perceptron. And two, the EFuNN in Table 4 was able to successfully predict yield for a given period of time in Figure 5. This indicates that the EFuNN has the ability to store a better representation of the temporal nature of the data and, to this end, generalize better than the other methods.

Results shown in Table 4 show the accuracy of our method compared to other classifiers like Bayesian, RBF

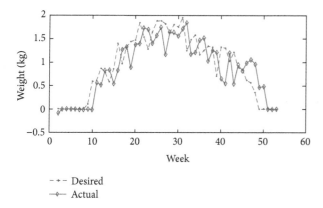

FIGURE 5: Training result with EFuNN.

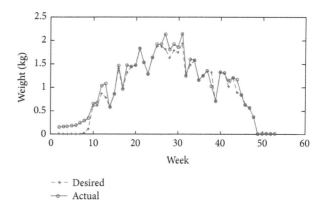

FIGURE 6: Test results and performance comparison of demand forecasts.

Network, and so forth. Results for those classifiers were constructed using Weka experimenter; Weka is a collection of machine learning algorithms for data mining tasks, and the algorithms can either be applied directly to a data set or called from your own Java code. Weka contains tools for data pre-processing, classification, regression, clustering, association rules, and visualization. It is also well suited for developing new machine learning schemes (http://www.cs.waikato.ac.nz/ml/weka/).

Performance of the learning algorithm is evaluated by the accuracy (%) on Cherry and Campari tomato data in different greenhouses, for four years (2004–2007).

In this paper, we have described how EFuNN can be applied in the domain of horticulture, especially in the challenging area of deciding support for yield prediction, which leads to the production of well-determined amounts. These results do not provide a mechanistic explanation of the factors influencing these fluctuations. However, knowing this information in advance could be valuable for growers for making decisions on climate and crop management. Some of the advantages of the neural network model implemented in this study include the following: (1) The input parameters of the model are currently recorded by most growers, which makes the model easy to implement; (2) the model can "learn" from datasets with new scenarios (new cultivars, different control strategies, improved climate control, etc.); (3) less-experienced growers could use the system because the decision-making process of the most experienced growers is captured by the data used in the trained networks, and production could thereby become more consistent.

5. Conclusion

It is feasible to implement Intelligent System (IS) techniques, including NN and fuzzy logic, for modeling and predicting of a greenhouse tomato production system. Data from experimental trials and from a commercial operation for complete production cycles allowed the modeling of tomato yields. IS techniques were robust in dealing with imprecise data, and they have a learning capability when presented with new scenarios and need to be tested on different tomato cultivars.

Experimentation results show that EFuNN performed better than other techniques like ANN in terms of low RMSE error and less computational loads (performance time). As showed in Figure 6, ANN training needs more epochs (longer training time) to achieve a better performance. EFuNN makes use of the knowledge of FIS and the learning done by NN. Hence, the neurofuzzy system is able to precisely model the uncertainty and imprecision within the data as well as to incorporate the learning ability of NN. Even though the performance of neurofuzzy systems is dependent on the problems domain, very often the results are better while compared to a pure neural network approach. Compared to NN, an important advantage of neurofuzzy systems is its reasoning ability (*If-Then* rules) within any particular state. A fully trained EFuNN could be replaced by a set of *If-Then* rules.

As EFuNN adopts a single pass training (1 epoch), it is more adaptable and easy for further online training which might be highly useful for online forecasting. However, an important disadvantage of EFuNN is the determination of the network parameters like number and type of MF for each input variable, sensitivity threshold, error threshold, and the learning rates.

Similar procedures might be used to automatically adapt the optimal combination of network parameters for the EFuNN.

Acknowledgments

The authers would like to thank the Wight Salads Group (WSG) Company and Warwick Horticultural Research Institute (WHRI) for providing the datasets which have been used in this research and for their help and cooperation in providing all the necessary information. They acknowledge the support of the Horticulture Development Company (HDC) who has provided the Ph.D. degree studentship support.

References

[1] J. W. Jones, E. Dayan, L. H. Allen, H. van Keulen, and H. Challa, "Dynamic tomato growth and yield model (TOMGRO)," *Transactions of the ASAE*, vol. 34, no. 2, pp. 663–672, 1991.

[2] J. W. Jones, A. Kening, and C. E. Vallejos, "Reduced state-variable tomato growth model," *Transactions of the ASAE*, vol. 42, no. 1, pp. 255–265, 1999.

[3] H. Heuvelink, "Growth, development and yield of a tomato crop: periodic destructive measurements in a greenhouse," *Scientia Horticulturae*, vol. 61, no. 1-2, pp. 77–99, 1995.

[4] E. Heuvelink, *Tomato growth and yield: quantitative analysis and synthesis [Ph.D. thesis]*, Wageningen Agricultural University, Wageningen, The Netherlands, 1996.

[5] P. Abreu, J. F. Meneses, and C. Gary, "Tompousse, a model of yield prediction for tomato crops: calibration study for unheated plastic greenhouses," *Acta Horticulturae*, vol. 519, pp. 141–150, 2000.

[6] S. R. Adams, "Predicting the weekly fluctuations in glasshouse tomato yields," *Acta Horticulturae*, vol. 593, pp. 19–23, 2002.

[7] R. M. de Moraes and L. dos Santos Machado, "Evaluation system based on EFuNN for on-line training evaluation in virtual reality," in *Proceedings of the 10th Iberoamerican Congress on Pattern Recognition, Image Analysis and Applications (CIARP '05)*, vol. 3773 of *Lecture Notes in Computer Science*, pp. 778–785, 2005.

[8] H. U. Frausto, J. G. Pieters, and J. M. Deltour, "Modelling greenhouse temperature by means of auto regressive models," *Biosystems Engineering*, vol. 84, no. 2, pp. 147–157, 2003.

[9] R. Linker, I. Seginer, and P. O. Gutman, "Optimal CO_2 control in a greenhouse modeled with neural networks," *Computers and Electronics in Agriculture*, vol. 19, no. 3, pp. 289–310, 1998.

[10] I. Seginer, "Some artificial neural network applications to greenhouse environmental control," *Computers and Electronics in Agriculture*, vol. 18, no. 2-3, pp. 167–186, 1997.

[11] I. Seginer, T. Boulard, and B. J. Bailey, "Neural network models of the greenhouse climate," *Journal of Agricultural Engineering Research*, vol. 59, no. 3, pp. 203–216, 1994.

[12] P. Salgado and J. B. Cunha, "Greenhouse climate hierarchical fuzzy modelling," *Control Engineering Practice*, vol. 13, no. 5, pp. 613–628, 2005.

[13] H. Ehrlich, M. Kühne, and J. Jäkel, "Development of a fuzzy control system for greenhouses," *Acta Horticulturae*, vol. 406, pp. 463–470, 1996.

[14] L. A. Zadeh, "Fuzzy sets," *Information and Control*, vol. 8, no. 3, pp. 338–353, 1965.

[15] B. T. Tien, *Neural-fuzzy approach for system identification [Ph.D. thesis]*, Wageningen Agricultural University, Wageningen, The Netherlands, 1997.

[16] B. Center and B. P. Verma, "A fuzzy photosynthesis model for tomato," *Transactions of the ASAE*, vol. 40, no. 3, pp. 815–821, 1997.

[17] M. W. Craven and J. W. Shavlik, "Using sampling and queries to extract rules from trained neural networks," in *Proceedings of the 11th International Conference on Machine Learning*, pp. 37–45, 1994.

[18] HortiMax, *Village Farms, USA, Reports Record Tomato Production*, HortiMax Growing Solutions, Rancho Santa Margarita, Calif, USA, 2008.

[19] I. Taha and J. Ghosh, "Three techniques for extracting rules from feedforward networks," *Intelligent Engineering Systems through Artificial Neural Networks*, vol. 6, pp. 5–10, 1996.

[20] R. Linker and I. Seginer, "Greenhouse temperature modeling: a comparison between sigmoid neural networks and hybrid models," *Mathematics and Computers in Simulation*, vol. 65, no. 1-2, pp. 19–29, 2004.

[21] J. Huysmans, B. Baesens, and J. Vanthienen, *Using Rule Extraction to Improve the Comprehensibility of Predictive Models*, Technical Report KBI, 0612, vol. 43, Department of Decision Sciences and Information Management, Katholieke Universiteit Leuven, Leuven, Belgium, 2006.

[22] P. Costa, *A quantified approach to tomato plant growth status for greenhouse production in a semi arid climate [Ph.D. thesis]*, University of Arizona, Tucson, Ariz, USA, 2007.

[23] N. Kasabov, "Adaptable neuro production systems," *Neurocomputing*, vol. 13, no. 2–4, pp. 95–117, 1996.

[24] N. Kasabov, *Foundations of Neural Networks, Fuzzy Systems, and Knowledge Engineering*, MIT Press, Cambridge, Mass, USA, 1996.

[25] M. H. Jensen, "Steering your tomatoes towards profit," in *Greenhouse Crop Production and Engineering Design Short Course*, Controlled Environment Agriculture Center, University of Arizona, Tucson, Ariz, USA, 2004.

[26] J. J. Buckley and E. Eslami, *An Introduction to Fuzzy Logic and Fuzzy Sets*, Physica, Heidelberg, Germany, 2002.

[27] M. T. Hagan, H. B. Demuth, and M. H. Beale, *Neural Network Design*, University of Colorado, Boulder, Colo, USA, 1995.

[28] E. Heuvelink, "Developmental process," in *Tomatoes*, E. Heuvelink, Ed., Crop Production Science in Horticulture Series, pp. 53–83, CABI Publishing, Wallingford, UK, 2005.

[29] E. Heuvelink and M. Dorais, "Crop growth and yield," in *Tomatoes*, E. Heuvelink, Ed., Crop Production Science in Horticulture Series, pp. 85–144, CABI Publishing, Wallingford, UK, 2005.

[30] H. Demuth, M. Beale, and M. Hagan, *Neural Network Toolbox 5: User's Guide*, The MathWorks, Inc., Natick, Mass, USA, 2007.

[31] H. Ishibuchi, T. Nakashima, and M. Nii, *Classification and Modeling with Linguistic Information Granules: Advanced Approaches to Linguistic Data Mining*, Springer, Berlin, Germany, 2004.

7

Comparison of Adaptive Information Security Approaches

Antti Evesti and Eila Ovaska

VTT Technical Research Centre of Finland, Kaitoväylä 1, 90571 Oulu, Finland

Correspondence should be addressed to Antti Evesti; antti.evesti@vtt.fi

Academic Editors: P. Kokol, Y. Liu, and Z. Liu

Dynamically changing environments and threat landscapes require adaptive information security. Adaptive information security makes it possible to change and modify security mechanisms at runtime. Hence, all security decisions are not enforced at design-time. This paper builds a framework to compare security adaptation approaches. The framework contains three viewpoints, that is, adaptation, security, and lifecycle. Furthermore, the paper describes five security adaptation approaches and compares them by means of the framework. The comparison reveals that the existing security adaptation approaches widely cover the information gathering. However, the compared approaches do not describe how to decide a method to perform a security adaptation. Similarly, means how to provide input knowledge for the security adaptation is not covered. Hence, these research areas have to be covered in the future. The achieved results are applicable for software developers when selecting a security adaptation approach and for researchers when considering future research items.

1. Introduction

Heterogeneous and dynamic environments create a need that software products and systems are able to manage their behaviour and functionality. The software system faces several situations during its lifecycle, and all of them cannot be dealt with at design-time. Moreover, various systems are so complex that setup, running, and updating are unmanageable tasks even for the professional users [1, 2]. In [3] Dobson et al. say that emphasis is moving from systems developed based on a priori sets requirements towards platforms that adapt themselves based on changing demands. Some years ago, the vision of autonomic computing was presented [1]. In the vision, the self-management is defined to be the essence of autonomic computing. In this paper, however, autonomic computing, self-managing, and self-adaptive terms are interchangeable. The similar decision is also made in previous surveys presented by Huebscher and McCann [2] and Salehie and Tahvildari [4].

The similar challenges, as mentioned above, can be also seen from the information security point of view, shortly called security. Evolving environments create new threats and static security mechanisms are not applicable in all situations. This development sets the requirement of self-adaptive software and adaptation of security mechanisms. The purpose of security adaptation is to ensure an appropriate security level in different situations. The self-adaptive software is a closed-loop system with a feedback loop aiming to adjust itself to changes during its operation [4]. This is achieved by means of sensors and executors. The sensors monitor the environment in order to reveal changes, and the executors perform the adaptation. From the security viewpoint, the monitored changes relate to environment or usage changes that affect the required or achieved security level. The adaptation executors concentrate on security mechanisms and policies.

Currently, several security adaptation approaches exist. On one hand, approaches concentrate on adapting a particular security mechanism or supporting a specific security attribute. On the other hand, some approaches are generic; that is, they support different attributes and mechanisms. Hence, it is difficult to select the most suitable adaptation approach for different usages. Moreover, it is difficult to know what research steps are needed in the future. Elkhodary and Whittle surveyed four approaches for adaptive security in [5]. The surveyed approaches were Extensible Security Infrastructure [6], Strata Security API [7], The Willow Architecture [8], and The Adaptive Trust Negotiation Framework [9].

Elkhodary and Whittle performed their survey in 2007 [5], and hence, new approaches have already appeared. Moreover, authors compare the type of adaptation achieved with different adaptation approaches. However, in this comparison the comparison addresses how the adaptation is performed.

The purpose of this comparison is to describe and compare existing security adaptation approaches presented in the literature. Consequently, the comparison framework is introduced. The framework combines three viewpoints: security, lifecycle, and adaptation. Hence, existing information security taxonomies and the surveys of general adaptation approaches have provided input for the framework definition. We have selected five security adaptation approaches for the comparison, namely, (i) an architectural approach for self-managing security services [10], (ii) a software framework for autonomic security in pervasive environments [11], (iii) context sensitive adaptive authentication [12], (iv) adaptive messaging middleware [13], and (v) adaptive security architecture based on EC-MQV algorithm in pervasive networks [14]. These five approaches are selected based on the following three requirements. Firstly, the selected approach has to combine adaptation and security aspects. Hence, approaches, which concentrate on adaptation without considering security, are left out of this paper. Secondly, at least the initial implementation of the selected approach has to be realised. Even though the approach is not validated, some kind of implementation is assumed to exist. Thirdly, all selected approaches are published after the survey performed by Elkhodary and Whittle [5], that is, in 2007 or after. The first and second requirements cut down eight approaches as total. Two of these approaches were presented in journal papers and six in conference and workshop papers. These eight approaches focused mostly on the adaptation aspect, and thus information security was not in the focal point. Naturally, it is possible to develop those approaches towards security adaptation. However, now the focus is in approaches, which already contain security aspects.

After the introduction background information is given, the comparison framework is built in Section 3. Section 4 describes the selected adaptation approaches, and Section 5 makes the comparison by means of the comparison framework and discusses the future research needs. Finally, conclusions close the paper.

2. Background for Security Adaptation

In this section the focus of the comparison is defined, and required background information is given. Figure 1 shows three essential knowledge areas required to achieve adaptive security. (1) The autonomic computing area has to be known, in order to utilise appropriate patterns, decision making algorithms, and so forth. (2) Knowledge from the security area is needed to select adaptive security mechanisms and sensing relevant information. (3) Experience from the software development is needed in order to combine security and autonomic computing areas. To complicate the wholeness, these three areas interact with each other, illustrated with arrows in Figure 1. Firstly, the software development has to take into account requirements and constraints both from

the security and autonomic computing areas. Similarly, the software development area declares which kind of security and adaptation features the final product contains. Secondly, autonomic computing sets requirements for the selected security mechanisms and their dynamism. Thirdly, security area sets requirements for decision making and sensing mechanisms used in autonomic computing.

All of these three areas form their own research field with their own terminology and research focuses, and thus it is not possible to cover all areas in one paper. Hence, in this paper the focus area is set as depicted with the dashed line circle in Figure 1. The compared security adaptation approaches are investigated from the autonomic computing viewpoint. In other words, how adaptability is achieved and what security attributes are to be adapted. The software development viewpoint is investigated from the evolution viewpoint; that is, how easily the adaptation approach can be utilised when new software is developed. Therefore, several aspects of the wholeness are enforced to exclude from the comparison, as depicted in Figure 1 outside the dash circle. Next, background information and related terminology for each of these three areas will be described.

2.1. Autonomic Computing. In the vision of autonomic computing—presented by IBM in [1]—the autonomic behaviour is achieved by means of the MAPE-K reference model (Monitor, Analyse, Plan, Execute, and Knowledge). The phases of the MAPE-K model constitute the adaptation loop, depicted in Figure 2. The similar structure is also followed in many adaptation approaches. The previous surveys, that is, Dobson et al. [3], Huebscher and McCann [2], and Salehie and Tahvildari [4], utilise the loop structure with similar four phases as a reference model. Hence, the MAPE-K model acts as the reference model also in this comparison to present self-adaptive software.

The purpose of the Monitor phase is to collect information from the managed element, that is, the adapted software, and execution environment. The monitoring utilises sensors, either hardware or software, to collect relevant data. The Analyse phase combines the collected data and possible history data to reveal if requirements are not fulfilled, which causes an adaptation need. Consequently, the Analyse phase calls the Plan phase, which creates the adaptation plan. The adaptation plan contains a decision on how the software will be adapted. In order to create the adaptation plan, different algorithms or rules are utilised. Moreover, the Plan phase takes possible contradicting requirements into account as trade-offs. Finally, the Execute phase enforces the adaptation plan by means of effectors, which affect the managed element.

The existing surveys of autonomic computing adopt this loop structure in some level and explain these four phases of the loop. Nevertheless, the Knowledge part is not clearly defined—even, authors of the MAPE-K model do not describe the Knowledge part. Huebscher and McCann discuss the Knowledge part from the planning point of view in [2]. Authors state that the division between planning and knowledge is not clear. Similarly, the boundary between knowledge and Monitor, Analyse, and Execute phases is vacillating. However, it is clear that right knowledge is

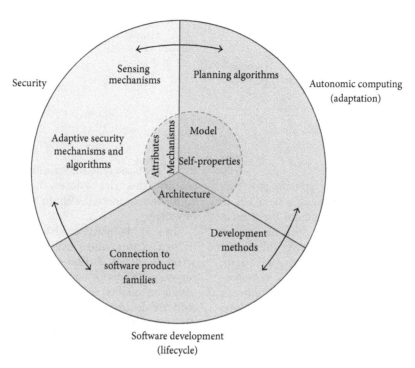

FIGURE 1: Scoping the comparison area.

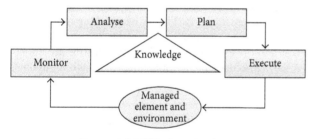

FIGURE 2: MAPE adaptation loop.

required in each of these phases. The Monitor phase needs knowledge to observe right attributes from the managed element and environment. On the contrary, the Analyse phase requires knowledge how to combine the monitored data in a meaningful way. The Plan phase has to know the right planning algorithm and means to perform trade-offs. Finally, the Execute phase requires knowledge how the particular adaptation plan can be enforced in the current implementation and environment. Naturally, all of this knowledge exists in each adaptation approach realisation. However, many approaches integrate knowledge inside the adaptation loop, and, consequently, a separated knowledge part is not presented. In other words, knowledge required in each phase is coded inside that phase.

2.2. Security. On one hand, ISO/IEC defines security in [15] as follows: "The capability of the software product to protect information and data so that unauthorised persons or systems cannot read or modify them and authorised persons or systems are not denied access to them." On the other hand, some sources [16, 17] define security as a composition of confidentiality, integrity, and availability, which are called security attributes. Based on the security definition from ISO/IEC above, it is clear that authentication and authorisation are also essential security attributes. In some sources terms security goal, objective, and property are also used. Moreover, other security attributes may also appear in the literature, for example, privacy, nonrepudiation, immunity, and so forth. However, this paper uses the term security attribute, containing confidentiality, integrity, availability, authentication, and authorisation. This attribute set is sufficient to cover the existing security adaptation approach.

Risk management is a process to identify risks, assess risks, and take steps to reduce risks to an acceptable level [18]. Herzog et al. [19] build an information security terminology and present it in an ontology form by utilising risk management terms, that is, asset, threat, vulnerability, and countermeasure. Common criteria [17] define an asset as an entity that someone presumably places value upon. Hence, asset can be almost anything that needs protection. National Institute of Standards and Technology (NIST) [18] defines that a threat is a possibility that vulnerability is exercised. The vulnerability is defined as a flaw or weakness in software that could be exercised (accidentally or intentionally) to cause a security breach [18]. Finally, countermeasures refer to means to mitigate risks caused by threats. However, in this paper the term security mechanism is used instead of countermeasure. Figure 3 illustrates security concepts described above and their relationships.

Chess et al. discuss security and privacy challenges in autonomic computing environments in [20]. Authors

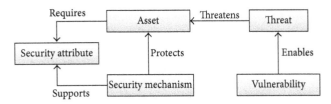

FIGURE 3: Relations of security concepts.

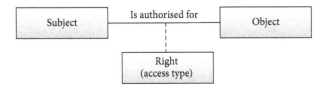

FIGURE 4: Authorisation pattern.

mention that the security of autonomic systems is not an entirely new kind of security. Nevertheless, system has to be secure in each configuration where it adapts itself. From the security point of view, autonomous systems support self-protection and/or self-healing. Chess et al. [20] characterize these as system capabilities to determine intrusions, eliminate the intrusion, and finally, restore the system to an uncompromised state. This categorization concentrates on reactive security approaches. In other words, it assumes that the system is already compromised. However, it is also possible to act proactively and perform self-protecting activities before the system is compromised. This means that system performs self-configuring and self-optimization for security mechanisms and architectures in order to achieve reasonable self-protection for various anticipated/predicted situations. It is notable that Chess et al. [20] concentrate security in autonomic computing environments, that is, the autonomic element performs functional or quality adaptation and achieving security also in a new state is important. The emphasise of this paper is on autonomic security, which naturally contains similarities with security in autonomic computing. However, by autonomic security we refer to adaptation approaches, whose primary purpose is to manage security.

2.3. Software Development. From the software development viewpoint, adaptation is a variability form where variation occurs at runtime [21, 22]. In this paper, the software development of security adaptation approaches is studied from the architecture viewpoint—as depicted in Figure 1. Hence, different variation techniques and methods to develop software product families are not covered. Bass et al. [23] define software architecture as follows: "The software architecture of a program or computing system is the structure or structures of the system, which comprise software elements, the externally visible properties of those elements and the relationships among them." In this paper, the purpose is to reveal the used architecture of each security adaptation approach. Hence, the architecture shows how the elements of adaptation approach are structured and related to each other. Furthermore, the architecture dictates how easily the particular security adaptation approach can be applied.

From the software development viewpoint, the MAPE model is a pattern to achieve the adaptation. Hence, the pattern is a reusable and generic model to achieve the particular solution. Similarly, dozens of patterns to achieve security in the software development exist. Security patterns are surveyed, for instance, in [24]. Figure 4 presents a pattern

to achieve basic type authorisation [25]. The subject presents an entity that tries to access the object entity and these two entities are connected with the access right, for example, read or write.

In [26] Matinlassi and Niemelä categorise software quality to execution and evolution qualities. Execution quality refers to quality attributes, which are visible at runtime, for example, performance and usability. On the contrary, evolution quality refers to quality attributes faced during software development and maintenance. This paper focuses on evolution qualities. Matinlassi and Niemelä list the following evolution qualities: maintainability, flexibility, modifiability, extensibility, portability, reusability, integrability, and testability; in this categorisation, maintainability acts as the parent quality for other evolution qualities. In the context of this paper, maintainability describes how easily the security adaptation approach can be updated or modified to a new environment, for security adaptation maintainability is an important property. Firstly, new vulnerabilities might be found. Moreover, new situations for software usage can appear and the existing adaptation mechanisms are not able to achieve a secure state in those situations without updates.

2.4. Related Work. As already referred to, few surveys from the autonomic computing field already exist. Moreover, as mentioned in the introduction, Elkhodary and Whittle [5] surveyed four approaches for adaptive security. The survey concentrates on evaluating systems that adapt application-level security mechanisms. On one hand, the evaluation concentrates on three security services, namely authentication, authorization, and tolerance. Each security service is thought to serve security attributes as follows: authentication supports identification and nonrepudiation, authorization for confidentiality and integrity, and, finally, tolerance for availability. Based on this security attribute categorization, authors were able to perform comparisons with three security services mentioned above. On the other hand, the adaptation viewpoint evaluates the achieved adaptation level. The adaptation dimensions for the security services were absent, fixed, and adaptive. Furthermore, authors utilise an evaluation scheme that contains the following aspects (content of each aspect is presented in parentheses): (i) computational paradigm (parameterization, component based, reflection, or aspect-orientation), (ii) reconfiguration scale (single unit, interunit, or architecture wide), and (iii) Conflict handling (user driven, autonomous, or interactive). The final conclusion of the survey notices that none of the presented approaches supports all security services. In addition, the authors summarise that maintainability and reusability seem

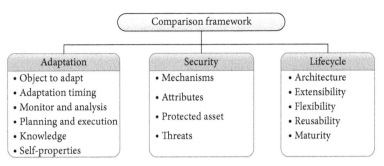

FIGURE 5: Comparison Framework.

challenging. In order to avoid overlapping, this paper does not reevaluate security adaptation approaches, which are already discussed by Elkhodary and Whittle in [5].

3. Comparison Framework

In this section a comparison framework for security adaptation approaches is defined. The framework is built around three viewpoints: (i) adaptation viewpoint, (ii) security viewpoint, and (iii) lifecycle viewpoint, following the areas presented in Section 2 and Figure 1. The adaptation viewpoint consists of generic adaptation related properties. Consequently, these properties are common for all adaptive software. The content for the adaptation viewpoint is collected from the existing adaptation surveys and landscape papers, which are mentioned above [2–4]. The security viewpoint contains properties, which relate to software security. These properties are a subset from the existing security taxonomies. Finally, the lifecycle viewpoint concentrates on the aspects of software development. Figure 5 depicts the framework and content of its three viewpoints. Next, the properties in the framework are described in more detail.

Adaptation Viewpoint. The purpose of this category is to collect adaptation features. Six properties are included as follows.

(i) *Object to adapt* describes what part of the software will be adapted. In the security adaptation approaches this usually refers to security mechanisms and their parameters in different layers and the behaviour of these mechanisms. although it is possible to adapt other parts, contrast to security mechanisms, in order to affect software security. On one hand, it is possible to change a communication protocol, which directly influences the achieved security. On the other hand, adapting resource utilisation indirectly affects security. These indirect objects play an important role of security as the wholeness. However, most security adaptation approaches have selected direct security mechanisms for objects to adapt.

(ii) *Adaptation timing* describes when the adaptation is intended to occur. A start-up time adaptation means that a configuration and parameters are bound when the software is started. In contrast, the runtime adaptation means that adaptation is able to occur when the software is up and running. Naturally, the runtime adaptation approach can perform adaptation during the start-up but the adaptation is not limited to that particular moment. Hence, the runtime adaptation refers to a more dynamic adaptation approach than the start-up, adaptation in this comparison. Furthermore, the runtime adaptation is able to occur reactively and/or proactively. As mentioned earlier, the reactive adaptation takes place when an attack is identified. On the opposite, the proactive adaptation predicts threats and adapts the software beforehand.

(iii) *Monitoring and analyses* describes how the adaptation approach recognises a need for adaptation. Each adaptation approach uses some method to collect information from its behaviour and/or environment. The collected information is aggregated or utilised as such in order to detect when the adaptation is required. The purpose of this property is to compare, which kind of information the adaptation approach requires, how the monitoring is performed, and what kinds of analyses will be performed for making adaptation decision from information.

(iv) *Planning and execution* describes how the adaptation approach makes an adaptation plan; that is, what object will be adapted and how and how the adaptation plan is enforced. In static solutions, the adaptation approach contains a set of predefined adaptation plans for different situations. Alternatively, the adaptation is dynamic, and the adaptation plan is made at runtime based on utility function or other models.

(v) *Knowledge* describes how the required input knowledge is provided for the adaptation approach. As mentioned earlier, each phase of the adaptation loop requires certain knowledge. It is possible that the required knowledge is hard coded inside the adaptation phases or alternatively a dedicated knowledge storage is utilised.

(vi) *Self-properties* describe which kind of self-properties the adaptation approach supports. (1) Self-configuring refers to a capability to automatically change a used software component. (2) Self-optimization is a capability to set and modify parameters. (3) Self-protection is a software capability to protect itself from the security breaches and mitigate attack effects. (4) Self-healing refers to a capability to determine failures and perform required recovering actions. (5) Self-awareness is a software capability to know its own state and behaviour. (6) Context-awareness means, in this comparison, a capability to know the operational environment of software.

Security Viewpoint. The purpose of this viewpoint is to collect security related features from the compared approach. The following properties are included.

   (i) *Attributes* list which security attributes are supported in an adaptive manner. Supported security attributes can be confidentiality, integrity, availability, authentication, and authorisation. If an adaptation approach focuses on one or few security attributes, the other security attributes are considered static ones. On the contrary, generic adaptation approaches do not nominate adapted security attributes.

  (ii) *Mechanisms* describe security mechanisms which can be adapted. Hence, this property is closely related to object to adapt—described above. It is possible to implement support for the same security attribute with several security mechanisms. The adaptation can concentrate on tuning the parameters of one specific mechanism (self-optimization), or, alternatively, the adaptation is able to change between different mechanisms (self-configuring). If the adaptation approach is tightly coupled to a particular security mechanism it affects generalization possibilities.

 (iii) *Protected assets* describe assets that are intended to be secured by means of the security adaptation approach. If a security adaptation approach does not explicitly define assets, the protected asset is identified implicitly.

 (iv) *Threats* describe which security threats the adaptation approach is able to cover in an adaptive manner. Security threats will be reasoned from the available material if not stated explicitly.

Lifecycle Viewpoint. The viewpoint concentrates on the aspects of the software development. From the evolution qualities, listed in Section 2, the framework contains reusability, extendibility, and flexibility. The lifecycle viewpoint has the following properties.

   (i) *Architecture* describes how the elements of the adaptation loop are connected and related to each other. Moreover, the architecture shows how the adaptation approach and software functionality are coupled. In some approaches adaptation mechanisms are built inside the software functionality, called internal approaches by Salehie and Tahvildari in [4]. On the contrary, external approaches separate adaptation mechanisms and software functionality to their own parts to support maintainability and reuse.

  (ii) *Extensibility* describes an ability to utilise new components and perform new functions. Different needs to extend the security adaptation approach can appear. Support for a new security mechanism or a security attribute is the most obviously required during the lifecycle. However, extension needs for adaptation mechanisms can also emerge. For example, a need to add a new monitoring component, a different analysis method, or a more sophisticated planning algorithm.

 (iii) *Reusability* describes how easily the components of the adaptation approach or the whole approach can be reused as such or slightly modified. Possibility to reuse components from the approach is strongly related to the selected architecture.

 (iv) *Flexibility* describes how easily the adaptation approach can be modified for use in a different environment. Some approaches are tightly coupled to the specific domain or environment. On the other hand, generic approaches can be utilised in various environments without major modifications. Again, the selected architecture dictates how flexible the solution is.

  (v) *Maturity* describes performed validation, available implementation guidelines, and current activity of the adaptation approach. Validation describes a type of validation performed for the approach. In case the validation is performed, the number of validation use cases and usage environment varies. Next, the implementation guidelines and reusable components offer valuable support for a new user. The type of publishing forum indicates the maturity of the approach. Conference papers typically introduce less mature solutions than journal papers. Similarly, current activity is an important attribute from the maturity viewpoint. A live community or project, behind the security adaptation approach, offers updates and support for the utilisation of the approach.

The presented framework is intended to offer a universal way to compare the properties of different security adaptation approaches. It is possible to argue the structure of the framework because its three viewpoints contain some overlapping. However, the purpose of the framework is to compare and raise up the differences between approaches, and, thus, all the attributes are vital instead of the most compact framework. In the next section, the above described information is collected from each adaptation approach and presented in Tables 1–5.

4. Security Adaptation Approaches

In this section, five security adaptation approaches are covered. Moreover, details selected to the comparison framework are described. Each approach is presented in its own subsection containing a description part and a data collection for the comparison framework.

4.1. An Architectural Approach for Self-Managing Security Services. In [10] Russello and Dulay present an architectural approach for self-managing security services by means of ESCA (Event, State, Condition, and Action) policies. The approach separates application logic to an application layer, and adaptation elements are located on a middleware layer. Furthermore, security mechanisms are separated from the application logic to the middleware layer. Authors have designed the middleware architecture to comply the Shared Data Space (SDS) model. The architecture contains a kernel component on the middleware layer and a proxy element, which handles communication between application and the kernel. The kernel component consists of three parts, that is, Operation subsystem, Security subsystem, and Context subsystem. The Operation subsystem contains functionality required to implement the SDS model, and thus, it is not directly related to security adaptation. On the contrary, the Security subsystem contains all security related parts. The first part is ESCA Policy manager, which manages and enforces policies. The ESCA policy language and enforcement are described in [27]. The second part of the Security subsystem is the set of security mechanisms, which are adapted based on the selected policy. Authors mention mechanisms for authentication, authorization, encryption, and fault tolerance. The approach is intended to be generic, and, thus, these mechanisms are not named in more detail. The final subsystem in the kernel component is the Context subsystem, which contains a set of services to provide contextual information for the Operational and Security subsystems. Authors present the following context services: Trust level, Threat level, Availability monitor, Memory monitor, and Bandwidth monitor service.

Authors have emphasised the importance of the separation of concerns. Hence, the presented approach is clearly structured to dedicated subsystems and components. However, mutual behaviour of these subsystems are not emphasised as much. The ECSA Policy manager is validated by means of the case study in [27, 28] but without security adaptation viewpoint. The validation focuses on sense and react applications, which utilise wireless sensor networks. Table 1 collects data by means of the comparison framework.

4.2. A Software Framework for Autonomic Security in Pervasive Environments. Saxena et al. present a software framework for autonomic security in [11]. The framework consists of an adaptation loop with monitoring, analysing, and responding modules. An architecture, which contains these modules and their mutual interactions, is also described. The monitoring modules are registered to observe security related events, called security context. Authors give an example list of security events, for example, new authentication schema available, user location change, low memory, and so forth. Hence, security-relevant events can occur in a device or execution environment. The analysing modules subscribe to events recognised by monitoring modules. Based on the received events, each analysing module suggests a high-level security action to reconfigure the system. The responding module maps these high-level security actions to implementation specific sub-systems, for example, communication, device authentication, application, and so forth. Authors give an example from the high-level security action

"increase encryption strength", which can be mapped to implementation to increase key size or perform additional encryption rounds. Added to monitoring, analysing, and responding nodes, the framework contains a support module. The support module offers a profile database for other modules. Events from the monitoring modules can be stored in the profile database for the future use. Moreover, the database provides information for the analysing modules to support decision making. Finally, the responding node stores the information of the current configuration in the profile database.

The framework is applicable to adapt both an individual device and the whole network. Both adaptation alternatives utilise the similar adaptation loop. In [29] He and Lacoste present these adaptation loops as the nested adaptation loop. Even though, the device level adaptation can be utilised independently, without network level adaptation. The framework is implemented on the Nokia 770 Internet tablet; that is, the required components exist. However, any use case that utilises the framework is not presented. Table 2 collects data by means of the comparison framework.

4.3. Context Sensitive Adaptive Authentication. Hulsebosch et al. took initial steps towards the adaptive security approaches in the paper *"Context Sensitive Access Control"* [30] by developing context awareness for security purposes. However, the main focus was in access control mechanism with context information without adaptation. Further development is made in [12], which presents the context sensitive adaptive authentication. The purpose of the approach is to make static security mechanisms more adaptive and less intrusive. The adaptive authentication approach utilises context information, namely, location and time, for adaptation purposes. Authors concentrate on user authentication. Hence, they propose that "where the user is and when" is one authentication class added to conventional "what the user is", "what the user has," and "what the user knows." The main idea is to approximate the authentication confidence with the probability of the user being at a certain location in an authentication time. Location information from user's different identity tokens is composed, which indicates the probability of being in the certain location. The authors present a fusion algorithm, which calculates a probability that the user is in a certain location based on the location information of user's devices. The results of the fusion algorithm are simulated by using the locations of the Bluetooth device and RFID badge in two different situations. In the first case, the location of Bluetooth device and RFID badge overlaps, and this increases authentication confidence. In the second case, devices' locations are not overlapping, causing decreased authentication confidence. Context management framework collects context information, that is, location information with timestamps, which are provided for the User Location Probability Calculator (ULPC). The ULPC component calculates probability values with the developed fusion algorithm, and the result is delivered to the application. The application utilises this information to decide the current authentication level. If the authentication level is not sufficient, the application uses alternative authentication

TABLE 1: Data for comparison framework.

Property	Description
	Adaptation
Object to adapt	Generic solution. Authors mention security mechanisms for authentication, authorization, encryption, and fault tolerance.
Adaptation timing	Runtime and reactive. It is possible to achieve proactive adaptation by the means of threat monitoring service. The service acts like the IDS (Intrusion Detection System), which reveals ongoing attacks. However, these monitoring services are not described in more detail, and how the results of these services will be utilised.
Monitoring and analyses	The Context subsystem performs monitoring and analyses by means of dedicated services. The Context subsystem offers the following: trust level, threat level, availability, memory usage, and bandwidth usage. The internal design of these services is not described.
Planning and execution	Planning and execution are performed inside the security subsystem by means of ECSA Policy manager. The specific action is executed when corresponding event occurs and certain condition is true. Hence, the planning is static; that is, actions are defined beforehand.
Knowledge	Inside the monitoring services and ECSA policies.
Self-properties	Authors describe their proposal to self-managing and self-adaptive. By using terms described in Section 3, the approach offers self-protection by using self-configuration and self-optimization. Context-awareness by means of services in the Context subsystem.
	Security
Attributes	Generic solution. Authors emphasise authentication, authorization, confidentiality, integrity, and availability
Mechanisms	Generic solution
Protected asset	Generic solution
Threats	Generic solution
	Lifecycle
Architecture	All elements, related to security and adaptation, are located on the middleware layer under the application layer. The structure of architecture is clearly described, but mutual behaviour of subsystems and components is not described.
Extensibility	The clearly defined architecture ensures that the approach can be extended easily. It is possible to bring new security mechanisms into the Security subsystem and new monitoring services into the Context subsystem. However, possibilities on how to extend the ECSA Policy manager are not described.
Flexibility	The defined architecture also supports flexibility. Applying the approach in different domains requires at least new policies. Based on the existing research papers it seems that there are no restrictions to add new policies afterwards.
Reusability	The approach is not tight into the application logic or particular security mechanisms. Thus, reusing will be a straightforward process. Reusing the whole adaptation approach requires that the presented middleware layer is implemented under the application layer. This might be challenging for the existing applications. Reusing monitoring services inside the Context subsystem will be easy.
Maturity	The approach is not validated from the security adaptation viewpoint. Existing papers do not describe how to build security adaptation by means of the approach. Several examples of ECSA policies are given, but implementation of the policy manager is not described. The latest article with the security viewpoint in 2009, and the latest article from ECSA policies in 2011. The software community or code libraries are not available.

mechanisms, for example, asks username and password. The approach is further developed in [31, 32] by developing an alternative fusion algorithm, which concentrates on the trust of location sensors. However, the initial idea of an adaptive authentication is similar regardless of the used fusion algorithm.

Based on the description given in papers [12, 31, 32] much focus has not been given for the security adaptation. This does not mean that the paper has not merited itself, but emphasis of the paper is more for context awareness and how to apply it. The presented approach can be thought as a means to monitor environment or user's behaviour or an authentication mechanism. Naturally, the monitored information can be utilised during the adaptation. Table 3 collects data by means of the comparison framework.

4.4. Adaptive Messaging Middleware. Abie et al. presents self-healing and secure adaptive messaging middleware called Genetic Messaging-Oriented Secure Middleware (GEMOM) in [13]. The GEMOM is a message oriented middleware that utilises the publish-subscribe messaging paradigm. The purpose of self-healing and adaptation features of the GEMOM is to ensure optimal security strength and uninterrupted operation in changing environments and threats. Self-healing is achieved by means of replication. In other words, GEMOM heals from faults by deploying a new instance from the

TABLE 2: Data for comparison framework.

Property	Description
	Adaptation
Object to adapt	Security services for authentication, authorization, and cryptography are directly mentioned. However, the Responder module produces configuration information, which can be delivered for any part in the device. Thus, the solution is generic.
Adaptation timing	Runtime and reactive
Monitoring and analyses	Dedicated components for monitoring and analysing. Monitoring components observe predefined security related events from environment or device and analysing components subscribe to these events. The analysing components propose high-level security actions based on information from the profile database. Consequently, analysing component covers also the planning phase.
Planning and execution	No dedicated planning component. The planning functionality is partially composed inside the Analyse and Respond components. The Respond components map high-level security actions from the Analyse component to the implementation specific subsystems. The implementation specific subsystem decides how to finally execute the adaptation. Thus, the adaptation approach does not dictate the content of plan and execution phases as a whole.
Knowledge	Separated support module, which contains the Profile database. The monitor, analyse, and respond components are able to retrieve knowledge from the Profile database. However, the content of the database is not described.
Self-properties	Self-configuration and self-optimization, that is, changing used security components or setting different parameters for those components. Self-protection by recognising events that decrease security. Context-awareness monitors security relevant events from the environment by means of Context Management Infrastructure (CMI).
	Security
Attributes	Generic solution, authors emphasize authentication, authorisation, confidentiality, and integrity attributes.
Mechanisms	Generic security services for authentication, authorisation, and cryptography.
Protected asset	Generic solution
Threats	Generic solution
	Lifecycle
Architecture	The adaptation loop is clearly defined, and Monitor, Analyse, and Respond components are separated for their own components. Events between the Monitor and Analyse components are specified to occur via Dbus based event bus. The Responder component sends events to implementation specific subsystems, which in turn support generalisation. Therefore, both structure and behaviour of the approach are described.
Extensibility	The presented architecture supports extensions; that is, new security mechanisms and monitoring techniques can be applied.
Flexibility	The presented architecture supports flexibility. No dependencies to specific domain or environment.
Reusability	The framework and its components are conceptually reusable. Internal functionality of components is not described, which complicates reusing.
Maturity	The adaptation approach is implemented by Java for the Nokia 770 Internet tablet, but validation use cases are not described. The framework is described in a research paper. The latest article from the approach appeared in 2010. The software community or code libraries are not available.

messaging system at runtime by utilising the replica nodes of the system. In the GEMOM the Adaptive Security Manager (ASM) component is intended to perform tasks related to adaptation. Hence, the ASM monitors and analyses security, plans actions, and executes planned actions. The high-level internal structure of the ASM is described in [33]. The structure follows a generic adaptation loop. However, plan and execute phases are combined into one adaptation phase. Moreover, learning functionality is added into the analyse phase. Unfortunately, the learning part is not described in more detail. In the presented approach monitoring is performed by means of anomaly detection, Quality of Service

(QoS) monitoring, and security measuring. From these monitoring techniques the security measuring is described in more detail in [34]. The same paper also describes how different measurements are combined to higher level security indicators. State of Security (SoS) is constituted from the security indicators. The purpose is to maintain past, current, and predicted SoS information, which is used for reactive and/or proactive security adaptation. Table 4 collects data by means of the comparison framework.

4.5. Adaptive Security Architecture Based on EC-MQV Algorithm in Personal Networks (PN). The approach is presented

TABLE 3: Data for comparison framework.

Property	Description
Adaptation	
Object to adapt	Authentication mechanism. In the demo case password based authentication is enforced when the sufficient authentication level is not reached from the location information.
Adaptation timing	Runtime and reactive
Monitoring and analyses	Locations of user's devices and timestamps are monitored by means of context management framework. The ULPC analyses monitor results by means of the developed fusion algorithms. Additional analyses are left for the application and not described in the paper. Hence, the application concludes the current authentication level.
Planning and execution	Each application has to contain its own planning and execution mechanism. Hence, these phases are left for the application developer.
Knowledge	Monitored attributes are selected beforehand, and the fusion algorithm contains knowledge for analyses. Moreover, planning and execution is intended to occur inside the application. Thus, the approach does not contain separated knowledge storage.
Self-properties	Self-configuration, that is, the approach selects among different authentication alternatives. Context awareness, that is, the approach monitors user's location and time.
Security	
Attributes	Authentication
Mechanisms	The approach makes it possible to select alternative user authentication mechanisms if the location based authentication does not offer reasonable authentication level.
Protected asset	User's identity
Threats	Identity theft
Lifecycle	
Architecture	Separated components for context monitoring and user's location analysing. These components are independent from the application. However, structure for additional analyses and adaptation planning is not described.
Extensibility	The whole approach is intended for authentication adaptation, and thus extending the approach will be laborious. The approach can be seen as a potential extension for other security adaptation approaches. Especially those that already contain analysing and planning components.
Flexibility	The used context information includes location and timestamps. The approach is strongly related to this information, and using different context information needs new algorithms and components.
Reusability	Presented components are not coupled to the application logic and interfaces are clear. Thus, reusing will be easy.
Maturity	Authors validated the approach with a laboratory case, called Buddy spotter application. In the case example, a user is able to see her current authentication level and which mechanisms are used in authentication. User is able to set a minimal authentication level that her buddies have to reach in order to get user's information. The use of the fusion algorithm is simulated.
	Information is available in the related publications. Implementation guidelines or available software components are not mentioned. However, the publications give descriptions of fusion algorithms. Thus, the algorithms can be implemented based on available information.
	The latest article from the approach appeared in 2011. The software community or code libraries are not available.

by Mihovska and Prasad in [14]. The proposed approach is a three level architecture for context-aware asymmetric key agreement. Three level means in this approach that three different algorithms for key agreement and exchange exist. The approach concentrates on the key agreement method in elliptic curve cryptosystem (EC-MQV) in Personal Network (PN). The PN contains a dynamic set of nodes and devices around a user and remote nodes and devices (from home, office, etc.) connected with the Internet or cellular network. Context-aware Security Manager (CaSM) manages security parameters used in the PN, and thus makes it possible to achieve adaptive security. Firstly, each device joining to the PN has to register for the CaSM, which inspects the device and stores its information. In the first phase, the long term shared key pair is created between device and CaSM. In the second phase, the shared secret key is created for devices communicating in the PN. A new shared secret key is created for each session. For each session, the used key agreement method depends on location and device constraints, that is, context information. In the presented approach, location information indicates different security levels. Hence, in the home environment the one-pass key agreement algorithm is used, which offers the lowest security level. In the known cluster, for example, office, the two-pass

TABLE 4: Data for comparison framework.

Property	Description
Adaptation	
Object to adapt	Generic approach. For the adaptive authorization, authors mention the following possibilities: security policy, algorithms, protocols, and encryption schemes.
Adaptation timing	Runtime, proactive, and reactive
Monitoring and analyses	Security measuring is the most emphasised form of monitoring. Moreover, anomaly and QoS monitoring are also mentioned. The component called Adaptive Analyser and Learner utilises the results of monitoring. The results from security measuring are composed for higher levels. However, the functionality of the component is not described in more detail.
Planning and execution	Composed together into the phase called Adapt. The content of this phase is not described in more detail.
Knowledge	The Analyser component communicates with the Adaptive database. However, the included knowledge is not described.
Self-properties	Self-healing by means of self-configuration, that is, selecting replicated component in failure situation. Self-protection by means of self-configuring and self-optimization.
Security	
Attributes	Generic approach. Adaptive authentication and authorization are emphasized in the above mentioned papers. However, means to monitor, other security attributes are also presented.
Mechanisms	Generic approach
Protected asset	Generic approach
Threats	Generic approach
Lifecycle	
Architecture	The Adaptive Security Manager (ASM) component performs all tasks related to adaptation. The component contains monitor, analyse, and adaptation parts. Furthermore, adapted security mechanisms are also included inside this component. The monitor part utilises security measurements from different layers of the GEMOM middleware.
Extensibility	The adaptation loop is located inside one component, which is closely related to the GEMOM middleware. Hence, extending the whole approach will be laborious. However, the monitoring part is described in an extensible manner.
Flexibility	The approach is tested in various environments. However, all of these utilise the GEMOM middleware as a whole.
Reusability	The security measuring is described in the reusable form. The adaptation loop is tightly coupled to the GEMOM middleware.
Maturity	Validation with five different scenarios, that is, a collaborative business portal, a dynamic linked exchange, a financial market data delivery system, a dynamic road management system, and a banking scenario for transaction processing. Implementation by means of deliverables and publications from the GEMOM project. The GEMOM project ended in 2010; software community is not available.

key agreement algorithm is utilised, which supports medium level security. Finally, in public networks the highest security level is required, which is achieved by means of the three-pass key agreement algorithm. Consequently, the main emphasis is on the key agreement. Unfortunately, the adaptation aspect has not got much visibility in the paper. Table 5 collects data by means of the comparison framework.

5. Comparisons and Analysis

This section collects all data from the approaches in a concise form (cf.) Table 6. The purpose of the table is to facilitate comparison of the presented approaches. In the table a line symbol (—) indicates that the aspect is not covered in the approach. In order to compare extensibility and flexibility, the following grades will be used: extensibility grades *Completely*, *Partially*, and *No* and Flexibility grades *Easy*, *Moderate*, and *Hard*.

For extensibility, completely means that the approach can be extended from the security and adaptation viewpoints. In other words, it is possible to add support for new security attributes and mechanisms. Moreover the approach can be extended to use new adaptation techniques, that is, new monitors, analyses, and planning algorithms. A Partially grade means that the approach supports either security or adaptation related extensions. Finally, a No grade means that extensions cannot be made or those are laborious. Similarly, flexibility is graded to three levels Easy, Moderate, and Hard. An Easy grade means that utilising the approach in a new usage environment or situation requires only slight modifications. Hence, the architecture follows the separation of concerns principle and required modifications are anticipated. A Moderate grade means that the approach can be applied in different environments. However, the amount of required changes is higher, or, alternatively, the selected architecture complicates changes. Lastly, a Hard grade implies that

TABLE 5: Data for comparison framework.

Property	Description
	Adaptation
Object to adapt	Key agreement algorithm
Adaptation timing	Start-up time adaptation, that is, at the beginning of each communication session. Considering proactive/reactive aspect is not applicable for start-up time adaptation.
Monitoring and analyses	Monitors: location (scenario/scene) and device's capability. It is assumed that particular attacks are not relevant in certain places, that is, analysed beforehand.
Planning and execution	The used key agreement algorithm depends on location and constraints of the device, that is, context information from the CaSM. The actions, which will be performed in different situations, are selected beforehand (hard coded actions), that is, static planning.
Knowledge	Knowledge source is not described.
Self-properties	Context awareness: location and device constraints.
	Security
Attributes	Confidentiality and integrity during the communication.
Mechanisms	Key agreement algorithm One-, two-, and three-pass EC-MQW
Protected asset	Data in communication channel.
Threats	Threats for the communication confidentiality and integrity.
	Lifecycle
Architecture	CaSM (Context-aware Security Manager) implemented as a layer between a user's application and security protocol. Architecture for the adaptation loop is not described.
Extensibility	The approach concentrates on key agreement with the specific crypto system. However, CaSM can be also applied to adapt to other security mechanisms.
Flexibility	The approach is not coupled to specific environment or usage scenario.
Reusability	The CaSM component (layer) can be reused in different applications.
Maturity	The approach is not validated. In addition, the paper, which presents the approach, is the only available information source. Hence, guidelines how to implement the adaptation approach is not available. There is not a community behind the approach.

the approach is closely related to particular environment or usage. Thus, changing the usage environment or situation will be laborious.

After the comparison table, the differences of these approaches are analysed.

5.1. Analysis. This paper developed the framework to compare security adaptation approaches. The framework contains three viewpoints, that is, adaptation, security, and lifecycle. Each of these viewpoints brought out different aspects from the compared security adaptation approaches.

In the adaptation viewpoint, the first attributes, that is, object to adapt and adaptation timing, do not show any surprises. In the presented adaptation approaches the most emphasis is put to the monitor and analyse phases. In other words, each approach monitors own behaviour and/or environment somehow and makes an adaptation decision based on the monitored data. The monitored data varies a lot from an approach to another. In some approaches, the monitoring concentrates on context related data, for example, location. In contrast, some approaches monitor directly security threats. Several aspects can affect security; and thus, it is natural that monitored attributes vary between approaches. However, means of how the monitoring has to

be performed is not described in these approaches. In other words, it is not always clear which kind of sensor, software or hardware, is needed to collect the required information.

Most of the compared approaches contain a separated component for the analyses. This separation facilitates reusing and extensibility. However, the approaches do not emphasise the content of the analyse phase as much as the monitoring phase. Approaches 3 and 4 (cf. numbers in the first row in Table 6) describe also the analyse phase. The approach 3 presents the fusion algorithm to compose location information, but the final authentication level has to be decided in the application. The approach 4 presents formulas to compose the results of security metrics, collected during the monitoring phase. On the contrary, the approach 5 utilises beforehand performed analyses; that is, security levels for different locations are decided statically beforehand. Finally, approaches 1 and 2 do not describe how the analyses are performed.

Moving forward to planning and execution reveals that these are the most uncovered phases of the adaptation loop in these approaches. Approaches 1 and 5 utilise static planning; that is, the adaptation plan is created beforehand and described in a policy description or in application logic. Other approaches do not describe algorithms or rules to

TABLE 6: Comparison of approaches.

Security adaptation approach	(1) An architectural approach for self-managing security services	(2) A software framework for autonomic security in pervasive environments	(3) Context sensitive adaptive authentication	(4) Adaptive messaging middleware	(5) Adaptive security architecture based on EC-MQV algorithm in personal networks
Adaptation viewpoint					
Object to adapt	Generic approach	Generic approach	Authentication mechanism	Generic approach	Key agreement algorithm
Adaptation timing	Runtime, reactive, and proactive	Runtime and reactive	Runtime and reactive	Runtime, reactive, and proactive	Start-up
Monitor and analyses	Monitoring and analysing composed inside the Context subsystem by means of dedicated services for trust level, threat level, availability, memory usage, and bandwidth usage. The internal design of services is not described.	Monitors: beforehand defined security events. Analyses: decides to reconfigure based on monitored events. How a decision is made is not described.	Monitors: location of user's devices and timestamps. Analyses: ULPC partially analyses monitoring results by means of the developed fusion algorithms. The application has to conclude the current authentication level.	Monitoring: security measuring is the most emphasised form of monitoring. Analyses: the separated component composes the monitoring results to the higher level. The internal design of this component is not described.	Monitors location and device capabilities. Analyses: beforehand analysed.
Planning and execution	Planning: static planning by the means of ECSA policies. Execution: ECSA Policy manager enforces beforehand defined actions.	Planning: in high level Execution: —	Planning: — Execution: —	Planning and execution are composed into the one phase called Adapt. However, the content of this phase is not described.	Planning: static planning, that is, beforehand defined actions for different locations. Execution: beginning of each communication session.
Knowledge	Inside the monitoring services and ECSA policies.	Profile database (content is not described)	—	Adaptive database (content is not described)	—
Self-properties	Self-configuration, optimization, and protection. Context-awareness	Self-configuration, optimization, and protection. Context-awareness	Self-configuration. Context-awareness	Self-configuration, optimization, protection, and healing.	Context-awareness
Security viewpoint					
Mechanisms	Generic approach	Generic approach	Authentication mechanism	Generic approach	Key agreement algorithm
Attributes	Generic approach	Generic approach	Authentication	Generic approach	Confidentiality and integrity
Protected asset	Generic approach	Generic approach	User's identity	Generic approach	Data in communication channel
Threats	Generic approach	Generic approach	Identity theft	Generic approach	Threats for the communication confidentiality and integrity.

TABLE 6: Continued.

Security adaptation approach	(1) An architectural approach for self-managing security services	(2) A software framework for autonomic security in pervasive environments	(3) Context sensitive adaptive authentication	(4) Adaptive messaging middleware	(5) Adaptive security architecture based on EC-MQV algorithm in personal networks
			Lifecycle viewpoint		
Architecture	Structure is described. Middleware under the application layer contains elements for adaptation. Behaviour is not described.	Structure and behaviour of the approach are described. Separated components for monitoring, analysing, and responding.	Structure and behaviour of the approach are described. Separated components for monitoring and analysing.	Structure is described. The ASM component performs all adaptation tasks. The component contains monitor, analyse, and adaptation parts. Behaviour is not described.	Structure is described. Layer between application and security protocol.
Extensibility	Completely	Completely	No	Partially	Partially
Flexibility	Easy	Easy	Hard	Moderate	Easy
Reusability	It is possible to reuse the whole approach or individual components.	It is possible to reuse the whole approach or individual components.	It is possible to reuse the whole approach. Individual components can be also reused, but the functionality is strongly related to this approach.	Reusing the whole adaptation approach requires that the GEMOM middleware is utilised as a whole, which causes additional work. Reusing individual monitoring (measuring) parts will be easy.	CaSM component can be reused. It is notable that the component is intended for the start-up phase adaptations.
Maturity	Validation No Guidelines No Community No	Validation No Guidelines No Community No	Validation Yes Guidelines partially Yes[a] Community No	Validation Yes Guidelines No Community No	Validation No Guidelines No Community No

[a] Separated guidelines are not available. However, the existing papers describe the monitored attributes and the fusion algorithm in detail, and thus these can be implemented by means of this input.

TABLE 7: Approaches mapped to the adaptation loop.

	(1) An architectural approach for self-managing security services	(2) A software framework for autonomic security in pervasive environments	(3) Context sensitive adaptive authentication	(4) Adaptive messaging middleware	(5) Adaptive security architecture based on EC-MQV algorithm in personal networks
Monitor	•	•	•	•	•
Analyse			•	•	•
Plan	•				•
Execute					
Knowledge					

define adaptation plans. Furthermore, means of how the adaptation plan will be enforced is not described, that is, the execution phase. This phase should not be underestimated because each adaptation plan might cause side effects and require totally different actions. For example, optimising parameters for a TLS connection requires that the whole connection is recreated, which in turn might affect application functionality. The approach 5 covers also the execution phase. However, the approach is intended to start-up phase adaptation; that is, adaptation occurs when a new connection is established. Hence, it is not proper to compare this approach to runtime phase adaptations.

As mentioned in Section 2, the adaptation loop requires also knowledge. Naturally, each adaptation approach contains the required knowledge in some form. However, the utilised knowledge, and how it is stored, is not described at all. Approaches 2 and 4 contain a database, which offers input for the adaptation phases. However, the content of the database is not described in these approaches. Approach 1 contains knowledge in policies and in the monitoring services. In this approach policies describe what security mechanism to use in different situations. Furthermore, monitoring services also perform the analyse phase, and required knowledge is integrated in these services. Thus, approaches 1, 2, and 4 address to place where the knowledge can be stored. Nevertheless, none of these approaches describe which kind of knowledge is required during the adaptation.

Utilising some adaptation approach requires that the knowledge is also available. If software components for the adaptation approach are available, but the required knowledge is missing, the components are useless. Without knowledge each component requires hard coded, that is, integrated, decisions to describe what to monitor, how to compose monitoring results, and how to adapt. Naturally, hard coding all these decisions is not sufficient for the autonomous adaptation. In other words, hard coding leads the adaptation approach with the huge set of if-then-else clauses, which is fairly a static approach and not flexible, extensible, or reusable as such. Hence, separating knowledge from the adaptation phases, instead of integrating them together, makes it easier to achieve evolution qualities. Furthermore, the lack of knowledge models is other aspect that complicates the achievement of evolution qualities. The knowledge model, which describes the form of the knowledge explicitly will facilitate the evolution of the approach.

Table 7 summarises the contributions of the presented approaches from the adaptation loop viewpoint. As a summary, in these security adaptation approaches, the most effort is put to first phases of the adaptation loop. Therefore, the plan and execute phases and knowledge are bypassed and described only with few sentences.

From the security viewpoint, the compared security adaptation approaches are quite similar. Approaches are either generic; that is, approaches are not intended to specific security attributes or mechanisms. Or alternatively, approaches are clearly dedicated for particular adaptations. Approach 5 is the most specified one, concentrating on the particular key agreement algorithm. In contrast, the approach 3 is intended to authentication but the authentication mechanism is not bound. Other three approaches are generic, and thus, the end user is able to utilise these approaches for various security attributes. However, it can be assumed that more implementation effort will be needed when utilising a generic approach instead of more specific one.

In the lifecycle viewpoint, architecture is the first comparison attribute. The used architecture affects also the achieved evolution qualities. Architecture structure is described in each approach. In other words, at least required software components are described. Furthermore, approaches 2 and 3 describe also architecture behavior; that is, how components call each other.

The level of extensibility varies between the approaches. Approaches 1 and 2 support extensibility completely; that is, approaches can be extended from the security and adaptation viewpoints. On the other hand, approaches 4 and 5 offer partial extensibility. In the approach 4 monitoring part, called security metrics in the approach, can be extended. On the contrary, the approach 5 can be extended to new security mechanisms. Finally, the approach 3 is strongly designed for the authentication adaptation with the particular fusion algorithm, and thus extending the approach will be laborious. Similarly, flexibility varies between approaches. Approaches 1, 2, and 5 can be easily applied to a new environment or usage situation. The approach 4 supports flexibility in a moderate level. The approach is already utilised in various environments. However, in this approach the selected architecture causes challenges for the flexibility. The approach 3 is strongly bound to location and timestamps context information. Therefore, utilising the approach in other way will need a lot of work. Finally, reusability of approaches is broadly supported. Approaches 1 and 2 can be reused as a whole, or alternatively, separated components can be reused. On the other hand, approach 3 can be reused as a whole. In this approach individual components are strongly related to the approach, and thus reusing them as such is not reasonable. Lastly, approaches 4 and 5 contain individual components, which can be reused easily.

In the lifecycle viewpoint, maturity attribute revealed that the validation is performed for approaches 3 and 4. On the contrary, none of these approaches provides support via a software community or even user guidelines. The lack of communities and guidelines is natural because each of these approaches is presented in research papers. Thus, utilising these approaches will be challenging and requires a lot of work. However, it is notable that authors of these approaches do not claim that their solutions are ready for the wider usage.

5.2. Future Work. The existing security adaptation approaches do not cover the whole adaptation loop and the knowledge part. Nevertheless, each approach offers viable components and ideas for the further utilisation. For instance, combining presented monitoring and analysing techniques will provide a novel security adaptation solution. Consequently, the new solution is able to observe security relevant attributes and events broadly from the execution environment and security mechanisms.

In the future it is important to achieve a solution, which is able to cover the whole adaptation loop. One possibility to achieve an appropriate solution is to utilise bottom-up development and reusing the existing approaches. Consequently, all elements are not needed to reinvent, and the evolution of the existing components will benefit the developed approach. Developing the whole adaptation loop for one security attribute first and then extending the approach for other attributes might be a reasonable way to proceed. Hence, each security attribute can be covered in detail level. Naturally, the utilised architecture has to be selected carefully, in order to ensure extensibility of the approach with new security attributes. In contrast, developing the whole adaptation loop in a generic manner, for all security attributes at once, will be challenging and error prone process.

As mentioned above, more emphasis is especially needed to planning and knowledge parts. For the planning, one possibility is to utilise existing decision making algorithms, developed in the autonomic computing field. Furthermore, applying techniques utilised in other adaptation approaches, for example, in performance adaptation, is able to offer valuable input for planning in security adaptation. For the knowledge part, required research is twofold. Firstly, the content of required knowledge has to be defined explicitly. Naturally, collecting knowledge has to be an iterative process; that is, new knowledge is defined in small pieces and the existing knowledge is updated. At least the following knowledge is needed: applicable sensors and what they monitor, how to use monitored data in the analyses, and how to create the adaptation plan. In other words, different knowledge is needed in different phases of the adaptation. In addition, security knowledge has to be included, containing

descriptions of security attributes, mechanisms, and their relationships. Similarly, knowledge of the execution environment is needed, that is, context information. Secondly, developing the knowledge base means that an appropriate format for the knowledge is selected. This is a technical viewpoint for the knowledge base development, containing data formats and used database solutions. However, this is important selection because it dictates how easily the knowledge base can be updated in the future.

Consequently, additional research is needed in order to combine monitoring and analysing phases coherently to planning and execution phases and support the adaptation with appropriate knowledge. Hence, the cross-discipline research and cooperation between security and autonomous computing experts are required. Furthermore, achieving reusable and long-lasting security adaptation approach demands that architecture and software development aspects are perceived during the future research.

6. Conclusions

Achieving appropriate security in dynamically changing environments and threat landscapes is not possible by means of static and beforehand selected security mechanisms. Therefore, information security has to be implemented in a self-adaptive way. In adaptive security, utilised security mechanisms can be changed and modified at runtime, and thus all security related decisions are not bound at design-time.

This paper developed a framework to compare security adaptation approaches. The framework constitutes of three viewpoints, namely, adaptation, security, and lifecycle viewpoints. The adaptation viewpoint concentrates on the used adaptation model. The security viewpoint covers software security related properties. Lastly, the lifecycle viewpoint compares architectures, evolution qualities, and maturity. The framework was utilised to compare five security adaptation approaches. The comparison showed that the monitor phase is described in each adaptation approach and most approaches contain also the analyse phase. However, the plan phase, where a decision of how to adapt will be made, is not described on an adequate level. In addition, the compared approaches do not offer means to manage knowledge required during the adaptation, or, alternatively, the content of the required knowledge is not described. Hence, these two areas have to be researched more in the future. In order to achieve coherent security adaptation approach, the cooperation between autonomous computing, security, and software development experts will be needed. As a result of collaboration, the approach which is secure, easy to utilise, and contains necessary adaptation aspects in the same time can be achieved.

Acknowledgments

This work has been carried out in the SOFIA ARTEMIS project (2009–2011) and SASER-Siegfried Celtic-Plus project (2012–2015) funded by the Finnish Funding Agency for

Technology and Innovation (Tekes), VTT Technical Research Centre of Finland, and the European Commission.

References

[1] J. O. Kephart and D. M. Chess, "The vision of autonomic computing," *Computer*, vol. 36, no. 1, pp. 4–50, 2003.

[2] M. C. Huebscher and J. A. McCann, "A survey of Autonomic computing—degrees, models, and applications," *ACM Computing Surveys*, vol. 40, no. 3, article 7, 2008.

[3] S. Dobson, S. Denazis, A. Fernández et al., "A survey of autonomic communications," *ACM Transactions on Autonomous and Adaptive Systems*, vol. 1, no. 2, pp. 223–259, 2006.

[4] M. Salehie and L. Tahvildari, "Self-adaptive software: landscape and research challenges," *ACM Transactions on Autonomous and Adaptive Systems*, vol. 4, no. 2, article 14, 2009.

[5] A. Elkhodary and J. Whittle, "A survey of approaches to adaptive application security," in *Proceedings of the Software Engineering for Adaptive and Self-Managing Systems Workshop*, pp. 16–23, Minneapolis, Minn, USA, May 2007.

[6] B. Hashii, S. Malabarba, R. Pandey, and M. Bishop, "Supporting reconfigurable security policies for mobile programs," *Computer Networks*, vol. 33, no. 1, pp. 77–93, 2000.

[7] W. Hu, J. Hiser, D. Williams et al., "Secure and practical defense against code-injection attacks using software dynamic translation," in *Proceedings of the 2nd International Conference on Virtual Execution Environments*, pp. 2–12, ACM, Ottawa, Canada, June 2006.

[8] J. C. Knight and E. A. Strunk, "Achieving critical system survivability through software architectures," in *Architecting Dependable Systems II*, R. Lemos, C. Gacek, and A. Romanovsky, Eds., pp. 51–78, Springer, Berlin, Germany, 2004.

[9] T. Ryutov, L. Zhou, C. Neuman, T. Leithead, and K. E. Seamons, "Adaptive trust negotiation and access control," in *Proceedings of 10th ACM Symposium on Access Control Models and Technologies*, pp. 139–146, Yorkshire, UK, June 2005.

[10] G. Russello and N. Dulay, "An architectural approach for self-managing security services," in *Proceedings of the IEEE International Conference on Advanced Information Networking and Applications Workshops*, pp. 153–158, Bradford, UK, May 2009.

[11] A. Saxena, M. Lacoste, T. Jarboui, U. Lücking, and B. A. Steinke, "Software framework for autonomic security in pervasive environments," in *Information Systems Security*, P. McDaniel and S. Gupta, Eds., pp. 91–109, Springer, Berlin, Germany, 2007.

[12] R. Hulsebosch, M. Bargh, G. Lenzini, P. Ebben, and S. Iacob, "Context sensitive adaptive authentication," in *Smart Sensing and Context*, G. Kortuem, J. Finney, R. Lea, and V. Sundramoorthy, Eds., pp. 93–109, Springer, Berlin, Germany, 2007.

[13] H. Abie, R. M. Savola, J. Bigham, I. Dattani, D. Rotondi, and G. Da Bormida, "Self-healing and secure adaptive messaging middleware for business-critical systems," *International Journal On Advances in Security*, vol. 3, pp. 34–51, 2010.

[14] A. Mihovska and N. R. Prasad, "Adaptive security architecture based on EC-MQV algorithm in personal network (PN)," in *Proceedings of the 4th Annual International Conference on Mobile and Ubiquitous Systems: Computing, Networking & Services (MobiQuitous '07)*, pp. 1–5, August 2007.

[15] ISO/IEC 9126-1, *2001 Software Engineering—Product Quality—Part 1: Quality Model*, International Organization of Standardization, 2001.

[16] A. Avižienis, J.-C. Laprie, B. Randell, and C. Landwehr, "Basic concepts and taxonomy of dependable and secure computing," *IEEE Transactions on Dependable and Secure Computing*, vol. 1, no. 1, pp. 11–33, 2004.

[17] ISO/IEC 15408-1, *2009 Common Criteria for Information Technology Security Evaluation—Part 1: Introduction and General Model*, 2009.

[18] G. Stoneburner, A. Goguen, and A. Feringa, "Risk management guide for information technology systems," Tech. Rep. 800-30, 2002.

[19] A. Herzog, N. Shahmehri, and C. Duma, "An ontology of information security," *Journal of Information Security and Privacy*, vol. 1, pp. 1–23, 2007.

[20] D. M. Chess, C. C. Palmer, and S. R. White, "Security in an autonomic computing environment," *IBM Systems Journal*, vol. 42, no. 1, pp. 107–118, 2003.

[21] M. Svahnberg, J. Van Gurp, and J. Bosch, "A taxonomy of variability realization techniques," *Software*, vol. 35, no. 8, pp. 705–754, 2005.

[22] E. Niemelä, A. Evesti, and P. Savolainen, "Modeling quality attribute variability," in *Proceedings of the 3rd International Conference on Evaluation of Novel Approaches to Software Engineering*, pp. 169–176, Madeira, Portugal, May 2008.

[23] L. Bass, P. Clements, and R. Kazman, *Software Architecture in Practice*, Addison-Wesley, Boston, Mass, USA, 2nd edition, 2003.

[24] N. Yoshioka, H. Washizaki, and K. Maruyama, "A survey on security patterns," *Progress in Informatics*, no. 5, pp. 35–47, 2008.

[25] T. Priebe, E. Fernandez, J. Mehlau, and G. Pernul, "A pattern system for access control," in *Research Directions in Data and Applications Security XVIII*, C. Farkas and P. Samarati, Eds., pp. 235–249, Springer, Boston, Mass, USA, 2004.

[26] M. Matinlassi and E. Niemelä, "The impact of maintainability on component-based software systems," in *Proceedings of the 29th IEEE Euromicro Conference*, pp. 25–32, Belek, Turkey, September, 2003.

[27] G. Russello, L. Mostarda, Dulay, and N. Escape, "A component-based policy framework for sense and react applications," in *Component-Based Software Engineering*, M. Chaudron, C. Szyperski, and R. Reussner, Eds., pp. 212–229, Springer, Berlin, Germany, 2008.

[28] G. Russello, L. Mostarda, and N. Dulay, "A policy-based publish/subscribe middleware for sense-and-react applications," *Journal of Systems and Software*, vol. 84, no. 4, pp. 638–654, 2011.

[29] R. He and M. Lacoste, "Applying component-based design to self-protection of ubiquitous systems," in *Proceedings of the the 3rd ACM Workshop on Software Engineering for Pervasive Services (ACM '08)*, pp. 9–14, Sorrento, Italy, July 2008.

[30] R. J. Hulsebosch, A. M. Salden, M. S. Bargh, P. W. G. Ebben, and J. Reitsma, "Context sensitive access control," in *Proceedings of 10th ACM Symposium on Access Control Models and Technologies*, pp. 111–119, Stockholm, Sweden, June 2005.

[31] G. Lenzini, M. S. Bargh, and B. Hulsebosch, "Trust-enhanced security in location-based adaptive authentication," *Electronic Notes in Theoretical Computer Science*, vol. 197, no. 2, pp. 105–119, 2008.

[32] J. M. Seigneur, G. Lenzini, and B. Hulsebosch, "Adaptive trust management," in *Self-Organising Software*, G. Di Marzo Serugendo, M. Gleizes, and A. Karageorgos, Eds., pp. 379–403, Springer, Berlin, Germany, 2011.

[33] H. Abie, "Adaptive security and trust management for auto-
     nomic message-oriented middleware," in *Proceedings of the 6th
     IEEE International Conference on Mobile Adhoc and Sensor
     Systems*, pp. 810–817, Macau, China, October 2009.

[34] R. Savola and H. Abie, "Development of measurable security
     for a distributed messaging system," *International Journal On
     Advances in Security*, vol. 2, pp. 358–380, 2009.

8

3D Gestural Interaction: The State of the Field

Joseph J. LaViola Jr.

Department of EECS, University of Central Florida, Orlando, FL 32816, USA

Correspondence should be addressed to Joseph J. LaViola Jr.; jjl@eecs.ucf.edu

Academic Editors: O. Castillo, R.-C. Hwang, and P. Kokol

3D gestural interaction provides a powerful and natural way to interact with computers using the hands and body for a variety of different applications including video games, training and simulation, and medicine. However, accurately recognizing 3D gestures so that they can be reliably used in these applications poses many different research challenges. In this paper, we examine the state of the field of 3D gestural interfaces by presenting the latest strategies on how to collect the raw 3D gesture data from the user and how to accurately analyze this raw data to correctly recognize 3D gestures users perform. In addition, we examine the latest in 3D gesture recognition performance in terms of accuracy and gesture set size and discuss how different applications are making use of 3D gestural interaction. Finally, we present ideas for future research in this thriving and active research area.

1. Introduction

Ever since Sutherland's vision of the ultimate display [1], the notion of interacting with computers naturally and intuitively has been a driving force in the field of human computer interaction and interactive computer graphics. Indeed, the notion of the post-WIMP interface (Windows, Icons, Menus, Point and Click) has given researchers the opportunity to explore alternative forms of interaction over the traditional keyboard and mouse [2]. Speech input, brain computer interfaces, and touch and pen-computing are all examples of input modalities that attempt to bring a synergy between user and machine and that provide a more direct and natural method of communication [3, 4].

Once such method of interaction that has received considerable attention in recent years is 3D spatial interaction [5], where users' motions are tracked in some way so as to determine their 3D pose (e.g., position and orientation) in space over time. This tracking can be done with sensors users wear or hold in their hands or unobtrusively with a camera. With this information, users can be immersed in 3D virtual environments and avateer virtual characters in video games and simulations and provide commands to various computer applications. Tracked users can also use these handheld devices or their hands, fingers, and whole bodies to generate specific patterns over time that the computer can

recognize to let users issue commands and perform activities. These specific recognized patterns we refer to as 3D gestures.

1.1. 3D Gestures. What exactly is a gesture? Put simply, gestures are movements with an intended emphasis and they are often characterized as rather short bursts of activity with an underlying meaning. In more technical terms, a gesture is a pattern that can be extracted from an input data stream. The frequency and size of the data stream are often dependent on the underlying technology used to collect the data and on the intended gesture style and type. For example, x, y coordinates and timing information are often all that is required to support and recognize 2D pen or touch gestures. A thorough survey on 2D gestures can be found in Zhai et al. [6].

Based on this definition, a 3D gesture is a specific pattern that can be extracted from a continuous data stream that contains 3D position, 3D orientation, and/or 3D motion information. In other words, a 3D gesture is a pattern that can be identified in space, whether it be a device moving in the air such as a mobile phone or game controller, or a user's hand or whole body. There are three different types of movements that can fit into the general category of 3D gestures. First, data that represents a static movement, like making and holding a fist or crossing and holding the arms together, is known as a posture. The key to a posture is that the user is moving to get into a stationary position and then holds that position for some length of time. Second, data that represents a dynamic movement with limited duration, like waving or drawing a circle in the air, is considered to be what we think of as a gesture. Previous surveys [7, 8] have distinguished postures and gestures as separate entities, but they are often used in the same way and the techniques for recognizing them are similar. Third, data that represents dynamic movement with an unlimited duration, like running in place or pretending to climb a rope, is known as an activity. In many cases these types of motions are repetitive, especially in the entertainment domain [9]. The research area known as activity recognition, a subset of computer vision, focuses on recognizing these types of motions [10, 11]. One of the main differences between 3D gestural interfaces and activity recognition is that activity recognition is often focused on detecting human activities where the human is not intending to perform the actions as part of a computer interface, for example, detecting unruly behavior at an airport or train station. For the purposes of this paper, unless otherwise stated, we will group all three movement types into the general category of 3D gestures.

1.2. 3D Gesture Interface Challenges. One of the unique aspects of 3D gestural interfaces is that it crosses many different disciplines in computer science and engineering. Since recognizing a 3D gesture is a question of identifying a pattern in a continuous stream of data, concepts from time series, signal processing and analysis, and control theory can be used. Concepts from machine learning are commonly used since one of the main ideas behind machine learning is to be able to classify data into specific classes and categories, something that is paramount in 3D gesture recognition. In many cases, cameras are used to monitor a user's actions, making computer vision an area that has extensively explored 3D gesture recognition. Given that recognizing 3D gestures is an important component of a 3D gestural user interface, human computer interaction, virtual and augmented reality, and interactive computer graphics all play a role in understanding how to use 3D gestures. Finally, sensor hardware designers also work with 3D gestures because they build the input devices that perform the data collection needed to recognize them.

Regardless of the discipline, from a research perspective, creating and using a 3D gestural interface require the following:

(i) monitoring a continuous input stream to gather data for training and classification,

(ii) analyzing the data to detect a specific pattern from a set of possible patterns,

(iii) evaluating the 3D gesture recognizer,

(iv) using the recognizer in an application so commands or operations are performed when specific patterns are detected.

Each one of these components has research challenges that must be solved in order to provide robust, accurate, and intuitive 3D gestural user interaction. For example, devices that collect and monitor input data need to be accurate with high sampling rates, as unobtrusive as possible, and capture as much of the user's body as possible without occlusion. The algorithms that are used to recognize 3D gestures need to be highly accurate, able to handle large gesture sets, and run in real time. Evaluating 3D gesture recognizers is also challenging given that their true accuracies are often masked by the constrained experiments that are used to test them. Evaluating these recognizers in situ is much more difficult because the experimenter cannot know what gestures the user will be performing at any given time. Finally, incorporating 3D gestures recognizers as part of a 3D gestural interface in an application requires gestures that are easy to remember and perform with minimal latency to provide an intuitive and engaging user experience. We will explore these challenges throughout this paper by examining the latest research results in the area.

1.3. Paper Organization. The remainder of this paper is organized in the following manner. In the next section, we will discuss various strategies for collecting 3D gesture data with a focus on the latest research developments in both worn and handheld sensors as well as unobtrusive vision-based sensors. In Section 3, we will explore how to recognize 3D gestures by using heuristic-based methods and machine learning algorithms. Section 4 will present the latest results from experiments conducted to examine recognition accuracy and gesture set size as well as discuss some applications that use 3D gestural interfaces. Section 5 presents some areas for future research that will enable 3D gestural interfaces to become more commonplace. Finally, Section 6 concludes the paper.

2. 3D Gesture Data Collection

Before any 3D gestural interface can be built or any 3D gesture recognizers can be designed, a method is required to collect the data that will be needed for training and classification. Training data is often needed (for heuristic recognition, training data is not required) for the machine learning algorithms that are used to classify one gesture from another. Since we are interested in 3D gestural interaction, information about the user's location in space or how the user moves in space is critical. Depending on what 3D gestures are required in a given interface, the type of device needed to monitor the user will vary. When thinking about what types of 3D gestures users perform, it is often useful to categorize them into hand gestures, full body gestures, or finger gestures. This categorization can help to narrow down the choice of sensing device, since some devices do not handle all types of 3D gestures. Sensing devices can be broken down into active sensors and passive sensors. Active sensors require users to hold a device or devices in their hands or wear the device in some way. Passive sensors are completely unobtrusive and mostly include pure vision sensing. Unfortunately, there is no perfect solution and there are strengths and weaknesses with each technology [12].

FIGURE 1: The SixSense system. A user wears colored fiducial markers for fingertip tracking [14].

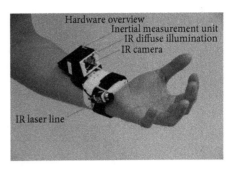

FIGURE 2: Digits hardware. A wrist worn camera that can optically image a user's hand to support hand and finger tracking [15].

2.1. Active Sensors. Active sensors use a variety of different technologies to support the collection and monitoring of 3D gestural data. In many cases, hybrid solutions are used (e.g., combining computer vision with accelerometers and gyroscopes) that combine more than one technology together in an attempt to provide a more robust solution.

2.1.1. Active Finger Tracking. To use the fingers as part of a 3D gestural interface, we need to track their movements and how the various digits move in relation to each other. The most common approach and the one that has the longest history uses some type of instrumented glove that can determine how the fingers bend. Accurate hand models can be created using these gloves and the data used to feed a 3D gesture recognizer. These gloves often do not provide where the hand is in 3D space or its orientation so other tracking systems are needed to complement them. A variety of different technologies are used to perform finger tracking including piezoresistive, fiber optic, and hall-effect sensors. These gloves also vary in the number of sensors they have which determines how detailed the tracking of the fingers can be. In some cases, a glove is worn without any instrumentation at all and used as part of a computer vision-based approach. Dipietro et al. [13] present a thorough survey on data gloves and their applications.

One of the more recent approaches to finger tracking for 3D gestural interfaces is to remove the need to wear an instrumented glove in favor of wearing a vision-based sensor that uses computer vision algorithms to detect the motion of the fingers. One example of such a device is the SixSense system [14]. The SixSense device is worn like a necklace and contains a camera, mirror, and projector. The user also needs to wear colored fiducial markers on the fingertips (see Figure 1). Another approach developed by Kim et al. uses a wrist worn sensing device called Digits [15]. With this system, a wrist worn camera (see Figure 2) is used to optically image the entirety of a user's hand which enables the sampling of fingers. Combined with a kinematic model, Digits can reconstruct the hand and fingers to support 3D gestural interfaces in mobile environments. Similar systems that make use of worn cameras or proximity sensors to track the fingers for 3D gestural interfaces have also been explored [16–19].

Precise finger tracking is not always a necessity in 3D gestural interfaces. It depends on how sophisticated the 3D gestures need to be. In some cases, the data needs only to provide distinguishing information to support different, simpler gestures. This idea has led to utilizing different sensing systems to support course finger tracking. For example, Saponas et al. have experimented with using forearm electromyography to differentiate fingers presses and finger tapping and lifting [20]. A device that contains EMG sensors is attached to a user's wrist and collects muscle data about fingertip movement and can then detect a variety of different finger gestures [21, 22]. A similar technology supports finger tapping that utilizes the body for acoustic transmission. Skinput, developed by Harrison et al. [23], uses a set of sensors worn as an armband to detect acoustical signals transmitted through the skin [18].

2.1.2. Active Hand Tracking. In some cases, simply knowing the position and orientation of the hand is all the data that is required for a 3D gestural interface. Thus, knowing about the fingers provides too much information and the tracking requirements are simplified. Of course, since the fingers are attached to the hand, many finger tracking algorithms will also be able to track the hand. Thus there is often a close relationship between hand and finger tracking. There are two main flavors of hand tracking in active sensing: the first is to attach a sensing device to the hand and the second is to hold the device in the hand.

Attaching a sensing device to the user's hand or hands is a common approach to hand tracking that has been used for many years [5]. There are several tracking technologies that support the attachment of an input device to the user's hand including electromagnetic, inertial/acoustic, ultrasonic, and others [12]. These devices are often placed on the back of the user's hand and provide single point pose information through time. Other approaches include computer vision techniques where users wear a glove. For example, Wang and Popović [24] designed a colored glove with a known pattern to support a nearest-neighbor approach to tracking hands at interactive rates. Other examples include wearing retroreflective fiducial markers coupled with cameras to track a user's hand.

The second approach to active sensor-based hand tracking is to have a user hold the device. This approach has both strengths and weaknesses. The major weakness is that the users have to hold something in their hands which can be problematic if they need to do something else with their hands during user interaction. The major strengths are that the devices users hold often have other functionalities such as buttons, dials, or other device tools which can be used in addition to simply tracking the user's hands. This benefit will become clearer when we discuss 3D gesture recognition and the segmentation problem in Section 3. There have been a variety of different handheld tracking devices that have been used in the virtual reality and 3D user interface communities [25–27].

Recently, the game industry has developed several video game motion controllers that can be used for hand tracking. These devices include the Nintendo Wii Remote (Wiimote), Playstation Move, and Razer Hydra. They are inexpensive and massproduced. Both the Wiimote and the Playstation Move use both vision and inertial sensing technology while the Hydra uses a miniaturized electromagnetic tracking system. The Hydra [28] and the Playstation Move [29] both provide position and orientation information (6 DOF) while the Wiimote is more complicated because it provides certain types of data depending on how it is held [30]. However, all three can be used to support 3D gestural user interfaces.

2.1.3. Active Full Body Tracking.

Active sensing approaches to tracking a user's full body can provide accurate data used in 3D gestural interfaces but can significantly hinder the user since there are many more sensors the user needs to wear compared with simple hand or finger tracking. In most cases, a user wears a body suit that contains the sensors needed to track the various parts of the body. This body suit may contain several electromagnetic trackers, for example, or a set of retroreflective fiducial markers that can be tracked using several strategically placed cameras. These systems are often used for motion capture for video games and movies but can also be used for 3D gestures. In either case, wearing the suit is not ideal in everyday situations given the amount of time required to put it on and take it off and given other less obtrusive solutions.

A more recent approach for supporting 3D gestural interfaces using the full body is to treat the body as an antenna. Cohn et al. first explored this idea for touch gestures [31] and then found that it could be used to detect 3D full body gestures [32, 33]. Using the body as an antenna does not support exact and precise tracking of full body poses but provides enough information to determine how the body is moving in space. Using a simple device either in a backpack or worn on the body, as long as it makes contact with the skin, this approach picks up how the body affects the electromagnetic noise signals present in an indoor environment stemming from power lines, appliances, and devices. This approach shows great promise for 3D full body gesture recognition because it does not require any cameras to be strategically placed in the environment, making the solution more portable.

2.2. Passive Sensors.

In contrast to active sensing, where the user needs to wear a device or other markers, passive sensing makes use of computer vision and other technologies (e.g., light and sound) to provide unobtrusive tracking of the hands, fingers, and full body. In terms of computer vision, 3D gestural interfaces have been constructed using traditional cameras [34–37] (such as a single webcam) as well as depth cameras. The more recent approaches to recognizing 3D gestures make use of depth cameras because they provide more information than a traditional single camera in that they support extraction of a 3D representation of a user, which then enables skeleton tracking of the hands, fingers, and whole body.

There are generally three different technologies used in depth cameras, namely, time of flight, structured light, and stereo vision [38]. Time-of-flight depth cameras (e.g., the depth camera used in the XBox One) determine the depth map of a scene by illuminating it with a beam of pulsed light and calculating the time it takes for the light to be detected on an imaging device after it is reflected off of the scene. Structured-light depth cameras (e.g., Microsoft Kinect) use a known pattern of light, often infrared, that is projected into the scene. An image sensor then is able to capture this deformed light pattern based on the shapes in the scene and finally extracts 3D geometric shapes using the distortion of the projected optical pattern. Finally. stereo based cameras attempt to mimic the human-visual system using two calibrated imaging devices laterally displaced from each. These two cameras capture synchronized images of the scene, and the depth for image pixels is extracted from the binocular disparity. The first two depth camera technologies are becoming more commonplace given their power in extracting 3D depth and low cost.

These different depth camera approaches have been used in a variety of ways to track fingers, hands, and the whole body. For example, Wang et al. used two Sony Eye cameras to detect both the hands and fingers to support a 3D gestural interface for computer aided design [39] while Hackenberg et al. used a time-of-flight camera to support hand and finger tracking for scaling, rotation, and translation tasks [40]. Keskin et al. used structured light-based depth sensing to also track hand and finger poses in real time [41]. Other recent works using depth cameras for hand and finger tracking for 3D gestural interfaces can be found in [42–44]. Similarly, these cameras have also been used to perform whole body tracking that can be used in 3D full body-based gestural interfaces. Most notably is Shotton et al.'s seminal work on using a structured light-based depth camera (i.e., Microsoft Kinect) to track a user's whole body in real time [45]. Other recent approaches that make use of depth cameras to track the whole body can be found in [46–48].

More recent approaches to passive sensing used in 3D gesture recognition are through acoustic and light sensing. In the SoundWave system, a standard speaker and microphone found in most commodity laptops and devices is used to sense user motion [49]. An inaudible tone is sent through the speaker and gets frequency-shifted when it reflects off moving objects like a user's hand. This frequency shift is measured by the microphone to infer various gestures. In the LightWave system, ordinary compact fluorescent light (CFL) bulbs are used as sensors of human proximity [50]. These CFL bulbs are sensitive proximity transducers when illuminated and the approach can detect variations in electromagnetic noise resulting from the distance from the human to the bulb. Since this electromagnetic noise can be sensed from any point in an electrical wiring system, gestures can be sensed using a simple device plugged into any electrical outlet. Both of these sensing strategies are in their early stages and currently do not support recognizing a large quantity of 3D gestures at any time, but their unobtrusiveness and mobility make them a potential powerful approach to body sensing for 3D gestural user interfaces.

3. 3D Gesture Recognition and Analysis

3D gestural interfaces require the computer to understand the finger, hand, or body movements of users to determine what specific gestures are performed and how they can then be translated into actions as part of the interface. The previous section examined the various strategies for continuously gathering the data needed to recognize 3D gestures. Once we have the ability to gather this data, it must be examined in real time using an algorithm that analyzes the data and determines when a gesture has occurred and what class that gesture belongs to. The focus of this section is to examine some of the most recent techniques for real-time recognition of 3D gestures. Several databases such as the ACM and IEEE Digital Libraries as well as Google Scholar were used to survey these techniques and the majority of those chosen reflect the state of the art. In addition, when possible, techniques that were chosen also had experimental evaluations associated with them. Note that other surveys that have explored earlier work on 3D gesture recognition also provide useful examinations of existing techniques [8, 51–53].

Recognizing 3D gestures is dependent on whether the recognizer first needs to determine if a gesture is present. In cases where there is a continuous stream of data and the users do not indicate that they are performing a gesture (e.g., using a passive vision-based sensor), the recognizer needs to determine when a gesture is performed. This process is known as gesture segmentation. If the user can specify when a gesture begins and ends (e.g., pressing a button on a Sony Move or Nintendo Wii controller), then the data is presegmented and gesture classification is all that is required. Thus, the process of 3D gesture recognition is made easier if a user is holding a tracked device, such as a game controller, but it is more obtrusive and does not support more natural interaction where the human body is the only "device" used. We will examine recognition strategies that do and do not make use of segmentation.

There are, in general, two different approaches to recognizing 3D gestures. The first, and most common, is to make use of the variety of different machine learning techniques in order to classify a given 3D gesture as one of a set of possible gestures [54, 55]. Typically, this approach requires extracting important features from the data and using those features as input to a classification algorithm. Additionally, varying amounts of training data are needed to seed and tune the classifier to make it robust to variability and to maximize accuracy. The second approach, which is somewhat underutilized, is to use heuristics-based recognition. With heuristic recognizers, no formal machine learning algorithms are used, but features are still extracted and rules are procedurally coded and tuned to recognize the gestures. This approach often makes sense when a small number of gestures are needed (e.g., typically 5 to 7) for a 3D gestural user interface.

3.1. Machine Learning. Using machine learning algorithms as classifiers for 3D gesture recognition represents the most common approach to developing 3D gesture recognition systems. The typical procedure for using a machine learning-based approach is to

(i) pick a particular machine learning algorithm,

(ii) come up with a set of useful features that help to quantify the different gestures in the gesture set,

(iii) use these features as input to the machine learning algorithm,

(iv) collect training and test data by obtaining many samples from a variety of different users,

(v) train the algorithm on the training data,

(vi) test the 3D gesture recognizer with the test data,

(vii) refine the recognizer with different/additional feature or with more training data if needed.

There are many different questions that need to be answered when choosing a machine learning-based approach to 3D gesture recognition. Two of the most important are what machine learning algorithm should be used and how accurate can the recognizer be. We will examine the former question by presenting some of the more recent machine learning-based strategies and discuss the latter question in Section 4.

3.1.1. Hidden Markov Models. Although Hidden Markov Models (HMMs) should not be considered recent technology, they are still a common approach to 3D gesture recognition. HMMs are ideally suited for 3D gesture recognition when the data needs to be segmented because they encode temporal information so a gesture can first be identified before it is recognized [37]. More formally, an HMM is a double stochastic process that has an underlying Markov chain with a finite number of states and a set of random functions, each associated with one state [56]. HMMs have been used in a variety of different ways with a variety of different sensor technologies. For example, Sako and Kitamura used multistream HMMs for recognizing Japanese sign language [57]. Pang and Ding used traditional HMMs for recognizing dynamic hand gesture movements using kinematic features such as divergence, vorticity, and motion direction from optical flow [58]. They also make use of principal component analysis (PCA) to help with feature dimensionality reduction. Bevilacqua et al. developed a 3D gesture recognizer that combines HMMs with stored reference gestures which helps to reduce the training amount required [59]. The method used only one single example for each gesture and the recognizer was targeted toward music and dance performances. Wan et al. explored better methods to generate efficient observations after feature extraction for HMMs [60]. Sparse coding is used for finding succinct representations of information in comparison to vector quantization for hand gesture recognition. Lee and Cho used hierarchical HMMs to recognize actions using 3D accelerometer data from a smart phone [61]. This hierarchical approach, which breaks up the recognition process into actions and activities, helps to overcome the memory storage and computational power concerns of mobile devices. Other work on 3D gesture recognizers that incorporate HMMs include [62–69].

3.1.2. Conditional Random Fields.

Conditional random fields (CRFs) are considered to be a generalization of HMMs and have seen a lot of use in 3D gesture recognition. Like HMMs they are a probabilistic framework for classifying and segmenting sequential data, however, they make use of conditional probabilities which relax any independence assumptions and also avoid the labeling bias problem [70]. As with HMMs, there have been a variety of different recognition methods that use and extend CRFs. For example, Chung and Yang used depth sensor information as input to a CRF with an adaptive threshold for distinguishing between gestures that are in the gesture set and those that are outside the gestures set [71]. This approach, known as T-CRF, was also used for sign language spotting [72]. Yang and Lee also combined a T-CRF and a conventional CRF in a two-layer hierarchical model for recognition of signs and finger spelling [73]. Other 3D gesture recognizers that make use of CRFs include [39, 74, 75].

Hidden conditional random fields (HCRFs) extend the concept of the CRF by adding hidden state variables into the probabilistic model which is used to capture complex dependencies in the observations while still not requiring any independence assumptions and without having to exactly specify dependencies [76]. In other words, HCRFs enable sharing of information between labels with the hidden variables but cannot model dynamics between them. HCRFs have also been utilized in 3D gesture recognition. For example, Sy et al. were one of the first groups to use HCRFs in both arm and head gesture recognition [77]. Song et al. used HCRFs coupled with temporal smoothing for recognizing body and hand gestures for aircraft signal handling [78]. Liu et al. used HCRFs for detecting hand poses in a continuous stream of data for issuing commands to robots [79]. Other works that incorporate HCRFs in 3D gesture recognizers include [80, 81].

Another variant to CRFs is the latent-dynamic hidden CRF (LDCRF). This approach builds upon the HCRF by providing the ability to model the substructure of a gesture label and learn the dynamics between labels, which helps in recognizing gestures from unsegmented data [82]. As with CRFs and HCRFs, LDCRFs have been examined for use as part of 3D gesture recognition systems and received considerable attention. For example, Elmezain and Al-Hamadi use LDCRFs for recognizing hand gestures in American sign language using a stereo camera [83]. Song et al. improved upon their prior HCRF-based approach [78] to recognizing

both hand and body gestures by incorporating the LDCRF [84]. Zhang et al. also used LDCRFs for hand gesture recognition but chose to use fuzzy-based latent variables to model hand gesture features with a modification to the LDCRF potential functions [85]. Elmezain et al. also used LDCRFs in hand gesture recognition to specifically explore how they compare with CRFs and HCRFs. They examined different window sizes and used location, orientation, and velocity features as input to the recognizers, with LDCRFs performing the best in terms of recognition accuracy [86].

3.1.3. Support Vector Machines.

Support vector machines (SVMs) are another approach that is used in 3D gesture recognition that has received considerable attention in recent years. SVMs are a supervised learning-based probabilistic classification approach that constructs a hyperplane or set of hyperplanes in high dimensional space used to maximize the distance to the nearest training data point in a given class [87]. These hyperplanes are then used for classification of unseen instances. The mappings used by SVMs are designed in terms of a kernel function selected for a particular problem type. Since not all the training data may be linearly separable in a given space, the data can be transformed via nonlinear kernel functions to work with more complex problem domains.

In terms of 3D gestures, there have been many recognition systems that make use of SVMs. For example, recent work has explored different ways of extracting the features used in SVM-based recognition. Huang et al. used SVMs for hand gesture recognition coupled with Gabor filters and PCA for feature extraction [88]. Hsieh et al. took a similar approach for hand gesture recognition but used the discrete Fourier transform (DFT) coupled with the Camshift algorithm and boundary detection to extract the features used as input to the SVM [89]. Hsieh and Liou not only used Haar features for their SVM-based recognizer but also examined the color of the user's face to assist in detecting and extracting the users' hands [90]. Dardas et al. created an SVM-based hand gesture detection and recognition system by using the scale invariance feature transform (SIFT) and vector quantization to create a unified dimensional histogram vector (e.g., bag of words) with K-means clustering. This vector was used as the input to a multiclass SVM [91, 92].

Other ways in which SVMs have been used for 3D gesture recognition have focused on fusing more than one SVM together or using the SVM as part of a larger classification scheme. For example, Chen and Tseng used 3 SVMs from 3 different camera angles to recognize 3D hand gestures by fusing the results from each with majority voting or using recognition performance from each SVM as a weight to the overall gesture classification score [93]. Rashid et al. combined an SVM and HMM together for American sign language where the HMM was used for gestures while the SVM was used for postures. The results from these two classifiers were then combined to provide a more general recognition framework [94]. Song et al. used an SVM for hand shape classification that was combined with a particle filtering estimation framework for 3D body postures and an LDCRF for overall recognition [84]. Other 3D gesture recognizers that utilize SVMs include [80, 95–101].

3.1.4. Decision Trees and Forests. Decision trees and forests are an important machine learning tool for recognizing 3D gestures. With decision trees, each node of the tree makes a decision about some gesture feature. The path traversed from the root to a leaf in a decision tree specifies the expected classification by making a series of decisions on a number of attributes. There are a variety of different decision tree implementations [102]. One of the most common is the C4.5 algorithm [103] which uses the notion of entropy to identify ranking of features to determine which feature is most informative for classification. This strategy is used in the construction of the decision tree. In the context of 3D gesture recognition, there have been several different strategies explored using decision trees. For example, Nisar et al. used standard image-based features such as area, centroid, and convex hull among others as input to a decision tree for sign language recognition [104]. Jeon et al. used decision trees for recognizing hand gestures for controlling home appliances. They added a fuzzy element to their approach, developing a multivariate decision tree learning and classification algorithm. This approach uses fuzzy membership functions to calculate the information gain in the tree [105]. Zhang et al. combined decision trees with multistream HMMs for Chinese sign language recognition. They used a 3-axis accelerometer and electromyography (EMG) sensors as input to the recognizer [106]. Other examples of using decision trees in 3D gesture recognition include [107, 108].

Decision forests are an extension of the decision tree concept. The main difference is that instead of just one tree used in the recognition process, there is an ensemble of randomly trained decision trees that output the class that is the mode of the classes output by the individual trees [115]. Given the power of GPUs, decision forests are becoming prominent for real-time gesture recognition because the recognition algorithm can be easily parallelized with potentially thousands of trees included in the decision forest [116]. This decision forest approach can be considered a framework that has several different parts that can produce a variety of different models. The shape of the decision to use for each node, the type of predictor used in each leaf, the splitting objective used to optimize each node, and the method for injecting randomness into the trees are all choices that need to be made when constructing a decision forest used in recognition. One of the most notable examples of the use of decision forests was Shotton et al.'s work on skeleton tracking for the Microsoft Kinect [45]. This work led researchers to look at decision forests for 3D gesture recognition. For example, Miranda et al. used decision forests for full body gesture recognition using the skeleton information from the Microsoft Kinect depth camera. Key poses from the skeleton data are extracted using a multiclass SVM and fed as input to the decision forest. Keskin et al. used a depth camera to recognize hand poses using decision forests [41]. A realistic 3D hand model with 21 different parts was used to create synthetic depth images for decision forest training. In another

example, Negin et al. used decision forests on kinematic time series for determining the best set of features to use from a depth camera [111]. These features are then fed into a SVM for gesture recognition. Other work that has explored the use of decision forests for 3D gesture recognition include [110, 117, 118].

3.1.5. Other Learning-Based Techniques. There are, of course, a variety of other machine learning-based techniques that have been used for 3D gesture recognition, examples include neural networks [119, 120], template matching [121, 122], finite state machines [121, 123], and using the Adaboost framework [112]. To cover all of them in detail would go beyond the scope of this paper. However, two other 3D gesture recognition algorithms are worth mentioning because they both stem from recognizers used in 2D pen gesture recognition, are fairly easy to implement, and provide good results. These recognizers tend to work for segmented data but can be extended to unsegmented data streams by integrating circular buffers with varying window sizes, depending on the types of 3D gestures in the gesture set and the data collection system. This first one is based on Rubine's linear classifier [124], first published in 1991. This classifier is a linear discriminator where each gesture has an associated linear evaluation function, and each feature has a weight based on the training data. The classifier uses a closed form solution for training which produces optimal classifiers given that the features are normally distributed. However, the approach still produces good results even when there is a drift from normality. This approach also always produces a classification so the false positive rate can be high. However a good rejection rule will remove ambiguous gestures and outliers. The extension of this approach to 3D gestures is relatively straightforward. The features need to be extended to capture 3D information with the main classifier and training algorithm remaining the same. This approach has been used successfully in developing simple, yet effective 3D gesture recognizers [112, 125, 126].

The second approach is based on Wobbrock et al.'s $1 2D recognizer [127]. Kratz and Rohs used the $1 recognizer as a foundation for the $3 recognizer, designed primarily for 3D gestures on mobile devices [113, 128]. In this approach, gesture traces are created using the differences between the current and previous acceleration data values and resampled to have the same number of points as any gesture template. These resampled traces are then corrected for rotational error using the angle between the gesture's first point and its centroid. Average mean square error is then used to determine the given gesture trace's distance to each template in the gesture class library. A heuristic scoring mechanism is used to help reject false positives. Note that a similar approach to constructing a 3D gesture recognizer was done by Li, who adapted the Protractor 2D gesture recognizer [129] and extended it to work with accelerometers and gyroscope data [114, 130].

3.2. Heuristic Recognizers. Heuristic 3D gesture recognizers make sense when there are a small number of easily identifiable gestures in an interface. The advantage of heuristic-based approaches is that no training data is needed and they are fairly easy to implement. For example, Williamson et al. [131] developed a heuristic recognition method using skeleton data from a Microsoft Kinect focused on jumping, crouching, and turning. An example of a heuristic recognizer for jumping would be to assume a jump was made when the head is at a certain height above its normal position, defined as

$$J = H_y - \overline{H}_y > C, \tag{1}$$

where J is true or false based on if a jump has occurred, H_y is the height of the head position, $\overline{H}_y$ is the calibrated normal height of the head position with the user standing, and C is some constant. C would then be set to a height that a person would only get to by jumping from the ground. Such recognition is very specialized but simple and explainable and can determine in an instant whether a jump has occurred.

Recent work has shown that heuristic 3D recognition works well with devices that primarily make use of accelerometers and/or gyroscopes (e.g., the Nintendo Wiimote, smart phones). For example, One Man Band used a Wiimote to simulate the movements necessary to control the rhythm and pitch of several musical instruments [132]. RealDance explored spatial 3D interaction for dance-based gaming and instruction [133]. By wearing Wiimotes on the wrists and ankles, players followed an on-screen avatar's choreography and had their movements evaluated on the basis of correctness and timing. These explorations led to several heuristic recognition schemes for devices which use accelerometers and gyroscopes.

Poses and Underway Intervals. A pose is a length of time during which the device is not changing position. Poses can be useful for identifying held positions in dance, during games, or possibly even in yoga. An underway interval is a length of time during which the device is moving but not accelerating. Underway intervals can help identify smooth movements and differentiate between, say, strumming on a guitar and beating on a drum.

Because neither poses nor underway intervals have an acceleration component, they cannot be differentiated using accelerometer data alone. To differentiate the two, a gyroscope can provide a frame of reference to identify whether the device has velocity. Alternatively, context can be used, such as tracking acceleration over time to determine whether the device is moving or stopped.

Poses and underway intervals have three components. First, the time span is the duration in which the user maintains a pose or an underway interval. Second, the orientation of gravity from the acceleration vector helps verify that the user is holding the device at the intended orientation. Of course, unless a gyroscope is used, the device's yaw cannot be reliably detected. Third, the allowed variance is the threshold value for the amount of acceleration allowed in the heuristic before rejecting the pose or underway interval. For example, in RealDance [133], poses were important for recognizing certain dance movements. For a pose, the user was supposed to stand still in a specific posture beginning at time t_0 and lasting until $t_0 + N$, where N is a specified number of beats.

A player's score could be represented as the percentage of the time interval during which the user successfully maintained the correct posture.

Impulse Motions. An impulse motion is characterized by a rapid change in acceleration, easily measured by an accelerometer. A good example is a tennis or golf club swing in which the device motion accelerates through an arc or a punching motion, which contains a unidirectional acceleration. An impulse motion has two components, which designers can tune for their use. First, the time span of the impulse motion specifies the window over which the impulse is occurring. Shorter time spans increase the interaction speed, but larger time spans are more easily separable from background jitter. The second component is the maximum magnitude reached. This is the acceleration bound that must be reached during the time span in order for the device to recognize the impulse motion.

Impulse motions can also be characterized by their direction. The acceleration into a punch is essentially a straight impulse motion, a tennis swing has an angular acceleration component, and a golf swing has both angular acceleration and even increasing acceleration during the follow-through when the elbow bends. All three of these impulse motions, however, are indistinguishable to an acceleration only device, which does not easily sense these orientation changes. For example, the punch has an acceleration vector along a single axis, as does the tennis swing as it roughly changes its orientation as the swing progresses. These motions can be differentiated by using a gyroscope as part of the device or by assuming that orientation does not change. As an example, RealDance used impulse motions to identify punches. A punch was characterized by a rapid deceleration occurring when the arm was fully extended. In a rhythm-based game environment, this instant should line up with a strong beat in the music. An impulse motion was scored by considering a one-beat interval centered on the expected beat.

Impact Events. An impact event is an immediate halt to the device due to a collision, characterized by an easily identifiable acceleration bursting across all three dimensions. Examples of this event include the user tapping the device on a table or dropping it so it hits the floor. To identify an impact event, the change in acceleration (jerk) vector is required for each pair of adjacent time samples. Here, t_k corresponds to the largest magnitude of jerk:

$$t_k = \arg\max_T \left\| \vec{a}_t - \vec{a}_{t-1} \right\|, \tag{2}$$

where $\vec{a}$ is the acceleration vector at time t. If the magnitude is larger than a threshold value, an impact occurs. As an example, RealDance used impact motions to identify stomps. If the interval surrounding a dance move had a maximal jerk value less than a threshold, no impact occurred. One Man Band also used impact events to identify when a Nintendo Nunchuk controller and Wiimote collided, which is how users played hand cymbals.

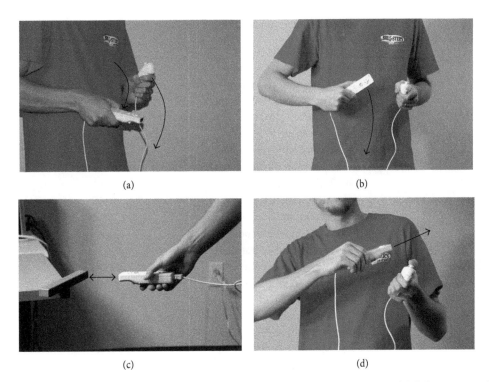

FIGURE 3: One Man Band differentiated between multiple Wiimote gestures using mostly simple modal differentiations for (a) drums, (b) guitar, (c) violin, and (d) theremin. To the player, changing instruments only required orienting the Wiimote to match how an instrument would be played.

Modal Differentiation. Herustics can also be used as a form of simple segmentation to support the recognition of different gestures. For example, in One Man Band [132], the multi-instrument musical interface (MIMI) differentiated between five different instruments by implementing modal differences based on a Wiimote's orientation. Figure 3 shows four of these. If the user held the Wiimote on its side and to the left, as if playing a guitar, the application interpreted impulse motions as strumming motions. If the user held the Wiimote to the left, as if playing a violin, the application interpreted the impulse motions as violin sounds. To achieve this, the MIMI's modal-differentiation approach used a normalization step on the accelerometer data to identify the most prominent orientation:

$$\vec{a}_{norm} = \frac{\vec{a}}{\|\vec{a}\|} \tag{3}$$

followed by two exponential smoothing functions

$$\vec{a}_{current} = \alpha \vec{a}_i + (1 - \alpha)\, \vec{a}_{i-1}. \tag{4}$$

The first function, with an $\alpha = 0.1$, removed jitter and identified drumming and strumming motions. The second function, with an $\alpha = 0.5$, removed jitter and identified short, sharp gestures such as violin strokes.

4. Experimentation and Accuracy

As we have seen in the last section, there have been a variety of different approaches for building 3D gesture recognition

systems for use in 3D gestural interfaces. In this section, we focus on understanding how well these approaches work in terms of recognition accuracy and the number of gestures that can be recognized. These two metrics help to provide researchers and developers guidance on what strategies work best. As with Section 3, we do not aim to be an exhaustive reference on the experiments that have been conducted on 3D gesture recognition accuracy. Rather, we present a representative sample that highlights the effectiveness of different 3D gesture recognition strategies.

A summary of the experiments and accuracy of various 3D gesture recognition systems is shown in Table 1. This table shows the authors of the work, the recognition approach or strategy, the number of recognized gestures, and the highest accuracy level reported. As can be seen in the table, there have been a variety of different methods that have been proposed and most of the results reported are able to achieve over 90% accuracy. However, the number of gestures in the gesture sets used in the experiments vary significantly. The number of gestures in the gesture set is often not indicative of performance when comparing techniques. In some cases, postures were used instead of more complex gestures and in some cases, more complex activities were recognized. For example, Lee and Cho recognized only 3 gestures, but these are classified as activities that included shopping, taking a bus, and moving by walking [61]. The gestures used in these actions are more complex than, for example, finger spelling. In other cases, segmentation was not done as part of the recognition process. For example, Hoffman et al. were able to recognize 25 gestures at 99% accuracy, but the data was

TABLE 1: A table summarizing different 3D gesture recognition approaches, the size of the gesture set, and the stated recognition accuracy.

Author	Recognition approach	Number of gestures	Accuracy
Pang and Ding [58]	HMMs with kinematic features	12	91.2%
Wan et al. [60]	HMMs with sparse coding	4	94.2%
Lee and Cho [61]	Hierarchical HMMs	3	Approx. 80.0%
Whitehead and Fox [68]	Standard HMMs	7	91.4%
Nguyen et al. [66]	Two-stage HMMs	10	95.3%
Chen et al. [63]	HMMs with Fourier descriptors	20	93.5%
Pylvänäinen [67]	HMMs without rotation data	10	99.76%
Chung and Yang [71]	Threshold CRF	12	91.9%
Yang et al. [72]	Two-layer CRF	48	93.5%
Yang and Lee [73]	HCRF with BoostMap embedding	24	87.3%
Song et al. [78]	HCRF with temporal smoothing	10	93.7%
Liu and Jia [80]	HCRF with manifold learning	10	97.8%
Elmezain and Al-Hamadi [83]	LDCRF with depth camera	36	96.1%
Song et al. [84]	LDCRF with filtering framework	24	75.4%
Zhang et al. [85]	Fuzzy LDCRF	5	91.8%
Huang et al. [88]	SVM with Gabor filters	11	95.2%
Hsieh et al. [89]	SVM with Fourier descriptors	5	93.4%
Hsieh and Liou [90]	SVM with Haar features	4	95.6%
Dardas and Georganas [92]	SVM with bag of words	10	96.2%
Chen and Tseng [93]	Fusing multiple SVMs	3	93.3%
Rashid et al. [94]	Combining SVM with HMM	18	98.0%
Yun and Peng [101]	Hu moments with SVM	3	96.2%
Ren and Zhang [99]	SVM with min enclosing ball	10	92.9%
Wu et al. [100]	Frame-based descriptor with SVM	12	95.2%
He et al. [96]	SVM with Wavelet and FFT	17	87.4%
Nisar et al. [104]	Decision trees	26	95.0%
Jeon et al. [105]	Multivariate fuzzy decision trees	10	90.6%
Zhang et al. [106]	Decision trees fused with HMMs	72	96.3%
Fang et al. [107]	Hierarchical Decision trees	14	91.6%
Miranda et al. [109]	Decision forest with key pose learning	10	91.5%
Keskin et al. [41]	Decision forest with SVM	10	99.9%
Keskin et al. [110]	Shape classification forest	24	97.8%
Negin et al. [111]	Feature selection with decision forest	10	98.0%
Ellis et al. [74]	Logistic regression	16	95.9%
Hoffman et al. [112]	Linear classifier	25	99.0%
Kratz and Rohs [113]	$3 gesture recognizer	10	80.0%
Kratz and Rohs [114]	Protractor 3D (rotation invariance)	11	Approx. 91.0%

presegmented using button presses to indicate the start and stop of a gesture [112].

It is often difficult to compare 3D gesture recognition techniques for a variety of reasons including the use of different data sets, parameters, and number of gestures. However, there have been several, more inclusive experiments that have focused on examining several different recognizers in one piece of research. For example, Kelly et al. compared their gesture threshold HMM with HMMs, transition HMMs, CRFs, HCRFs, and LDCRFs [64] and found their approach to be superior, achieving over 97% accuracy on 8 dynamic sign language gestures. Wu et al. compared their frame-based descriptor and multiclass SVM to dynamic time warping, a naive Bayes classifier, C4.5 decision trees, and HMMs and showed their approach has better performance compared to the other methods for both user dependent (95.2%) and user independent cases (89.3%) for 12 gestures [100]. Lech et al. compared a variety of different recognition systems for building a sound mixing gestural interface [118]. They compared the nearest neighbor algorithm with nested generalization, naive Bayes, C4.5 decision trees, random trees, decision forests, neural networks, and SVMs on a set of four gestures and found the SVM to be the best approach for their application. Finally, Cheema et al. compared a linear classifier, decision trees, Bayesian networks, SVM, and AdaBoost using decision trees as weak learners on a gesture set containing 25

FIGURE 4: A user performing a gesture in a video game application [9].

gestures [125]. They found that the linear classifier performed the best under different conditions which is interesting given its simplicity compared to the other 3D gesture recognition methods. However, SVM and AdaBoost also performed well under certain user independent recognition conditions when using more training samples per gesture.

Experiments on 3D gesture recognition systems have also been carried out in terms of how they can be used as 3D gestural user interfaces and there have been a variety of different application domains explored [134]. Entertainment and video games are just one example of an application domain where 3D gestural interfaces are becoming more common. This trend is evident since all major video game consoles and the PC support devices that capture 3D motion from a user. In other cases, video games are being used as the research platform for 3D gesture recognition. Figure 4 shows an example of using a video game to explore what the best gesture set should be for a first person navigation game [9], while Figure 5 shows screenshots of the video game used in Cheema et al.'s 3D gesture recognition study [125]. Other 3D gesture recognition research that has focused on the entertainment and video game domain include [132, 135–137].

Medical applications and use in operating rooms are an area where 3D gestures have been explored. Using passive sensing enables the surgeon or doctor to use gestures to gather information about a patient on a computer while still maintaining a sterile environment [138, 139]. 3D gesture recognition has also been explored with robotic applications in the human robot interaction field. For example, Pfeil et al. (shown in Figure 6) used 3D gestures to control unmanned aerial vehicles (UAVs) [140]. They developed and evaluated several 3D gestural metaphors for teleoperating the robot. Other examples of 3D gesture recognition technology used in human robot interaction applications include [141–143]. Other application areas include training and interfacing with vehicles. Williamson et al. developed a full body gestural interface for dismounted soldier training [29] while Riener explored how 3D gestures could be used to control various components of automotive vehicles [144]. Finally, 3D gesture recognition has recently been explored in consumer electronics, specifically for control of large screen smart TVs [145, 146].

5. Future Research Trends

Although there have been great strides in 3D gestural user interfaces from unobtrusive sensing technologies to advanced machine learning algorithms that are capable of robustly recognizing large gesture sets, there still remains a significant amount of future research that needs to be done to make 3D gestural interaction truly robust, provide compelling user experiences, and support interfaces that are natural and seamless to users. In this section, we highlight three areas that need to be explored further to significantly advance 3D gestural interaction.

5.1. Customized 3D Gesture Recognition. Although there has been some work on customizable 3D gestural interfaces [147], customization is still an open problem. Customization can take many forms and in this case, we mean the ability for users to determine the best gestures for themselves for a particular application. Users should be able to define the 3D gestures they want to perform for a given task in an application. This type of customization goes one step further than having user-dependent 3D gesture recognizers (although this is still a challenging problem in cases where many people are using the interface).

There are several problems that need to be addressed to support customized 3D gestural interaction. First, how do users specify what gestures they want to perform for a given task. Second, once these gestures are specified, if using machine learning, how do we get enough data to train the classification algorithms without burdening the user? Ideally, the user should only need to specify a gesture just once. This means that synthetic data needs to be generated based on user profiles or more sophisticated learning algorithms that deal with small training set sized are required. Third, how do we deal with user defined gestures that are very similar to each other? This problem occurs frequently in all kinds of gestures recognition, but the difference in this case is that the users are specifying the 3D gesture and we want them to use whatever gesture they come up with. These are all problems that need to be solved in order to support truly customized 3D gestural interaction.

5.2. Latency. 3D gesture recognition needs to be both fast and accurate to make 3D gestural user interfaces usable and compelling. In fact, the recognition component needs to be somewhat faster than real time because responses based on 3D gestures need to occur at the moment a user finishes a gesture. Thus, the gesture needs to be recognized a little bit before the user finishes it. This speed requirement makes latency an important problem that needs to be addressed to ensure fluid and natural user experiences. In addition, as sensors get better at acquiring a user's position, orientation, and motion in space, the amount of data that must be processed will increase making the latency issue a continuing problem.

Latency can be broken up into computational latency and observational latency [74, 148]. Computational latency is the delay that is based on the amount of computation needed

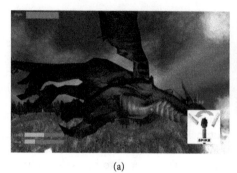

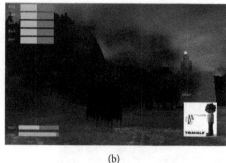

(a)   (b)

FIGURE 5: Screenshots of a video game used to explore different 3D gesture recognition algorithms [125].

FIGURE 6: A user controlling a UAV using a 3D gesture [140].

to recognize 3D gestures. Observational latency is the delay based on the minimum amount of data that needs to be observed to recognize a 3D gesture. Both latencies present an important area in terms of how to minimize and mitigate them. Parallel processing can play an important role in reducing computational latency while better understanding the kinematics of the human body is one of many possible ways to assist in reducing observational latency.

5.3. Using Context. Making use of all available information for recognizing 3D gestures in a 3D gestural interface makes intuitive sense because it can assist the recognizer in several ways. First, it can help to reduce the amount of possible 3D gestures that could be recognized at any one time and it can assist in improving the recognition accuracy. Using context is certainly an area that has received considerable attention [149–151], especially in activity recognition [152–154], but there are several questions that need to be answered specifically related to context in 3D gestural interfaces. First, what type of context can be extracted that is most useful to improve recognition. As an example, in a video game, the current state of the player and the surrounding environment could provide useful information to trivially reject certain gestures that do not make sense in a given situation. Second, how can context be directly integrated into 3D gesture

recognizers? As we have seen, there are a variety of different approaches to recognize 3D gestures, yet it is unclear how context can be best used in all of these algorithms. Finally, what performance benefits do we gain making use of context both in terms of accuracy and in latency reduction when compared to recognizers that do not make use of context? It is important to know how much more of an improvement we can get in accuracy and latency minimization so we can determine what the best approaches are for a given application.

5.4. Ecological Validity. Perhaps, one of the most important research challenges with 3D gestural interfaces is determining exactly how accurate the 3D gesture recognizer is that makes up the 3D gestural interface from a usability standpoint. In other words, how accurate is the 3D gestural interface when used in its intended setting. Currently most studies that explore a recognizer's accuracy are constrained experiments intended to evaluate the recognizer by having users perform each available gesture *n* number of times. As seen in Section 4, researchers have been able to get very high accuracy rates. However, we have also seen from Cheema et al. [125, 126] that accuracy can be severely reduced when tests are conducted in more realistic, ecologically valid scenarios. Even in the case of Cheema et al.'s work, their experiments do not come close to the ecological validity required to truly test a 3D gestural interface. Thus, these studies act more as an upper bound on gesture recognition performance than a true indicator of the recognition accuracy in everyday settings.

The open research problem here is how to design an ecologically valid experiment to test a 3D gestural interface. To illustrate the challenge, consider a 3D gestural interface for a video game. To adequately test the 3D gesture recognizer, we need to evaluate how accurately the recognizer can handle each gesture in the gesture set. However, to be ecologically valid, the game player should be able to use any gesture that makes sense at any given time. Thus, we do not know what gestures the user will be doing at any given time nor if they will provide enough test samples to adequately test the recognizer. That presents a difficult challenge. One option is to try to design the game so that each gesture is needed for an integral multiple of times, but this may not be the best user experience, if, for example, a user likes one particular gesture over another. Another option is to have many users test the system, video tape the sessions, and then watch them to determine which gestures they appear to perform. With enough users, the number of gestures in the test set would approach the appropriate amount. Neither of these two options seem ideal and more research is needed to determine the best way to deal with the ecological validity issue.

6. Conclusion

3D gestural interaction represents a powerful and natural method of communication between humans and computers. The ability to use 3D gestures in a computer application requires a method to capture 3D position, orientation, and/or motion data through sensing technology. 3D gesture recognizers then need to be developed to detect specific pattern in the data from a set of known patterns. These 3D gesture recognizers can be heuristic-based, where a set of rules are encoded based on observation of the types of gestures needed in an application or through machine learning techniques where classifiers are trained using training data. These recognizers must then be evaluated to determine their accuracy and robustness.

In this paper, we have examined 3D gesture interaction research by exploring recent trends in these areas including sensing, recognition, and experimentation. These trends show that there are both strengths and weaknesses with the current state of 3D gesture interface technology. Strengths include powerful sensing technologies that can capture data from a user's whole body unobtrusively as well as new sensing technology directions that go beyond computer vision-based approaches. In addition, we are seeing better and faster 3D gesture recognition algorithms (that can make use of parallel processing) that can reach high recognition accuracies with reasonably sized gesture sets. However, 3D gestural interaction still suffers from several weaknesses. One of the most important is that although accuracy reported for various 3D gesture recognizers is high, these results are often considered a theoretical upper bound given that the accuracy will often degrade in more ecologically valid settings. Performing accuracy tests in ecologically valid settings is also a challenge making it difficult to determine the best ways to improve 3D gesture recognition technology. In addition, latency is still a concern in that delays between a user's gesture and the intended response can hamper the overall user experience. In spite of these issues, the field of 3D gesture interfaces is showing maturity as evidenced by 3D gestural interfaces moving into the commercial sector and becoming more commonplace. However, it is clear that there is still work that needs to be done to make 3D gesture interfaces truly mainstream as a significant part of human computer interfaces.

References

[1] I. E. Sutherland, "The ultimate display," in *Proceedings of the IFIP Congress*, pp. 506–508, 1965.

[2] A. van Dam, "Post-WIMP User Interfaces," *Communications of the ACM*, vol. 40, no. 2, pp. 63–67, 1997.

[3] P. Kortum, "HCI beyond the GUI: design for haptic, speech, olfactory, and other nontraditional interfaces," in *Interactive Technologies*, Elsevier Science, New York, NY, USA, 2008.

[4] D. Wigdor and D. Wixon, *Brave NUI World: Designing Natural User Interfaces for Touch and Gesture*, Elsevier Science, New York, NY, USA, 2011.

[5] D. A. Bowman, E. Kruijff, J. J. LaViola Jr., and I. Poupyrev, "An introduction to 3-D user interface design," *Presence*, vol. 10, no. 1, pp. 96–108, 2001.

[6] S. Zhai, P. O. Kristensson, C. Appert, T. H. Andersen, and X. Cao, "Foundational issues in touch-surface stroke gesture design-an integrative review," *Foundations and Trends in Human-Computer Interaction*, vol. 5, no. 2, pp. 97–205, 2012.

[7] J. J. LaViola Jr., "A survey of hand posture and gesture recognition techniques and technology," Technical Report, Brown University, Providence, RI, USA, 1999.

[8] S. Mitra and T. Acharya, "Gesture recognition: a survey," *IEEE Transactions on Systems, Man and Cybernetics C*, vol. 37, no. 3, pp. 311–324, 2007.

[9] J. Norton, C. A. Wingrave, and J. J. LaViola Jr., "Exploring strategies and guidelines for developing full body video game interfaces," in *Proceedings of the 5th International Conference on the Foundations of Digital Games (FDG '10)*, pp. 155–162, ACM, New York, NY, USA, June 2010.

[10] J. K. Aggarwal and M. S. Ryoo, "Human activity analysis: a review," *ACM Computing Surveys*, vol. 43, no. 3, p. 16, 2011.

[11] R. Poppe, "A survey on vision-based human action recognition," *Image and Vision Computing*, vol. 28, no. 6, pp. 976–990, 2010.

[12] G. Welch and E. Foxlin, "Motion tracking: no silver bullet, but a respectable arsenal," *IEEE Computer Graphics and Applications*, vol. 22, no. 6, pp. 24–38, 2002.

[13] L. Dipietro, A. M. Sabatini, and P. Dario, "A survey of glove-based systems and their applications," *IEEE Transactions on Systems, Man and Cybernetics C*, vol. 38, no. 4, pp. 461–482, 2008.

[14] P. Mistry and P. Maes, "SixthSense: a wearable gestural interface," in *Proceedings of the ACM SIGGRAPH ASIA 2009 Sketches (SIGGRAPH ASIA '09)*, p. 11:1, ACM, New York, NY, USA, December 2009.

[15] D. Kim, O. Hilliges, S. Izadi et al., "Digits: freehand 3d interactions anywhere using a wrist-worn gloveless sensor," in *Proceedings of the 25th annual ACM symposium on User interface software and technology (UIST '12)*, pp. 167–176, ACM, New York, NY, USA, 2012.

[16] G. Bailly, J. Muller, M. Rohs, D. Wigdor, and S. Kratz, "Shoesense: a new perspective on gestural interaction and wearable applications," in *Proceedings of the SIGCHI Conference on Human Factors in Computing Systems (CHI '12)*, pp. 1239–1248, ACM, New York, NY, USA, 2012.

[17] T. Starner, J. Auxier, D. Ashbrook, and M. Gandy, "Gesture Pendant: a self-illuminating, wearable, infrared computer vision system for home automation control and medical monitoring," in *Proceedings of the 4th International Symposium on Wearable Computers*, pp. 87–94, October 2000.

[18] C. Harrison, H. Benko, and A. D. Wilson, "OmniTouch: wearable multitouch interaction everywhere," in *Proceedings of the 24th Annual ACM Symposium on User Interface Software and Technology (UIST '11)*, pp. 441–450, ACM, New York, NY, USA, October 2011.

[19] J. Kim, J. He, K. Lyons, and T. Starner, "The Gesture Watch: a wireless contact-free Gesture based wrist interface," in *Proceedings of the 11th IEEE International Symposium on Wearable*

Computers (ISWC '07), pp. 15–22, IEEE Computer Society, Washington, DC, USA, October 2007.

[20] T. S. Saponas, D. S. Tan, D. Morris, and R. Balakrishnan, "Demonstrating the feasibility of using forearm electromyography for muscle-computer interfaces," in *Proceedings of the 26th Annual CHI Conference on Human Factors in Computing Systems (CHI '08)*, pp. 515–524, ACM, New York, NY, USA, April 2008.

[21] T. S. Saponas, D. S. Tan, D. Morris, R. Balakrishnan, J. Turner, and J. A. Landay, "Enabling always-available input with muscle-computer interfaces," in *Proceedings of the 22nd Annual ACM Symposium on User Interface Software and Technology (UIST '09)*, pp. 167–176, ACM, New York, NY, USA, October 2009.

[22] T. S. Saponas, D. S. Tan, D. Morris, J. Turner, and J. A. Landay, "Making muscle-computer interfaces more practical," in *Proceedings of the 28th Annual CHI Conference on Human Factors in Computing Systems (CHI '10)*, pp. 851–854, ACM, New York, NY, USA, April 2010.

[23] C. Harrison, D. Tan, and D. Morris, "Skinput: appropriating the body as an input surface," in *Proceedings of the 28th Annual CHI Conference on Human Factors in Computing Systems (CHI '10)*, pp. 453–462, ACM, New York, NY, USA, April 2010.

[24] R. Y. Wang and J. Popović, "Real-time hand-tracking with a color glove," *ACM Transactions on Graphics*, vol. 28, no. 3, p. 63, 2009.

[25] D. F. Keefe, D. A. Feliz, T. Moscovich, D. H. Laidlaw, and J. LaViola J.J., "CavePainting: a fully immersive 3D artistic medium and interactive experience," in *Proceedings of the 2001 symposium on Interactive 3D graphics (I3D '01)*, pp. 85–93, ACM, New York, NY, USA, March 2001.

[26] C. Ware and D. R. Jessome, "Using the BAT: a six-dimensional mouse for object placement," *IEEE Computer Graphics and Applications*, vol. 8, no. 6, pp. 65–70, 1988.

[27] R. C. Zeleznik, J. J. La Viola Jr., D. Acevedo Feliz, and D. F. Keefe, "Pop through button devices for VE navigation and interaction," in *Proceedings of the IEEE Virtual Reality 2002*, pp. 127–134, March 2002.

[28] A. Basu, C. Saupe, E. Refour, A. Raij, and K. Johnsen, "Immersive 3dui on one dollar a day," in *Proceedings of the IEEE Symposium on 3D User Interfaces (3DUI '12)*, pp. 97–100, 2012.

[29] B. Williamson, C. Wingrave, and J. LaViola, "Full body locomotion with video game motion controllers," in *Human Walking in Virtual Environments*, F. Steinicke, Y. Visell, J. Campos, and A. Lecuyer, Eds., pp. 351–376, Springer, New York, NY, USA, 2013.

[30] C. A. Wingrave, B. Williamson, P. D. Varcholik et al., "The wiimote and beyond: spatially convenient devices for 3D user interfaces," *IEEE Computer Graphics and Applications*, vol. 30, no. 2, pp. 71–85, 2010.

[31] G. Cohn, D. Morris, S. N. Patel, and D. S. Tan, "Your noise is my command: sensing gestures using the body as an antenna," in *Proceedings of the 29th Annual SIGCHI Conference on Human Factors in Computing Systems (CHI '11)*, pp. 791–800, ACM, New York, NY, USA, May 2011.

[32] G. Cohn, S. Gupta, T.-J. Lee et al., "An ultra-low-power human body motion sensor using static electric field sensing," in *Proceedings of the 2012 ACM Conference on Ubiquitous Computing (UbiComp '12)*, pp. 99–102, ACM, New York, NY, USA, 2012.

[33] G. Cohn, D. Morris, S. Patel, and D. Tan, "Humantenna: using the body as an antenna for real-time whole-body interaction," in *Proceedings of the 2012 ACM annual conference on Human Factors in Computing Systems (CHI '12)*, pp. 1901–1910, ACM, New York, NY, USA, 2012.

[34] J. H. Hammer and J. Beyerer, "Robust hand tracking in realtime using a single head-mounted rgb camera," in *Human-Computer Interaction. Interaction Modalities and Techniques*, M. Kurosu, Ed., vol. 8007 of *Lecture Notes in Computer Science*, pp. 252–261, Springer, Berlin, Germany, 2013.

[35] S.-H. Choi, J.-H. Han, and J.-H. Kim, "3D-position estimation for hand gesture interface using a single camera," in *Human-Computer Interaction. Interaction Techniques and Environments*, J. A. Jacko, Ed., vol. 6762 of *Lecture Notes in Computer Science*, pp. 231–237, Springer, Berlin, Germany, 2011.

[36] S. Rodriguez, A. Picon, and A. Villodas, "Robust vision-based hand tracking using single camera for ubiquitous 3D gesture interaction," in *Proceedings of the IEEE Symposium on 3D User Interfaces 2010 (3DUI '10)*, pp. 135–136, March 2010.

[37] T. Starner, J. Weaver, and A. Pentland, "Real-time american sign language recognition using desk and wearable computer based video," *IEEE Transactions on Pattern Analysis and Machine Intelligence*, vol. 20, no. 12, pp. 1371–1375, 1998.

[38] A. K. Bhowmik, "3D computer vision," in *SID Seminar Lecture Notes, M9*, 2012.

[39] R. Y. Wang, S. Paris, and J. Popović, "6D hands: markerless hand tracking for computer aided design," in *Proceedings of the 24th Annual ACM Symposium on User Interface Software and Technology (UIST '11)*, pp. 549–557, ACM, New York, NY, USA, October 2011.

[40] G. Hackenberg, R. McCall, and W. Broll, "Lightweight palm and finger tracking for real-time 3D gesture control," in *Proceedings of the 18th IEEE Virtual Reality Conference (VR '11)*, pp. 19–26, March 2011.

[41] C. Keskin, F. Kıraç, Y. E. Kara, and L. Akarun, "Real time hand pose estimation using depth sensors," in *Consumer Depth Cameras for Computer Vision, Advances in Computer Vision and Pattern Recognition*, A. Fossati, J. Gall, H. Grabner, X. Ren, and K. Konolige, Eds., pp. 119–137, Springer, 2013.

[42] Z. Feng, S. Xu, X. Zhang, L. Jin, Z. Ye, and W. Yang, "Real-time fingertip tracking and detection using kinect depth sensor for a new writing-in-the air system," in *Proceedings of the 4th International Conference on Internet Multimedia Computing and Service (ICIMCS '12)*, pp. 70–74, ACM, New York, NY, USA, 2012.

[43] H. Liang, J. Yuan, and D. Thalmann, "3D fingertip and palm tracking in depth image sequences," in *Proceedings of the 20th ACM international conference on Multimedia (MM '12)*, pp. 785–788, ACM, New York, NY, USA, 2012.

[44] Z. Ren, J. Yuan, and Z. Zhang, "Robust hand gesture recognition based on finger-earth mover's distance with a commodity depth camera," in *Proceedings of the 19th ACM International Conference on Multimedia ACM Multimedia (MM '11)*, pp. 1093–1096, ACM, New York, NY, USA, December 2011.

[45] J. Shotton, T. Sharp, A. Kipman et al., "Real-time human pose recognition in parts from single depth images," *Communications of the ACM*, vol. 56, no. 1, pp. 116–124, 2011.

[46] V. Ganapathi, C. Plagemann, D. Koller, and S. Thrun, "Real time motion capture using a single time-of-flight camera," in *Proceedings of the IEEE Computer Society Conference on Computer Vision and Pattern Recognition (CVPR '10)*, pp. 755–762, June 2010.

[47] L. A. Schwarz, A. Mkhitaryan, D. Mateus, and N. Navab, "Human skeleton tracking from depth data using geodesic distances and optical flow," *Image and Vision Computing*, vol. 30, no. 3, pp. 217–226, 2012.

[48] X. Wei, P. Zhang, and J. Chai, "Accurate realtime full-body motion capture using a single depth camera," *ACM Transactions on Graphics*, vol. 31, no. 6, pp. 188:1–188:12, 2012.

[49] S. Gupta, D. Morris, S. Patel, and D. Tan, "Soundwave: using the doppler effect to sense gestures," in *Proceedings of the 2012 ACM annual conference on Human Factors in Computing Systems (CHI '12)*, pp. 1911–1914, ACM, New York, NY, USA, 2012.

[50] S. Gupta, K. Chen, M. S. Reynolds, and S. N. Patel, "LightWave: using compact fluorescent lights as sensors," in *Proceedings of the 13th International Conference on Ubiquitous Computing (UbiComp '11)*, pp. 65–74, ACM, New York, NY, USA, September 2011.

[51] J. Suarez and R. R. Murphy, "Hand gesture recognition with depth images: a review," in *Proceedings of the 21st IEEE International Symposium on Robot and Human Interactive Communication (RO-MAN '12)*, pp. 411–417, IEEE, 2012.

[52] A. D. Wilson, "Sensor- and recognition-based input for interaction," in *The Human Computer Interaction Handbook*, chapter 7, pp. 133–156, 2012.

[53] Y. Wu and T. S. Huang, "Vision-based gesture recognition: a review," in *Gesture-Based Communication in Human-Computer Interaction*, A. Braffort, R. Gherbi, S. Gibet, D. Teil, and J. Richardson, Eds., vol. 1739 of *Lecture Notes in Computer Science*, pp. 103–115, Springer, Berlin, Germany, 1999.

[54] C. M. Bishop, *Pattern Recognition and Machine Learning (Information Science and Statistics)*, Springer, New York, NY, USA, 2006.

[55] R. O. Duda, P. E. Hart, and D. G. Stork, *Pattern Classification (2nd Edition)*, Wiley-Interscience, New York, NY, USA, 2000.

[56] L. R. Rabiner, "Tutorial on hidden markov models and selected applications in speech recognition," *Proceedings of the IEEE*, vol. 77, no. 2, pp. 257–286, 1989.

[57] S. Sako and T. Kitamura, "Subunit modeling for japanese sign language recognition based on phonetically depend multistream hidden markov models," in *Universal Access in Human-Computer Interaction. Design Methods, Tools, and Interaction Techniques for EInclusion*, C. Stephanidis and M. Antona, Eds., vol. 8009 of *Lecture Notes in Computer Science*, pp. 548–555, Springer, Berlin, Germany, 2013.

[58] H. Pang and Y. Ding, "Dynamic hand gesture recognition using kinematic features based on hidden markov model," in *Proceedings of the 2nd International Conference on Green Communications and Networks (GCN '12)*, Y. Yang and M. Ma, Eds., vol. 5–227 of *Lecture Notes in Electrical Engineering*, pp. 255–262, Springer, Berlin, Germany, 2013.

[59] F. Bevilacqua, B. Zamborlin, A. Sypniewski, N. Schnell, F. Guédy, and N. Rasamimanana, "Continuous realtime gesture following and recognition," in *Gesture in Embodied Communication and Human-Computer Interaction*, S. Kopp and I. Wachsmuth, Eds., vol. 5934 of *Lecture Notes in Computer Science*, pp. 73–84, Springer, Berlin, Germany, 2009.

[60] J. Wan, Q. Ruan, G. An, and W. Li, "Gesture recognition based on hidden markov model from sparse representative observations," in *Proceedings of the IEEE 11th International Conference on Signal Processing (ICSP '12)*, vol. 2, pp. 1180–1183, 2012.

[61] Y. Lee and S. Cho, "Activity recognition using hierarchical hidden markov models on a smartphone with 3D accelerometer," *Lecture Notes in Computer Science (including subseries Lecture Notes in Artificial Intelligence and Lecture Notes in Bioinformatics)*, vol. 6678, no. 1, pp. 460–467, 2011.

[62] S. Bilal, R. Akmeliawati, A. A. Shafie, and M. J. E. Salami, "Hidden Markov model for human to computer interaction: a study on human hand gesture recognition," *Artificial Intelligence Review*, 2011.

[63] F. Chen, C. Fu, and C. Huang, "Hand gesture recognition using a real-time tracking method and hidden Markov models," *Image and Vision Computing*, vol. 21, no. 8, pp. 745–758, 2003.

[64] D. Kelly, J. McDonald, C. Markham, and editors, "Recognition of spatiotemporal gestures in sign language using gesture threshold hmms," in *Machine Learning for Vision-Based Motion Analysis, Advances in Pattern Recognition*, L. Wang, G. Zhao, L. Cheng, and M. Pietikainen, Eds., pp. 307–348, Springer, London, UK, 2011.

[65] A. Just and S. Marcel, "A comparative study of two state-of-the-art sequence processing techniques for hand gesture recognition," *Computer Vision and Image Understanding*, vol. 113, no. 4, pp. 532–543, 2009.

[66] N. Nguyen-Duc-Thanh, S. Lee, and D. Kim, "Two-stage hidden markov model in gesture recognition for human robot interaction," *International Journal of Advanced Robotic Systems*, vol. 9, no. 39, 2012.

[67] T. Pylvänäinen, "Accelerometer based gesture recognition using continuous HMMs," in *Proceedings of the 2nd Iberian Conference on Pattern Recognition and Image Analysis (IbPRIA '05)*, J. S. Marques, N. P. de la Blanca, and P. Pina, Eds., vol. 3522 of *Lecture Notes in Computer Science*, pp. 639–646, Springer, Berlin, Germany, June 2005.

[68] A. Whitehead and K. Fox, "Device agnostic 3D gesture recognition using hidden Markov models," in *Proceedings of the GDC Canada International Conference on the Future of Game Design and Technology (FuturePlay '09)*, pp. 29–30, ACM, New York, NY, USA, May 2009.

[69] P. Zappi, B. Milosevic, E. Farella, and L. Benini, "Hidden Markov Model based gesture recognition on low-cost, low-power Tangible User Interfaces," *Entertainment Computing*, vol. 1, no. 2, pp. 75–84, 2009.

[70] J. D. Lafferty, A. McCallum, and F. C. N. Pereira, "Conditional random fields: probabilistic models for segmenting and labeling sequence data," in *Proceedings of the 18th International Conference on Machine Learning (ICML '01)*, pp. 282–289, Morgan Kaufmann, San Francisco, Calif, USA, 2001.

[71] H. Chung and H.-D. Yang, "Conditional random field-based gesture recognition with depth information," *Optical Engineering*, vol. 52, no. 1, p. 017201, 2013.

[72] H. Yang, S. Sclaroff, and S. Lee, "Sign language spotting with a threshold model based on conditional random fields," *IEEE Transactions on Pattern Analysis and Machine Intelligence*, vol. 31, no. 7, pp. 1264–1277, 2009.

[73] H. Yang and S. Lee, "Simultaneous spotting of signs and fingerspellings based on hierarchical conditional random fields and boostmap embeddings," *Pattern Recognition*, vol. 43, no. 8, pp. 2858–2870, 2010.

[74] C. Ellis, S. Z. Masood, M. F. Tappen, J. J. LaViola Jr., and R. Sukthankar, "Exploring the trade-off between accuracy and observational latency in action recognition," *International Journal of Computer Vision*, vol. 101, no. 3, pp. 420–436, 2013.

[75] M. Elmezain, A. Al-Hamadi, S. Sadek, and B. Michaelis, "Robust methods for hand gesture spotting and recognition using Hidden Markov Models and Conditional Random Fields," in *Proceedings of the 10th IEEE International Symposium on Signal Processing and Information Technology (ISSPIT '10)*, pp. 131–136, December 2010.

[76] A. Quattoni, S. Wang, L. Morency, M. Collins, and T. Darrell, "Hidden conditional random fields," *IEEE Transactions on Pattern Analysis and Machine Intelligence*, vol. 29, no. 10, pp. 1848–1853, 2007.

[77] B. W. Sy, A. Quattoni, L. Morency, D. Demirdjian, and T. Darrell, "Hidden conditional random fields for gesture recognition," in *Proceedings of the IEEE Computer Society Conference on Computer Vision and Pattern Recognition (CVPR '06)*, vol. 2, pp. 1521–1527, June 2006.

[78] Y. Song, D. Demirdjian, and R. Davis, "Multi-signal gesture recognition using temporal smoothing hidden conditional random fields," in *Proceedings of the IEEE International Conference on Automatic Face and Gesture Recognition and Workshops (FG '11)*, pp. 388–393, March 2011.

[79] T. Liu, K. Wang, A. Tsai, and C. Wang, "Hand posture recognition using hidden conditional random fields," in *Proceedings of the IEEE/ASME International Conference on Advanced Intelligent Mechatronics (AIM '09)*, pp. 1828–1833, July 2009.

[80] F. Liu and Y. Jia, "Human action recognition using manifold learning and hidden conditional random fields," in *Proceedings of the 9th International Conference for Young Computer Scientists (ICYCS '08)*, pp. 693–698, November 2008.

[81] C. R. Souza, E. B. Pizzolato, M. S. Anjo, and editors, "Fingerspelling recognition with support vector machines and hidden conditional random fields," in *Proceedings of the Ibero-American Conference on Artificial Intelligence (IBERAMIA '12)*, J. Pavon, N. D. Duque-Mendez, and R. Fuentes-Fernandez, Eds., vol. 7637 of *Lecture Notes in Computer Science*, pp. 561–570, Springer, 2012.

[82] L. Morency, A. Quattoni, and T. Darrell, "Latent-dynamic discriminative models for continuous gesture recognition," in *Proceedings of the IEEE Computer Society Conference on Computer Vision and Pattern Recognition (CVPR '07)*, pp. 1–8, June 2007.

[83] M. Elmezain and A. Al-Hamadi, "Ldcrfs-based hand gesture recognition," in *Proceedings of the IEEE International Conference on Systems, Man, and Cybernetics (SMC '12)*, pp. 2670–2675, 2012.

[84] Y. Song, D. Demirdjian, and R. Davis, "Continuous body and hand gesture recognition for natural human-computer interaction," *ACM Transactions on Interactive Intelligent Systems*, vol. 2, no. 1, pp. 5:1–5:28, 2012.

[85] Y. Zhang, K. Adl, and J. Glass, "Fast spoken query detection using lower-bound dynamic time warping on graphical processing units," in *Proceedings of the IEEE International Conference on Acoustics, Speech and Signal Processing (ICASSP '12)*, pp. 5173–5176, March 2012.

[86] M. Elmezain, A. Al-Hamadi, and B. Michaelis, "Discriminative models-based hand gesture recognition," in *Proceedings of the 2nd International Conference on Machine Vision (ICMV '09)*, pp. 123–127, December 2009.

[87] V. Vapnik, *The Nature of Statistical Learning Theory*, Springer, New York, NY, USA, 1995.

[88] D. Huang, W. Hu, and S. Chang, "Vision-based hand gesture recognition using PCA+Gabor filters and SVM," in *Proceedings of the 5th International Conference on Intelligent Information Hiding and Multimedia Signal Processing (IIH-MSP '09)*, pp. 1–4, September 2009.

[89] C. T. Hsieh, C. H. Yeh, K. M. Hung, L. M. Chen, and C. Y. Ke, "A real time hand gesture recognition system based on dft and svm," in *Proceedings of the 8th International Conference on Information Science and Digital Content Technology (ICIDT '12)*, vol. 3, pp. 490–494, 2012.

[90] C.-C. Hsieh and D.-H. Liou, "Novel haar features for real-time hand gesture recognition using svm," *Journal of Real-Time Image Processing*, 2012.

[91] N. Dardas, Q. Chen, N. D. Georganas, and E. M. Petriu, "Hand gesture recognition using bag-of-features and multi-class support vector machine," in *Proceedings of the 9th IEEE International Symposium on Haptic Audio-Visual Environments and Games (HAVE '10)*, pp. 163–167, October 2010.

[92] N. H. Dardas and N. D. Georganas, "Real-time hand gesture detection and recognition using bag-of-features and support vector machine techniques," *IEEE Transactions on Instrumentation and Measurement*, vol. 60, no. 11, pp. 3592–3607, 2011.

[93] Y. Chen and K. Tseng, "Multiple-angle hand gesture recognition by fusing SVM classifiers," in *Proceedings of the 3rd IEEE International Conference on Automation Science and Engineering (IEEE CASE '07)*, pp. 527–530, September 2007.

[94] O. Rashid, A. Al-Hamadi, and B. Michaelis, "A framework for the integration of gesture and posture recognition using HMM and SVM," in *Proceedings of the IEEE International Conference on Intelligent Computing and Intelligent Systems (ICIS '09)*, vol. 4, pp. 572–577, November 2009.

[95] K. K. Biswas and S. K. Basu, "Gesture recognition using Microsoft Kinect," in *Proceedings of the 5th International Conference on Automation, Robotics and Applications (ICARA '11)*, pp. 100–103, December 2011.

[96] Z. He, L. Jin, L. Zhen, and J. Huang, "Gesture recognition based on 3D accelerometer for cell phones interaction," in *Proceedings of the IEEE Asia Pacific Conference on Circuits and Systems (APCCAS '08)*, pp. 217–220, December 2008.

[97] S. H. Lee, M. K. Sohn, D. J. Kim, B. Kim, and H. Kim, "Smart tv interaction system using face and hand gesture recognition," in *Proceedings of the IEEE International Conference on Consumer Electronics (ICCE '13)*, pp. 173–174, 2013.

[98] R. C. B. Madeo, C. A. M. Lima, and S. M. Peres, "Gesture unit segmentation using support vector machines: segmenting gestures from rest positions," in *Proceedings of the 28th Annual ACM Symposium on Applied Computing (SAC '13)*, pp. 46–52, ACM, New York, NY, USA, 2013.

[99] Y. Ren and F. Zhang, "Hand gesture recognition based on MEB-SVM," in *Proceedings of the International Conference on Embedded Software and System (ICESS '09)*, pp. 344–349, May 2009.

[100] J. Wu, G. Pan, D. Zhang, G. Qi, and S. Li, "Gesture recognition with a 3-D accelerometer," *Lecture Notes in Computer Science (including subseries Lecture Notes in Artificial Intelligence and Lecture Notes in Bioinformatics)*, vol. 5585, pp. 25–38, 2009.

[101] L. Yun and Z. Peng, "An automatic hand gesture recognition system based on Viola-Jones method and SVMs," in *Proceedings of the 2nd International Workshop on Computer Science and Engineering (WCSE '09)*, vol. 2, pp. 72–76, October 2009.

[102] W.-Y. Loh, "Classification and regression trees," *Wiley Interdisciplinary Reviews*, vol. 1, no. 1, pp. 14–23, 2011.

[103] J. R. Quinlan, *C4.5: Programs for Machine Learning (Morgan Kaufmann Series in Machine Learning)*, Morgan Kaufmann, Boston, Mass, USA, 1st edition, 1993.

[104] S. Nisar, A. A. Khan, and M. Y. Javed, "A statistical feature based decision tree approach for hand gesture recognition," in *Proceedings of the 7th International Conference on Frontiers of Information Technology (FIT '09)*, vol. 27, pp. 1–6, ACM, New York, NY, USA, December 2009.

[105] M. Jeon, S. Yang, and Z. Bien, "User adaptive hand gesture recognition using multivariate fuzzy decision tree and fuzzy garbage model," in *Proceedings of the IEEE International Conference on Fuzzy Systems*, pp. 474–479, August 2009.

[106] X. Zhang, X. Chen, Y. Li, V. Lantz, K. Wang, and J. Yang, "A framework for hand gesture recognition based on accelerometer and EMG sensors," *IEEE Transactions on Systems, Man, and Cybernetics Part A: Systems and Humans*, vol. 41, no. 6, pp. 1064–1076, 2011.

[107] G. Fang, W. Gao, and D. Zhao, "Large vocabulary sign language recognition based on hierarchical decision trees," in *Proceedings of the 5th International Conference on Multimodal Interfaces (ICMI '03)*, pp. 125–131, ACM, New York, NY, USA, November 2003.

[108] S. Oprisescu, C. Rasche, and B. Su, "Automatic static hand gesture recognition using tof cameras," in *Proceedings of the 20th European Signal Processing Conference (EUSIPCO '12)*, pp. 2748–2751, 2012.

[109] L. Miranda, T. Vieira, D. Martinez, T. Lewiner, A. W. Vieira, and M. F. M. Campos, "Real-time gesture recognition from depth data through key poses learning and decision forests," in *Proceedings of the 25th SIBGRAPI Conference on Graphics, Patterns and Images (SIBGRAPI '12)*, pp. 268–275, 2012.

[110] C. Keskin, F. Kirac, Y. Kara, and L. Akarun, "Hand pose estimation and hand shape classification using multi-layered randomized decision forests," in *Proceedings of the 12th European Conference on Computer Vision (ECCV '12)*, A. Fitzgibbon, S. Lazebnik, P. Perona, Y. Sato, and C. Schmid, Eds., vol. 7577 of *Lecture Notes in Computer Science*, pp. 852–863, Springer, Berlin, Germany, 2012.

[111] F. Negin, F. Ozdemir, C. Akgul, K. Yuksel, and A. Ercil, "A decision forest based feature selection framework for action recognition from rgb-depth cameras," in *Image Analysis and Recognition*, M. Kamel and A. Campilho, Eds., vol. 7950 of *Lecture Notes in Computer Science*, pp. 648–657, Springer, Berlin, Germany, 2013.

[112] M. Hoffman, P. Varcholik, and J. J. LaViola Jr., "Breaking the status quo: improving 3D gesture recognition with spatially convenient input devices," in *Proceedings of the 2010 IEEE Virtual Reality Conference (VR '10)*, pp. 59–66, IEEE Computer Society, Washington, DC, USA, March 2010.

[113] S. Kratz and M. Rohs, "A % gesture recognizer: simple gesture recognition for devices equipped with 3D acceleration sensors," in *Proceedings of the 14th ACM International Conference on Intelligent User Interfaces (IUI '10)*, pp. 341–344, ACM, New York, NY, USA, February 2010.

[114] S. Kratz and M. Rohs, "Protractor3D: a closed-form solution to rotation-invariant 3D gestures," in *Proceedings of the 15th ACM International Conference on Intelligent User Interfaces (IUI '11)*, pp. 371–374, ACM, New York, NY, USA, February 2011.

[115] A. Criminisi, J. Shotton, and E. Konukoglu, "Decision forests: a unified framework for classification, regression, density estimation, manifold learning and semi-supervised learning," *Foundations and Trends in Computer Graphics and Vision*, vol. 7, no. 2-3, pp. 81–227, 2011.

[116] A. Criminisi and J. Shotton, *Decision Forests for Computer Vision and Medical Image Analysis*, Springer, New York, NY, USA, 2013.

[117] S. Fothergill, H. Mentis, P. Kohli, and S. Nowozin, "Instructing people for training gestural interactive systems," in *Proceedings of the SIGCHI Conference on Human Factors in Computing Systems (CHI '12)*, pp. 1737–1746, ACM, New York, NY, USA, 2012.

[118] M. Lech, B. Kostek, A. Czyzewski, and editors, "Examining classifiers applied to static hand gesture recognition in novel sound mixing systemvolume," in *Multimedia and Internet Systems: Theory and Practice*, A. Zgrzywa, K. Choros, and A. Sieminski, Eds., vol. 183 of *Advances in Intelligent Systems and Computing*, pp. 77–86, Springer, Berlin, Germany, 2013.

[119] K. R. Konda, A. Königs, H. Schulz, and D. Schulz, "Real time interaction with mobile robots using hand gestures," in *Proceedings of the 7th Annual ACM/IEEE International Conference on Human-Robot Interaction (HRI '12)*, pp. 177–178, ACM, New York, NY, USA, March 2012.

[120] K. Murakami and H. Taguchi, "Gesture recognition using recurrent neural networks," in *Proceedings of the SIGCHI Conference on Human Factors in Computing Systems (CHI '91)*, pp. 237–242, ACM, New York, NY, USA, 1991.

[121] Z. Li and R. Jarvis, "Real time hand gesture recognition using a range camera," in *Proceedings of the Australasian Conference on Robotics and Automation (ACRA '09)*, pp. 21–27, December 2009.

[122] X. Liu and K. Fujimura, "Hand gesture recognition using depth data," in *Proceedings of the 6th IEEE International Conference on Automatic Face and Gesture Recognition (FGR '04)*, pp. 529–534, May 2004.

[123] P. Hong, M. Turk, and T. S. Huang, "Gesture modeling and recognition using finite state machines," in *Proceedings of the 4th IEEE International Conference on Automatic Face and Gesture Recognition*, pp. 410–415, 2000.

[124] D. Rubine, "Specifying gestures by example," in *Proceedings of the 18th Annual Conference on Computer Graphics and Interactive Techniques (SIGGRAPH '91)*, pp. 329–337, ACM, New York, NY, USA, 1991.

[125] S. Cheema, M. Hoffman, and J. J. LaViola Jr., "3D gesture classification with linear acceleration and angular velocity sensing devices for video games," *Entertainment Computing*, vol. 4, no. 1, pp. 11–24, 2013.

[126] S. Cheema and J. J. LaViola Jr., "Wizard of Wii: toward understanding player experience in first person games with 3D gestures," in *Proceedings of the 6th International Conference on the Foundations of Digital Games (FDG '11)*, pp. 265–267, ACM, New York, NY, USA, July 2011.

[127] J. O. Wobbrock, A. D. Wilson, and Y. Li, "Gestures without libraries, toolkits or training: a $1 recognizer for user interface prototypes," in *Proceedings of the 20th Annual ACM Symposium on User Interface Software and Technology (UIST '07)*, pp. 159–168, ACM, New York, NY, USA, October 2007.

[128] S. Kratz and M. Rohs, "The % recognizer: simple 3D gesture recognition on mobile devices," in *Proceedings of the 14th ACM International Conference on Intelligent User Interfaces (IUI '10)*, pp. 419–420, ACM, New York, NY, USA, February 2010.

[129] Y. Li, "Protractor: a fast and accurate gesture recognizer," in *Proceedings of the 28th Annual CHI Conference on Human Factors in Computing Systems (CHI '10)*, pp. 2169–2172, ACM, New York, NY, USA, April 2010.

[130] S. Kratz, M. Rohs, and G. Essl, "Combining acceleration and gyroscope data for motion gesture recognition using classifiers with dimensionality constraints," in *Proceedings of the 2013 international conference on Intelligent user interfaces (IUI '13)*, pp. 173–178, ACM, New York, NY, USA, 2013.

[131] B. Williamson, C. Wingrave, J. LaViola, T. Roberts, and P. Garrity, "Natural full body interaction for navigation in dismounted

soldier training," in *Proceedings of the Interservice/Industry Training, Simulation, and Education Conference (I/ITSEC '11)*, pp. 2103–2110, 2011.

[132] J. N. Bott, J. G. Crowley, and J. J. LaViola Jr., "Exploring 3D gestural interfaces for music creation in video games," in *Proceedings of the 4th International Conference on the Foundations of Digital Games (ICFDG '09)*, pp. 18–25, ACM, New York, NY, USA, April 2009.

[133] E. Charbonneau, A. Miller, C. Wingrave, and J. J. LaViola Jr., "Understanding visual interfaces for the next generation of dance-based rhythm video games," in *Proceedings of the 2009 ACM SIGGRAPH Symposium on Video Games (Sandbox '09)*, pp. 119–126, ACM, New York, NY, USA, August 2009.

[134] J. P. Wachs, M. Kölsch, H. Stern, and Y. Edan, "Vision-based hand-gesture applications," *Communications of the ACM*, vol. 54, no. 2, pp. 60–71, 2011.

[135] H. Kang, C. W. Lee, and K. Jung, "Recognition-based gesture spotting in video games," *Pattern Recognition Letters*, vol. 25, no. 15, pp. 1701–1714, 2004.

[136] J. Payne, P. Keir, J. Elgoyhen et al., "Gameplay issues in the design of spatial 3D gestures for video games," in *Proceedings of the CHI '06 Extended Abstracts on Human Factors in Computing Systems (CHI EA '06)*, pp. 1217–1222, ACM, New York, NY, USA, 2006.

[137] T. Starner, B. Leibe, B. Singletary, and J. Pair, "MIND-WARPING: towards creating a compelling collaborative augmented reality game," in *Proceedings of the 5th International Conference on Intelligent User Interfaces (IUI '00)*, pp. 256–259, ACM, New York, NY, USA, January 2000.

[138] A. Bigdelou, L. A. Schwarz, and N. Navab, "An adaptive solution for intra-operative gesture-based human-machine interaction," in *Proceedings of the 17th ACM International Conference on Intelligent User Interfaces (IUI '12)*, pp. 75–83, ACM, New York, NY, USA, February 2012.

[139] L. A. Schwarz, A. Bigdelou, and N. Navab, "Learning gestures for customizable human-computer interaction in the operating room," in *Proceedings of the Medical Image Computing and Computer-Assisted Intervention (MICCAI '11)*, G. Fichtinger, A. Martel, and T. Peters, Eds., vol. 6891 of *Lecture Notes in Computer Science*, pp. 129–136, Springer, Berlin, Germany, 2011.

[140] K. Pfeil, S. L. Koh, and J. LaViola, "Exploring 3D gesture metaphors for interaction with unmanned aerial vehicles," in *Proceedings of the 2013 International Conference on Intelligent User Interfaces (IUI '13)*, pp. 257–266, ACM, New York, NY, USA, 2013.

[141] B. Burger, I. Ferrané, F. Lerasle, and G. Infantes, "Two-handed gesture recognition and fusion with speech to command a robot," *Autonomous Robots*, pp. 1–19, 2011.

[142] M. Sigalas, H. Baltzakis, and P. Trahanias, "Gesture recognition based on arm tracking for human-robot interaction," in *Proceedings of the 23rd IEEE/RSJ 2010 International Conference on Intelligent Robots and Systems (IROS '10)*, pp. 5424–5429, October 2010.

[143] M. Van Den Bergh, D. Carton, R. De Nijs et al., "Real-time 3D hand gesture interaction with a robot for understanding directions from humans," in *Proceedings of the 20th IEEE International Symposium on Robot and Human Interactive Communication (RO-MAN '11)*, pp. 357–362, August 2011.

[144] A. Riener, "Gestural interaction in vehicular applications," *Computer*, vol. 45, no. 4, Article ID 6165247, pp. 42–47, 2012.

[145] S. H. Lee, M. K. Sohn, D. J. Kim, B. Kim, and H. Kim, "Smart tv interaction system using face and hand gesture recognition," in *Proceedings of the IEEE International Conference on Consumer Electronics (ICCE '13)*, pp. 173–174, IEEE, 2013.

[146] M. Takahashi, M. Fujii, M. Naemura, and S. Satoh, "Human gesture recognition system for TV viewing using time-of-flight camera," *Multimedia Tools and Applications*, vol. 62, no. 3, pp. 761–783, 2013.

[147] H. I. Stern, J. P. Wachs, and Y. Edan, "Designing hand gesture vocabularies for natural interaction by combining psycho-physiological and recognition factors," *International Journal of Semantic Computing*, vol. 2, no. 1, pp. 137–160, 2008.

[148] S. Z. Masood, C. Ellis, A. Nagaraja, M. F. Tappen, J. J. Laviola, and R. Sukthankar, "Measuring and reducing observational latency when recognizing actions," in *Proceedings of the IEEE International Conference on Computer Vision Workshops (ICCV '11)*, pp. 422–429, November 2011.

[149] M. Baldauf, S. Dustdar, and F. Rosenberg, "A survey on context-aware systems," *International Journal of Ad Hoc and Ubiquitous Computing*, vol. 2, no. 4, pp. 263–277, 2007.

[150] W. Liu, X. Li, and D. Huang, "A survey on context awareness," in *Proceedings of the International Conference on Computer Science and Service System (CSSS '11)*, pp. 144–147, June 2011.

[151] A. Saeed and T. Waheed, "An extensive survey of context-aware middleware architectures," in *Proceedings of the IEEE International Conference on Electro/Information Technology (EIT '10)*, pp. 1–6, May 2010.

[152] D. Han, L. Bo, and C. Sminchisescu, "Selection and context for action recognition," in *Proceedings of the 12th International Conference on Computer Vision (ICCV '09)*, pp. 1933–1940, October 2009.

[153] D. J. Moore, I. A. Essa, and M. H. Hayes, "Object spaces: context management for human activity recognition," in *Proceedings of 2nd International Conference on Audio-Vision-based Person Authentication*, 1998.

[154] D. J. Moore, I. A. Essa, and M. H. Hayes III, "Exploiting human actions and object context for recognition tasks," in *Proceedings of the 1999 7th IEEE International Conference on Computer Vision (ICCV'99)*, pp. 80–86, September 1999.

9

PSO-Based PID Controller Design for a Class of Stable and Unstable Systems

K. Latha,[1] V. Rajinikanth,[2] and P. M. Surekha[2]

[1] *Department of Instrumentation Engineering, Anna University, M.I.T Campus, Chennai 600 044, India*
[2] *Department of Electronics and Instrumentation Engineering, St. Joseph's College of Engineering, Chennai 600 119, India*

Correspondence should be addressed to V. Rajinikanth; rajinisjceeie@gmail.com

Academic Editors: K. W. Chau and J. M. Molina López

Nonlinear processes are very common in process industries, and designing a stabilizing controller is always preferred to maximize the production rate. In this paper, tuning of PID controller for a class of time delayed stable and unstable process models using Particle Swarm Optimization (PSO) algorithm is discussed. The dimension of the search space is only three (K_p, K_i, and K_d); hence, a fixed weight is assigned for the inertia parameter. A comparative study is presented between various inertia weights such as 0.5, 0.75, and 1. From the result, it is evident that the proposed method helps to attain better controller settings with reduced iteration number. The efficacy of the proposed scheme has been validated through a comparative study with classical controller tuning methods and heuristic methods such as Genetic Algorithm (GA) and Ant Colony Optimization (ACO). Finally, a real-time implementation of the proposed method is carried on a nonlinear spherical tank system. From the simulation and real-time results, it is evident that the PSO algorithm performs well on the stable and unstable process models considered in this work. The PSO tuned controller offers enhanced process characteristics such as better time domain specifications, smooth reference tracking, supply disturbance rejection, and error minimization.

1. Introduction

In process industries, many important real-time processing units such as Continuous Stirred Tank Reactor (CSTR), biochemical reactor, and spherical tank system are highly nonlinear in nature. Tuning of controllers to stabilize these nonlinear chemical process loops and impart adequate disturbance rejection is critical because of their complex nature. Based on the operating regions, most of the chemical loops exhibit stable and/or unstable steady states.

Controller tuning is an essential preliminary procedure in almost all industrial process control systems. In control literature, a number of controller structures are available to stabilize stable, unstable, and nonlinear processes [1–5]. Designing controller for process with stable operating region is quite simple. For unstable systems, there exist minimum and maximum values of controller gain, and the average of this limiting value is considered to design the controller to stabilize the system. The increase in time delay in the process narrows down the limiting value and restricts

the performance of closed loop system under control. In addition, these systems show unusual overshoot or inverse response due to the presence of positive zeros [4].

Despite the significant developments in advanced process control schemes such as predictive control, internal model control, and sliding mode control, PID controllers are still widely used in industrial control application because of their structural simplicity, reputation, robust performance, and easy implementation [2]. Many researchers proposed PID tuning rules to control various stable and unstable systems by different schemes to enhance closed loop performance [1]. For stable systems, PID controller offers a viable result for both reference tracking and disturbance rejection operations. However, for unstable systems, it can effectively work either for reference tracking or disturbance rejection. The proportional and derivative kick in the controller also results in large overshoot and large settling time [3].

Conventional controller tuning methods proposed by most of the researchers are model dependent, and they require a reduced order models such as first-order or

TABLE 1: Optimized PID parameters for Example 1.

W	Best values	Iteration number	K_p	K_i	K_d
0.5	1	58	0.6749	0.6525	0.0228
	2	35	0.6800	0.6415	0.0170
	3	41	0.6904	0.6965	0.0332
0.75	1	45	0.6976	0.6597	0.1136
	2	43	0.8579	0.6827	0.0781
	3	52	0.5779	0.6413	0.0812
1	1	44	0.4885	0.839	0.1013
	2	39	0.6781	0.9102	0.2954
	3	63	1.0119	0.7781	0.1377

TABLE 2: Quantitative analysis for Example 1.

W	Best values	M_p	t_r (s)	t_s (s)	ISE	IAE
0.5	1	0	5.5	5.5	9.395	3.065
	2	0	6.5	6.5	9.72	3.118
	3	0.004	3.9	8.5	8.245	2.871
0.75	1	0.0055	4.3	6.6	9.191	3.030
	2	0	8.1	8.1	8.582	2.929
	3	0.0185	4.0	9.8	9.726	3.119
1	1	0.13	2.6	9.5	5.682	2.384
	2	0.112	2.6	10	4.828	2.197
	3	0	6.5	6.5	6.606	2.570

second-order process model with time delay. Particularly for unstable systems, the tuning rule proposed for a particular reduced order model will not offer a fitting response for other models (higher order models, model with a positive or negative zero, model with a large delay time to process time constant ratio, etc.). Most of the classical PID tuning methods require numerical computations in order to get the best possible controller parameters. Due to these reasons, in recent years, heuristic algorithm-based controller tuning has greatly attracted the researchers.

From recent literature, it is observed that heuristic algorithm-based optimization procedures have emerged as a powerful tool for finding the solutions for variety of control engineering problems [6–12]. Heuristic algorithms are widely used in process control because of their structural simplicity, better optimization ability, and speed of response. Heuristic algorithms can effectively work for higher dimensional optimization problems compared to the existing classical optimization procedures. Due to their flexibility, they can easily adapt to the existing classical controller design procedures. They can be used as a vital tool to design classical and modified structured controllers for a class of unstable process models, irrespective of its model order. Most recent heuristic methods such as Genetic Algorithm (GA) [11], Ant Colony Optimization (ACO) [13], Bacterial Foraging Optimization (BFO) [14], and Particle Swarm Optimization (PSO) [12, 15] are extensively addressed by the researchers to tune controllers for a class of process models.

In this paper, PID controller parameter tuning is attempted using the PSO algorithm introduced by Kennedy

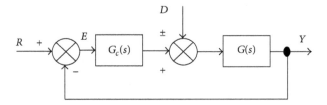

FIGURE 1: Block diagram of closed loop control system.

and Eberhart [16]. The main advantage of PSO algorithm is that it is an autotuning method; it does not require detailed mathematical description of the process and finds the best possible K_p, K_i, and K_d based on the Objective Function (OF) provided to guide the algorithm. A detailed study is presented with a PSO algorithm using various inertia weights such as 0.5, 0.75, and 1. A comparative study is also carried out between GA, ACO, BFO, and classical controller tuning methods existing in the literature.

The remaining part of the paper is organized as follows. Section 2 presents the outline of classical PID and setpoint filter-based PID controller. A brief description of PSO- and OF-based controller tuning is provided in Section 3. PSO based PID controller design is discussed in Section 4. Section 5 presents the simulated results on different process models and a real-time implementation using a spherical tank system. Section 6 provides conclusion of the present research work.

2. Controller Structure

2.1. PID Controller. PID controller has a simple structure and is usually available as a packaged form. To perform well with the industrial process problems, the controller should have optimally tuned K_p, K_i, and K_d values. Figure 1 shows the basic block diagram of the closed loop systemm where $G_c(s)$ is responsible to maintain Y based on R, by eliminating the redundant input disturbance (D) [3].

The closed loop response of the above system can be expressed as

$$Y(s) = \left[\frac{G(s)\, G_c(s)}{1 + G(s)\, G_c(s)} \right] R(s) \pm \left[\frac{G(s)}{1 + G(s)\, G_c(s)} \right] D(s).$$

(1)

Let us assume that $G(s) = K \cdot (\text{num}(s)/\text{den}(s))$, $R(s) = A/s$, and

$$G_c(s) = K_p \left(1 + \frac{1}{\tau_i s} + \tau_d s \right) = \left[K_p + \frac{K_i}{s} + K_d s \right]$$

$$= \left[\frac{K_i + K_p s + K_d s^2}{s} \right],$$

(2)

where $\tau_i = K_p/K_i$, $\tau_d = K_d/K_p$.

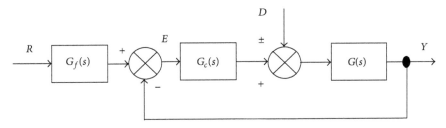

FIGURE 2: Block diagram of PID controller with prefilter.

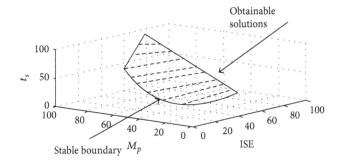

FIGURE 3: Obtainable solutions from search universe U.

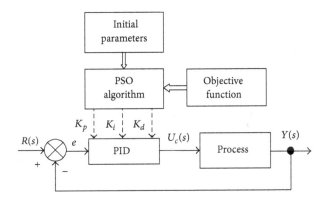

FIGURE 4: PSO-based PID controller design.

TABLE 3: PID parameters for Example 2.

Sl. Number	Method	K_p	K_i	K_d
1	ZN	2.808	1.712	1.151
2	GA	2.391	2.391	1.458
3	ACO	2.4911	0.8158	1.3540
4	MACO	2.808	1.021	1.668
5	PSO (0.75)	1.452	0.4259	0.5084

TABLE 4: Performance measure for Example 2.

Sl. Number	Method	% M_p	t_r (s)	t_s (s)	ISE
1	ZN	31.59%	0.664	4.78	0.854
2	GA	5.84%	0.676	3.63	0.797
3	ACO	4.95%	0.701	5.90	0.809
4	MACO	2.84%	0.700	3.00	0.772
5	PSO (0.75)	0.00%	2.713	9.836	4.108

TABLE 5: Controller values for various W.

Sl. Number	Method	K_p	K_i	K_d	ISE
1	ZN	−1.6722	−1.8580	−0.3762	1.782
2	GA	−1.2440	−1.3980	−0.2427	3.148
3	MOPSO	−0.5612	−2.0712	0.0133	1.434
4	PSO (0.75)	−0.6313	−1.7103	0.0159	1.603

TABLE 6: Controller settings for Example 4.

W	Best values	Iteration number	K_p	K_i	K_d
	1	77	−0.5697	−0.0803	0.0199
0.5	2	83	−0.6030	−0.0918	0.0099
	3	59	−0.5774	−0.1091	−0.0288
	1	63	−0.7027	−0.1968	0.0443
0.75	2	76	−0.6412	−0.1633	0.1990
	3	47	−0.7076	−0.2288	0.1669
	1	62	−0.6962	−0.1432	−0.4182
1	2	58	−0.6405	−0.1569	−0.4680
	3	83	−0.8869	−0.1671	−0.5309

The final steady-state response $Y(\infty)$ of the system $G(s)$ for reference tracking and supply disturbance rejection is presented correspondingly as follows:

$$Y_R(\infty) = \lim_{t \to \infty} sY_R(s)$$

$$= \lim_{t \to \infty} sx \left[\frac{G(s)G_c(s)}{1 + G(s)G_c(s)} \right] \left(\frac{A}{s} \right) = A, \tag{3}$$

$$Y_D(\infty) = \lim_{t \to \infty} sx \left[\frac{G(s)}{1 + G_p(s)G_c(s)} \right] \left(\frac{D}{s} \right) = 0, \tag{4}$$

where A is the amplitude of reference signal and D is the amplitude of disturbance.

2.2. PID Controller with Prefilter.
Figure 2 depicts the structure of prefilter/setpoint filter-based PID controller discussed by Araki and Taguchi [17], where $G_f(s)$ is a first-order prefilter with the following structure $1/(1 + \tau_f s)$.

Jung et al. reported that, when the filter time constant τ_f is set equal to integral time constant τ_i, the controller offers a smooth reference tracking performance [18]. Recently, Vijayan and Panda developed a detailed analytical expression

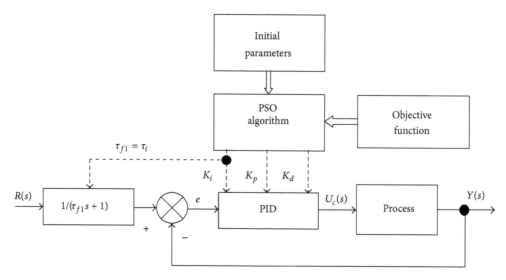

FIGURE 5: PSO-based PID controller with prefilter design.

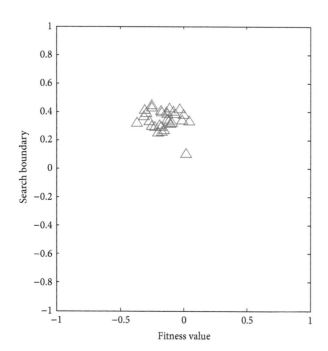

FIGURE 6: Convergence of particles with optimal solution.

to assign the above controller parameters and validated using a class of process models [19].

3. Methodology

3.1. PSO Algorithm. Particle Swarm Optimization (PSO) technique, proposed by Kennedy and Eberhart [16], is an evolutionary-type global optimization technique developed due to the inspiration of social activities in flock of birds and school of fish and is widely applied in various engineering problems due to its high computational efficiency [6–10, 20–23]. Compared with other population-based stochastic optimization methods, such as GA and ACO, PSO has comparable or even superior search performance for many

hard optimization problems, with faster and more stable convergence rates. It has been proved to be an effective optimum tool in system identification and PID controller tuning for a class of processes [24].

In PSO algorithm, the number of parameters to be assigned is very few compared to other nature-inspired algorithms. In this, a group of artificial birds is initialized with arbitrary positions X_i and velocities V_i. At early searching stage, each bird in the swarm is scattered randomly throughout the D dimensional search space. With the supervision of the Objective Function (OF), own flying experience, and their companions flying experience, each particle in the swarm dynamically adjusts its flying position and velocity. During the optimization search, each particle remembers its best position attained so far (i.e., *pbest*—$(P_{i,D}^t)$) and also obtains the global best position information achieved by any particle in the population (i.e., *gbest*—$(G_{i,D}^t)$).

At iteration t, each particle i has its position defined by $X_{i,n}^t = [X_{i,1}, X_{i,2}, \ldots, X_{i,D}]$ and velocity defined as $V_{i,n}^t = [V_{i,1}, V_{i,2}, \ldots, V_{i,D}]$ in search space D. Velocity and position of each particle in the next iteration can be calculated as

$$V_{i,D}^{t+1} = W * V_{i,D}^t + C_1 * R_1 * \left(P_{i,D}^t - X_{i,D}^t \right) \\ + C_2 * R_2 * \left(G_{i,D}^t - X_{i,D}^t \right), \tag{5}$$

$$X_{i,D}^{t+1} = X_{i,D}^t + V_{i,D}^{t+1}, \tag{6}$$

where $i = 1, 2, \ldots, N$; and acceleration constant C_1 called cognitive parameter pulls each particle towards local best position, and constant C_2 called social parameter pulls the particle towards global best position. R_1 and R_2 are known as random numbers in the range 0-1.

In (5), the inertia of weight W represented is an important factor for the PSO's convergence. It is used to control the impact of previous velocities on the current velocity at the current time step. The basic PSO, initially proposed by Kennedy and Eberhart, has no inertia weight, and this feature is first introduced by Shi and Eberhart [25]. The work reports that a large inertia weight factor facilitates global exploration while small weight factor facilitates local exploration.

Further, for high-dimensional problems, dynamical adjusting of inertia weight was introduced by many researchers which can increase the search capabilities of PSO. A review of inertia weight strategies in PSO is given chronologically in subsequent paragraphs.

Eberhart and Shi [26] proposed a Random Inertia Weight strategy and experimentally found that this strategy increases the convergence of PSO in early iterations of the algorithm. The linearly decreasing strategy enhances the efficiency and performance of PSO. In spite of its ability to converge optimum, it gets into the local optimum solving the question of more apices function. In global-local best inertia weight, the inertia weight is based on the function of local best and global best of the particles in each generation. It neither takes a constant value nor a linearly decreasing time-varying value. To overcome the weakness of premature convergence to local minimum, adaptive inertia weight strategy [27] is proposed to improve its searching capability. Chen et al. [28] present two natural exponent inertia weight strategies which are based on the basic idea of decreasing inertia weight. Malik et al. [29] presented a Sigmoid Increasing Inertia Weight (SIIW). They found that sigmoid function has contributed in getting minimum fitness function while linearly increasing inertia weight gives contribution to quick convergence ability. So they combine sigmoid function and linear increasing inertia weight and provide an SIIW which has produced a great improvement in quick convergence ability and aggressive movement narrowing towards the solution region. Oscillating inertia weight provides periodically alternates between global and local search waves, and the conclusion was drawn that this strategy appears to be generally competitive and, in some cases, PSO outperforms particularly in terms of convergence speed. Gao et al. [30] proposed a new PSO algorithm which combined the logarithm decreasing inertia weight with chaos mutation operator. The logarithm decreasing inertia weight can improve the convergence speed, while the chaos mutation can enhance the ability to jump out of the local optima. In order to overcome the premature convergence and later period oscillatory occurrences of the standard PSO, an exponent decreasing inertia weight and stochastic mutation to produce an improved PSO has been proposed by Gao et al. [30], which uses the exponent decreasing inertia weight along with stochastic piecewise mutation for current global optimal particle during the running time, to support better optimization search.

In this paper, we considered constant inertia weight-based velocity updation. The implementation of PSO has the following steps.

Step 1 (initialization of swarm). For a population size N, the particles are randomly generated between the minimum and maximum limits of parameter values.

Step 2 (evaluation of objective function). Objective function values of particles are evaluated using the performance criteria for algorithm convergence.

Step 3 (initialization of *pbest* and *gbest*). The objective values obtained above for the initial particles of swarm are set as the initial *pbest* values of particles. The best value among all the *pbest* values is identified as *gbest*.

Step 4 (evaluation of velocity). The new velocity for each particle is computed using (5).

Step 5 (update the swarm). The particle position is updated using (6). The values of the objective function are calculated for updated positions of particles. If the new value is better than the previous *pbest*, the new value is set to *pbest*. Similarly, *gbest* value is also updated as the best *pbest*.

Step 6 (stopping criteria). If the stopping criteria are met, positions of particles represented by *pbest* are the optimal values. Otherwise, the above said procedure is repeated from Step 4 until the specified iteration is completed.

3.2. Objective Function. The overall performance (speed of convergence, efficiency, and optimization accuracy) of PSO algorithm depends on Objective Function (OF), which monitors the optimization search. The OF is chosen to maximize the domain constrains or to minimize the preference constrains. During the search, without loss of generality, the constrained optimization problem minimizes a scalar function "J" of some decision variable vector "D" in a universe "U." The objective function is to be framed by assuming, at least, that there exists one set of optimal parameters in "U" which satisfies all the constraints.

The minimization problem of preference constrains can be mathematically expressed as

$$\min_{D \in U} J(D). \tag{7}$$

The majority of controller design problems are multiobjective in nature. Multiobjective optimization always provides improved result compared to single-objective function. Without loss of generality, the multiobjective optimization problem simultaneously minimizes n objectives $\phi_i(p)$, $i = 1, \ldots, n$ of a variable vector D in a universe U:

$$\min_{D \in U} (\phi_1(p), \phi_2(p), \ldots, \phi_n(p)). \tag{8}$$

Weighted sum method is widely adopted by most of the researchers, and it converts the multiobjective problem of minimizing the objectives into a scalar form [31]. The general form of weighted sum of multiple objective functions is presented in (7). In this method, the constraints which are to be minimized are arranged as weighted sum:

$$\min_{D \in U} \sum_{k=1}^{n} W_k J_k(D), \tag{9}$$

where W_k is the weighting coefficient, n is the number of constrains to be solved, D is the dimension of the problem, and U is the search universe. Generally, the weight for W_k (between 0 and 1 or 0 and 100%) is assigned based on the preference constraints to be minimized.

In the control literature, there exist a number of weighted-sum-based objective functions [31]. In this paper, we considered three-parameter-based objective function by considering the error and important time domain constraints such as overshoot M_p and settling time t_s:

$$J(\theta) = w_1 \cdot \text{ISE} + w_2 \cdot M_p + w_3 \cdot t_s,$$
$$\theta = \left[K_p K_i K_d\right], \tag{10}$$

where θ are parameters to be optimized, M_p is peak overshoot, t_s is settling time, and the weighting function $w_1 = w_2 = 1$ and $w_3 = 0.5$.

In many optimization cases, it is very difficult to satisfy all the considered constraints. Hence, there should be some negotiation between the preference constraint parameters without compromising the domain constraint [31]. In this work, we assigned more preference for ISE and M_p compared to t_s. Figure 3 depicts the obtainable optimal solution and stability boundary in the three-dimensional search space.

Search boundary for controller parameters is assigned as follows:

$$K_p : \text{min} -60\% \text{ to } \text{max} +60\%,$$
$$K_i : \text{min} -30\% \text{ to } \text{max} +30\%, \tag{11}$$
$$K_d : \text{min} -50\% \text{ to } \text{max} +50\%.$$

The algorithm continuously varies the values of controller parameters until the objective function J is minimised to J_{min}.

4. Controller Tuning

The controller design process is to find the optimal values for controller parameters form the search space that minimizes the considered objective function. Figure 4 illustrates the basic block diagram of PSO algorithm-based PID controller tuning. Initially, PSO algorithm assigns arbitrary values for K_p, K_i, and K_d and computes the OF. This procedure continues until the J reaches J_{min} or the final iteration number is reached.

Figure 5 shows the block diagram of PSO tuned PID controller with a prefilter setup. For this procedure, dimension of the search is three, and the algorithm finds the best possible controller parameters along with filter time constant τ_f. This setup provides better result for both the stable and unstable process models.

PSO-based controller design procedure is developed with number of swarms $N = 20$, swarm step size = 20, $C_1 = C_2 = 2$, and maximum generation value of 200. Optimal tuning procedure is repeated 10 times independently, and the best value among the trials is considered to stabilize the process.

5. Results and Discussion

Example 1. The first-order stable process with the following transfer function model is considered [19]:

$$G(s) = \frac{1}{s+1}e^{-0.5s}. \tag{12}$$

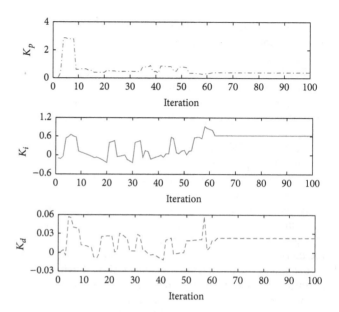

FIGURE 7: Optimal controller parameters.

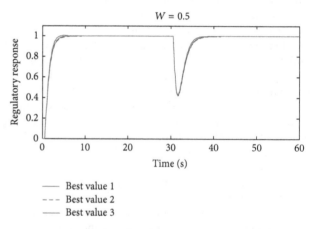

—— Best value 1
--- Best value 2
—— Best value 3

FIGURE 8: Regulatory response for $W = 0.5$.

PSO-based PID tuning is proposed with the method as shown in Figure 4. The final convergence of swarm is depicted in Figure 6. The multiple OF-based controller design procedure is converged at 58th iteration (for $W = 0.5$) as shown in Figure 7, and the final PID parameters with various W values and the corresponding iteration number are tabulated in Table 1.

Table 1 presents three best values among 10 trials. These values are individually evaluated using the process model (12). Figure 8 represents the reference tracking and input disturbance rejection performance of PID controller obtained when $W = 0.5$. Figure 9 shows the corresponding controller performance.

Similar responses are obtained for the above process model for $W = 0.75$ and $W = 1$, and the obtained performance measures are tabulated in Table 2.

From Table 2 and Figure 10, it is observed that, even though the total iteration taken by the best value 3 (for $W = 1$) is considerably large, it provides better overall performance compared to other values considered in this study.

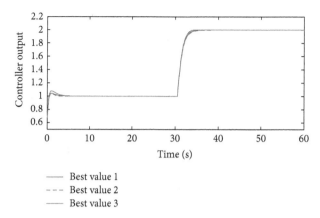

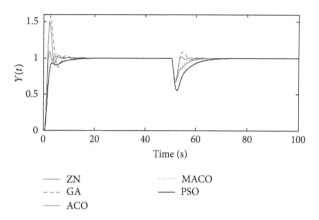

FIGURE 9: Controller output for $W = 0.5$.

FIGURE 11: Regulatory response for $W = 0.5$.

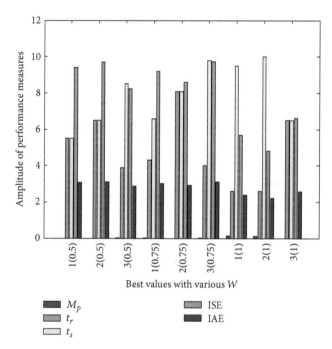

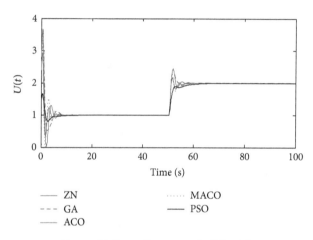

FIGURE 12: Controller output for $W = 0.5$.

FIGURE 10: Process performance with various W.

Example 2. The stable second-order model discussed by Chiha et al. is considered [13];

$$G(s) = \frac{1}{(s+1)^2} e^{-0.1s}. \tag{13}$$

Chiha et al. proposed a Multiobjective Ant Colony Optimization (MACO) algorithm and validated the result with Ziegler-Nichols (ZN), GA, and ACO tuned PID controller. In this work, we considered the PSO tuned PID controller, and the controller values and its performance measure values are presented in Tables 3 and 4 respectively.

Figure 11 shows the process output for Example 2 for various controller settings. Initially a unity reference input signal is applied to the system. An unity input disturbance signal is applied at 50 s to study the disturbance rejection performance. The performance by the present method is smooth compared to other methods considered in this study.

The ZN, GA, ACO, and MACO methods show oscillations during the reference tracking and the disturbance rejection cases compared to the PSO tuned PID. But the response by the present controller is sluggish than other methods. From Figure 12, it is observed that the controller performance is also very smooth. Even though the parameters such as t_r, t_s, and ISE are large, the present controller provides approximately null % overshoot (Table 4).

Example 3. The stable second-order steady-state model of the bioreactor is presented below [11]:

$$G(s) = \frac{-1.53s - 0.4588}{s^2 + 2.564s + 0.6792} e^{-0.1s}. \tag{14}$$

For this model, Kumar et al. [11] proposed a GA-based PID controller. Recently Rajinikanth and Latha proposed and validated the multiple-objective PSO-based PID tuning procedure using nonlinear process model [33].

In this work, PSO-based PID is proposed for the above process model with $W = 0.75$, and the final converged controller parameters are presented in Table 5. Figures 13 and 14 show the process response and controller output, respectively. The proposed methods provide improved reference tracking and disturbance rejection performance compared to the

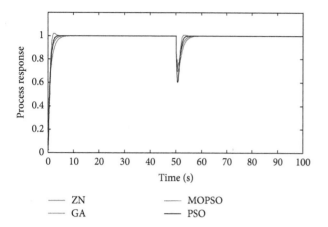

FIGURE 13: Process response for stable bioreactor model.

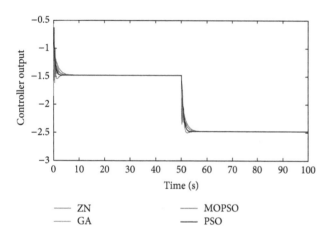

FIGURE 14: $U(t)$ for bioreactor model.

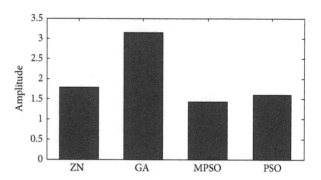

FIGURE 15: Graphical representation of ISE.

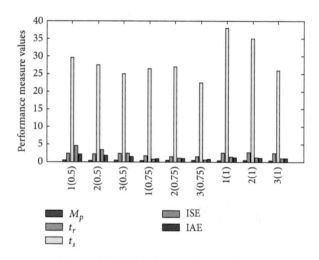

FIGURE 16: Graphical representation of ISE.

other methods considered. From Figure 15 the observation is that, ISE value by the proposed method is considerably smaller than ZN and GA.

Example 4. The unstable steady-state model of the bioreactor presented below is widely considered by the researchers [14, 15]:

$$G(s) = \frac{-0.9951s - 0.2985}{s^2 + 0.1302s - 0.0509}e^{-0.1s}$$
$$= \frac{-5.8644}{5.89s - 1}e^{-0.1s}. \tag{15}$$

The above process model is a bench mark problem in the unstable controller design problem. In this paper, initially, the PSO controller is designed for the process later a prefilter-based PID structure is implemented as shown in Figure 5. The previous work by Rajinikanth and Latha provided the following controller parameters: $K_p = -0.5374$, $K_i = -0.0702$, and $K_d = -0.0537$ using the BFO algorithm [14].

The controller setting by the proposed method for various W values is presented in Table 6, and the corresponding performance values are tabulated in Table 7 (best three values among 10 trials). The performance measure values are

TABLE 7: Performance measure values for Example 4.

W	Best values	M_p	t_r (s)	t_s (s)	ISE	IAE
0.5	1	0.434	2.3	29.6	4.497	2.121
	2	0415	2.25	27.5	3.446	1.856
	3	0.454	2.3	25	2.447	1.564
0.75	1	0.409	1.7	26.5	0.75	0.886
	2	0.435	1.5	27	1.09	1.044
	3	0.423	1.5	22.5	0.557	0.746
1	1	0.39	2.56	38.1	1.419	1.19
	2	0.44	2.7	35	1.178	1.05
	3	0.32	2.5	26	1.04	1.020

graphically represented in Figure 16, and the PSO-based PID setting for $W = 0.75$ (third best value) provides improved performance compared to other values. Hence the above-mentioned value is considered for the comparative work with the BFO algorithm (with PID and prefilter-based PID controller).

In this study, a disturbance of 50% (of setpoint value) is applied at 50 s to analyze the supply disturbance rejection performance. Figure 17 shows the regulatory response for the unstable bioreactor model, and Figure 18 shows the corresponding controller output. Even though the reference

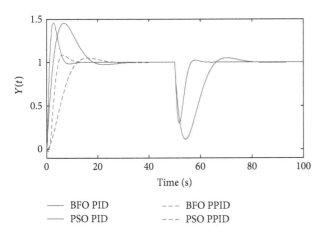

FIGURE 17: Output response with PID and PID with prefilter (PPID).

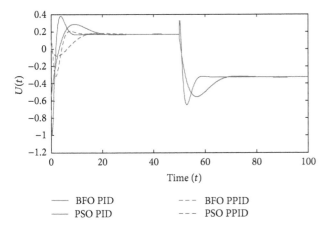

FIGURE 18: Controller output for PID and PID with prefilter (PPID).

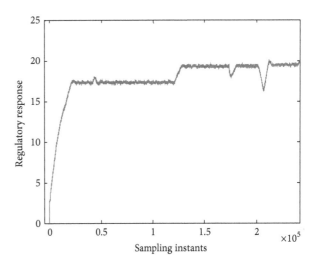

FIGURE 19: Real-time process response for nonlinear spherical tank system.

tracking response of the PID and prefilter-based PID (PPID) is different, both show a similar response for the disturbance rejection problem, where the proposed PSO tuned PID and PPID show enhanced performance compared to the existing BFO tuned PID and PPID controller. From this, it is observed that the fixed inertia weight-based PID controller provides best optimized values when the dimension of the problem is small.

Example 5. The nonlinear spherical tank system recently discussed by Rajinikanth and Latha is considered to show the real-time implementation of the proposed method [34]. The transfer function model of the system for an operating range of 18 cm is

$$G(s) = \frac{3.6215}{330.46s + 1} e^{-11.7s}. \quad (16)$$

A simulation time of 500 s is considered in the PSO-based PID tuning procedure, and the algorithm is converged at 41th iteration for $W = 0.75$ with $K_p = 6.8115$, $K_i = 1.0042$, and $K_d = 1.9016$. The obtained PID values are then transferred to the real-time controller hardware installed in the process loop through the monitoring and control program developed in MATLAB Simulink with ODE 45 solver, which is directly

interfaced with the real-time process system through DAQ module. It is enabled with National Instruments VISA serial communication interface. The module supports ASCII data format with a sampling time of 0.1 s and a baud rate of 38400. With this, monitoring and control of the real-time process can be easily established with MATLAB software. In real-time implementation, the maximum controller output is set as 90% in order to reduce the thrust on the control valve which allows the flow rate to the tank.

Figure 19 shows the variation of level for the reference tracking, multiple reference tracking, supply disturbance, and load disturbance rejection problems.

Initially a reference input of 18 cm is assigned. When the process output reaches a final steady-state value, then the reference input is increased by 2 cm (i.e., 20 cm) at 1.3×10^5th sampling instant. Later a supply disturbance of 10% of the setpoint and a load disturbance of 25% of the setpoint are applied at 1.75×10^5th sampling instant and 2×10^5th sampling instants, respectively.

In the real-time study, the ISE and IAE values are obtained as 455.81 and 196.33, respectively. From this result, it can be noted that the PSO algorithm presents a smooth servo and regulatory response for the spherical tank level control problem and it can be easily implemented in real time using a MATLAB-supported real-time process loop.

6. Conclusion

This paper attempted a controller parameter optimization work with PSO algorithm with various inertia weights. The fixed inertia weight method helps to improve the speed of convergence and also maintains good accuracy in optimized parameters. Proposed weighted sum of multiple-objective function provides the necessary controller parameters and supports enhanced performance for both the reference tracking and disturbance rejection problems. The real-time implementation also confirms the adaptability of the proposed method on the MATLAB supportable real-time hardware.

The real-time result with PSO tuned PID offers better result for reference tracking, multiple reference tracking, and disturbance rejection problems.

References

[1] A. O'Dwyer, *Handbook of PI and PID Controller Tuning Rules*, Imperial College Press, London, UK, 3rd edition, 2009.

[2] R. C. Panda, "Synthesis of PID controller for unstable and integrating processes," *Chemical Engineering Science*, vol. 64, no. 12, pp. 2807–2816, 2009.

[3] M. A. Johnson and M. H. Moradi, *PID Control: New Identification and Design Methods*, chapter 2, Springer, London, UK, 2005.

[4] R. Padmasree and M. Chidambaram, *Control of Unstable Systems*, Narosa Publishing House, New Delhi, India, 2006.

[5] B. W. Bequette, *Process Control—Modeling, Design and Simulation*, Prentice Hall, New Delhi, India, 2003.

[6] U. S. Banu and G. Uma, "Fuzzy gain scheduled continuous stirred tank reactor with particle swarm optimization based PID control minimizing integral square error," *Instrumentation Science and Technology*, vol. 36, no. 4, pp. 394–409, 2008.

[7] M. S. Arumugam and M. V. C. Rao, "On the performance of the particle swarm optimization algorithm with various inertia weight variants for computing optimal control of a class of hybrid systems," *Discrete Dynamics in Nature and Society*, vol. 2006, Article ID 79295, 17 pages, 2006.

[8] M. S. Arumugam and M. V. C. Rao, "On the optimal control of single-stage hybrid manufacturing systems via novel and different variants of particle swarm optimization algorithm," *Discrete Dynamics in Nature and Society*, vol. 2005, no. 3, pp. 257–279, 2005.

[9] R. M. Chen and C. M. Wang, "Project scheduling heuristics-based standard PSO for task-resource assignment in heterogeneous grid," *Abstract and Applied Analysis*, vol. 2011, Article ID 589862, 20 pages, 2011.

[10] R. F. Abdel-Kader, "Particle swarm optimization for constrained instruction scheduling," *VLSI Design*, vol. 2008, Article ID 930610, 7 pages, 2008.

[11] S. M. G. Kumar, R. Jain, N. Anantharaman, V. Dharmalingam, and K. M. M. S. Begam, "Genetic algorithm based PID controller tuning for a model bioreactor," *Indian Institute of Chemical Engineers*, vol. 50, no. 3, pp. 214–226, 2008.

[12] M. Zamani, M. Karimi-Ghartemani, N. Sadati, and M. Parniani, "Design of a fractional order PID controller for an AVR using particle swarm optimization," *Control Engineering Practice*, vol. 17, no. 12, pp. 1380–1387, 2009.

[13] I. Chiha, N. Liouane, and P. Borne, "Tuning PID controller using multiobjective ant colony optimization," *Applied Computational Intelligence and Soft Computing*, vol. 2012, Article ID 536326, 7 pages, 2012.

[14] V. Rajinikanth and K. Latha, "Bacterial foraging optimization algorithm based pid controller tuning for time delayed unstable systems," *Mediterranean Journal of Measurement and Control*, vol. 7, no. 1, pp. 197–203, 2011.

[15] V. Rajinikanth and K. Latha, "Identification and control of unstable biochemical reactor," *International Journal of Chemical Engineering Applications*, vol. 1, no. 1, pp. 106–111, 2010.

[16] J. Kennedy and R. C. Eberhart, "Particle swarm optimization," in *Proceedings of the IEEE International Conference on Neural Networks*, vol. 4, pp. 1942–1948, 1995.

[17] M. Araki and H. Taguchi, "Two-degree-of-freedom PID controllers," *International Journal of Control, Automation and Systems*, vol. 1, no. 4, pp. 401–411, 2003.

[18] C. S. Jung, H. K. Song, and J. C. Hyun, "Direct synthesis tuning method of unstable first-order-plus-time-delay processes," *Journal of Process Control*, vol. 9, no. 3, pp. 265–269, 1999.

[19] V. Vijayan and R. C. Panda, "Design of a simple setpoint filter for minimizing overshoot for low order processes," *ISA Transactions*, vol. 51, no. 2, pp. 271–276, 2012.

[20] C. H. Lin, J. L. Chen, and Z. L. Gaing, "Combining biometric fractal pattern and particle swarm optimization-based classifier for fingerprint recognition," *Mathematical Problems in Engineering*, vol. 2010, Article ID 328676, 14 pages, 2010.

[21] J. Zhang and K. W. Chau, "Multilayer ensemble pruning via novel multi-sub-swarm particle swarm optimization," *Journal of Universal Computer Science*, vol. 15, no. 4, pp. 840–858, 2009.

[22] K. W. Chau, "Application of a PSO-based neural network in analysis of outcomes of construction claims," *Automation in Construction*, vol. 16, no. 5, pp. 642–646, 2007.

[23] K. Chau, "Predicting construction litigation outcome using particle swarm optimization," in *Innovations in Applied Artificial Intelligence*, vol. 3533 of *Lecture Notes in Computer Science*, pp. 571–578, Springer, New York, NY, USA, 2005.

[24] A. Alfi and H. Modares, "System identification and control using adaptive particle swarm optimization," *Applied Mathematical Modelling*, vol. 35, no. 3, pp. 1210–1221, 2011.

[25] Y. Shi and R. Eberhart, "A modified particle swarm optimizer," in *Proceedings of the IEEE World Congress on Computational Intelligence*, pp. 69–73, 1998.

[26] R. C. Eberhart and Y. Shi, "Tracking and optimizing dynamic systems with particle swarms," in *Proceedings of the Congress on Evolutionary Computation*, vol. 1, pp. 94–100, Seoul, Republic of Korea, 2001.

[27] A. Nikabadi and M. Ebadzadeh, "Particle swarm optimization algorithms with adaptive inertia weight: a survey of the state of the art and a novel method," *IEEE Journal of Evolutionary Computation*, 2008.

[28] G. Chen, X. Huang, J. Jia, and Z. Min, "Natural exponential inertia weight strategy in particle swarm optimization," in *Proceedings of the 6th World Congress on Intelligent Control and Automation (WCICA '06)*, pp. 3672–3675, Dalian, China, June 2006.

[29] R. F. Malik, T. A. Rahman, S. Z. M. Hashim, and R. Ngah, "New particle swarm optimizer with sigmoid increasing inertia weight," *International Journal of Computer Science and Security*, vol. 1, no. 2, pp. 35–44, 2007.

[30] Y. Gao, X. An, and J. Liu, "A particle swarm optimization algorithm with logarithm decreasing inertia weight and chaos mutation," in *Proceedings of the International Conference on Computational Intelligence and Security (CIS '08)*, vol. 1, pp. 61–65, 2008.

[31] G. P. Liu, J. B. Yang, and J. F. Whidborne, *Multiobjective Optimization and Control*, Printice Hall, New Delhi, India, 2008.

[32] J. G. Ziegler and N. B. Nichols, "Optimum settlings for automatic controllers," *Transactions of the ASME*, vol. 64, pp. 759–768, 1942.

[33] V. Rajinikanth and K. Latha, "Optimization of PID controller parameters for unstable chemical systems using soft computing technique," *International Review of Chemical Engineering*, vol. 3, no. 3, pp. 350–358, 2011.

[34] V. Rajinikanth and K. Latha, "Controller parameter optimization for nonlinear systems using enhanced bacteria foraging algorithm," *Applied Computational Intelligence and Soft Computing*, vol. 2012, Article ID 214264, 12 pages, 2012.

10

Belief Revision in the GOAL Agent Programming Language

Johannes Svante Spurkeland, Andreas Schmidt Jensen, and Jørgen Villadsen

Algorithms, Logic and Graphs Section, Department of Applied Mathematics and Computer Science,
Technical University of Denmark, Matematiktorvet, Building 303B, 2800 Kongens Lyngby, Denmark

Correspondence should be addressed to Jørgen Villadsen; jovi@dtu.dk

Academic Editors: C. Kotropoulos, L. Mikhailov, and B. Schuller

Agents in a multiagent system may in many cases find themselves in situations where inconsistencies arise. In order to properly deal with these, a good belief revision procedure is required. This paper illustrates the usefulness of such a procedure: a certain belief revision algorithm is considered in order to deal with inconsistencies and, particularly, the issue of inconsistencies, and belief revision is examined in relation to the GOAL agent programming language.

1. Introduction

When designing artificial intelligence, it is desirable to mimic the human way of reasoning as closely as possible to obtain a realistic intelligence albeit still artificial. This includes the ability to not only construct a plan for solving a given problem but also to be able to adapt the plan or discard it in favor of a new. In these situations the environment in which the agents act should be considered as dynamic and complicated as the world it is representing. This will lead to situations where an agent's beliefs may be *inconsistent* and need to be revised. Therefore, an important issue in the subject of modern artificial intelligence is that of *belief revision*.

This paper presents an algorithm for belief revision proposed in [1] and shows some examples of situations where belief revision is desired in order to avoid inconsistencies in an agent's knowledge base. The agent programming language GOAL will be introduced and belief revision will be discussed in this context. Finally, the belief revision algorithm used in this paper will be compared to other approaches dealing with inconsistency.

2. Motivation

In many situations, assumptions are made in order to optimize and simplify an artificial intelligent system. This often leads to solutions which are elegant and planning can be done without too many complications. However, such systems tend to be more difficult to realize in the real world—simply because the assumptions made are too restrictive to model the complex real world.

The first thing to notice when modeling intelligence is that human thoughts are themselves inconsistent as considered in [2]. It also considers an example of an expert system from [3], where the classical logical representation of the experts' statements leads to inconsistency when attempting to reason with it. From this, one can realize how experts of a field not necessarily agree with one another and in order to properly reason with their statements inconsistencies need to be taken into account. This is an example where it is not possible to uniquely define the cause and effect in the real world. The experts might all have the best intentions but this might not be the case with entities interaction with an agent. Malicious entities may want to mislead the agent or otherwise provide false information which again may lead to inconsistencies. One example of this is when using multiagent systems to model computer security; agents may represent hackers or other attackers on the system in question.

Another important fact about the real world is that it is constantly changing. Agents which find themselves in changing environments need to be able to adapt to such changes; the changes may not lead to inconsistencies. When programming multiagent systems, it might not always be possible or it might be too overwhelming to foresee all consequences and outcomes that the environment provides.

In this paper, a small example will now be presented for the purpose of illustration. The example is inspired by [4, 5], where an agent-based transport information system is considered in order to improve the parking spot problem. That is, having an agent represent each car, they can communicate and coordinate to find an available parking spot nearby. In this paper, cars are considered as autonomous entities which drive their passengers around the city. Each car thus poses as an agent. Such an agent may have the following trivial rules for how to behave in traffic lights,

$$green(X) \longrightarrow go(X) \tag{1}$$

$$red(X) \longrightarrow stop(X) \tag{2}$$

Furthermore, the agent may have a rule specifying that if the brakes of a car malfunction, it cannot stop:

$$failing(brakes, X) \longrightarrow \neg stop(X). \tag{3}$$

Imagine now the situation where the light is *perceived* as green and a car in the crossing lane sends to the agent that its brakes fail. That is, the agent now also believes the following:

$$green(me) \tag{4}$$

$$red(other) \tag{5}$$

$$failing(brakes, other) \tag{6}$$

This situation will now lead to inconsistencies when the agent attempts to reason with its beliefs. From (2) and (5), it is straightforward to deduce $stop(other)$, whereas from (3) and (6), $\neg stop(other)$ is deduced. Furthermore, by adding rules for the mutual exclusion of the go and $stop$ predicates and having the rule $go(other) \rightarrow stop(me)$ saying to stop if the other does not, the agent will also be able to deduce that it both should go and should not go. The obvious choice for the agent here is to discard the thought of going onwards and stop to let the other car pass. Notice that the exclusion of go and $stop$ might be achieved by simply using $\neg go$ instead of $stop$ or vice versa. Depending on the interpretation of the two predicates, one might want to distinguish the two though— saying that failing brakes of a car means it should go seems wrong if it never started.

Assume that the agent makes the right choice and escapes the car crash. The passenger of the car wants to go shopping and the agent thus needs to find an available parking lot. To represent that the agent wants to get to the destination of the shop, it has the following:

$$dest(shop_1) \tag{7}$$

The agent currently does not know the whereabouts of the shop that the passenger wants to go to; so it broadcasts a request for such information. The agent receives a response,

$$dest(shop_1) \longrightarrow goto(lot_1) \tag{8}$$

This basically tells the agent that if it wants to reach $shop_1$ it needs to get to parking lot_1. This is straightforward; however, shortly after the agent receives a second response from a third agent:

$$dest(shop_1) \longrightarrow \neg goto(lot_1) \tag{9}$$

$$dest(shop_1) \longrightarrow goto(lot_2) \tag{10}$$

The third agent has experienced that the parking lot_1 is full which makes it send the first rule. It then also sends the second rule as a *plan* for getting parked desirably and thereby enabling the passenger to reach the destination shop.

Blissfully adding both responses to the belief base will, however, lead to inconsistencies again. Obviously, (7) can be used with (8) and (9) to obtain $goto(lot_1)$ and $\neg goto(lot_1)$, respectively. Since the agent does not currently have any more information about the two, it does not know which of them to trust.

For more examples, refer to [6]. They are of a more theoretical nature, but may illustrate how one can deal with inconsistencies efficiently. The examples are explained in relation to a tool which was developed by the author and which lets one apply a belief revision algorithm on formulas given to the program. The algorithm will be considered in more details in the next section.

It should be noted that in the above example, one might discuss several ways of trying to fix the problem. For instance, one might suggest that the problem is that the rules should not be strict, and therefore one could introduce a deontic operator meaning "should." This is not considered in this paper—instead the problem considered is that different rules may end up concluding contradictory information (and as such there is negation in actions and beliefs). This is only really a problem for larger and more complex systems, since one may find situation-specific ways of fixing the problem for smaller systems while avoiding a general solution. The example might be fixed by refining the rules and similarly for the expert system presented in [3]. However, consider if the expert system had a huge amount of statements or if all of the huge complexity of the real world had to be considered in the car example, then it might not be as easy to manually find and fix all the sources of inconsistencies. The example is simple but still provides some nice points and illustrates the main problem considered.

Notice that the example above is presented in a form of first-order logic. That is, the exact relation to the actions has not been given. Considering firing rules as adding beliefs, the agent adds information that it believes that it can for example, go. This is kind of metareasoning about the actions. Depending on the language, it might be more natural to have the rules execute actions directly. This way firing rules may execute actions instead of adding beliefs.

3. Belief Revision Algorithm

The algorithm considered in this paper is the one proposed by [1] (and [6]). It is based on a combination of the two main approaches to belief revision introduced in [7, 8] and is

```
for all j = (B, s) ∈ dependencies(A) do
    remove(j)
end for
for all j = (A, s) ∈ justifications(A) do
    if s = [] then
        remove(j)
    else
        contract(w(s))
    end if
end for
remove(A)
```

ALGORITHM 1: Contraction by belief A.

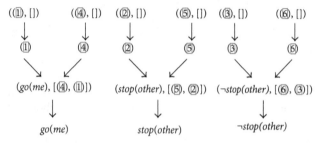

FIGURE 1: Graph over the beliefs and justifications in the first part of the example from Section 2.

extending work done in, for example, [9, 10] by treating rules and facts the same.

The basic principle of the algorithm is to keep track of what beliefs the agent has and how the agent may *justify* these beliefs. The idea is based on the human reasoning process: if two contradictory beliefs arise, one of them is selected and the other is discarded. Of course, one must also discard whatever beliefs may end up concluding the discarded belief as they can no longer be trusted either. This process of discarding beliefs is referred to as *contraction* by beliefs. This will be made more concrete in the following.

The agent is defined as having beliefs consisting of ground literals, l or $\neg l$, and rules. The rules take the form of universally quantified positive Horn clauses, $l_1 \wedge l_2 \wedge \cdots \wedge l_n \rightarrow l$ and the agent is required to reason with a weak logic, W, which only has generalized modus ponens as inference rule (i.e., if the antecedent of an implication holds, the consequent can be inferred). The inference rule is formally as follows, where δ is a substitution function replacing all variables with constants:

$$\frac{\delta(l_1), \ldots, \delta(l_n) \quad l_1 \wedge \cdots \wedge l_n \longrightarrow l}{\delta(l)} \quad (11)$$

The approach is now to detect inconsistencies in the belief base. Notice that this is a simple rule, $l \wedge \neg l \rightarrow \neg consistent(l)$. If an inconsistency is detected, the least preferred belief is removed. Furthermore, the rules from which the belief can be derived are removed along with the beliefs, which can only be derived from the removed belief. This assumes two things. First, that we keep track of how the beliefs relate to each other,

and second, that there is a measure of how preferred a belief is.

To deal with the first problem, the notion of justifications is used. A justification is a pair, (A, s), of a belief A and a support list s. The support list contains the rule used to derive A together with all the premises used for firing that rule. This means that the percepts and initial knowledge will have an empty support list. The justifications for $green(me)$ and $\neg stop(other)$ from the example in Section 2 are then as follows:

$$(green(me), [])$$

$$(\neg stop(other), [failing(brakes, other),$$
$$failing(brakes, X) \longrightarrow \neg stop(X)])$$
$$(12)$$

Notice that a belief may have several justifications. If the light had been green for the other and there was an exclusivity rule $go(X) \rightarrow \neg stop(X)$, then $\neg stop(other)$ would also have the justification:

$$(\neg stop(other), [go(other), go(X) \longrightarrow \neg stop(X)]) \quad (13)$$

Having this data structure, the beliefs and justifications can be regarded as a directed graph: incoming edges from the justifications of a belief and outgoing edges to justifications containing the belief in its support list. Figure 1 shows such a graph for the first part of the presented example. The elements at an odd depth are justifications, whereas elements of an even depth are beliefs. To make the graph fit, references to the formulas have been used instead of the actual formula where possible. One may also notice that the agent has the two contradictory nodes, which means that either of the two subgraphs holding one of the two nodes must be contracted.

In [9, 10], the successors of a belief (justifications with the belief in the support list) are denoted dependencies. The algorithm is then simply considered to have a list of justifications and dependencies for each belief and recursively traverses the elements of these two lists to remove beliefs which are justifying or justified only by the belief selected for contraction. More specifically, Algorithm 1 provides pseudo code for the contraction algorithm similar to that from [9, 10]. The contraction algorithm assumes that an inconsistency has

```
Knowledge {
    % Mutual exclusion rules of go and stop predicates.
    neg (stop (X)) :- go (X).
    neg (go (X)) :- stop (X).
}
```

ALGORITHM 2

been detected and the least preferred belief is given as input. The $w(x)$ function takes a support list as input and returns the least preferred belief of that list.

It is worth noting that the belief base needs to be in the quiescent setting in order for the algorithm to work properly. Basically what this means is that all the rules which may add new information must have been fired before executing the algorithm. This is due to that if more beliefs can be inferred, the belief for contraction might be inferred again by other beliefs than the ones removed by the algorithm. Consider, for example, the belief base consisting of $\{A \rightarrow C, B \rightarrow C, A, B, \neg C\}$. Then firing the first rule adds a contradiction and if contracting on C without firing the second rule then C may again be derived, introducing the inconsistency again. Notice, however, that this requirement is only for the algorithm to work optimally. Not firing the second rule does not make the algorithm work incorrectly but simply does so that it cannot be guaranteed that the contracted belief cannot be inferred from the current beliefs again after contraction.

It may be desirable for the algorithm to also contract beliefs which no longer have justifications because they have been removed in the contraction process, cf. [9, 10]. Even though keeping the beliefs in the belief base might not currently lead to inconsistencies, something is intuitively wrong with keeping beliefs which are derived from what has been labeled wrong or untrustworthy information.

The problem of measuring how preferred a belief is does not have a trivial solution. In fact, the problem is passed on to the designer of the multiagent system in question. The requirement from the perspective of the algorithm is that there is an ordering relation such that for any two beliefs it is decidable which one is more preferable to the other. However, in [9] an algorithm is presented for preference computation.

Consider again the example from Section 2. Intuitively, percepts of the agent should be of highest preference since the agent ought to trust what it itself sees. However, in the example, this would lead to the contraction of the belief $\neg stop(other)$ which will mean that the agent will decide to move forward and crash with the other car. Instead here the belief received from the other agent should actually have a higher preference than the percepts. This is, however, in general, not desirable as other agents might not be trustworthy. This is even though the other agents might have good intentions. Consider, for example, the plan exchange between the agents in the example. Here, the first agent sends a plan for getting to the closest parking lot not knowing it is full. If the agent chose to follow this plan and on the way perceived a sign showing the number of free spots in the parking lot, this percept should be of higher preference than following the plan through. This illustrates the care which needs to be taken in the process of deciding upon nonpreferred beliefs.

4. GOAL

GOAL is a language for programming rational agents and as such is a target of interest in relation to belief revision. This section will examine GOAL and how it conforms to belief revision of inconsistent information. First, the basic concepts of GOAL are explained and afterwards belief revision is considered in GOAL. This paper will not explain how to set up and use GOAL, instead the reader is referred to [11].

4.1. The Basics. The basic structure of a GOAL multiagent system consists of an environment and the agents which interact within this environment. The agents are according to [12] connected to the environment by means of entities. That is, an agent is considered to be the mind of the physical entity it is connected to in the multiagent system. Agents need not be connected to an entity though; however, they cannot interact with the environment if they are not. Having agents that are not part of the environment can be useful in, for example, organizational centralized multiagent systems, where there may be an agent whose only task is to coordinate the organization.

Agents may consist of the following components:

(1) knowledge;

(2) beliefs;

(3) goals;

(4) module sections;

(5) action specification.

Knowledge is what is known to be true. It should be considered as axioms and as such should not be allowed to be inconsistent. Beliefs, however, represent what the agent thinks is true and may be both false and ambiguous. That is, different rules may lead to inconsistent beliefs. The representation of knowledge, beliefs, and goals is all in a Prolog based manner by standard (see [12] for more details). While it may be arguably very few things in the real world that are certain enough to be declared axioms, the mutual exclusion of the *go* and *stop* predicates should be. Since the two predicates are direct opposites, it does not make sense to have both, for example, *go(me)* and *stop(me)*. Declaring these rules as initial knowledge may look as Algorithm 2.

```
beliefs {
    % Green and red light rules.
    go (X) :- green (X).
    stop (X) :- red (X).
}
```

ALGORITHM 3

```
actionspec {
    /* Action for the car agent to drive towards Dest provided it is desired and
        that it can go onwards. */
    drive (Dest) {
        Pre {dest (Dest), me (Me), go (Me)}
        post {true}
    }
}
```

ALGORITHM 4

The two *neg* predicates represent strong negation and will be explained in Section 4.2.

One might argue that the rules for green and red lights are accepted worldwide and thus should be considered axioms. However, global consensus and being a universal truth are not the same. First, the trend may change, and second, the agent may find itself in unforeseen situations in which such a rule cannot apply. Consider the example where green light should not allow for *go* since the other car cannot fulfill the rule of the red light. Another example is that of [1], where there is global consensus that birds fly and yet penguins, which are birds, cannot fly. These are both examples of why one cannot assume not to face inconsistencies when exposing multiagent systems to the real world. We therefore choose to declare the two traffic light rules as beliefs rather than knowledge as shown in Algorithm 3.

The action specification follows a STRIPS-style specification (see e.g., [13, ch. 10]) and actions are defined using a name, parameters, preconditions, and postconditions. Imagine that the car agent has a drive action which represents the agent driving to a desired destination. The action takes the destination to drive to as parameter, and has as preconditions that it must desire to get to the destination and that it can go onwards. The *me* predicate is a built-in predicate for the agent to obtain its own ID and the action specification may now look as Algorithm 4.

The postcondition may seem to be somewhat odd—driving somewhere ought to change the agent's state. This is due to thinking of the drive action as a *durative* action. In GOAL, there is a distinction between the two types of actions: *instantaneous* and *durative* [12]. Durative actions take time to perform, whereas instant actions to will finish immediately and thereby affect the system immediately. Therefore, the approach seems to be to let the outcome of durative actions be a consequence of their effect on the environment. That way durative actions can also be interrupted and their effect might not (entirely) come through. Thus, the drive action is durative, since the agent will not instantly reach its destination. Furthermore, the environment can send percepts to the agent (such as a red light), which will interrupt the action (if the agent chooses to react to the percept). When the agent perceives that the lights become green, it may resume driving.

If one wants to avoid the kind of metareasoning discussed in Section 2, the premise of the green rule might have been used directly when defining the requirements of the drive action. That is, instead of the *go(Me)* precondition, one might use *green(Me)*. Notice, however, that this requires instantiation of the premise and makes the rule less general. This also means that the rule cannot be used in other contexts if desired (unless again explicitly defined). Basically, these considerations depend on how one wants to design the system. Yet another approach would be to use the premise in the motivation for taking the action (see the part about the main module below); however, this implies the same considerations.

The environment is specified by means of an environment interface standard; for more information about this standard [12], refer to, for example, [14]. It is beyond the scope of this paper to uncover how to program environments for GOAL programs; however, we assume that there is an environment in which the agents can perceive the traffic lights. The agent has a percept base which contains the percepts of the current reasoning cycle. It is up to the programmer to make the agent capable of reacting to such percepts. This can be done by using the predicate *percept*, which is a predicate holding the current percepts of the agent.

The module sections define the agent's behavior. There are two modules by standard: the event module and the main module. The purpose of the main module is to define how the agent should decide what actions to perform, whereas the purpose of the event module is to handle events such as percepts and incoming messages so that the belief base is always up to date when deciding upon actions cf. [12].

```
event module {
    program {
        % Green and red light percepts - on.
        forall bel (percept (green (X)), not (green (X))) do insert (green (X)).
        forall bel (percept (red (X)), not (red (X))) do insert (red (X)).

        % Green and red light percepts - off.
        forall bel (green (X), percept (not (green (X)))) do delete (green (X)).
        forall bel (red (X), percept (not (red (X)))) do delete (red (X)).
    }
}
```

ALGORITHM 5

```
main module {
    program {
        % Drive economically if low on gas.
        if bel (low (gas), dest (X)) then drive (dest (X), eco).

        % Drive fast if busy.
        if bel (busy, dest (X)) then drive (dest (X), fast).

        % Drive comfortably otherwise.
        if bel (dest (X)) then drive (dest (X), comfort).

        % If no driving options the car simply idles.
        if true then skip.
    }
}
```

ALGORITHM 6

Therefore, the event module is always the first to run in an agent's reasoning cycle. To add the logic for actually making the agent believe the light perceptions, the event module of Algorithm 5 may be used where *insert* and *delete* are two built-in functions for adding and deleting beliefs, respectively.

The *bel* predicate is a built-in predicate to indicate that the agent believes the argument(s) of the predicate.

The main module is not that interesting when the agent does not have more actions defined since there are not really any strategic choices to regard in relation to the choice of action. It might consider whether or not to drive or brake. Depending on how the environment is defined, braking might be implicitly assumed by saying that if the car is not driving, it has stopped. Instead of considering a brake action, here is considered a more sophisticated *drive* action. One may assume that the *drive* action takes an extra argument which defines the mode that the car should drive in. Assuming that when low on gas it drives economically, and if busy it drives fast; the main module of Algorithm 6 may define the choice of actions.

Notice that the precondition stating that the *drive* action must have a destination is actually obsolete now since this is ensured when deciding upon action in the main module. The main module may evaluate actions in different kinds of orders. The default is linear which means that, for example, the economical option is chosen over the others if applicable. The *skip* action is not built-in but may be defined by simply having *true* as pre- and postconditions.

Agents communicate using a mailbox system. Mails are handled similarly to percepts, with the main difference that the mailbox is not emptied in every reasoning cycle. GOAL supports three moods of messages: indicative, declarative, and interrogative. These three moods basically represent a statement, a request and a question and are denoted using an operator in front of the message. Similar to the *percept* predicate, there is a *received* predicate over received messages. This predicate takes two arguments: the agent who sent the message and the message itself. Messages must be a conjunction of positive literals. Therefore, handling the message that the other agent's brakes fail can be done by adding Algorithm 7 to the program shown in Algorithm 5 in the event module where : is being the indicative operator.

By requiring messages to be a conjunction of positive literals, agents cannot share rules or plans. It is simply not possible to send or receive the rules (8), (9), and (10) from the second part of the example. This also means that the rule base of an agent will be static and is designed *offline*. Thus, the graph of Algorithm 1 will be less complex during runtime.

Another lack of expressiveness in GOAL is that of representing inconsistencies. This will be examined further in the next section.

% Add the belief received from another agent that its brakes fail.
if bel (received (A,:failing (brakes, A))) **then insert** (failing (brakes, A))
+ **delete** (received (A,:failing (brakes, A))).

Algorithm 7

4.2. Inconsistencies. While having the tools for implementing the algorithm dealing with inconsistencies, a rather crucial point is to be noted. Since the knowledge representation language of the belief base in GOAL is Prolog, the rules will all take the form of positive Horn clauses with a positive consequent. This means only positive literals can be concluded using the rules in the belief base. Furthermore, the action specifications ensure that if a negative literal is added then it is not actually added to the belief base. Instead, if the positive literal is in the belief base it is removed and otherwise nothing happens. This is due to the closed world assumption. This means that an agent will never be able to represent both the positive and the negative of a literal in its belief base. That is, GOAL simply does not allow for representing inconsistencies when using Prolog as knowledge representation language.

One of the advantages of GOAL is that its structure allows for selecting different knowledge representation languages depending on what is best with regard to modeling the system at hand. At current stage, it is only Prolog which has been implemented as knowledge representation language; however, work is done on implementing answer set programming. This allows for both negation as failure as in Prolog but also for a notion of strong negation (see, e.g., [15] for more information about answer set programming) which allows for representing incomplete information. This means that using answer set programming as knowledge representation language would be quite powerful when dealing with systems in which inconsistencies might arise. It is not implemented yet though; so in the following, strong negation will be discussed in relation to GOAL using Prolog.

In order to allow for the representation of inconsistencies, the notion of strong negation is introduced in Prolog. In [16], this kind of negation does not rely on the closed world assumption. It explicitly says that the negation of a formula succeeds whereas negation as failure says that the formula does not succeed, but also that it does not explicitly fail either. In other words, negation as failure can be read as "it is not currently believed that."

The basic principle is now to consider the strong negation, ¬, of a predicate as a positive literal. That is, for literal, p, p' can be regarded as a positive literal with the meaning $\neg p$. In terms of Prolog, this means querying p will succeed if p holds, fail if $\neg p$ holds, and be inconsistent if both holds. In [16], it is furthermore considered possible to return the value unknown to such queries if neither p nor $\neg p$ can be proven in the current Prolog program. Another interesting observation they made is that the closed world assumption

can be defined for any literal in the following way (where *not* denotes negation as failure):

$$\neg p(X_1, \ldots, X_n) \longleftarrow not\,(p(X_1, \ldots, X_n)) \qquad (14)$$

The interested reader might also see [17] in relation to strong negation and logic programming.

In the terms of GOAL, this means that it is fairly straightforward to introduce the notion of strong negation, and the *neg* predicate introduced in Section 4.1 serves exactly this purpose. There is no explicit problem in having both the belief and its negation in the belief base: it is required in the event module to check if the belief base is still consistent by querying whether or not $neg(X)$, X follows from the belief base and act accordingly. It may be necessary to introduce a *pos* predicate denoting positive literals as GOAL does not allow for the query $bel(X)$.

4.3. Belief Revision. This section will consider how to implement the belief revision algorithm described in Section 3 in GOAL.

The event module is the first thing that is executed in an agent's reasoning cycle and since it is desirable to have an up-to-date belief base when performing belief revision, the belief revision algorithm should be implemented as the last procedure in the event module.

GOAL relies on Prolog as representation language (in most cases), which conforms well to the weak logic defined for use with the belief revision algorithm in [1] since Prolog programs consist of Horn clauses and literals.

The question is then how to associate and represent the justification and dependency lists. One idea is to simply let them be beliefs of the agent. This way one just has to make sure to add a justification when adding a belief. The rules for adding percepts to the agent from Section 4.1 may be extended to also constructing a justification as shown in Algorithm 8.

Similarly, the justification is deleted when the percept is no longer valid, as shown above. While the case is rather trivial when dealing with percepts (as they do not have any justifications), a similar approach may be taken for the rules, the actions, and when adding beliefs from messages of other agents. We need to consider the actions carefully, since the motivation for executing an action is specified in the main module, whereas the postconditions (i.e., effect) of the actions are specified in the action specification. Each effect of an action should be supported by a conjunction of the motivation for taking the action and the preconditions of the action. There are several ways for obtaining this

```
% Add beliefs and justifications from red light percepts.
forall bel (percept (red (X)), not (red (X))) do insert (red (X))
    + insert (just (red (X), [], p)).

% Remove belief and justification when no longer red light.
forall bel (red (X), percept (not (red (X)))) do delete (red (X))
    + delete (just (red (X), [], _)).
```

ALGORITHM 8

```
actionspec {
% Action for the car agent to drive which also adds justifications.
    drive (Dest, Pre) {
        pre {dest (Dest), me (Me), go (Me), append (Pre, [dest (Dest), go (Me),
            action (drive)], S)}
        post {at (Dest), just (at (Dest), S)}
    }
}
```

ALGORITHM 9

conjunction. A simple one is to simply let the action take them as parameters. The provided action is instantaneous; the agent is immediately at its destination; so the action specification could look like Algorithm 9.

The idea is to include the motivation from the main module as an argument to the action and then append it to a list of preconditions of the action to obtain s. The *action* predicate then corresponds to the rule used for deriving the belief. In this case it is a plan, which has been executed. Since actions and main modules cannot be altered dynamically, another predicate might be added as precondition, for example, *not contracted(action(drive))*. If an action or particular instance of an action is then contracted using the belief revision algorithm, for example, the belief *contracted(action(drive))* may simply be added to invalidate any future run of that action. If the agent finds reason to believe in the action again, it may simply remove the belief again.

The case of durative actions is more difficult to handle. The effects of a durative action appear as changes in the environment, which the agent will then perceive. However, since percepts create a justification with an empty support list, there is no way of telling whether the percept is from a change in the environment due to an action that the agent has performed or simply due to the environment itself (or even other agents interacting in the environment). In other words, durative actions cannot be contracted. One might attempt to solve this problem by implementing the environment such that it provides justifications for changes happening as a result of actions and then keep track of how these justifications relate to the percepts. However, it seems wrong to let the environment handle part of the agent's reasoning and it might couple the agent and the environment too much.

One might raise the questions why include actions in the contraction process and what does it actually mean to contract an action? Actions may be reasons for adding new beliefs (e.g., changes in the environment as a result of an action). The agent will need some way of justifying these beliefs, especially because a rule might trigger an action, which then adds a belief that renders the belief base inconsistent. If there is no justification; for the action, then it is not possible to trace back to the rule originally triggering the action leading to the inconsistency. Furthermore, it might be that some actions simply lead to undesirable outcomes and therefore the agent should not want to do them again. Therefore, one might decide to contract them and thereby disable executing them in the future. Since actions are not deleted, they may be enabled again in the future if desirable.

We have provided means for representing justifications, so the next step is to check for inconsistencies, which, as argued above, will be done as the last thing in the event module. Then if two contradictory beliefs are found, the less preferred of the two is marked for contraction.

The contraction itself then happens by three blocks. In the first all the positive beliefs marked for contraction are contracted and in the second all the negative. These two blocks follow contraction Algorithm 1 with the exception of the recursive call. This is what the third block is for. The recursive call is emulated by marking all the least preferred elements of the support lists to contract and in the third block the first of the recursive calls are then performed on these. Again, the recursive call is emulated by marking beliefs for contraction. However, since the program is executed sequentially, it has now passed the three blocks for contraction. The idea is then to prohibit the agent from performing any actions until there are no beliefs marked for contraction. Then the agent will

```
% Detect inconsistencies
#define poscontract (X) bel (p (neg (X), Pn), p (X, Pp), Pn > Pp).
#define negcontract (X) bel (p (neg (X), Pn), p (X, Pp), Pn < Pp).

% Contract all least preferred positive beliefs
listall C <- poscontract (X) do {
    forall just (Y, S), member (Z, C), member (Z, S) do delete (just (Y, S)).
    forall just (Y, []), member (Y, C) do delete (just (Y, _)).
    forall member (Y, C), just (Y, S) bel (w (just (Y, S), Z)) do insert (contract (Z)).
    forall member (Y, C) do delete (Y).
}

% Contract all least preferred negative beliefs
listall C <- negcontract (X) do {
    forall just (Y, S), member (Z, C), member (Z, S) do delete (just (Y, s)).
    forall just (Y, []), member (Y, C) do delete (just (Y, _)).
    forall member (Y, C), just (Y, S) bel (w (just (Y, S), Z)) do insert (contract (Z)).
    forall member (Y, C) do delete (Y).
}

% Recursive contraction
listall C <- contract (X) do {
    forall just (Y, S), member (Z, C), member (Z, S) do delete (just (Y, S)).
    forall just (Y, []), member (Y, C) do delete (just (Y, _)).
    forall member (Y, C), just (Y, S) bel (w (just (Y, S), Z)) do insert (contract (Z)).
    forall member (Y, C) do delete (Y).
}
```

ALGORITHM 10

do nothing and the next reasoning cycle will start. This time it will go directly to the third cycle and continue emulating recursive calls by doing this until no more beliefs are marked for contraction and the agent is allowed to perform actions again (Algorithm 10).

However, this solution is not optimal, since it lets the agent idle for several cycles while it is revising its thoughts. Though the number of recursive calls is most likely quite low because of the simplified graph due to static rules as mentioned in Section 4.1, it would be better to have a Prolog contraction procedure, which can make use of recursion. One might, for example, import such a procedure in the knowledge section such that it will mark all the beliefs for contraction recursively and in the next cycle actually do the removal of them. This way only one extra cycle is used for contracting beliefs.

Another possibility is to recursively contract beliefs in the event module. This is done by moving the contraction algorithm into a separate module, which is then imported in the event module (see, e.g., [11] for how to import) and can be called recursively within itself. This would obviously be the most efficient solution as it only takes the calculation time and no reasoning cycles.

Until now, the implementation of the preference relations has not been discussed. In the above code, it is assumed that a preference of a belief is added as a predicate cf. justification. Furthermore, it is assumed that when adding a nonempty support list of a justification, a predicate w, which specifies the least preferred belief in a support list, is added to the belief base. This simplifies the least preferred belief queries; however, one should keep in mind that these predicates all should be deleted when also deleting the corresponding belief.

In [9, 10], the algorithm was considered with regards to an implementation in Jason, and they argued that the quiescent setting could not be guaranteed. In our implementation, an action may not be activated for a long time, but it may still lead to inconsistencies. Therefore, the same argument can be made in our case. However, when querying the belief base for inconsistencies (which is done every reasoning cycle), the Prolog engine will attempt to evaluate all the rules in the belief base in order to search for a proof. This means that the quiescent setting is guaranteed for the belief base, but not for the action rules.

5. Other Approaches

Previous work, [2], considered a four-valued logic proposed by [3] in order to deal with inconsistent information. The main difference between this approach and the algorithm considered here is that the algorithm attempts to recover the belief base from an inconsistent state to a consistent state. It does so by attempting to get rid of the information which was the cause of the inconsistency. The four-valued logic on the other hand attempts to reason with the inconsistent knowledge base while actually preserving the inconsistency in the system.

At first glance, it seems to be more desirable to recover the belief base from an inconsistent state to a consistent state.

However, just like determining the preferences of the beliefs, this also has some complications. For instance, if the agent makes the right choice in the example from Section 2, it will contract the rules for the light signal. This means that when the danger has passed, then the agent will not know to go when it is green light and stop when it is red light. That is, deleting information from the knowledge base might not always be the best choice as the agent might actually delete some vital beliefs. The problem is that the beliefs might hold in most situations where they should be applied but in some more rare cases they may lead to inconsistencies.

Handling inconsistencies is still a debated topic and there is no full solution yet. One might take several different approaches for dealing with the above problem. One is to do as with the actions where one simply disables rules instead of completely deleting them. Then they may be reconsidered later. One could also attempt to combine the four-valued approach with the contraction algorithm. That is, use contraction and if a requirement arises that a rule which is known to lead to inconsistencies needs to be used again, one can attempt to use the paraconsistent logic to reason with this rule. Yet another approach is rule refinement instead of rule contraction. If the agent, for example, detects the cause of the inconsistency, it might be able to repair or refine the rules in question. If, for instance the car agent realizes that the cause of the problem is the failing brakes with regard to the red light rule, it could refine it into the following rule:

$$red\,(X) \wedge not\ failing\,(brakes, X) \longrightarrow stop\,(X) \qquad (15)$$

Even though it might seem to be the smartest solution, this is not guaranteed to always have a solution and finding such a solution might prove very complicated.

6. Conclusion

It has been argued why belief revision is an important issue. A particular algorithm for belief revision has been considered. It has the advantages of being efficient and straightforward to implement; however, it has the disadvantages that it is only defined for a weak logic of the agent and that it requires the nontrivial question of a preference ordering. Issues of such an ordering have been pointed out. Furthermore, issues with deleting information, which may be important in many cases even though it is inconsistent, have been pointed out.

GOAL has been examined in relation to belief revision. It has the strengths of using logic programming which means that it is very easy to learn for people with a background in logic programming and it provides elegant logical solutions. Furthermore, the restrictions of logic programming conform well to the restrictions of the weak logic of the belief revision algorithm. However, it has been identified that at current state, the GOAL language is actually more restrictive than required for the algorithm which results in that inconsistencies cannot be represented at all. The introduction of strong negation has been considered in order to mitigate this problem. Furthermore, using answer set programming as knowledge representation language may also deal with this problem when it is supported by GOAL. Another less critical issue with GOAL is that it does not provide the means for plan sharing.

Acknowledgments

The authors would like to thank Koen V. Hindriks and M. Birna van Riemsdijk for their comments.

References

[1] H. H. Nguyen, "Belief revision in a fact-rule agents belief base," in *Agent and Multi-Agent Systems: Technologies and Applications*, A. Håkansson, N. T. Nguyen, L. Ronald Hartung, R. J. Howlett, and L. C. Jain, Eds., vol. 5559 of *Lecture Notes in Computer Science*, pp. 120–130, Springer, Berlin, Germany, 2009.

[2] J. S. Spurkeland, *Using paraconsistent logics in knowledge-based systems [B.Sc. thesis]*, Technical University of Denmark, 2010.

[3] J. Villadsen, "Paraconsistent knowledge bases and many-valued logic," in *Proceedings of the International Baltic Conference on Databases and Information Systems (Baltic DB&IS '02)*, H.-M. Haav and A. Kalja, Eds., vol. 2, pp. 77–90, Institute of Cybernetics at Tallinn Technical University, 2002.

[4] N. Bessghaier, M. Zargayouna, and F. Balbo, "An agent-based community to manage urban parking," in *Advances on Practical Applications of Agents and Multi-Agent Systems*, Y. Demazeau, J. P. Müller, J. M. C. Rodríguez, and J. B. Pérez, Eds., vol. 155 of *Advances in Intelligent and Soft Computing*, pp. 17–22, Springer, Berlin, 2012.

[5] N. Bessghaier, M. Zargayouna, and F. Balbo, "Management of urban parking: an agent-based approach," in *Artificial Intelligence: Methodology, Systems, and Applications*, A. Ramsay and G. Agre, Eds., vol. 7557 of *Lecture Notes in Computer Science*, pp. 276–285, Springer, Berlin, Germany, 2012.

[6] H. H. Nguyen, *A belief revision system [B.Sc. thesis]*, University of Nottingham, 2009.

[7] C. E. Alchourron, P. Gärdenfors, and D. Makinson, "On the logic of theory change: partial meet contraction and revision functions," *The Journal of Symbolic Logic*, vol. 50, pp. 510–530, 1985.

[8] J. Doyle, *Truth Maintenance Systems for Problem Solving*, Massachusetts Institute of Technology, Cambridge, Mass, USA, 1978.

[9] N. Alechina, M. Jago, and B. Logan, "Resource-bounded belief revision and contraction," in *Declarative Agent Languages and Technologies III*, M. Baldoni, U. Endriss, A. Omicini, and P. Torroni, Eds., vol. 3904 of *Lecture Notes in Computer Science*, pp. 141–154, Springer, Berlin, Germany, 2005.

[10] N. Alechina, R. H. Bordini, J. F. Hübner, M. Jago, and B. Logan, "Automating belief revision for AgentSpeak," in *Declarative Agent Languages and Technologies IV*, M. Baldoni and U. Endriss, Eds., vol. 4327 of *Lecture Notes in Computer Science*, pp. 61–77, Springer, Berlin, Germany, 2006.

[11] K. V. Hindriks and W. Pasman, *GOAL User Manual*, 2012.

[12] K. V. Hindriks, *Programming Rational Agents in GOAL*, 2011.

[13] S. Russell and P. Norvig, *Artificial Intelligence—A Modern Approach*, Pearson Education, 3rd edition, 2010.

[14] T. M. Behrens, K. V. Hindriks, and J. Dix, "Towards an environment interface standard for agent platforms," *Annals of Mathematics and Artificial Intelligence*, vol. 61, no. 4, pp. 261–295, 2011.

[15] V. Lifschitz, *What Is Answer Set Programming*, University of Texas at Austin, 2008.

[16] C. Baral and M. Gelfond, "Logic programming and knowledge representation," *The Journal of Logic Programming*, vol. 19-20, no. 1, pp. 73–148, 1994.

[17] G. Wagner, "Logic programming with strong negation and inexact predicates," in *Vivid Logic*, vol. 764 of *Lecture Notes in Computer Science*, pp. 89–110, Springer, Berlin, Germany, 1994.

11

Probabilistic Multiagent Reasoning over Annotated Amalgamated F-Logic Ontologies

Markus Schatten

University of Zagreb, Faculty of Organization and Informatics, Pavlinska 2, 42000 Varaždin, Croatia

Correspondence should be addressed to Markus Schatten; markus.schatten@foi.hr

Academic Editors: H. A. Guvenir, J. A. Hernandez, and C. Kotropoulos

In a multiagent system (MAS), agents can have different opinions about a given problem. In order to solve the problem collectively they have to reach consensus about the ontology of the problem. A solution to probabilistic reasoning in such an environment by using a social network of trust is given. It is shown that frame logic can be annotated and amalgamated by using this approach which gives a foundation for collective ontology development in MAS. Consider the following problem: a set of agents in a multiagent system (MAS) model a certain domain in order to collectively solve a problem. Their opinions about the domain differ in various ways. The agents are connected into a social network defined by trust relations. The problem to be solved is how to obtain consensus about the domain.

1. Introduction

To formalize the problem let $A = \{a_1,\ldots,a_n\}$ be a set of agents, let τ be a trust relation defined over $A \times A$, and let $D = \{o_1,\ldots,o_m\}$ be a problem domain consisting of a set of objects. Let further S be a set of all possible statements about D, and let O be a relation over $A \times S$. We will denote by O the social ontology expressed by the agents. What is the probability that a certain statement from the expressed statements in O is true?

By modeling some domains of interest (using a formalism like ontologies, knowledge bases, or other models) a person expresses his/her knowledge about it. Thus the main concept of interest in modeling any domain is knowledge. Nonaka and Takeuchi once defined knowledge as a "justified true belief" [1] whereby this definition is usually credited to Plato. This means that the modeling person implicitly presumes that the expressed statements in his/her model are true. On the other hand if one asks the important question *what is the truth?*, we arrive at one of the fundamental philosophical questions. Nietzsche once argued in [2] that a person is unable to prove the truth of a statement which is nothing more than the invention of fixed conventions for merely practical purposes, like repose, security, and/or consistence. According to this view, no one can prove that this paper is not just a fantasy of the reader reading it.

The previously outlined definition of knowledge includes, intentionally or not, two more crucial concepts: *justified* and *belief*. An individual will consider something to be true that he believes in, and, from that perspective, the overall truth will be a set of statements that the community believes in. This mutual belief makes this set of statements justified. The truth was once that the Earth was the center of the universe until philosophers and scientists started to question that theory. The Earth was also once a flat surface residing on the back of an elephant. So an interesting fact about the truth, from this perspective, is that it evolves depending on the different beliefs of a certain community.

In an environment where a community of agents collaborates in modeling a domain there is a chance that there will be disagreements about the domain which can yield certain inconsistencies in the model. A good example of such disagreements is the so-called "editor wars" on Wikipedia the popular free online encyclopedia. A belief about the war in ex-Yugoslavia will likely differ between a Croat and a Serb, but they will probably share the same beliefs about fundamental mathematical algebra.

Following this perspective, our conceptualization of statements as units of formalized knowledge will consider the probability of giving a true statement a matter of justification. An agent is justified if other members of a social system believe in his statements. Herein we would like to outline a social network metric introduced by Bonacich [3] called eigenvector centrality which calculates the centrality of a node based on the centrality's of its adjacent nodes. Eigenvector centrality assigns relative values to all nodes of a social network based on the principle that connections to nodes with high values contribute more to the value of the node in question than equal connections to nodes with low values. In a way, if we interpret the network under consideration as a network of trust, it yields an approximation of the probability that a certain agent will say the truth in a statement as perceived by the other agents of the network. The use of eigenvector centrality here is arbitrary; any other metric with the described properties could be used as well.

In order to express knowledge about a certain domain, one needs an adequate language. Herein we will use frame logic or F-logic introduced by [4], which is an object-oriented, deductive knowledge base and ontology language. The use of F-logic here is arbitrary, and any other formal (or informal) language could be used that allows expressing an ontology of a given domain. Nevertheless, F-logic allows us to reason about concepts (classes of objects), objects (instances of classes), attributes (properties of objects) and methods (behavior of objects), by defining rules over the domain, which makes it much more user friendly than other approaches.

2. Introducing Frame Logic

The syntax of F-logic is defined as follows [4].

Definition 1. The alphabet $\Sigma_{\mathscr{F}}$ of an F-logic language $\mathscr{L}_{\mathscr{F}}$ consists of the following:

(i) a set of object constructors, $\mathscr{F}$;

(ii) an infinite set of variables, $\mathscr{V}$;

(iii) auxiliary symbols, such as, $(,), [,], \rightarrow, \twoheadrightarrow, \longmapsto, \bullet\!\!\twoheadrightarrow, \Rightarrow$, and $\Rrightarrow$; and

(iv) usual logical connectives and quantifiers, $\vee, \wedge, \neg, \leftarrow, \forall$, and $\exists$.

Object constructors (the elements of $\mathscr{F}$) play the role of function symbols in F-logic whereby each function symbol has an arity. The arity is a nonnegative integer that represents the number of arguments the symbol can take. A constant is a symbol with arity 0, and symbols with arity ≥1 are used to construct larger terms out of simpler ones. An id term is a usual first-order term composed of function symbols and variables, as in predicate calculus. The set of all variable free or ground id terms is denoted by $U(\mathscr{F})$ and is commonly known as Herbrand Universe. Id terms play the role of logical object identities in F-logic which is a logical abstraction of physical object identities.

A language in F-logic consists of a set of formulae constructed out of alphabet symbols. The simplest formulae in F-logic are called F-molecules.

Definition 2. A molecule in F-logic is one of the following statements:

(i) an is-a assertion of the form $C :: D$ (C is a nonstrict subclass of D) or of the form $O : C$ (O is a member of class C), where C, D, and O are id terms;

(ii) an object molecule of the form O [a ";" separated list of method expressions], where O is an id term that denotes an object. A method expression can be either a noninheritable data expression, an inheritable data expression, or a signature expression.

(a) Noninheritable data expressions can be in either of the following two forms.

(1) A non-inheritable scalar expression $\text{ScalMethod}@Q_1,\ldots,Q_k \rightarrow T$, $(k \geq 0)$.

(2) A non-inheritable set-valued expression $\text{SetMethod}@R_1,\ldots,R_l \twoheadrightarrow \{S_1,\ldots,S_m\}$ $(l, m \geq 0)$.

(b) Inheritable scalar and set-valued expression are equivalent to their non-inheritable counterparts except that $\rightarrow$ is replaced with $\longmapsto$ and $\twoheadrightarrow$ with $\bullet\!\!\twoheadrightarrow$.

(c) Signature expression can also take two different forms.

(1) A scalar signature expression $\text{ScalMethod}@V_1,\ldots,V_n \Rightarrow (A_1,\ldots,A_r)$, $(n, r \geq 0)$.

(2) A set-valued signature expression $\text{SetMethod}@W_1,\ldots,W_s \Rrightarrow (B_1,\ldots,B_t)$ $(s, t \geq 0)$.

All methods' left hand sides (e.g., Q_i, R_i, V_i, and W_i) denote arguments, whilst the right hand sides (e.g., T, S_i, A_i, and B_i) denote method outputs. Single-headed arrows ($\rightarrow, \longmapsto$, and $\Rightarrow$) denote scalar methods, and double-headed arrows ($\twoheadrightarrow, \bullet\!\!\twoheadrightarrow$, and $\Rrightarrow$) denote set-valued methods.

As in a lot of other logic, F-formulae are built out of simpler ones by using the usual logical connectives and quantifiers mentioned above.

Definition 3. A formula in F-logic is defined recursively:

(i) F-molecules are F-formulae;

(ii) $\varphi \vee \psi$, $\varphi \wedge \psi$, and $\neg\varphi$ are F-formulae if so are φ and ψ;

(iii) $\forall X\varphi$ and $\exists Y\psi$ are F-formulae if so are φ and ψ, and X and Y are variables.

F-logic further allows us to define logic programs. One of the popular class of logic programs is Horn programs.

Definition 4. A Horn F-program consists of Horn rules, which are statements of the form

$$head \longleftarrow body. \tag{1}$$

Whereby *head* is an F-molecule, and *body* is a conjunction of F-molecules. Since the statement is a clause, we consider all variables to be implicitly universally quantified.

For our purpose these definitions of F-logic are sufficient, but the interested reader is advised to consult [4] for profound logical foundations of object-oriented and frame based languages.

3. Introducing Social Network Analysis

A formal approach to defining social networks is graph theory [5].

Definition 5. A *graph* $\mathscr{G}$ is the pair $(\mathscr{N}, \mathscr{A})$ whereby $\mathscr{N}$ represents the set of *verticles* or *nodes* and $\mathscr{A} \subseteq \mathscr{N} \times \mathscr{N}$ the set of *edges* or *arcs* connecting pairs from $\mathscr{N}$.

A graph can be represented with the so-called adjacency matrix.

Definition 6. Let $\mathscr{G}$ be a graph defined with the set of nodes $\{n_1, n_2, \ldots, n_m\}$ and edges $\{e_1, e_2, \ldots, e_l\}$. For every i, j ($1 \leqslant i \leqslant m$ and $1 \leqslant j \leqslant m$) one defines

$$a_{ij} = \begin{cases} 1, & \text{if there is an edge between nodes } n_i \text{ and } n_j, \\ 0, & \text{otherwise.} \end{cases} \quad (2)$$

Matrix $A = [a_{ij}]$ is then the adjacency matrix of graph $\mathscr{G}$. The matrix i is symmetric since if there is an edge between nodes n_i and n_j, then clearly there is also an edge between n_j and n_i. Thus $A = [a_{ij}] = [a_{ji}]$.

The notion of directed and valued-directed graphs is of special importance to our study.

Definition 7. A *directed graph* or *digraph* $\mathscr{G}$ is the pair $(\mathscr{N}, \mathscr{A})$, whereby $\mathscr{N}$ represents the set of *nodes* and $\mathscr{A} \subseteq \mathscr{N} \times \mathscr{N}$ the set of ordered pairs of elements from $\mathscr{N}$ that represents the set of graph *arcs*.

Definition 8. A *valued* or *weighted digraph* $\mathscr{G}_{\mathscr{V}}$ is the triple $(\mathscr{N}, \mathscr{A}, \mathscr{V})$ whereby $\mathscr{N}$ represents the set of *nodes* or *verticles*, $\mathscr{A} \subseteq \mathscr{N} \times \mathscr{N}$ the set of ordered pairs of elements from $\mathscr{N}$ that represent the set of graph *arcs*, and $\mathscr{V} : \mathscr{N} \to \mathbb{R}$ a function that attaches values or weights to nodes.

A social network can be represented as a graph $\mathscr{G} = (\mathscr{N}, \mathscr{A})$ where $\mathscr{N}$ denotes the set of actors and $\mathscr{A}$ denotes the set of relations between them [6]. If the relations are directed (e.g. support, influence, message sending, trust, etc.), we can conceptualize a social network as a directed graph. If the relations additionally can be measured in a numerical way, social networks can be represented as valued digraphs.

One of the main applications of graph theory to social network analysis is the identification of the "most important" actors inside a social network. There are lots of different methods and algorithms that allow us to calculate the importance, prominence, degree, closeness, betweenness, information, differential status, or rank of an actor. As previously mentioned we will use the eigenvector centrality to annotate agents' statements.

Definition 9. Let p_i denote the value or weight of node n_i, and let $[a_{ij}]$ be the adjacency matrix of the network. For node n_i let the centrality value be proportional to the sum of all values of nodes which are connected to it. Hence

$$p_i = \frac{1}{\lambda} \cdot \sum_{j \in M(j)} p_j = \frac{1}{\lambda} \cdot \sum_{j=1}^{N} a_{ij} \cdot p_j, \quad (3)$$

where $M(i)$ is the set of nodes that are connected to the ith node, N is the total number of nodes, and λ is a constant. In vector notation this can be rewritten as

$$p = \frac{1}{\lambda} \cdot A \cdot p \text{ or as the eigenvector equation } A \cdot p = \lambda \cdot p. \quad (4)$$

PageRank is a variant of the eigenvector centrality measure, which we decided to use herein. PageRank was developed by Google or more precise by Larry Page (from where the word play PageRank comes from) and Sergey Brin. They used this graph analysis algorithm, for the ranking of web pages on a web search engine. The algorithm uses not only the content of a web page but also the incoming and outgoing links. Incoming links are hyperlinks from other web pages pointing to the page under consideration, and outgoing links are hyperlinks to other pages to which the page under consideration points.

PageRank is iterative and starts with a random page following its outgoing hyperlinks. It could be understood as a Markov process in which states are web pages, and transitions (which are all of equal probability) are the hyperlinks between them. The problem of pages which do not have any outgoing links, as well as the problem of loops, is solved through a jump to a random page. To ensure fairness (because of a huge base of possible pages), a transition to a random page is added to every page which has the probability q and is in most cases 0.15. The equation which is used for rank calculation (which could be thought of like the probability that a random user will open this particular page) is as follows:

$$\text{PageRank}(p_i) = \frac{q}{N} + (1 - q) \sum_{p_j \in M(p_i)} \frac{\text{PageRank}(p_j)}{L(p_j)}, \quad (5)$$

where $p_1, p_2, \ldots, p_N$ are nodes under consideration, $M(p_i)$ the set of nodes pointing to p_i, $L(p_i)$ the number of arcs which come from node p_j, and N the number of all nodes [7, 8].

A very convenient feature of PageRank is that the sum of all ranks is 1. Thus, semantically, we can interpret the ranking value of agents (or actors in the social network) participating in a given MAS as *the probability that an agent will say the truth in the perception of the others*. In the following we will use the ranking, obtained through such an algorithm in this sense.

4. Probability Annotation

As shown in Section 2 there are basically three types of statements agents can make: (1) is-a relations, (2) object molecules, and (3) Horn rules. While is-a relations and Horn rules can be considered atomic, object molecules can be compound since object molecules of the form

$$o[a_1 \longrightarrow v_1; \ldots; a_n \longrightarrow v_n]$$

$$o[a_1 \twoheadrightarrow v_1; \ldots; a_n \twoheadrightarrow v_n]$$

$$o[a_1 \bullet\!\!\longrightarrow v_1; \ldots; a_n \bullet\!\!\longrightarrow v_n]$$

$$o[a_1 \bullet\!\!\twoheadrightarrow v_1; \ldots; a_n \bullet\!\!\twoheadrightarrow v_n]$$

$$o[a_1 \Longrightarrow v_1; \ldots; a_n \Longrightarrow v_n]$$

$$o[a_1 \Longrightarrow\!\!\!\!\twoheadrightarrow v_1; \ldots; a_n \Longrightarrow\!\!\!\!\twoheadrightarrow v_n] \tag{6}$$

can be rewritten as corresponding atomic F-molecules

$$o[a_1 \longrightarrow v_1] \cdots o[a_n \longrightarrow v_n]$$

$$o[a_1 \twoheadrightarrow v_1] \cdots o[a_n \twoheadrightarrow v_n]$$

$$o[a_1 \bullet\!\!\longrightarrow v_1] \cdots o[a_n \bullet\!\!\longrightarrow v_n]$$

$$o[a_1 \bullet\!\!\twoheadrightarrow v_1] \cdots o[a_n \bullet\!\!\twoheadrightarrow v_n]$$

$$o[a_1 \Longrightarrow v_1] \cdots o[a_n \Longrightarrow v_n]$$

$$o[a_1 \Longrightarrow\!\!\!\!\twoheadrightarrow v_1] \cdots o[a_n \Longrightarrow\!\!\!\!\twoheadrightarrow v_n]. \tag{7}$$

We will consider in the following that all F-molecule statements are atomic. Now we are able to define the annotation scheme of agent statements as follows.

Definition 10. Let $S = \{s_1, s_2, \ldots, s_n\}$ be a set of statements, let $A = \{a_1, a_2, \ldots, a_n\}$ be a set of agents, let $O : S \times A$ be a corresponding social ontology, let τ be a trust relation between agents over $A \times A$, and let $\phi : A \to [0,1]$ be a function that assigns ranks to agents based on τ. Then the *annotation* $\overline{\overline{\wedge}}$ of the statements is defined as follows:

$$s \overline{\overline{\wedge}} \pi, \quad \pi = \sum_{(a,s) \in O} \phi(a). \tag{8}$$

An extension to such a probability annotation is the situation when statements can have a negative valency. This happens when a particular agent disagrees to a statement of another agent. Such an annotation would be defined as follows.

Definition 11. Let $S = \{s_1, s_2, \ldots, s_n\}$ be a set of signed statements, let $A = \{a_1, a_2, \ldots, a_n\}$ be a set of agents, let $O : S \times A$ be a corresponding social ontology, let τ be a trust relation between agents over $A \times A$, and let $\phi : A \to [0,1]$ be a function that assigns ranks to agents based on τ. Then the *annotation* $\overline{\wedge}$ of the statements is defined as follows:

$$s \overline{\overline{\wedge}} \pi, \pi$$

$$= \begin{cases} \sum_{(a,s) \in O} \phi(a) - \sum_{(a,-s) \in O} \phi(a) & \text{if } \sum_{(a,s) \in O} \phi(a) > \sum_{(a,-s) \in O} \phi(a), \\ 0 & \text{if } \sum_{(a,s) \in O} \phi(a) \leqslant \sum_{(a,-s) \in O} \phi(a). \end{cases} \tag{9}$$

Such a definition is needed in order to avoid possible negative probability (the case when disagreement is greater than approvement).

5. Query Execution

In a concrete system we need to provide a mechanism for query execution that will allow agents to issue queries of the following form:

$$Q_p : F \overline{\overline{\wedge}} p, \tag{10}$$

where F is any formula in frame logic and p a probability. The semantics of the query is: *does the formula F hold with probability p with regard to the social ontology?*

The solution of this problem is equivalent to finding the probabilities of all possible solutions of query F

$$Q : F. \tag{11}$$

Definition 12. Let $R_Q = \{r_1, r_2, \ldots, r_n\}$ be a set of solutions to query Q; then R_{Q_p} is a subset of R_Q consisting of those solutions from R_Q which probability is greater or equal to p and represents the set of solutions to query Q_p.

The probability of a solution $p(r_i)$ is obtained by a set of production rules.

Rule 1. If r_i is a conjunction of two formulas r_{i1} and r_{i2}, then $p(r_i) = p(r_{i1}) \cdot p(r_{i2})$.

Rule 2. If r_i is a disjunction of two formulas r_{i1} and r_{i2}, then $p(r_i) = p(r_{i1}) + p(r_{i2})$.

Rule 3. If r_i is an F-molecule if the form is $i[an \to av]$, then $p(r_i) = \min(p(an), p(av))$.

The implications of these three definitions are given in the following four theorems.

Theorem 13. *If r_i is an F-molecule of the form $i[an_1 \to av_1, \ldots, an_n \to av_n]$, then $p(r_i) = \prod_{i=1}^{n} \min(p(an_i), p(av_i))$.*

Proof. Since r_i in this case can be written as:

$$i[an_1 \longrightarrow av_1] \wedge \cdots \wedge i[an_v \longrightarrow av_v], \tag{12}$$

and due to Rule 3 the probabilities of the components of this conjunction are $\min(p(an_1), p(av_1)), \ldots, \min(p(an_n), p(av_n))$. Due to Rule 1 the probability of a conjunction is the product of the probabilities of its elements which yields $\prod_{i=1}^{n} \min(p(an_i), p(av_i))$. $\square$

Theorem 14. *If r_i is an F-molecule of the form $i : c[an_1 \to av_1, \ldots, an_n \to av_n]$, then $p(r_i) = p(i : c) \cdot \prod_{i=1}^{n} \min(p(an_i), p(av_i))$.*

Proof. Since the given F-molecule can be written as

$$i : c \wedge i[an_1 \longrightarrow av_1] \wedge \cdots \wedge i[an_n \longrightarrow av_n], \tag{13}$$

the proof is analogous to the proof of Theorem 13. $\square$

Theorem 15. *If r_i is a statement of generalization of the form $c_1 :: c_2$, if P is the set of all paths between c_1 and c_2, and if $\blacktriangleright$ is the relation of immediate generalization, then*

$$p(r_i) = \sum_{pa \in P} \prod_{c_j \blacktriangleright c_i \in pa} p(c_j \blacktriangleright c_i). \qquad (14)$$

Proof. Since any class hierarchy can be presented as a directed graph, it is obvious that there has to be at least one path from c_1 to c_2. If the opposite was true, the statement would not hold and thus wouldn't be in the initial solution set.

For the statement $c_1 :: c_2$ to hold, at least one path statement of the form

$$pa_x = c_1 \blacktriangleright c_{x1} \wedge c_{x1} \blacktriangleright c_{x2} \wedge \cdots \wedge c_{xn} \blacktriangleright c_2 \qquad (15)$$

has to hold as well. This yields according to Rule 1 that the probability of one path would be

$$p(pa_x) = \prod_{c_j \blacktriangleright c_i \in pa} p(c_j \blacktriangleright c_i). \qquad (16)$$

Since there is a probability that there are multiple paths which are alternative possibilities for proving the same premise, it holds that

$$pa_1 \vee pa_2 \vee \cdots \vee pa_m. \qquad (17)$$

Thus from Rule 2 we get

$$p(c_1 :: c_2) = \sum_{pa \in P} \prod_{c_j \blacktriangleright c_i \in pa} p(c_j \blacktriangleright c_i) \qquad (18)$$

what we wanted to prove. $\qquad \square$

Theorem 16. *If r_i is a statement of classification of the form $i : c$, then*

$$p(r_i) = p(i) \cdot \sum_{pa \in P} \prod_{c_j \blacktriangleright c_i \in pa} p(c_j \blacktriangleright c_i). \qquad (19)$$

Proof. Since the statement r_i can be written as

$$r_i = i : c_1 \wedge c_1 :: c, \qquad (20)$$

the given probability is a consequence of Rule 1 and Theorem 15. $\qquad \square$

A special case of query execution is when the social ontology contains Horn rules. Such rules are also subject to probability annotation. Thus we have

$$rule : Head \longleftarrow Body \overline{\wedge} p, \qquad (21)$$

where p is the annotated probability of the rule. In order to provide a mechanism to deal with such probability annotated rules, we will establish an extended definition by using an additional counter predicate for each Horn rule. Thus, each rule is extended as

$$Head \longleftarrow Body \wedge CounterPredicate, \qquad (22)$$

whereby *CounterPredicate* is a predicate which will count the number of times the particular rule has been successfully executed for finding a given solution.

The query execution scheme has to be altered as well. Instead of finding only the solutions from formula F an additional variable for every rule in the social ontology is added to the formula. For n rules we would thus have

$$Q : F \wedge count(?r_1) \wedge count(?r_2) \wedge \cdots \wedge count(?r_n). \qquad (23)$$

In order to calculate the probability of a result obtained by using some probability annotated rule we establish the following definition.

Definition 17. Let r be a result obtained with probability p_F by query F from a social ontology, let p_r be the probability of rule R, and let c be the number of times rule R was executed during the derivation of result r. The final probability of r is then defined as

$$p(r) = p_F \cdot p_r^c. \qquad (24)$$

This definition is intuitive since for the obtainment of result r the rule R has to hold c times. Thus if a social ontology contains n rules $(R_1, \ldots, R_n)$ their corresponding annotated probabilities are $p_{r1}, \ldots, p_{rn}$, and numbers of execution during derivation of result r are $c_1, \ldots, c_n$, then the final probability is defined as

$$p(r) = p_F \cdot \prod_{i=1}^{n} p_{ri}^{c_i}. \qquad (25)$$

6. Annotated Reasoning Example

In order to demonstrate the approach we will take the following (imaginary) example of an MAS (all images, names, and motives are taken from the 1968 movie "Yellow Submarine" produced by United Artists (UA) and King Features Syndicate). Presume we have a problem domain entitled "Pepperland" with objects entitled "Music" and "Purpose of life." Let us further presume that we have six agents collaborating on this problem, namely, "John," "Paul," "Ringo," "George," "Max," and "Glove."

Another intelligent agent "Jeremy Hilary Boob Ph.D (Nowhere man)" tries to reason about the domain, but as it comes out, the domain is inconsistent. Table 1 shows the different viewpoints of agents.

Due to the disagreement on different issues a normal query would yield at least questionable results. For instance, if the disagreement statements are ignored in frame logic syntax, the domain would be represented with a set of sentences similar to the following:

$$
\begin{aligned}
o_{\text{Music}} &: \quad \text{evil noise} \\
o_{\text{Music}} &: \quad \text{harmonious sounds} \\
o_{\text{Purpose of life}} & \quad [\text{main purpose} \rightarrow \\
& \qquad \{\text{glove, love, drums}\}].
\end{aligned}
\qquad (26)
$$

TABLE 1: Viewpoints of "Pepperland" agents.

	Music	Purpose of life
John	: harmonious sounds	Main purpose $\rightarrow$ love
Paul	: harmonious sounds	Main purpose $\rightarrow$ love
Ringo	: harmonious sounds	Main purpose $\rightarrow$ drums
George	Disagrees to (: evil noise)	Main purpose $\rightarrow$ love
Max	: evil noise	Disagrees to (main purpose $\rightarrow$ love)
Glove	: evil noise	Main purpose $\rightarrow$ glove

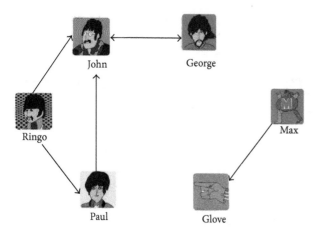

FIGURE 1: Social network of "Pepperland."

Thus a query asking for the class to which the object entitled "Music" belongs

$$? - o_{\text{Music}} : ?class \qquad (27)$$

would yield two valid answers, namely, "evil noise" and "harmonious sounds." Likewise if querying for the value of the "main purpose" attribute of object $o_{\text{Purpose of life}}$, for example,

$$? - o_{\text{Purpose of life}} \left[\text{main purpose} \longrightarrow ?purpose\right] \qquad (28)$$

the valid answers would be "glove," "love," and "drums." But, these answers do not reflect the actual state of the MAS, since one answer is more meaningful to it than the others.

Nowhere man thinks hard and comes up with a solution. The agents form a social network of trust are shown in Figure 1.

The figure reads as follows: Ringo trusts Paul and John, Paul trusts John, John trusts George, George trusts John, Max trusts Glove, and Glove does not trust anyone. Using the previously described PageRank algorithm Nowhere man was able to order the agents by their respective rank (Table 2).

Now, Nowhere man uses these rankings to annotate the statements given by the agents:

$$p\,(\text{evil noise}) = \text{Rank}\,(\text{Max})$$
$$+ \text{Rank}\,(\text{Glove})$$
$$- \text{Rank}\,(\text{George}) \qquad (29)$$
$$= 0.065609.$$

As we can see the probability that object o_{Music} is and "evil noise" is equal to the sum of agents' rankings who agree to this

TABLE 2: Trust ranking of the "Pepperland" agents.

Agent	Ranking
John	0.303391
Glove	0.289855
George	0.267724
Paul	0.060667
Max	0.043478
Ringo	0.034884

statement (Glove and Max) minus the sum of agents' rankings who disagree (George). Note that if an agent had expressed the same statement twice with the same attribute name, his ranking would be counted only once. Also note that, if an agent would have agreed and disagreed to a statement, his sum would be zero, since he would be at the agreed and disagreed side.

From this probability calculation Nowhere man is able to conclude that the formula o_{Music} : evil noise holds with probability 0.065609. Likewise he calculates the probability of o_{Music} : harmonious sounds

$$p\,(\text{harmonious sounds}) = \text{Rank}\,(\text{John})$$
$$+ \text{Rank}\,(\text{Paul})$$
$$+ \text{Rank}\,(\text{Ringo}) \qquad (30)$$
$$= 0.398942.$$

He can now conclude that o_{Music} : harmonious sounds holds more likely than o_{Music} : evil noise with regard to the social network of agents. From these calculations Nowhere man concludes that the final solutions to query $? - o_{\text{Music}}$: $?class$ are

$$?class = \text{evil noise} \overline{\overline{\wedge}} \, 0.065609$$
$$?class = \text{harmonious sounds} \overline{\overline{\wedge}} \, 0.398942. \qquad (31)$$

Nowhere man continues reasoning and calculates the probabilities for the other queries

$$p\,(\text{main purpose}) = \text{Rank}\,(\text{John})$$
$$+ \text{Rank}\,(\text{Paul})$$
$$+ \text{Rank}\,(\text{Ringo})$$
$$+ \text{Rank}\,(\text{George})$$
$$- \text{Rank}\,(\text{Max})$$
$$+ \text{Rank}\,(\text{Glove})$$
$$= 0.913043,$$

$$p \,(\text{love}) = \text{Rank} \,(\text{John})$$

$$+ \,\text{Rank} \,(\text{Paul})$$

$$+ \,\text{Rank} \,(\text{George})$$

$$- \,\text{Rank} \,(\text{Max})$$

$$= 0.588304,$$

$$p \,(\text{glove}) = \text{Rank} \,(\text{Glove})$$

$$= 0.289855,$$

$$p \,(\text{drums}) = \text{Rank} \,(\text{Ringo})$$

$$= 0.034884. \tag{32}$$

From these calculations Nowhere man concludes that $o_{\text{Purpose of life}}$ [main purpose $\rightarrow$ love] is most likely to hold with $p = 0.588304$. The final result of the query

$$? - o_{\text{Purpose of life}} \,[\text{main purpose} \longrightarrow ?purpose] \tag{33}$$

is then

$$?purpose = love \,\overline{\overline{\wedge}}\, 0.588304$$

$$?purpose = glove \,\overline{\overline{\wedge}}\, 0.289855 \tag{34}$$

$$?purpose = drums \,\overline{\overline{\wedge}}\, 0.034884.$$

Now we can complicate things a bit to see the other parts of the approach in action. Assume now that John has expressed a statement that relates the object entitled "Music" to the object entitled "Purpose of life" and named the attribute "has to do with." We would now have the following social ontology:

$$o_{\text{Music}} \;:\; \text{evil noise}$$

$$o_{\text{Music}} \;:\; \text{harmonious sounds}$$

$$o_{\text{Music}} \,\left[\longrightarrow \; o_{\text{Purpose of life}} \right]$$

$$o_{\text{Purpose of life}} \;\;[\text{main purpose} \;\twoheadrightarrow\; \{\text{glove; love, drums}\}] \,. \tag{35}$$

Now suppose that Nowhere man wants to issue the following query:

$$?- \,?o1 \;:\; ?c \,[?a \longrightarrow ?o2] \,\wedge\, ?o2 \,[\text{main purpose} \longrightarrow ?p] \,. \tag{36}$$

The solutions using "normal" frame logic are

s_1 :

$\quad ?o1 = o_{\text{Music}}$

$\quad ?c = \text{evil noise}$

$\quad ?a = \text{has to do with}$

$\quad ?o2 = o_{\text{Purpose of life}}$

$\quad ?p = \text{glove},$

s_2 :

$\quad ?o1 = o_{\text{Music}}$

$\quad ?c = \text{evil noise}$

$\quad ?a = \text{has to do with}$

$\quad ?o2 = o_{\text{Purpose of life}}$

$\quad ?p = \text{love},$

s_3 :

$\quad ?o1 = o_{\text{Music}}$

$\quad ?c = \text{evil noise}$

$\quad ?a = \text{has to do with}$

$\quad ?o2 = o_{\text{Purpose of life}}$

$\quad ?p = \text{drums},$

s_4 :

$\quad ?o1 = o_{\text{Music}}$

$\quad ?c = \text{harmonious sounds}$

$\quad ?a = \text{has to do with}$

$\quad ?o2 = o_{\text{Purpose of life}}$

$\quad ?p = \text{glove},$

s_5 :

$\quad ?o1 = o_{\text{Music}}$

$\quad ?c = \text{harmonious sounds}$

$\quad ?a = \text{has to do with}$

$\quad ?o2 = o_{\text{Purpose of life}}$

$\quad ?p = \text{love},$

s_6 :

$\quad ?o1 = o_{\text{Music}}$

$\quad ?c = \text{harmonious sounds}$

$\quad ?a = \text{has to do with}$

$\quad ?o2 = o_{\text{Purpose of life}}$

$\quad ?p = \text{drums}. \tag{37}$

To calculate the probabilities Nowhere man uses the following procedure. The variables in the query are exchanged with the actual values for a given solution:

s_1: o_{Music} : evil noise [has to do with $\longrightarrow$ $o_{\text{Purpose of life}}$] $\wedge$ $o_{\text{Purpose of life}}$ [main purpose $\longrightarrow$ glove],

s_2: o_{Music} : evil noise [has to do with $\longrightarrow$ $o_{\text{Purpose of life}}$] $\wedge$ $o_{\text{Purpose of life}}$[main purpose $\longrightarrow$ love],

s_3: o_{Music} : evil noise [has to do with $\longrightarrow$ $o_{\text{Purpose of life}}$] $\wedge$ $o_{\text{Purpose of life}}$[main purpose $\longrightarrow$ drums],

s_4: o_{Music} : harmonious sounds [has to do with $\longrightarrow$ $o_{\text{Purpose of life}}$] $\wedge$ $o_{\text{Purpose of life}}$[main purpose $\longrightarrow$ glove],

s_5: o_{Music} : harmonious sounds [has to do with $\longrightarrow$ $o_{\text{Purpose of life}}$] $\wedge$ $o_{\text{Purpose of life}}$[main purpose $\longrightarrow$ love],

s_6: o_{Music} : harmonious sounds [has to do with $\longrightarrow$ $o_{\text{Purpose of life}}$] $\wedge$ $o_{\text{Purpose of life}}$[main purpose $\longrightarrow$ drums].

Now according to rule 1 the conjunction becomes

$$p(s_1) = p\left(o_{\text{Music}} : \text{evil noise}\left[\text{has to do with} \longrightarrow o_{\text{Purpose of life}}\right]\right)$$
$$\cdot p\left(o_{\text{Purpose of life}}\left[\text{main purpose} \longrightarrow \text{glove}\right]\right),$$

$$p(s_2) = p\left(o_{\text{Music}} : \text{evil noise}\left[\text{has to do with} \longrightarrow o_{\text{Purpose of life}}\right]\right)$$
$$\cdot p\left(o_{\text{Purpose of life}}\left[\text{main purpose} \longrightarrow \text{love}\right]\right),$$

$$p(s_3) = p\left(o_{\text{Music}} : \text{evil noise}\left[\text{has to do with} \longrightarrow o_{\text{Purpose of life}}\right]\right)$$
$$\cdot p\left(o_{\text{Purpose of life}}\left[\text{main purpose} \longrightarrow \text{drums}\right]\right),$$

$$p(s_4) = p\left(o_{\text{Music}} : \text{harmonious sounds}\left[\text{has to do with} \longrightarrow o_{\text{Purpose of life}}\right]\right)$$
$$\cdot p\left(o_{\text{Purpose of life}}\left[\text{main purpose} \longrightarrow \text{glove}\right]\right),$$

$$p(s_5) = p\left(o_{\text{Music}} : \text{harmonious sounds}\left[\text{has to do with} \longrightarrow o_{\text{Purpose of life}}\right]\right)$$
$$\cdot p\left(o_{\text{Purpose of life}}\left[\text{main purpose} \longrightarrow \text{love}\right]\right),$$

$$p(s_6) = p\left(o_{\text{Music}} : \text{harmonious sounds}\left[\text{has to do with} \longrightarrow o_{\text{Purpose of life}}\right]\right)$$
$$\cdot p\left(o_{\text{Purpose of life}}\left[\text{main purpose} \longrightarrow \text{drums}\right]\right).$$
$$(38)$$

The second parts of the equations were already calculated, and according to Theorem 14 the first parts of the equations become

$$p(s_1) = p\left(o_{\text{Music}} : \text{evil noise}\right)$$
$$\cdot \min\left(p(\text{has to do with}), p\left(o_{\text{Purpose of life}}\right)\right)$$
$$\cdot 0.289855,$$

$$p(s_2) = p\left(o_{\text{Music}} : \text{evil noise}\right)$$
$$\cdot \min\left(p(\text{has to do with}), p\left(o_{\text{Purpose of life}}\right)\right)$$
$$\cdot 0.588304,$$

$$p(s_3) = p\left(o_{\text{Music}} : \text{evil noise}\right)$$
$$\cdot \min\left(p(\text{has to do with}), p\left(o_{\text{Purpose of life}}\right)\right)$$
$$\cdot 0.034884,$$

$$p(s_4) = p\left(o_{\text{Music}} : \text{harmonious sounds}\right)$$
$$\cdot \min\left(p(\text{has to do with}), p\left(o_{\text{Purpose of life}}\right)\right)$$
$$\cdot 0.289855,$$

$$p(s_5) = p\left(o_{\text{Music}} : \text{harmonious sounds}\right)$$
$$\cdot \min\left(p(\text{has to do with}), p\left(o_{\text{Purpose of life}}\right)\right)$$
$$\cdot 0.588304,$$

$$p(s_6) = p\left(o_{\text{Music}} : \text{harmonious sounds}\right)$$
$$\cdot \min\left(p(\text{has to do with}), p\left(o_{\text{Purpose of life}}\right)\right)$$
$$\cdot 0.034884.$$
$$(39)$$

We already know the probabilities of the is-a statement, and since

$$p(\text{has to do with}) = p\left(o_{\text{Purpose of life}}\right)$$
$$= \phi(\text{John}) = 0.303391,$$
$$(40)$$

the equations become

$$p(s_1) = 0.065609 \cdot 0.303391 \cdot 0.289855,$$
$$p(s_2) = 0.065609 \cdot 0.303391 \cdot 0.588304,$$
$$p(s_3) = 0.065609 \cdot 0.303391 \cdot 0.034884,$$
$$p(s_4) = 0.398942 \cdot 0.303391 \cdot 0.289855,$$
$$p(s_5) = 0.398942 \cdot 0.303391 \cdot 0.588304,$$
$$p(s_6) = 0.398942 \cdot 0.303391 \cdot 0.034884,$$
$$(41)$$

and finally

$$p(s_1) = 0.005770,$$
$$p(s_2) = 0.011710,$$
$$p(s_3) = 0.000694,$$
$$p(s_4) = 0.035083,$$
$$p(s_5) = 0.071206,$$
$$p(s_6) = 0.004222.$$

(42)

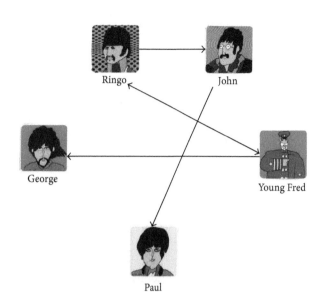

FIGURE 2: Social network of "Yellow submarine."

7. Amalgamation

To provide a mechanism for agents to query multiple annotated social ontologies we decided to use the principles of amalgamation. The model of knowledge base amalgamation which is based on online querying of underlaying sources is described in [9]. The intention of amalgamation is to show if a given solution holds in any of the underlaying sources.

Since the local annotations of different ontologies that are subject to amalgamation do not necessarily hold for the global ontology, we need to introduce a mechanism to integrate the ontologies in a coherent way which will yield global annotations. Since the set of ontologies is a product of a set of respective social agent networks surrounding them, we decided to firstly integrate the social networks in order to provide the necessary foundation for global annotation.

Definition 18. The integration of n social networks represented with the valued digraphs $(\mathcal{N}_1, \mathcal{A}_1, \mathcal{V}_1), \ldots,$ $(\mathcal{N}_n, \mathcal{A}_n, \mathcal{V}_n)$ is given as the valued digraph $(\mathcal{N}_1 \cup \cdots \cup \mathcal{N}_z, \mathcal{A}_1 \cup \cdots \cup \mathcal{A}_n, \mathcal{V})$, where $\mathcal{V}$ is a function $\mathcal{V} : \mathcal{N}_1 \cup \cdots \cup \mathcal{N}_n \to \mathbb{R}$ that attaches values to nodes.

In particular $\mathcal{V}$ will be a social network analysis metric or in our case a variant of the eigenvector centrality. Now we can define the integration of ontologies as follows.

Definition 19. Let $O_1, \ldots, O_n$ be sets of statements as defined above representing particular social ontologies. The integration is given as $O_1 \cup \cdots \cup O_n$.

What remains is to provide the annotation that is at the same time the amalgamation scheme.

Definition 20. Let $(\mathcal{N}_1 \cup \cdots \cup \mathcal{N}_n, \mathcal{A}_1 \cup \cdots \cup \mathcal{A}_n, \mathcal{V})$ be the integration of n social networks of agents, let $O_1 \cup \cdots \cup O_n$ be the integration of their corresponding social ontologies, let τ be a trust relation between agents, and let $\phi : A \to [0, 1]$ be a function that assigns ranks to agents based on τ; then the amalgamated annotation scheme $\overline{\overline{\wedge}}$ of the metadata statements is defined as follows:

$$s \overline{\overline{\wedge}} \pi, \quad \pi = \sum_{(a,s) \in O_1 \cup \cdots \cup O_n} \phi(a).$$

(43)

8. Amalgamated Annotated Reasoning Example

To demonstrate the amalgamation approach proposed here let us again assume that our intelligent agent "Jeremy Hilary Boob Ph.D. (Nowhere man)" tries to reason about the "Pepperland" domain, but this time he wants to draw conclusions from the domain "Yellow submarine" as well. The "Yellow submarine" domain is being modeled by "Ringo," "John," "Paul," "George," and "Young Fred" which form the social network shown in Figure 2. Since the contents of this domain as well as the particular ranks of the agents in it will not be used further in the example, they have been left out.

Since Nowhere man wants to reason about both domains he needs to find a way to amalgamate these two domains.

Again he thinks hard and comes up with the following solution. All he needs to do is to integrate the two social networks together and recalculate the ranks of all agents of this newly established social network in order to reannotate the metainformation in both domains.

Since the networks of "Pepperland" and "Yellow submarine" can be represented as the following sets of tuples:

$$\mathcal{G}_{\text{Pepperland}} = \{$$
$$(\text{Ringo, John}),$$
$$(\text{Ringo, Paul}),$$
$$(\text{Paul, John}),$$
$$(\text{John, George}),$$
$$(\text{George, John}),$$
$$(\text{Max, Glove})$$
$$\},$$

(44)

$$\mathcal{G}_{\text{Yellow submarine}} = \{$$

$$(\text{Ringo}, \text{John}),$$

$$(\text{Ringo}, \text{Young Fred}),$$

$$(\text{John}, \text{Paul}), \qquad (45)$$

$$(\text{Young Fred}, \text{Ringo}),$$

$$(\text{Young Fred}, \text{George})$$

$$\},$$

all he needs is to find $\mathcal{G}_A = \mathcal{G}_{\text{Pepperland}} \cup \mathcal{G}_{\text{Yellow submarine}}$ and recalculate the ranks of this new network. Thus

$$\mathcal{G}_A = \{$$

$$(\text{Ringo}, \text{John}),$$

$$(\text{Ringo}, \text{Paul}),$$

$$(\text{Paul}, \text{John}),$$

$$(\text{John}, \text{George}),$$

$$(\text{George}, \text{John}),$$

$$(\text{Max}, \text{Glove}) \qquad (46)$$

$$(\text{Ringo}, \text{Young Fred}),$$

$$(\text{John}, \text{Paul}),$$

$$(\text{Young Fred}, \text{Ringo}),$$

$$(\text{Young Fred}, \text{George})$$

$$\}.$$

The newly established integrated social network is shown in Figure 3.

Now Nowhere man calculates the ranks of this new network and uses the previously described procedure to annotate the meta information (Section 4) and reason about the amalgamated domain (Section 5).

9. Towards a Distributed Application

As we could see from the previous examples, in order to gain accurate knowledge and accurate probabilities about a certain domain, we had to introduce an all-knowing agent (Nowhere man). This agent had to be aware of all knowledge of each agent and all trust relations they engage in. Such a scenario is not feasible for large-scale MAS (LSMAS). Thus we need to provide a mechanism to let agents reason in a distributed manner and still get accurate enough results.

This problem consists of two parts; namely, an agent needs (1) to acquire an accurate approximation of the ranks of each agent in its network and (2) to acquire knowledge about the knowledge of other agents. The first part deals with annotation and the second with amalgamation of the ontology.

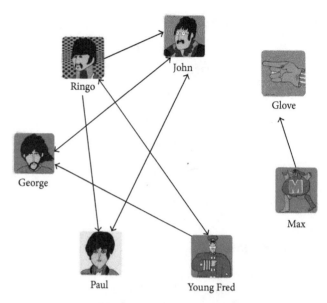

FIGURE 3: The integration of two social networks.

A solution to the first problem might be to calculate ranks in a distributed manner, as has been shown in [10]. In this way agents acquire approximate knowledge about the ranks of their neighbouring agents.

The second problem could be used by the proposed algorithm for amalgamation. Each agent can ask agents it trusts about their knowledge and then amalgamate their ontology with its own. In this way the agent acquires continuously better knowledge about its local environment. We could have easily considered Nowhere man in the last example to be doing the just described procedure—asking one agent after another about their knowledge.

10. Possible Application areas

In order to provide a practical example, consider a network of store-and-forward e-mail routing agents in which spam bots try to send unsolicited messages. Some routers (agents) might be under the control of spam bots and send out messages which might be malicious to users and other routers. The domain these agents reason about is the domain of spam messages—for example, which message from which user forwarded by which router and what kind of content is spam and should be discarded.

This scenario can be modeled by using the previously described approach: agents form trust relations and mutually exchange new rules about spam filtering. An agent will amalgamate rules (ontologies) of other agents with its own but will decide about a message (using an adequate query) based not only on the given rules but also on the probability annotation given by the network of trust.

11. Related Work

Alternative approaches to measuring trust in the form of the reputation inference and the SUNNY algorithm are presented in [11, 12], respectively. Both of these could have been used instead of PageRank in the approach outlined herein. A much more elaborated system of measuring reputation and likewise trust in MAS called the *Regret* system is presented in [13]. It is based on three different dimensions of reputation (individual, social, and ontological) and allows for measuring several types of reputation in parallel. The approach is partly incompatible with our approach, but several adjustments would allow us to combine both approaches.

A different approach to a similar problem related to trust management in the Semantic Web is presented in [14]. It provides a profound model based on path algebra and inspired by Markov models. It provides a method of deriving the degree of belief in a statement that is explicitly asserted by one or more individuals in a network of trust, whilst a calculus for computing the belief in derived statements is left to future research. Herein a formalism for deriving the belief in any computable statement is presented for F-logic.

12. Conclusion

When agents have to solve a problem collectively, they have to reach consensus about the domain since their opinions can differ. Especially when agents are self-interested, their goals in a given situation can vary quite intensively. Herein an approach to reaching this consensus based on a network of trust between agents has been presented which is a generalization of the work done in [15, 16] which dealt with semantic wiki systems and semantic social networks, respectively. By using a network analysis trust ranks of agents can be calculated which can be interpreted as an approximation of the probability that a certain agent will say the truth. Using this interpretation an annotation scheme for F-logic based Horn programs has been developed which allows agents to reason about the modeled domain and make decisions based on the probability that a certain statement (derived or explicit) is true. Based on this annotation scheme and the network of trust an amalgamation scheme has been developed as well, which allow agents to reason about multiple domains.

Still, there are open questions: how does the approach scale in fully decentralized environments like LSMAS? What are the implications of self-interest or could agents develop strategies to "lie" on purpose to attain their goals? These and similar questions are subject to our future research.

References

[1] I. Nonaka and H. Takeuchi, *The Knowledge-Creating Company, How Japanese Companies Create the Dynamics of Innovation*, Oxford University Press, 1995.

[2] F. Nietzsche, "Über wahrheit und lüge im außermoralischen sinn," 1873, http://www.textlog.de/455.html.

[3] P. Bonacich, "Factoring and weighting approaches to clique identification," *Journal of Mathematical Sociology*, vol. 2, pp. 113–120, 1972.

[4] M. Kifer, G. Lausen, and J. Wu, "Logical foundations of object-oriented and frame-based languages," *Journal of the Association for Computing Machinery*, vol. 42, no. 4, pp. 741–843, 1995.

[5] S. Wasserman and K. Faust, "Social network analysis, methods and applications," in *Structural Analysis in the Social Sciences*, Cambridge University Press, 1994.

[6] P. Mika, *Social Networks and the Semantic Web*, Springer, New York, NY, USA, 2007.

[7] S. Brin, "The anatomy of a large-scale hypertextual Web search engine," *Computer Networks*, vol. 30, pp. 107–117, 1998.

[8] L. Page, S. Brin, R. Motwani, and T. Winograd, "The pagerank citation ranking: bringing order to the web," 1999.

[9] A. Lovrenčić and M. Čubrilo, "Amalgamation of heterogeneous data sources using amalgamated annotated hilog," in *Proceedings of the 3rd IEEE Conference on Intelligent Engineering Systems (INES'99)*, 1999.

[10] Y. Zhu and X. Li, "Distributed pagerank computation based on iterative aggregation-disaggregation methods," in *Proceedings of the 14th ACM international conference on Information and knowledge management*, pp. 578–585, 2005.

[11] J. Golbeck and J. Hendler, "Accuracy of metrics for inferring trust and reputation in semantic web-based social networks," in *Proceedings of the 14th International Conference (EKAW '04)*, pp. 116–131, October 2004.

[12] U. Kuter and J. Golbeck, "Using probabilistic confidence models for trust inference in web-based social networks," *ACM Transactions on Internet Technology*, vol. 10, no. 2, article 8, 2010.

[13] J. Sabater and C. Sierra, "Reputation and social network analysis in multi-agent systems," in *Proceedings of the 1st International Joint Conference on Autonomous Agents adn Multiagent Systems (AAMAS '02)*, pp. 475–482, New York, NY, USA, July 2002.

[14] M. Richardson, R. Agrawal, and P. Domingos, "Trust management for the semantic web," in *Proceedings of the 2nd International Semantic Web Conference*, pp. 351–368, 2003.

[15] M. Schatten, *Programming Languages for Autopoiesis Facilitating Semantic Wiki Systems [Ph.D. thesis]*, University of Zagreb, Faculty of Organization and Informatics, Varaždin, Croatia, 2010.

[16] M. Schatten, "Knowledge management in semantic social networks," *Computational and Mathematical Organization Theory*, pp. 1–31, 2012.

12

Multiobjective Stochastic Programming for Mixed Integer Vendor Selection Problem Using Artificial Bee Colony Algorithm

Mostafa Ekhtiari[1] and Shahab Poursafary[2]

[1] Department of Industrial Management, Management and Accounting, Shahid Beheshti University, Tehran, Iran
[2] Department of Industrial Engineering, Mazandaran University of Science and Technology, Babol, Iran

Correspondence should be addressed to Mostafa Ekhtiari; m ektiari@yahoo.com

Academic Editors: R.-C. Hwang, P. Kokol, and Q. K. Pan

It has been always critical and inevitable to select and assess the appropriate and efficient vendors for the companies such that all the aspects and factors leading to the importance of the select process should be considered. This paper studies the process of selecting the vendors simultaneously in three aspects of multiple criteria, random factors, and reaching efficient solutions with the objective of improvement. Thus, selecting the vendors is introduced in the form of a mixed integer multiobjective stochastic problem and for the first time it is converted by CCGC (min-max) model to a mixed integer nonlinear single objective deterministic problem. As the converted problem is nonlinear and solving it in large scale will be time-consuming then the artificial bee colony (ABC) algorithm is used to solve it. Also, in order to better understand ABC efficiency, a comparison is performed between this algorithm and the particle swarm optimization (PSO) and the imperialist competitive algorithm (ICA) and Lingo software output. The results obtained from a real example show that ABC offers more efficient solutions to the problem solving in large scale and PSO spends less time to solve the same problem.

1. Introduction

In a competitive environment, to select and evaluate vendors are among the most important issues ahead of manufacturing companies as the expenses of procuring raw materials largely contribute to the final cost of a product. Vendor selection is one of the most important activities of a purchasing department and the selection of an appropriate vendor could largely result in decreases in purchase costs, delivery time, and an increase in customers' satisfaction and company's competition power. Companies are better off selecting as many appropriate vendors as they could commensurate with the production capacity of all potential vendors and establishing long lasting and useful relationships with them.

What brings about desirable results for companies managers in their decisions on selecting vendors is the selection of vendors based on three aspects of multiple criteria, random factors, and the quality of the obtained results simultaneously. The selection process and the evaluation of vendors are a multiple objective issue indeed so that more than one criterion could be considered during this process. Moreover, decisions related to the selection of vendors become more intricate when different criteria are to be simultaneously dealt with in the decision making process. In the various evaluation methods proposed in the available literature, price, delivery performance, and quality are the most common criteria in evaluating suppliers [1].

Several studies have been so far conducted on the selection of vendor problem with multiple objectives/criteria some of which are dealt with as follows.

Weber and Current [2] presented a multiobjective approach to systematically analyze the inherent trade-offs involved in multiple criteria vendor selection problems. Yahya and Kingsman [3] proposed a new approach based on the use of analytic hierarchy process (AHP) method and applied it into vendor rating for a government sponsored entrepreneur development program in Malaysia. Lam and Tang [4] proposed a new integrated supply chain model for vendor allocation in a multiechelon supply chain. This model takes into account the usual cost objective and other important criteria in a multiechelon supply chain ranging from the most upstream suppliers' quality to end customers' satisfaction level through a large-scale multi-objective linear programming (MOLP).

Lin et al. [5] proposed a novel hybrid multiple criteria decision making (MCDM) technique to cope with the complex and interactive vendor evaluation and selection problem which can determine the structural relationships and the interrelationships amongst all the evaluation's dimensions and support the analytic network process (ANP) method to arrange appropriate weightings to each dimension and criterion in the evaluation model by summarizing the opinions of the experts. Hsu et al. [6] proposed how the best selection to conduct the recycled materials can be implemented for enhancing and increasing the efficiency of using resources in the manufacturing process through recycled materials vendor selection. They used the MCDM model combining DEMATEL-based on ANP (called DANP) with VIKOR to solve the recycled materials vendor selection problems of multiple dimensions and criteria that were interdependent. Furthermore, some of the latest works concerning multiple criteria decision making in vendor selection problem can be searched in Zanjirani Farahani and Fadaei [7], Li et al. [8], Zhang et al. [9], and Arunkumar et al. [10].

One of the issues to be always accounted for in selecting vendors is to consider random factors and conditions that are likely to occur due to the existence of changing conditions and a dearth of information. To this end, some conventional techniques and methods, which consider the stochastic conditions of problem, should be used to select vendors. Stochastic programming deals with a class of optimization models and algorithms, in which all or some of the parameters may be subject to significant uncertainty. Stochastic programming is capable of inserting random factors in selecting and evaluating vendors.

Leung et al. [11] illustrated the production planning problem in supply chain management, with additional constraints, such as production plant preference selection. To deal with the uncertain demand data, they proposed a stochastic programming approach to determine optimal medium-term production loading plans under an uncertain environment. Talluri et al. [12] presented a chance-constrained data envelopment analysis (CCDEA) approach in the presence of multiple performance measures of vendors that were uncertain. Xu and Ding [13] presented a class of chance-constrained multi-objective linear programming models with birandom coefficients for vendor selection problem. They designed a genetic algorithm (GA) based on bi-random simulation for solving a birandom multiobjective vendor selection problem. Zhimin et al. [14] developed a multiple objective mixed integer stochastic programming model for the vendor selection problem (VSP) with stochastic demand under multiproducts purchases. Kasilingam and Lee [15] proposed a mixed integer programming model to select vendors and determine the order quantities. The model considers the stochastic nature of demand, the quality of supplied parts, the cost of purchasing and transportation, the fixed cost for establishing vendors, and the cost of receiving poor quality parts. Their proposed model also considers the lead time requirements for the parts.

Alonso-Ayuso et al. [16] presented a two-stage stochastic one-zero modeling and a related algorithmic approach for supply chain management under uncertainty. Zang et al. [17] developed a new chance-constrained programming model for supplier selection problem. In their proposed optimization problem, costs, quality, and lead times were characterized by random variables.

A review of the researches conducted in this regard shows that the selection of vendors has been modeled in the form of zero and one variables. For example, Keskin et al. [18] proposed a mixed integer nonlinear model for integrated vendor selection under capacity constraints. On the other hand, the issues that are modeled on a large scale and based on zero and one increase the time to achieve a solution. Hence, the researchers make use of metaheuristic algorithms to overcome this problem. Many algorithms such as GA, ABC, and PSO have been introduced so far. In the literature, there are several researches on the use of these algorithms in optimizing the vendor selection problem as follows.

He et al. [19] developed a class of special chance-constrained programming models and a GA designed for the vendor selection problem. They considered quality and service as uncertain parameters. Taleizadeh et al. [20] presented a multibuyer multivendor supply chain problem, in which the demand of each product was stochastic and was following a uniform distribution. The model of this problem was of an integer nonlinear programming type and in order to solve it a harmony search algorithm was employed. Also, to validate the solution and to compare the performance of the proposed algorithm, a GA was utilized as well. Huang et al. [21] used PSO algorithm to solve partner selection problem under uncertainty. Kuo et al. [22] developed an intelligent vendor decision support system by the collection of quantitative data such as profit and productivity, a PSO-based fuzzy neural network to derive the rules for qualitative data.

ABC is one of the new metaheuristic algorithms that can be used for solving nonlinear problems on a large scale. The algorithm was first introduced by Karaboga [23]. This paper studies the performance of ABC in solving the stochastic problem of selecting vendors on a large scale. It is conducted with the objective to improve the vendors' selection and evaluation process simultaneously at three aspects, that is, multiple criteria, random factors, and achievement of efficient solutions. For this purpose, the problem of vendor selection is introduced in the form of a mixed integer multiobjective stochastic problem as converted by CCGC (min-max) [24] into a mixed integer nonlinear single objective deterministic problem. The converted problem is nonlinear and its solution on the larger scale could be more time-consuming; therefore, in order to solve it, not only Lingo software; but also ABC, PSO, and ICA have been used and their performance is compared and evaluated from the view of solutions quality and the speed of reaching solutions.

The rest of this paper is organized as follows. Section 2 introduces the main structure of mixed integer multiobjective stochastic problem for vendor selection and the CCGC (min-max) model is reviewed in Section 3. In Section 4, some basic concepts on the ABC, the PSO, and the ICA are briefly introduced, respectively, for optimization of mixed integer nonlinear problem of vendor selection. Section 5 provides the background information for the case study problem and obtains the results. Also in this section, comparative evaluations are made to contrast the performances of these algorithms and discussions. Finally, conclusion remarks are drawn in Section 6.

2. The Mixed Integer Multiobjective Stochastic of Vendor Selection Problem

A general model for the multi-objective stochastic problem of vendor selection can be stated as follows:

$$\max \quad Z_k(\mathbf{x}) = \sum_{j=1}^{n} \tilde{c}_{ki} x_i y_i, \quad k = 1, \ldots, K,$$

$$\min \quad Z_r(\mathbf{x}) = \sum_{j=1}^{n} \tilde{c}_{ri} x_i y_i, \quad r = K+1, \ldots, R,$$

$$\text{subject to} \quad \sum_{i=1}^{n} y_i \le N_y, \tag{1}$$

$$\mathbf{x} \in S,$$

$$y_i \in \{0, 1\}, \ i = 1, \ldots, n,$$

$$x_i \in \{0, \mathbf{Z}^+\}, \ i = 1, \ldots, n.$$

The objectives of Program (1) can be generally divided into two categories as follows. Some objectives are positive, and the aim is to maximize them. Some of these objectives are profit and/or quality, so that the aim is to select vendors, which increase these cases. The other category of the objectives is of negative type with the aim of minimizing. Some of these objectives are cost, wastes, and/or lead time. Therefore, our objective is to select vendors that decrease these objectives. The constraints of the model are such total demand volume from the vendors, minimum and maximum goods vendors being capable of providing and/or maximum vendors selected (N_y), where have been in brief displayed with $\mathbf{x} \in S$ in Program (1). In Program (1), $y_i, i = 1, \ldots, n$, is a one-zero variable, where if y_i is equal to 1, that is to say, the vendor i is selected; otherwise, vendor i is not selected.

Also, vector $\mathbf{x}$ takes positive integer or zero values and if $\mathbf{x} \in S$ are system constraints that make solution space of the model and $\tilde{c}_{ki}$ and $\tilde{c}_{ri}$ are normal random parameters with known means and variances, then the objective is to maximize $\sum_{i=1}^{n} \tilde{c}_{ki} x_i y_i$ (for $k = 1, \ldots, K$) and minimize $\sum_{i=1}^{n} \tilde{c}_{ri} x_i y_i$ (for $r = K+1, \ldots, R$).

Program (1) can be solved by an appropriate optimization technique. Next section introduces the CCGC (min-max) model to solve Program (1) and multi-objective stochastic problems.

3. The CCGC (Min-Max) Model

The CCGC (min-max) model was proposed by Ekhtiari and Ghoseiri [24]. They introduced their deterministic equivalent programming model for solving multi-objective stochastic

problems such as Program (1). The CCGC (min-max) model, which is equivalent to Program (1), can be stated as

$$\min \quad v,$$

$$\text{subject to} \quad v \ge w_k \times \left(U_k - \sum_{j=1}^{n} E(\tilde{c}_{ki}) x_i y_i \right.$$

$$+ \Phi^{-1}(1 - \alpha_k)$$

$$\left. \times \sqrt{\sum_{i=1}^{n} \mathrm{Var}(\tilde{c}_{ki}) x_i^2 y_i} \right),$$

$$k = 1, \ldots, K,$$

$$v \ge w_r \times \left(\sum_{i=1}^{n} E(\tilde{c}_{ri}) x_i y_i - U_r \right.$$

$$+ \Phi^{-1}(1 - \alpha_r)$$

$$\left. \times \sqrt{\sum_{i=1}^{n} \mathrm{Var}(\tilde{c}_{ri}) x_i^2 y_i} \right),$$

$$r = K+1, \ldots, R,$$

$$\sum_{i=1}^{n} y_i \le N_y,$$

$$\mathbf{x} \in S,$$

$$y_i \in \{0, 1\}, \ i = 1, \ldots, n,$$

$$x_i \in \{0, \mathbf{Z}^+\}, \ i = 1, \ldots, n,$$

$$v \ge 0, \tag{2}$$

where w_k and w_r, respectively, are preference weights of objective k ($k = 1, \ldots, K$) and r ($r = K+1, \ldots, R$), and $\sum_{k=1}^{K} w_k + \sum_{r=K+1}^{R} w_r = 1$ ($w_k, w_r > 0$, for $k = 1, \ldots, K$ and $r = K+1, \ldots, R$). Also in Program (2), α_k and α_r, respectively, are the threshold value of objective k ($k = 1, \ldots, K$) and $\Phi(z) = \mathrm{prob}(N(0, 1) \le z)$ represents the probability distribution function of a standard normal distribution. Meanwhile, r ($r = K+1, \ldots, R$) and U_k and U_r, respectively, are the utopia value of objective k ($k = 1, \ldots, K$) and r ($r = K+1, \ldots, R$).

Let us consider c_{ki}^* as the maximum value observed for objective k, variable i for all the state of nature $\omega(c_{ki}^* = \max_\omega \tilde{c}_{ki})$. In Program (2), U_k is the best solution of the objective function $\sum_{i=1}^{n} c_{ki}^* x_i y_i$ subject to system constraints. In other words,

$$U_k = \max \quad \sum_{i=1}^{n} c_{ki}^* x_i y_i, \quad k = 1, \ldots, K,$$

$$\text{subject to} \quad \mathbf{x} \in S, \tag{3}$$

$$y_i \in \{0, 1\}, \ i = 1, \ldots, n,$$

$$x_i \in \{0, \mathbf{Z}^+\}, \ i = 1, \ldots, n.$$

Also, let us consider c_{ri}^* as the minimum value observed for objective r, variable i for all the state of nature $\omega(c_{ri}^* = \min_\omega \tilde{c}_{ri})$. In Program (2), U_r is the best solution of the objective function $\sum_{i=1}^n c_{ri}^* x_i y_i$ subject to system constraints. In other words,

$$U_r = \min \quad \sum_{i=1}^n c_{ri}^* x_i y_i, \quad r = K+1,\ldots,R,$$

$$\text{subject to} \quad \mathbf{x} \in S \tag{4}$$

$$y_i \in \{0,1\}, i = 1,\ldots,n,$$

$$x_i \in \{0,\mathbf{Z}^+\}, i = 1,\ldots,n.$$

Program (2) is a nonlinear programming model whose solution by Lingo software results in local solutions. Therefore, in order to obtain effective solutions, one may make use of metaheuristic algorithms, which, in addition to original ABC, PSO, and ICA, will be reviewed in brief for solving the problem of selecting vendors.

4. Metaheuristic Algorithms

One of the common methods for solving optimization problems is metaheuristic algorithms. In some problems with structural complication, mathematical methods and software packages based on mathematical methods are not capable of solving them or their solution time is too lengthy. Some metaheuristic algorithms can be recommended for such problems. The structure of such algorithms is that, at first, they produce primary random population in the searching space, and then they make use of latent calculation intelligence in their structure; they move the solutions in such a way as to be directed towards optimal point.

The main advantages of metaheuristic algorithms are as follows [25].

(1) *Being robust to dynamic changes*: traditional methods of optimization are not robust to dynamic changes in the environment and they require a complete restart for providing a solution. In contrary, evolutionary computation can be used to adapt solutions to the changing circumstances.

(2) *Broad applicability*: metaheuristic algorithms can be applied to any problems that can be formulated as function optimization problems.

(3) *Hybridization with other methods*: metaheuristic algorithms can be combined with more traditional optimization techniques.

(4) *Solves problems that have no solutions*: the advantages of metaheuristic algorithms includes the ability to address problems for which there is no human expertise. Even though human expertise should be used when it is needed and available, it often proves less adequate for automated problem-solving routines.

Some of meta-heuristic algorithms as introduced are reviewed in brief as follows.

4.1. The ABC. ABC is one of the metaheuristic algorithms recently introduced. The stages of original ABC are as follows [26].

In ABC algorithm, the position of a food source represents a possible solution to the optimization problem and the nectar amount of a food source corresponds to the quality (fitness) of the associated solution. The number of the employed bees or the onlooker bees is equal to the number of solutions in the population. At the first step, the ABC generates randomly distributed initial population P ($C = 0$) of SN solutions (food source positions), where SN denotes the size of employed bees or onlooker bees. Each solution x_i ($i = 1,\ldots,SN$) is a D-dimensional vector. Here, D is the number of optimization parameters. After initialization, the population of the positions (solutions) is subject to repeated cycles, $C = 1,\ldots,MCN$, of the search processes of the employed bees, the onlooker bees, and the scout bees. An employed bee produces a modification on the position (solution) in her memory depending on the local information (visual information) and tests the nectar amount (fitness value) of the new source (new solution). If the nectar amount of the new one is higher than that of the previous one, the bee memorizes the new position and forgets the old one. Otherwise she keeps the position of the previous one in her memory. After all employed bees complete the search process, they share the nectar information of the food sources and their position information with the onlooker bees. An onlooker bee evaluates the nectar information taken from all employed bees and chooses a food source with a probability related to its nectar amount. As in the case of the employed bee, she produces a modification on the position in her memory and checks the nectar amount of the candidate source. If the nectar is higher than that of the previous one, the bee memorizes the new position and forgets the old one.

The main steps of the algorithm are as follows.

(1) Initialize population.

(2) *repeat*.

(3) Place the employed bees on their food sources.

(4) Place the onlooker bees on the food sources depending on their nectar amounts.

(5) Send the scouts to the search area for discovering new food sources.

(6) Memorize the best food source found so far.

(7) *until* requirements are met.

In ABC algorithm, each cycle of the search consists of three steps: sending the employed bees onto their food sources and evaluating their nectar amounts; after sharing the nectar information of food sources, selecting food source regions by the onlookers and evaluating the nectar amount of the food sources; determining the scout bees and then sending them randomly onto possible new food sources. At the initialization stage, a set of food sources is randomly selected by the bees and their nectar amounts are determined. At the first step of the cycle, these bees come into the hive and share the nectar information of the sources with the bees waiting on the dance area. A bee waiting on the dance area for making decision to choose a food source is called onlooker and the bee going to the food source visited by herself just before is named as employed bee. After sharing their information with onlookers, every employed bee goes to the food source area visited by herself at the previous cycle since that food source exists in her memory and then chooses a new food source by means of visual information in the neighborhood of the one in her memory and evaluates its nectar amount. At the second step, an onlooker prefers a food source area depending on the nectar information distributed by the employed bees on the dance area. As the nectar amount of a food source increases, the probability of that food source chosen also increases. After arriving at the selected area, the bee chooses a new food source in the neighborhood of the one in the memory depending on visual information as in the case of employed bees. The determination of the new food source is carried out by the bees based on the comparison process of food source positions visually. At the third step of the cycle, when the nectar of a food source is abandoned by the bees, a new food source is randomly determined by a scout bee and replaced with the abandoned one. In our model, at each cycle at most one scout goes outside for searching a new food source, and the number of employed and onlooker bees is selected to be equal to each other. These three steps are repeated through a predetermined number of cycles called maximum cycle number (MCN) or until a termination criterion is satisfied. An artificial onlooker bee chooses a food source depending on the probability value associated with that food source, p_i, calculated by

$$p_i = \frac{\text{fit}_i}{\sum_{n=1}^{SN} \text{fit}_n}, \tag{5}$$

where fit_i is the fitness value of the solution i which is proportional to the nectar amount of the food source in the position i and SN is the number of food sources which is equal to the number of employed bees or onlooker bees.

In order to produce a candidate food position from the old one in memory, the ABC uses

$$v_{ij} = x_{ij} + \varphi_{ij} \left(x_{ij} - x_{kj} \right), \tag{6}$$

where $k \in \{1, \dots, SN\}$ and $j \in \{1, \dots, D\}$ are randomly chosen indexes. Although k is determined randomly, it has to be different from i. φ_{ij} is a random number between $[-1, 1]$. It controls the production of neighbor food sources around x_{ij} and represents the comparison of two food positions visually by a bee. As can be seen from (6), as the difference between the parameters of the x_{ij} and x_{kj} decreases, the perturbation on the position x_{ij} gets decreased, too. Thus, as the search approaches the optimum solution in the search space, the step length is adaptively reduced.

If a parameter value produced by this operation exceeds its predetermined limit, the parameter can be set to an acceptable value. In this work, the value of the parameter exceeding its limit is set to its limit value.

The food source of which the nectar is abandoned by the bees is replaced with a new food source by the scouts.

In ABC, this is simulated by producing a position randomly and replacing it with the abandoned one. In ABC, if a position cannot be improved further through a predetermined number of cycles, then that food source is assumed to be abandoned. The value of predetermined number of cycles is an important control parameter of the ABC algorithm, which is called "*limit*" for abandonment. Assume that the abandoned source is x_i and $j \in \{1, \dots, D\}$; then the scout discovers a new food source to be replaced with x_i. This operation can be defined as

$$x_i^j = x_{\min}^j + \text{rand}\,[0, 1] \left(x_{\max}^j - x_{\min}^j \right). \tag{7}$$

After each candidate source position v_{ij} is produced and then evaluated by the artificial bee, its performance is compared with that of its old one. If the new food source has an equal or better nectar than the old source, it is replaced with the old one in the memory. Otherwise, the old one is retained in the memory. In other words, a greedy selection mechanism is employed as the selection operation between the old and the candidate one.

Totally, ABC algorithm employs four different selection processes: (1) a global probabilistic selection process, in which the probability value is calculated by (5), used by the onlooker bees for discovering promising regions, (2) a local probabilistic selection process carried out in a region by the employed bees and the onlookers depending on the visual information such as the color, shape and fragrance of the flowers (sources) (bees will not be able to identify the type of nectar source until they arrive at the right location and discriminate among sources growing there based on their scent) for determining a food source around the source in the memory in a way described by (6), (3) a local selection called greedy selection process carried out by onlooker and employed bees in which if the nectar amount of the candidate source is better than that of the present one, the bee forgets the present one and memorizes the candidate source produced by (6), otherwise, the bee keeps the present one in the memory, and (4) a random selection process carried out by scouts as defined in (7).

It is clear from the above explanation that there are three control parameters in the basic ABC: the number of food sources which is equal to the number of employed or onlooker bees (SN), the value of limit, and the maximum cycle number (MCN).

In the case of honeybees, the recruitment rate represents a measure of how quickly the bee colony finds and exploits a newly discovered food source. Artificial recruiting could similarly represent the measurement of the speed with which the feasible solutions or the good quality solutions of the difficult optimization problems can be discovered. The survival and progress of the bee colony are dependent upon the rapid discovery and efficient utilization of the best food resources. Similarly, the successful solution of difficult engineering problems is connected to the relatively fast discovery of good solutions especially for the problems that need to be solved in real time. In a robust search process, exploration and exploitation processes must be carried out together. In the ABC algorithm, while onlookers and employed bees carry out the exploitation process in the search space, the scouts control the exploration process. Detailed pseudocode of the ABC algorithm is given as follows.

(1) Initialize the population of solutions $x_i, i = 1, \ldots, SN$.

(2) Evaluate the population.

(3) cycle = 1.

(4) *repeat*.

(5) Produce new solutions v_i for the employed bees by using (6) and evaluate them.

(6) Apply the greedy selection process for the employed bees.

(7) Calculate the probability values p_i for the solutions x_i by (5).

(8) Produce the new solutions v_i for the onlookers from the solutions x_i selected depending on p_i and evaluate them.

(9) Apply the greedy selection process for the onlookers.

(10) Determine the abandoned solution for the scout, if exists, and replace it with a new randomly produced solution x_i by (7).

(11) Memorize the best solution achieved so far.

(12) cycle = cycle + 1.

(13) *until* cycle = MCN.

4.2. The PSO.

This subsection will introduce the original PSO algorithm developed by Kennedy and Eberhart [27] for optimization of continues nonlinear functions. PSO was inspired by the motion of a flock of birds searching for food. During the search, each bird, called a particles adjust, its searching direction according to two factors, its own best previous experience (pbest) and the experience of all other members (gbest).

Mathematically, assume that the searching space is D-dimensional. Let $X_i^t = (x_{i1}^t, x_{i2}^t, \ldots, x_{id}^t)$ be the particle i in D-dimensional vector, where X_i^t is treated as a potential solution that explores the search space by the rate of position change called velocity. The velocity is denoted as $V_i^t = (v_{i1}^t, v_{i2}^t, \ldots, v_{id}^t)$. Let $P_i^t = (p_{i1}^t, p_{i2}^t, \ldots, p_{id}^t)$ be the best particle i obtained until iteration t and let $P_g^t = (p_{g1}^t, p_{g2}^t, \ldots, p_{gd}^t)$ be the global best in the population at iteration t. The basic procedure for implementing original PSO is described as follows [28].

(1) Create population of particles with random positions and velocities on the searching space.

(2) For each particle, evaluate the desired optimization fitness function and compare the evaluated fitness with its pbest. If the current particle is better than pbest, then set pbest to the current particle.

(3) Update particle velocities according to the following equation:

$$v_{id}^t = w v_{id}^{t-1} + c_1 \text{rand}\,(\cdot)\left(p_{id}^t - x_{id}^t\right) \\ + c_2 \text{rand}\,(\cdot)\left(p_{gd}^t - x_{id}^t\right), \tag{8}$$

where c_1 is the cognition learning factor, c_2 is the social learning factor, rand$(\cdot)$ are random numbers uniformly distributed in $U(0, 1)$, and w is the inertia weight.

(4) Particles are changed to their new positions according to the following equation:

$$x_{id}^{t+1} = x_{id}^t\,(t) + v_{id}^t. \tag{9}$$

(5) Stop the algorithm if the stopping criterion is satisfied; return to Step 2 otherwise.

The velocity update can improve the diversification of the search. To assure that the velocity would not lead the particles to move beyond boundaries, a maximum $(V_{\max})$ is set to limit the velocity range; any velocity tending to exceed it is brought back to it [29]. An inertia weight w is used to balance between global and local searches when updating the velocity in (8). The swarm population sizes ranging from 10 to 30 are the most common ones, and it has been learned that PSO requires a smaller population than is generally used in genetic algorithms to search for high quality solution [30].

4.3. The ICA.

ICA is a novel global search strategy and inspired by the imperialistic competition based on the human's sociopolitical evolution. This algorithm was first introduced by Atashpaz-Gargari and Lucas [31]. Imperialistic competition forms the core of the algorithm. This causes all countries to converge to an absolute minimum cost function. The original ICA starts with some countries as initial population, which is classified into two groups. Some of the countries with more power are selected to be the imperialist and all other countries with less power than the imperialists form colonies of them. The imperialist countries absorb the colonies based on their power using the absorption policy. The total power of an empire depends on both of its constituents, the imperialist country and the colonies. The mathematical expression of this relationship is defined as a power made up of the power of the imperialist country plus a percentage of the average power of the colonies.

After the initial imperialists were formed, the imperialist competition step starts between them. Each imperialist that cannot act successfully in this competition to increase its power (or at least to prevent the loss of its influence) will collapse. Therefore, the survival of an imperialist depends directly on its ability to absorb the rival imperialists' colonies and its ability to rule them out. Consequently, during the imperialist competition, gradually the power of larger imperialist is added and weaker imperialists will be removed. Those empires that want to increase their power will be forced to develop their own colonies. Thus, over time, colonies will be closer to imperialists, and a convergence will be seen. The convergence condition will be achieved when a single imperialist is created along with the colonies whose statues are very close to the imperialist country.

In the next section, original ABC performance in solving a stochastic problem of selecting vendors in the form of a real example is reviewed in comparison to original PSO and ICA and Lingo software.

5. Case Study

In this section, the performance of the proposed methodology is validated on a real problem. For this purpose, a real data set is obtained from a home appliances manufacturer as a case study in the manufacturing industry in Iran. This company manufactures a wide range of home appliances in its factory near Tehran in Iran. Besides, the company also markets its products in various cities.

In order to procure some materials and components, the company is always in need of keeping contact with vendors. At present, the company works with ten vendors only. They are its first priority. What the company is looking for is a planning based on two issues: first, if the company wants to continue its activities with these ten vendors according to certain criteria and limits, which vendors could meet how much demand of the company? Second, if the company wants to increase its potential vendors for its future development, which vendor can meet how much need of the company?

As the problem propounded by the company revolves around the selection of vendors and determination of the good number they provide, it can be defined in the form of a mixed integer multi-objective stochastic programming problem by taking some random parameters into account. They will be described in detail as follows.

5.1. Objectives

(i) Objective Function of Purchase Cost. If c_i ($i = 1, \ldots, n$) is fixed cost of purchase of a good unit from vendor i, n is number of vendors, x_i is number of products bought from vendor i in such a way that its value is an integer, y_i is a zero and one variable, which is equal to 1 if it is bought from vendor i and zero if not, and Z_1 is objective function of the purchase cost from vendors, then we have

$$\min Z_1 = \sum_{i=1}^{n} c_i x_i y_i. \tag{10}$$

(ii) Objective Function of Wastes. If $\tilde{\gamma}_i$ is a normal random variable of waste percentage for the vendor i and Z_2 is the objective function of wastes for vendors, then we have

$$\min Z_2 = \sum_{i=1}^{n} \tilde{\gamma}_i x_i y_i. \tag{11}$$

The best value of the random variable of $\tilde{\gamma}_i$ is the least waste percentage observed for the vendor i in accordance with the historical data. Meanwhile, mean and variance of this random variable are calculated based on its relevant historical data.

(iii) Objective Function of Lead Time. If $\tilde{t}_i$ is normal random variable for lead time of vendor i and Z_3 is the objective function for lead time of vendors, then we have

$$\min Z_3 = \sum_{i=1}^{n} \tilde{t}_i x_i y_i. \tag{12}$$

The best value for $\tilde{t}_i$ is the least lead time observed for vendor i in accordance with the historical data. Meanwhile, mean and variance of random variable can be calculated based on its relevant historical data.

(iv) Objective Function of Quality. If $\tilde{q}_i$ is normal random variable for quality percentage of products provided by vendor i and if Z_4 is quality objective function of vendors, then we have

$$\max Z_4 = \sum_{i=1}^{n} \tilde{q}_i x_i y_i. \tag{13}$$

The best value of $\tilde{q}_i$ is the highest percentage observed by vendor i in accordance with historical data. Meanwhile, mean and variance of this random variable can be calculated based on its relevant historical data.

5.2. Constraints

(i) Demand Volume. If X stands for total purchase demand volume from vendors, then we have

$$\sum_{i=1}^{n} x_i y_i = X. \tag{14}$$

(ii) Selection of Maximum Number of Vendors. If N_y is the maximum number of vendors to whom we can refer to purchase goods, then we have

$$\sum_{i=1}^{n} y_i \leq N_y. \tag{15}$$

(iii) Minimum and Maximum Numbers of Products Each Provider Can Provide. If $\underline{x}_i$ and $\overline{x}_i$ are minimum and maximum numbers of products that vendor i can provide, then we have

$$\underline{x}_i y_i \leq x_i \leq \overline{x}_i y_i, \quad i = 1, \ldots, n. \tag{16}$$

Therefore, the general form of mixed integer multi-objective stochastic model for vendor selection can be as follows

$$\min \quad Z_1 = \sum_{i=1}^{n} c_i x_i y_i,$$

$$\min \quad Z_2 = \sum_{i=1}^{n} \tilde{\gamma}_i x_i y_i,$$

$$\min \quad Z_3 = \sum_{i=1}^{n} \tilde{t}_i x_i y_i,$$

$$\max \quad Z_4 = \sum_{i=1}^{n} \tilde{q}_i x_i y_i,$$

subject to $\sum_{i=1}^{n} x_i y_i = X,$

$$\sum_{i=1}^{n} y_i \le N_y,$$

$$\underline{x}_i y_i \le x_i \le \overline{x}_i y_i, \quad i = 1, \dots, n,$$

$$x_i \in \{0, \mathbf{Z}^+\}, \quad i = 1, \dots, n,$$

$$y_i \in \{0, 1\}, \quad i = 1, \dots, n.$$

$\hspace{6cm}$ (17)

Due to the existence of varying conditions and inadequate information, Program (17) is a mixed integer multi-objective stochastic model whose some of its parameters are normal random variables with known mean and variance. Therefore, based on Program (2), Program (17) can be converted into a deterministic equivalent model like Program (18):

min $v,$

subject to $v \ge w_1 \times \left(\sum_{i=1}^{n} c_i x_i y_i - U_1 \right),$

$$v \ge w_2 \times \left(\sum_{i=1}^{n} E\left(\tilde{\gamma}_i\right) x_i y_i - U_2 + \Phi^{-1} \right.$$

$$\left. \times (1 - \alpha_2) \sqrt{\sum_{i=1}^{n} \mathrm{Var}\left(\tilde{\gamma}_i\right) x_i^2 y_i} \right)$$

$$v \ge w_3 \times \left(\sum_{i=1}^{n} E\left(\tilde{t}_i\right) x_i y_i - U_3 + \Phi^{-1} \right.$$

$$\left. \times (1 - \alpha_3) \sqrt{\sum_{i=1}^{n} \mathrm{Var}\left(\tilde{t}_i\right) x_i^2 y_i} \right),$$

$$v \ge w_4 \times \left(U_4 - \sum_{j=1}^{n} E\left(\tilde{q}_i\right) x_i y_i + \Phi^{-1} \right.$$

$$\left. \times (1 - \alpha_4) \sqrt{\sum_{i=1}^{n} \mathrm{Var}\left(\tilde{q}_i\right) x_i^2 y_i} \right),$$

$$\sum_{i=1}^{n} x_i y_i = X,$$

$$\sum_{i=1}^{n} y_i \le N_y,$$

$$\underline{x}_i y_i \le x_i \le \overline{x}_i y_i, \quad i = 1, \dots, n,$$

$$x_i \in \{0, \mathbf{Z}^+\}, \quad i = 1, \dots, n,$$

$$y_i \in \{0, 1\}, \quad i = 1, \dots, n,$$

$$v \ge 0.$$

$\hspace{6cm}$ (18)

5.3. Data Set.

At present, the company has 10 vendors, which are considered its top priority. The whole set of data related to the performance of each of them is presented in Table 1.

The information presented in Table 1 is in accordance with the two-year performance of 10 main vendors of the company. As it can be seen in this table, waste percentage, lead time, and the quality are normal random variables with known means and variances that have been calculated based on each vendor's historical data. Meanwhile, as the costs of the purchases from the vendors have been fixed, the purchase cost is considered as certain parameter. Given the data of Table 1, the demand volume from all vendors being 200 and the maximum selection of vendors' number being 5, Program (18) was solved by Lingo software package and its results have been shown in Table 2 (the complete shape of the model inserted in Lingo software is presented in appendix section of the paper). The preference weights, w_k (for $k = 1, 2, 3, 4$), have been equally considered to be 0.25 and the values of α_2, α_3, and α_4 are determined to be 0.1, 0.025 and 0.05, respectively. As the problem modeled in Program (18) is nonlinear and the solution obtained is local, therefore, in order to increase the accuracy of the results, this problem in the presence of 10 main vendors was repeated for 25 times. All results have been similarly saved for the solution achievement time at each execution time.

Considering the results presented in Table 2, four of the main vendors have been selected only, so that the optimal value of the objective function of Program (18) is equal to $v = 145.94$ and the average time for obtaining solution is some 1.4 seconds. As the problem of selecting vendors as commercial partners is of high importance for the company and as the model inserted in Lingo software is nonlinear, the results shown in Table 2 are local and better solutions are likely. For this purpose, three metaheuristic algorithms, ABC, PSO, and ICA, which are among the most updated metaheuristic algorithms, are used to solve the problem of Program (18).

5.4. Parameters Tuning.

For tuning the ABC for the mixed integer vendor selection stochastic problems, extensive experiments were conducted with differing sets of parameters in a competence against PSO, and ICA. At the end, the following sets were found to be effective in terms of solutions quality. Table 3 presents the parameters tuned by ABC, PSO and ICA for solving the problem of selecting vendors.

5.5. Solving the Problem of Main Vendors by ABC, PSO and ICA.

In order to omit random consequences of the results, the problem of Program (18) was repeated for 25 times in the presence of data related to 10 main vendors, and here the mean value of the objective function, v, and the mean CPU time obtained by ABC, PSO, and ICA are considered as the basis of comparisons. In this research, the said algorithms were executed by Matlab 7.12.0 under Microsoft Windows 7 in a personal computer with Dual Core CPU, 2.2 GHz, and a 4 GB RAM. The results obtained by ABC, PSO, and ICA in 25 repetitions are shown in Figure 1. Number of population for

TABLE 1: The primal and historical data related to 10 main vendors.

i	1	2	3	4	5	6	7	8	9	10
$\underline{x}_i$	40	53	65	45	40	33	28	46	55	63
$\overline{x}_i$	50	63	75	55	50	43	38	56	65	73
c_i (\$)	13	14	6	15	11	6	8	11	15	15
$E(\widetilde{y}_i)$ (%)	0.037	0.03	0.023	0.05	0.023	0.023	0.042	0.023	0.05	0.05
$\mathrm{Var}(\widetilde{y}_i)$	452×10^{-9}	721×10^{-9}	252×10^{-9}	8×10^{-7}	613×10^{-9}	252×10^{-9}	111×10^{-9}	613×10^{-9}	7×10^{-7}	825×10^{-9}
$E(\widetilde{t}_i)$ (day)	3.1	3.2	3.1	3.55	3.37	3.4	3.87	3.35	3.59	3.41
$\mathrm{Var}(\widetilde{t}_i)$	0.61	0.62	0.59	0.61	0.91	0.59	0.68	0.95	0.61	0.69
$E(\widetilde{q}_i)$ (%)	0.83	0.84	0.825	0.85	0.87	0.825	0.88	0.87	0.841	0.85
$\mathrm{Var}(\widetilde{q}_i)$	53×10^{-5}	54×10^{-5}	6×10^{-4}	55×10^{-5}	535×10^{-6}	6×10^{-4}	58×10^{-5}	53×10^{-5}	45×10^{-5}	55×10^{-5}

TABLE 2: Results obtained from solving Program (18) with 10 main vendors by Lingo software.

				x_i					
x_1	x_2	x_3	x_4	x_5	x_6	x_7	x_8	x_9	x_{10}
0	53	65	0	40	42	0	0	0	0

				y_i					
y_1	y_2	y_3	y_4	y_5	y_6	y_7	y_8	y_9	y_{10}
0	1	1	0	1	1	0	0	0	0

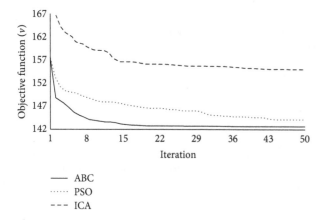

FIGURE 1: Changes trend of objective function for selection problem of 10 main vendors.

all three algorithms is 10 and maximum repetition number for each algorithm is considered to be 50.

As specified in Figure 1, ABC shows better results as compared to PSO and ICA. ABC practically reaches the final optimal solution from iteration 23 on, while PSO and ICA do not reach the solution in all 25 repetitions. Table 4 presents the mean time for achieving the solution to the problem of Program (18) in the presence of 10 main vendors as well as the least value of v obtained via ABC, PSO, and ICA and Lingo software. From the time view, ABC with the mean time of 0.517 seconds enjoys better status considering Lingo software with the mean time of 1.4 seconds. Of course, in a general comparison, PSO takes lower mean time as compared to ABC and ICA and Lingo software, and this result is not surprising considering its simple structure. Considering that the problem modeled by Program (17) is of multi-objective

problems, the best solution is the nearest solution to utopia point (where considering the space solution, each and every one of the objectives has its own best value). This issue can be obtained through the least value of v in Program (18). In this study, the most efficient solution is the one which presents the least possible value for v. Hence, from the viewpoint of the quality and efficiency of the solutions obtained here, ABC with the least possible value for v presents the best solution compared to PSO and ICA and Lingo. Also it should be noted that ICA is ranked last in obtainment of the least possible value for v.

As seen already, ABC is ranked first in achieving an efficient solution by obtaining the least possible value for v compared to PSO and ICA and Lingo software. Therefore, Table 5 presents the results obtained from solving Program (18) by ABC in the presence of 10 main vendors.

5.6. Company's Future Development Strategy with the Policy to Increase the Number of Vendors. Given the reports obtained from R&D unit of the company, one of the important strategies used by company is future development, increase in products, and further acquisition of competitive market share. Therefore, considering the constraint of minimum and maximum good number company can purchase from vendors, the company intends to also consider the policy of increasing the number of vendors commensurate with increased production volume. For this purpose, Table 6 presents the scenarios defined for the company's future strategy within the framework of changes in production volume and maximum number of vendors required.

To review the scenarios defined in Table 6, we act according to the following steps.

(1) The problem modeled in Program (18) is repeated by Lingo software and ABC, PSO, and ICA for each and every one of the scenarios defined in Table 6, another 9 times, so that, with each repetition, the data related to 10 vendors is added to the previous problem. In other words, the first problem is modeled with the data of 20 vendors and the last problem with that of 100 vendors. It should also be noted that the data related to the volume of products and maximum number of vendors required changes commensurate with each scenario. Meanwhile, other data inserted

TABLE 3: Parameters tuned by ABC, PSO, and ICA for solving the problem of Program (18) in the presence of 10 main vendors.

ABC		PSO			ICA			
Food number	Limit	w	c_1	c_2	Number of initial imperialists	Revolution rate	β	γ
5	15	0.7298	1.4962	1.4962	2	0.4	2	0.1

TABLE 4: The average solution achievement time and the least value for v in ABC, PSO, and ICA and Lingo software.

Algorithm	Average of min v	Average of CPU time (seconds)
Lingo	145.9443	1.4
ABC	142.6703	0.517
PSO	144.2132	0.43
ICA	152.5845	0.565

TABLE 5: The results obtained from solving Program (18) by ABC in the presence of 10 main vendors.

				x_i					
x_1	x_2	x_3	x_4	x_5	x_6	x_7	x_8	x_9	x_{10}
49	53	65	0	0	33	0	0	0	0
				y_i					
y_1	y_2	y_3	y_4	y_5	y_6	y_7	y_8	y_9	y_{10}
1	1	1	0	0	1	0	0	0	0

for each vendor comply with the available historical data of their performances during the past cycles.

(2) For each scenario, the value of utopia of each and everyone of the objectives is calculated separately.

(3) Optimization of each and everyone of the problems of Step 1 is repeated 25 times so that the average of the results is finally reported for each algorithm.

It should be noted that in all scenarios, w_k (for $k = 1, 2, 3, 4$) are considered to be equal to 0.25, and α_2, α_3, and α_4 are 0.1, 0.025, and 0.05, respectively. Table 7 illustrates a summary of the results, which are obtained by Lingo software and ABC, PSO, and ICA according to the above steps.

One of the important parameters in the presented problem is the maximum number of vendors required. The existence of this parameter increases not only the complexity of the problem but also its solution time by the algorithms. In fact, the relation between the parameter and the company's purchase volume and the volume any vendor could provide could result in increased complexity; therefore, the population number and maximum iterations (maxiter) for algorithms are based on the complexity rate of these problems so that the solution time is lower than that of Lingo. The results presented in Table 7 imply that from the view of reaching an efficient solution, ABC provides better performance compared to other algorithms and Lingo, to the extent that only ABC presents the lowest value for v in all scenarios. Meanwhile, PSO is ranked first from the view of the least solution achievement time.

6. Conclusion

In this paper, the problem of selecting vendors was modeled within the framework of a mixed integer multi-objective stochastic programming problem. With the objective to improve, the paper studied selection and evaluation process of vendors from the view of multiple criteria, random factors and achievement to efficient solutions. To this end, the problem of selecting vendors was presented as a mixed integer multi-objective stochastic problem its for solution; CCGC (min-max) model was used. As the presented problem was of nonlinear and mixed integer type, the original ABC was described to achieve efficient solutions. The proposed methodology was illustrated in the form of a real example so that the problem of selecting vendors was modeled on a large scale, and apart from original ABC and Lingo software, meta-heuristic algorithms PSO and ICA were also used for solving it. The results obtained indicated that the performance of ABC was better compared to PSO, ICA and Lingo output from the view of achieving efficient solutions; and PSO has a better performance compared to other algorithms from the view of the speed of reaching solution.

Appendix

Consider

$$\min \quad v,$$

$$\text{subject to} \quad v \geq 0.25 \times (13x_1 y_1 + 14x_2 y_2 + 6x_3 y_3$$
$$+ 15x_4 y_4 + 11x_5 y_5 + 6x_6 y_6$$
$$+ 8x_7 y_7 + 11x_8 y_8 + 15x_9 y_9$$
$$+ 15x_{10} y_{10} - U_1),$$

$$v \geq 0.25 \times \Big(0.037x_1 y_1 + 0.03x_2 y_2$$
$$+ 0.023x_3 y_3 + 0.05x_4 y_4$$
$$+ 0.023x_5 y_5 + 0.023x_6 y_6$$
$$+ 0.042x_7 y_7 + 0.023x_8 y_8$$
$$+ 0.05x_9 y_9 + 0.05x_{10} y_{10}$$
$$- U_2 + \Phi^{-1}(1 - \alpha_2)$$
$$\times (452 \times 10^{-9} x_1^2 y_1$$
$$+ 721 \times 10^{-9} x_2^2 y_2$$
$$+ 252 \times 10^{-9} x_3^2 y_3$$
$$+ 8 \times 10^{-7} x_4^2 y_4$$
$$+ 613 \times 10^{-9} x_5^2 y_5$$

TABLE 6: Scenarios defined for the company's future development.

Scenario	1	2	3	4	5	6	7	8	9
Number of available vendors	20	30	40	50	60	70	80	90	100
Purchase demand volume (X)	400	600	1050	1200	2200	3000	3500	4000	4500
Maximum number of vendors required (N_y)	6	9	15	20	30	40	45	50	60

TABLE 7: The results obtained by ABC, PSO, and ICA and Lingo considering the scenarios related to the company's future development.

Scenario	1	2	3	4	5	6	7	8	9
Lingo									
Average of min v	272.08	391.07	617.56	678.05	1212.78	1629.56	1856.94	2166.92	2423.74
Average of CPU time (seconds)	1.2	1.3	17.1	51.3	70.9	47.9	55	15.9	89
ABC									
Average of min v	267.82	375.68	610.34	675.74	1226.78	1598.91	1857.32	2097.85	2338.65
Average of CPU time (seconds)	0.95	1.05	9.56	39.54	43.51	39.65	47.31	14.58	43.41
Population	20	10	40	50	120	140	100	70	120
Maxiter	50	20	50	100	50	50	50	30	50
PSO									
Average of min v	274.324	389.86	643.16	714.3	1538.44	1678.22	1965.17	2258.42	2463.15
Average of CPU time (seconds)	0.923	0.99	6.76	10.29	18.44	34.17	35.54	8.65	24.15
Population	20	10	40	50	120	140	100	70	120
Maxiter	50	20	50	100	50	50	50	30	50
ICA									
Average of min v	278.35	384.88	636.92	708.24	1235.99	1646.22	1928.48	2206.17	2340.42
Average of CPU time (seconds)	1.17	1.22	12.33	43.54	65.56	61.1	71.93	21.46	60.8
Population	20	10	40	50	120	140	100	70	120
Maxiter	50	20	50	100	50	50	50	30	50

$$+ 252 \times 10^{-9} x_6^2 y_6$$
$$+ 111 \times 10^{-9} x_7^2 y_7$$
$$+ 613 \times 10^{-9} x_8^2 y_8$$
$$+ 7 \times 10^{-7} x_9^2 y_9 + 825$$
$$\left. \times 10^{-9} x_{10}^2 y_{10} \right)^{1/2} \Big),$$

$$v \geq 0.25 \times \Big(3.1 x_1 y_1 + 3.2 x_2 y_2 + 3.1 x_3 y_3$$
$$+ 3.55 x_4 y_4 + 3.37 x_5 y_5 + 3.4 x_6 y_6$$
$$+ 3.87 x_7 y_7 + 3.35 x_8 y_8 + 3.59 x_9 y_9$$
$$+ 3.41 x_{10} y_{10} - U_3 + \Phi^{-1} (1 - \alpha_3)$$
$$\left(0.61 x_1^2 y_1 + 0.62 x_2^2 y_2 + 0.59 x_3^2 y_3 \right.$$
$$+ 0.61 x_4^2 y_4 + 0.91 x_5^2 y_5$$
$$+ 0.59 x_6^2 y_6 + 0.68 x_7^2 y_7$$
$$+ 0.95 x_8^2 y_8 + 0.61 x_9^2 y_9$$
$$\left. + 0.69 x_{10}^2 y_{10} \right)^{1/2} \Big),$$

$$v \geq 0.25 \times \Big(U_4 - (0.83 x_1 y_1 + 0.84 x_2 y_2$$
$$+ 0.825 x_3 y_3 + 0.85 x_4 y_4 + 0.87 x_5 y_5$$
$$+ 0.825 x_6 y_6 + 0.88 x_7 y_7 + 0.87 x_8 y_8$$
$$+ 0.841 x_9 y_9 + 0.85 x_{10} y_{10}) + \Phi^{-1}$$
$$\times (1 - \alpha_4)$$
$$\times \left(53 \times 10^{-5} x_1^2 y_1 + 54 \times 10^{-5} x_2^2 y_2 \right.$$
$$+ 6 \times 10^{-4} x_3^2 y_3 + 55 \times 10^{-5} x_4^2 y_4$$
$$+ 535 \times 10^{-6} x_5^2 y_5$$
$$+ 6 \times 10^{-4} x_6^2 y_6$$
$$+ 58 \times 10^{-5} x_7^2 y_7$$
$$+ 53 \times 10^{-5} x_8^2 y_8$$
$$+ 45 \times 10^{-5} x_9^2 y_9$$
$$\left. + 55 \times 10^{-5} x_{10}^2 y_{10} \right)^{1/2} \Big),$$

$$\sum_{i=1}^{10} x_i y_i = 200,$$

$$\sum_{i=1}^{10} y_i \le 5,$$

$$40y_1 \le x_1 \le 50y_1, \quad 53y_2 \le x_2 \le 63y_2,$$

$$65y_3 \le x_3 \le 75y_3, \quad 45y_4 \le x_4 \le 55y_4,$$

$$40y_5 \le x_5 \le 50y_5, \quad 33y_6 \le x_6 \le 43y_6,$$

$$28y_7 \le x_7 \le 38y_7, \quad 46y_8 \le x_8 \le 56y_8,$$

$$55y_9 \le x_9 \le 65y_9, \quad 63y_{10} \le x_{10} \le 73y_{10},$$

$$x_i \in \{0, \mathbf{Z}^+\}, \quad i = 1, \dots, 10,$$

$$y_i \in \{0, 1\}, \quad i = 1, \dots, 10,$$

$$v \ge 0,$$

(A.1)

where

$U_1: \min \quad 13x_1 y_1 + 14x_2 y_2 + 6x_3 y_3 + 15x_4 y_4 + 11x_5 y_5$

$\qquad + 6x_6 y_6 + 8x_7 y_7 + 11x_8 y_8$

$\qquad + 15x_9 y_9 + 15x_{10} y_{10},$

subject to $\displaystyle \sum_{i=1}^{10} x_i y_i = 200,$

$$\sum_{i=1}^{10} y_i \le 5,$$

$$40y_1 \le x_1 \le 50y_1, 53y_2 \le x_2 \le 63y_2,$$

$$65y_3 \le x_3 \le 75y_3, 45y_4 \le x_4 \le 55y_4,$$

$$40y_5 \le x_5 \le 50y_5, 33y_6 \le x_6 \le 43y_6,$$

$$28y_7 \le x_7 \le 38y_7, 46y_8 \le x_8 \le 56y_8,$$

$$55y_9 \le x_9 \le 65y_9, 63y_{10} \le x_{10} \le 73y_{10},$$

$$x_i \in \{0, \mathbf{Z}^+\}, i = 1, \dots, 10,$$

$$y_i \in \{0, 1\}, i = 1, \dots, 10,$$

(A.2)

$U_2: \min \quad 0.037x_1 y_1 + 0.03x_2 y_2 + 0.023x_3 y_3 + 0.05x_4 y_4$

$\qquad + 0.023x_5 y_5 + 0.023x_6 y_6 + 0.042x_7 y_7$

$\qquad + 0.023x_8 y_8 + 0.05x_9 y_9 + 0.05x_{10} y_{10},$

subject to $\displaystyle \sum_{i=1}^{10} x_i y_i = 200,$

$$\sum_{i=1}^{10} y_i \le 5,$$

$$40y_1 \le x_1 \le 50y_1, 53y_2 \le x_2 \le 63y_2,$$

$$65y_3 \le x_3 \le 75y_3, 45y_4 \le x_4 \le 55y_4,$$

$$40y_5 \le x_5 \le 50y_5, 33y_6 \le x_6 \le 43y_6$$

$$28y_7 \le x_7 \le 38y_7, 46y_8 \le x_8 \le 56y_8,$$

$$55y_9 \le x_9 \le 65y_9, 63y_{10} \le x_{10} \le 73y_{10}$$

$$x_i \in \{0, \mathbf{Z}^+\}, i = 1, \dots, 10,$$

$$y_i \in \{0, 1\}, i = 1, \dots, 10,$$

(A.3)

$U_3: \min \quad 3.1x_1 y_1 + 3.2x_2 y_2 + 3.1x_3 y_3 + 3.55x_4 y_4$

$\qquad + 3.37x_5 y_5 + 3.4x_6 y_6 + 3.87x_7 y_7$

$\qquad + 3.35x_8 y_8 + 3.59x_9 y_9 + 3.41x_{10} y_{10},$

subject to $\displaystyle \sum_{i=1}^{10} x_i y_i = 200,$

$$\sum_{i=1}^{10} y_i \le 5,$$

$$40y_1 \le x_1 \le 50y_1, 53y_2 \le x_2 \le 63y_2$$

$$65y_3 \le x_3 \le 75y_3, 45y_4 \le x_4 \le 55y_4,$$

$$40y_5 \le x_5 \le 50y_5, 33y_6 \le x_6 \le 43y_6,$$

$$28y_7 \le x_7 \le 38y_7, 46y_8 \le x_8 \le 56y_8,$$

$$55y_9 \le x_9 \le 65y_9, 63y_{10} \le x_{10} \le 73y_{10}$$

$$x_i \in \{0, \mathbf{Z}^+\}, i = 1, \dots, 10,$$

$$y_i \in \{0, 1\}, i = 1, \dots, 10,$$

(A.4)

$U_4: \max \quad 0.83x_1 y_1 + 0.84x_2 y_2 + 0.825x_3 y_3 + 0.85x_4 y_4$

$\qquad + 0.87x_5 y_5 + 0.825x_6 y_6 + 0.88x_7 y_7$

$\qquad + 0.87x_8 y_8 + 0.841x_9 y_9 + 0.85x_{10} y_{10},$

subject to $\displaystyle \sum_{i=1}^{10} x_i y_i = 200,$

$$\sum_{i=1}^{10} y_i \le 5,$$

$$40y_1 \le x_1 \le 50y_1, 53y_2 \le x_2 \le 63y_2,$$

$$65y_3 \le x_3 \le 75y_3, 45y_4 \le x_4 \le 55y_4,$$

$$40y_5 \le x_5 \le 50y_5, 33y_6 \le x_6 \le 43y_6,$$

$$28y_7 \le x_7 \le 38y_7, 46y_8 \le x_8 \le 56y_8$$

$$55y_9 \le x_9 \le 65y_9, 63y_{10} \le x_{10} \le 73y_{10},$$

$$x_i \in \{0, \mathbf{Z}^+\}, i = 1, \dots, 10,$$

$$y_i \in \{0, 1\}, i = 1, \dots, 10.$$

(A.5)

References

[1] G. W. Dickson, "An analysis of vendor selection systems and decisions," *Journal of Purchasing*, vol. 2, no. 1, pp. 5–17, 1966.

[2] C. A. Weber and J. R. Current, "A multiobjective approach to vendor selection," *European Journal of Operational Research*, vol. 68, no. 2, pp. 173–184, 1993.

[3] S. Yahya and B. Kingsman, "Vendor rating for an entrepreneur development programme: a case study using the analytic hierarchy process method," *Journal of the Operational Research Society*, vol. 50, no. 9, pp. 916–930, 1999.

[4] S. W. Lam and L. C. Tang, "Multiobjective vendor allocation in multiechelon inventory systems: a spreadsheet model," *Journal of the Operational Research Society*, vol. 57, no. 5, pp. 561–578, 2006.

[5] Y.-T. Lin, C.-L. Lin, H.-C. Yu, and G.-H. Tzeng, "A novel hybrid MCDM approach for outsourcing vendor selection: a case study for a semiconductor company in Taiwan," *Expert Systems with Applications*, vol. 37, no. 7, pp. 4796–4804, 2010.

[6] C.-H. Hsu, F.-K. Wang, and G.-H. Tzeng, "The best vendor selection for conducting the recycled material based on a hybrid MCDM model combining DANP with VIKOR," *Resources, Conservation and Recycling*, vol. 66, pp. 95–111, 2012.

[7] R. Zanjirani Farahani and M. Fadaei, "A MCDM-based model for vendor selection: a case study in the particleboard industry," *Journal of Forestry Research*, vol. 23, no. 4, pp. 685–690, 2012.

[8] W. Li, X. Zhang, and Y. Chen, "Information integration approach to vendor selection group decision making under multiple criteria," in *Advances in Neural Networks—ISNN 2009*, vol. 5551 of *Lecture Notes in Computer Science*, pp. 1138–1143, 2009.

[9] H. Zhang, X. Li, and W. Liu, "An AHP/DEA methodology for 3PL vendor selection in 4PL," in *Computer Supported Cooperative Work in Design II*, vol. 3865 of *Lecture Notes in Computer Science*, pp. 646–655, 2006.

[10] N. Arunkumar, L. Karunamoorthy, S. Anand, and T. Ramesh Babu, "Linear approach for solving a piecewise linear vendor selection problem of quantity discounts using lexicographic method," *International Journal of Advanced Manufacturing Technology*, vol. 28, no. 11-12, pp. 1254–1260, 2006.

[11] S. C. H. Leung, Y. Wu, and K. K. Lai, "A stochastic programming approach for multi-site aggregate production planning," *Journal of the Operational Research Society*, vol. 57, no. 2, pp. 123–132, 2006.

[12] S. Talluri, R. Narasimhan, and A. Nair, "Vendor performance with supply risk: a chance-constrained DEA approach," *International Journal of Production Economics*, vol. 100, no. 2, pp. 212–222, 2006.

[13] J. Xu and C. Ding, "A class of chance constrained multiobjective linear programming with birandom coefficients and its application to vendors selection," *International Journal of Production Economics*, vol. 131, no. 2, pp. 709–720, 2011.

[14] G. Zhimin, J. Zhihong, and Z. Baogang, "A multi-objective mixed-integer stochastic programming model for the vendor selection problem under multi-product purchases," *International Journal of Information and Management Sciences*, vol. 18, no. 3, pp. 241–252, 2007.

[15] R. G. Kasilingam and C. P. Lee, "Selection of vendors—a mixed-integer programming approach," *Computers and Industrial Engineering*, vol. 31, no. 1-2, pp. 347–350, 1996.

[16] A. Alonso-Ayuso, L. F. Escudero, A. Garín, M. T. Ortuño, and G. Pérez, "An approach for strategic supply chain planning under uncertainty based on stochastic 0-1 programming," *Journal of Global Optimization*, vol. 26, no. 1, pp. 97–124, 2003.

[17] W. Zang, Y. Liu, and Z. Li, "Optimizing supplier selection with disruptions by chance-constrained programming," in *Advances in Swarm Intelligence*, vol. 7332 of *Lecture Notes in Computer Science*, pp. 108–116, 2012.

[18] B. B. Keskin, H. Ster, and S. Etinkaya, "Integration of strategic and tactical decisions for vendor selection under capacity constraints," *Computers and Operations Research*, vol. 37, no. 12, pp. 2182–2191, 2010.

[19] S. He, S. S. Chaudhry, Z. Lei, and W. Baohua, "Stochastic vendor selection problem: chance-constrained model and genetic algorithms," *Annals of Operations Research*, vol. 168, no. 1, pp. 169–179, 2009.

[20] A. A. Taleizadeh, S. T. A. Niaki, and F. Barzinpour, "Multiple-buyer multiple-vendor multi-product multi-constraint supply chain problem with stochastic demand and variable lead-time: a harmony search algorithm," *Applied Mathematics and Computation*, vol. 217, no. 22, pp. 9234–9253, 2011.

[21] B. Huang, C. Gao, and L. Chen, "Partner selection in a virtual enterprise under uncertain information about candidates," *Expert Systems with Applications*, vol. 38, no. 9, pp. 11305–11310, 2011.

[22] R. J. Kuo, S. Y. Hong, and Y. C. Huang, "Integration of particle swarm optimization-based fuzzy neural network and artificial neural network for supplier selection," *Applied Mathematical Modelling*, vol. 34, no. 12, pp. 3976–3990, 2010.

[23] D. Karaboga, "An idea based on honey bee swarm for numerical optimization," Tech. Rep. TR06, Erciyes University, Engineering Faculty, Computer Engineering Department, 2005.

[24] M. Ekhtiari and K. Ghoseiri, "Multi-objective stochastic programming to solve manpower allocation problem," *International Journal of Advanced Manufacturing Technology*, vol. 65, no. 1, pp. 183–196, 2013.

[25] S. N. Sivanandam and S. N. Deepa, *Introduction to Genetic Algorithms*, Springer, Berlin, Germany, 2008.

[26] D. Karaboga and B. Akay, "A comparative study of Artificial Bee Colony algorithm," *Applied Mathematics and Computation*, vol. 214, no. 1, pp. 108–132, 2009.

[27] J. Kennedy and R. Eberhart, "Particle swarm optimization," in *Proceedings of the IEEE International Conference on Neural Networks*, pp. 1942–1948, Perth WA, Australia, December 1995.

[28] C.-J. Liao, E. Tjandradjaja, and T.-P. Chung, "An approach using particle swarm optimization and bottleneck heuristic to solve hybrid flow shop scheduling problem," *Applied Soft Computing Journal*, vol. 12, no. 6, pp. 1755–1764, 2012.

[29] M. Clerc, *Particle Swarm Optimization*, ISTE, London, UK, 2006.

[30] A. P. Engelbrecht, *Fundamentals of Computational Swarm Intelligent*, John Wiley & Sons, 2005.

[31] E. Atashpaz-Gargari and C. Lucas, "Imperialist competitive algorithm: an algorithm for optimization inspired by imperialistic competition," in *Proceedings of the IEEE Congress on Evolutionary Computation (CEC '07)*, pp. 4661–4667, Singapore, September 2007.

13

Gamma-Poisson Distribution Model for Text Categorization

Hiroshi Ogura, Hiromi Amano, and Masato Kondo

Department of Information Science, Faculty of Arts and Sciences, Showa University, 4562 Kamiyoshida, Fujiyoshida City, Yamanashi 403-0005, Japan

Correspondence should be addressed to Hiroshi Ogura; ogura@cas.showa-u.ac.jp

Academic Editors: K. W. Chau, C. Chen, G. L. Foresti, and M. Loog

We introduce a new model for describing word frequency distributions in documents for automatic text classification tasks. In the model, the gamma-Poisson probability distribution is used to achieve better text modeling. The framework of the modeling and its application to text categorization are demonstrated with practical techniques for parameter estimation and vector normalization. To investigate the efficiency of our model, text categorization experiments were performed on 20 Newsgroups, Reuters-21578, Industry Sector, and TechTC-100 datasets. The results show that the model allows performance comparable to that of the support vector machine and clearly exceeding that of the multinomial model and the Dirichlet-multinomial model. The time complexity of the proposed classifier and its advantage in practical applications are also discussed.

1. Introduction

The Poisson distribution is one of the most commonly used models for describing the number of random occurrences of a phenomenon in a specified unit of space or time. This means that if we want to model the number of discrete occurrences that take place during a given length, we should first check whether or not the Poisson distribution provides a good approximation. For text modeling, it is justified to adopt the Poisson distribution for describing the number of occurrences of a certain word in documents of fixed length when the independent assumption of each word occurrence holds in an approximate sense. It has been well established, however, that the Poisson model does not fit observed data [1, 2]. The reason for the failure of the Poisson model is that, for most words, the predicted variance, which is equal to the Poisson mean (the expected number of occurrences during the given interval), systematically underestimates the actual variance. Although this inadequate description of words distribution with the Poisson model can be used for key words selection in information retrieval [1] and for feature selection in text categorization [2–4] improvement in the accuracy of description is inevitably needed in order to build a high-performance text classifier using the model.

As has been proposed by Church and Gale [5], it is natural to extend the simple Poisson to a Poisson mixture in order to describe the observed variance in actual documents. Here, a Poisson mixture is a probability density function that is expressed as a sum of infinite Poisson distributions with a certain weighting function. The Poisson mixture is therefore considered to be a hierarchical model because a two-step process is required to generate a sample; to get a sample, we first pick a Poisson distribution with a certain probability according to the weighting function and then pick the sample from the chosen Poisson distribution. A reasonable choice of the weighting function is the conjugate prior of the Poisson, that is, the gamma distribution, because it greatly simplifies mathematical treatments [6], and this choice leads to the joint gamma-Poisson distribution.

In this paper, we focus on the use of the gamma-Poisson distribution to construct a new generative probabilistic text classifier. We believe that this is worthwhile for the following reasons.

(i) Several attempts to extend the original generative probabilistic classifier by using a conjugate prior for better text modeling have already been suggested; the reported conjugate prior-likelihood pairs are the Dirichlet-multinomial [7], the beta-negative binomial [8], and the beta-binomial [9]. To the best of our knowledge, the gamma-Poisson distribution has not yet been used to construct a generative probabilistic text classifier. As mentioned above, since the model using the gamma-Poisson distribution can be regarded as one of the most fundamental and natural for modeling texts, it is useful to illustrate its framework.

(ii) It will be shown in a later section that our new classifier using the gamma-Poisson distribution clearly outperforms the original generative probabilistic classifier (multinomial naive Bayes) and is highly competitive with the support vector machine (SVM), which is the state of the art in terms of classification accuracy. This means that gamma-Poisson modeling is attractive not only for theoretical work but also for practical applications.

Note that the negative binomial distribution, which is the resultant posterior distribution of the gamma-Poisson pair [6], has been used for text modeling [5] and for text categorization [10]. In those studies, however, the hierarchical structure of gamma-Poisson modeling of texts was not taken into account, and the negative binomial distribution was merely used as a simple tool for describing word distributions. In the present work, the proposed classifier is based on hierarchical modeling; in other words, parameter estimation and classification procedures directly reflect the hierarchical structure of the gamma-Poisson distribution. In this sense, our approach is fundamentally different from the previous works.

To demonstrate that the proposed modeling is useful in practical applications, the classification accuracy and the computation time of the algorithm are examined using four standard datasets. The results lead us to conclude that the classifier with the proposed modeling is the most suitable among several tested classifiers in the case of noisy datasets. Furthermore, the advantage of the proposed model in incremental learning tasks that are frequently needed in practical application will be reported in detail.

The rest of the paper is organized as follows. Section 2 summarizes related works on the improvement of the generative probabilistic classifier in which some conjugate priors are utilized for better text modeling. In Section 3, we describe the framework of gamma-Poisson modeling of texts and how to construct a classifier by using the framework. Section 4 describes our experiments on automatic text classification. We summarize these results in Section 5 and discuss the characteristics of gamma-Poisson modeling in Section 6. In the last section, we give our conclusions.

2. Related Work

We first give a brief overview of the text categorization problem and introduce notation for later use. For the sake of completeness and later reference, we then review the original generative probabilistic classifier and its descendants, in which conjugate priors are used for better text modeling. Except for the beta-negative binomial model, all the models described in this section will be used in corresponding classifiers, and their performance will be compared with that of our new classifier through experiments.

2.1. *Text Categorization Problem.* Text classification/categorization is defined as the task of classifying documents into a fixed number of predefined categories. Categories are also called classes. Let $\mathcal{D}$ denote a domain of possible text documents, and let $C = \{c_1, c_2, \ldots, c_{|C|}\}$ be a finite set of predefined categories. In the conventional text categorization setting used in this study, each document $d \in \mathcal{D}$ is assigned to a single category $c \in C$. (Note that to simplify the problem, we consider here the categorization where each document is assigned to only one class. In other words, every document is assumed to be single labeled, not multilabeled. This assumption is made throughout this work.) We are given a set of training documents $D = \{d_1, d_2, \ldots, d_{|D|}\}$ which is a subset of $\mathcal{D}$, that is, $D \subset \mathcal{D}$. We assume that there is a target concept $\Phi : \mathcal{D} \rightarrow C$ that maps documents to categories. The result of the mapping $\Phi(d)$ is known for documents in the training set D; that is, each training document $d_i \in D$ has a class label $y_i \in \{c_1, c_2, \ldots, c_{|C|}\}$, which indicates that document d_i belongs to a category corresponding to the label. In the training phase, we attempt to find the classification function $f : \mathcal{D} \rightarrow C$, which approximates Φ from the information contained in training set D. In the test phase, f is used to classify new documents, the labels of which are unknown. The most important objective is to find f that maximizes accuracy (i.e., the percentage of times f and Φ agree).

To obtain a good f, the training set D must contain sample documents of all possible categories. If this is the case, D is expressed as

$$D = \bigcup_{c=c_1}^{c_{|C|}} D_c, \tag{1}$$

where D_c denotes a set of training documents that belong to a class c.

2.2. *The Generative Probabilistic Classifier.* The generative probabilistic classifier, often referred to as the *multinomial classifier* or *multinomial naive Bayes*, is one of the most popular classifiers for text categorization because it sometimes achieves good performance in various tasks, and because it is simple enough to be practically implemented even with a great number of features [11, 12]. The simplicity is mainly due to the following two assumptions. First, an individual document is assumed to be represented as a vector of word counts (bag-of-words representation). Since this representation greatly simplifies further processing, all the descendants including our new classifier inherit this first assumption. Next, documents are assumed to be generated by repeatedly drawing words from a fixed multinomial distribution for a given class, and word emissions are thus independent.

From the first assumption, documents can be represented as vectors of count-valued random variables. The ith document in a considered class c is then expressed as

$$d_{ci} = \left(x_{i1}, x_{i2}, \ldots, x_{ij}, \ldots, x_{i|V|} \right), \tag{2}$$

where x_{ij} is the count of the jth term t_j in the ith document in D_c and $|V|$ is a vocabulary size; in other words, we have assumed here that the vocabulary of the considered dataset is given as $V = \{t_1, t_2, \ldots, t_{|V|}\}$ where t_j is the jth word in the vocabulary. From the second assumption, the probability of the document d_{ci} given by vector (2) is

$$p(d_{ci} \mid \theta_c) = \frac{\left(\sum_{j=1}^{|V|} x_{ij}\right)!}{\prod_{j=1}^{|V|} \left(x_{ij}!\right)} \prod_{j=1}^{|V|} \theta_{cj}^{x_{ij}}, \tag{3}$$

where θ_{cj} is the probability for the emission of t_j and is subject to the constraints $\sum_{j=1}^{|V|} \theta_{cj} = 1$. Note that for text classification, the parameters θ_{cj} must be evaluated for each possible class c. We use the estimator for θ_{cj} given by

$$\hat{\theta}_{cj} = \frac{1 + \sum_{i=1}^{|D_c|} x_{ij}}{|V| + \sum_{i=1}^{|D_c|} \sum_{j=1}^{|V|} x_{ij}}, \tag{4}$$

where $|D_c|$ is the number of training documents belonging to the considered class c. To classify a new document with a given feature vector $d = (x_1, x_2, \ldots, x_{|V|})$, the multinomial classifier calculates a class-specific probability for class c as

$$p(c \mid d) \propto p(c) \, p(d \mid \theta_c) = p(c) \frac{\left(\sum_{j=1}^{|V|} x_j\right)!}{\prod_{j=1}^{|V|} \left(x_j!\right)} \prod_{j=1}^{|V|} \theta_{cj}^{x_j}, \tag{5}$$

where $p(c)$ is the prior probability of class c which is estimated from a training set by $p(c) = |D_c|/|D|$. We estimate θ_{cj} in (5) by using (4) for each specified class c. The document is assigned to the class with the highest probability $p(c \mid d)$.

The framework of the multinomial classifier described above usually works well in practical text classification tasks [11]. It has been pointed out, however, that the multinomial distribution used in the multinomial naive Bayes cannot describe the word burstiness phenomena that are inherently encountered in natural language documents [7]. Here, *bursti-ness* means the tendency of words in a document to appear in bursts; that is, if a word appears once, it is more likely to appear again. Since multinomial modeling is based on the assumption of independent word emissions with a fixed multinomial distribution for a considered class, the resultant word distribution fails to capture the burstiness especially for the words with moderate and low frequencies [7].

2.3. Dirichlet-Multinomial Model.

A substantial improvement to describe the word burstiness phenomena has been achieved by introducing the Dirichlet-multinomial model, which models texts in a hierarchical manner to capture the burstiness [7]. In the model, the word count vector representing each document is generated by a multinomial distribution whose parameters are generated by its conjugate prior, that is, the Dirichlet distribution. The Dirichlet distribution is defined as

$$p(\theta_c \mid \alpha_c) = \frac{\Gamma\left(\sum_{j=1}^{|V|} \alpha_{cj}\right)}{\prod_{j=1}^{|V|} \Gamma\left(\alpha_{cj}\right)} \prod_{j=1}^{|V|} \theta_{cj}^{\alpha_{cj}-1}, \tag{6}$$

where $\alpha_c = (\alpha_{c1}, \alpha_{c2}, \ldots, \alpha_{c|V|})$ is a parameter vector of the Dirichlet of which components determine the density

of the θ_c vector and where $\Gamma(\cdot)$ is the gamma function. The likelihood of a document $d = (x_1, x_2, \ldots, x_{|V|})$ with length n ($\sum_{j=1}^{|V|} x_j = n$) is given as an integral over θ_c vectors weighted by a Dirichlet distribution:

$$p(d \mid \alpha_c) = \int_{\theta_c} p(d \mid \theta_c) \, p(\theta_c \mid \alpha_c) \, d\theta_c$$
$$= \frac{n!}{\prod_{j=1}^{|V|} x_j!} \frac{\Gamma\left(\sum_{j=1}^{|V|} \alpha_{cj}\right) \prod_{j=1}^{|V|} \Gamma\left(x_j + \alpha_{cj}\right)}{\prod_{j=1}^{|V|} \Gamma\left(\alpha_{cj}\right) \Gamma\left(\sum_{j=1}^{|V|} x_j + \alpha_{cj}\right)}, \tag{7}$$

where we use the multinomial distribution function, (3), for $p(d \mid \theta_c)$. The classifier using Dirichlet-multinomial modeling computes class-specific probability of a given document d as

$$p(c \mid d) \propto p(c) \, p(d \mid \alpha_c)$$
$$\propto p(c) \frac{\Gamma\left(\sum_{j=1}^{|V|} \alpha_{cj}\right) \prod_{j=1}^{|V|} \Gamma\left(x_j + \alpha_{cj}\right)}{\prod_{j=1}^{|V|} \Gamma\left(\alpha_{cj}\right) \Gamma\left(\sum_{j=1}^{|V|} x_j + \alpha_{cj}\right)} \tag{8}$$

for each class c and assigns the document to the class with the highest probability. In the second expression of (8), we drop the term $n!/(\prod_{j=1}^{|V|} x_j!)$, which does not depend on class c. As in the case of θ_{cj} in multinomial modeling, one set of parameters for the Dirichlet, $\alpha_{cj}(j = 1 \cdots |V|)$, must be evaluated for each possible class. For the evaluation, we use the leave-one-out likelihood maximization method proposed by Minka [13] which offers a convergent fixed-point iteration for the update as

$$\alpha_{cj}^{new} = \alpha_{cj} \frac{\sum_{i=1}^{|D_c|} \left(x_{ij}/\left(x_{ij} + \alpha_{cj} - 1\right)\right)}{\sum_{i=1}^{|D_c|} \left(\sum_{j=1}^{|V|} x_{ij}/\left(\sum_{j=1}^{|V|} x_{ij} + \sum_{j=1}^{v} \alpha_{cj} - 1\right)\right)}. \tag{9}$$

It has been confirmed that the Dirichlet-multinomial leads to better text modeling in the sense that it can describe the burstiness for all word types ranging from frequent words to rare words. This success has recently led to two major modeling approaches along the lines of hierarchical modeling of texts: beta-binomial modeling and beta-negative binomial modeling.

2.4. Beta-Binomial Model.

The beta-binomial distribution model is derived with consideration of a serious drawback in Dirichlet-multinomial modeling [9]. If we use the Dirichlet distribution, (6), to describe the probability density of θ_{cj}, then it is concluded that words having the same expectation value in θ_{cj} also have the same variance in θ_{cj}; that is, if $E[\theta_{cl}] = E[\theta_{cm}]$ then $\mathrm{Var}[\theta_{cl}] = \mathrm{Var}[\theta_{cm}]$. This is an undesirable property of the Dirichlet for text modeling because we aim to model different words as having the same expected value but different variances in order to describe various word occurrence patterns.

Allison [9] addressed this problem with the following assumptions.

(i) The probability of the occurrence of a document d is a product of independent terms, each of which represents the probability of the number of emissions (i.e., the count) of an individual word.

(ii) The probability of the number of emissions is the average of a product $p(x_j \mid \theta_j)p(\theta_j \mid \alpha_j, \beta_j)$ over θ_j where θ_j is the probability for the emission of jth word t_j, $p(x_j \mid \theta_j)$ is the binomial distribution representing the probability of x_j times occurrence of t_j, and $p(\theta_j \mid \alpha_j, \beta_j)$ is beta-distributed weighting function of θ_j.

The assumptions described above allow means and variances for each θ_j to be specified separately and lead us to an expression of the probability of document d as

$$
\begin{aligned}
p(d \mid \alpha_c, \beta_c) &= \prod_{j=1}^{|V|} p\left(x_j \mid \alpha_{cj}, \beta_{cj}\right) \\
&= \prod_{j=1}^{|V|} \int_{\theta_{cj}} p\left(x_j \mid \theta_{cj}\right) p\left(\theta_{cj} \mid \alpha_{cj}, \beta_{cj}\right) d\theta_{cj} \\
&= \prod_{j=1}^{|V|} \binom{n}{x_j} \frac{B\left(x_j + \alpha_{cj}, n - x_j + \beta_{cj}\right)}{B\left(\alpha_{cj}, \beta_{cj}\right)},
\end{aligned}
\tag{10}
$$

where $B(\cdot)$ is the beta function and α_{cj} and β_{cj} are the parameters of the beta distribution. Note that the parameters α_j and β_j in the second assumption are replaced with α_{cj} and β_{cj} in the above equation since we aim to calculate $p(d \mid \alpha_c, \beta_c)$ for each class c to build a classifier. The classifier computes the class-specific probability $p(c \mid d) \propto p(c)p(d \mid \alpha_c, \beta_c)$ and the document d is assigned to the most probable class. Following Allison [9], we use the method of moments to evaluate sets of parameters α_{cj} and β_{cj} for each class.

2.5. Beta-Negative Binomial Model. The beta-negative binomial model is derived from consideration of the adequate empirical fit of the negative binomial distribution for text modeling [8]. The classifier using the model has been proved to be comparable to the multinomial naive Bayes in terms of classification performance, and this has been confirmed experimentally [8]. Hence, we do not test this model in the present experiment.

3. Gamma-Poisson Modeling of Text

3.1. Framework of the Model. As stated above, the Poisson distribution expresses the probability of a number of events occurring in a fixed period of time or in a specified unit of space. In text modeling, the "number of events" corresponds to the number of occurrences of a considered word in each document, all of which have a specified length in word count. Of course, documents are different from one another in length, and thus normalization, which will be described later, is necessary. A further step of text modeling is possible by extending the simple Poisson to a hierarchical gamma-Poisson description. The gamma-Poisson distribution is a Poisson distribution whose probability of the mean parameter λ follows a gamma distribution with a shape parameter

α and a rate parameter β. The mass function of the Poisson describing the probability of x_j occurrences of the jth word is

$$
p\left(x_j \mid \lambda_j\right) = \frac{\lambda_j^{x_j} \exp\left(-\lambda_j\right)}{x_j!}.
\tag{11}
$$

Its conjugate prior determining the density of λ_j is given by the gamma distribution, the density function of which is

$$
p\left(\lambda_j \mid \alpha_j, \beta_j\right) = \frac{\beta_j^{\alpha_j}}{\Gamma\left(\alpha_j\right)} \lambda_j^{\alpha_j - 1} \exp\left(-\beta_j \lambda_j\right).
\tag{12}
$$

We incorporate the gamma-Poisson description in our model under assumptions that are similar to the beta-binomial case.

(i) The probability of document d can be decomposed to a product of independent terms, each of which represents the probability of a number of emissions for each individual word.

(ii) Each term can be expressed as the average of a product $p(x_j \mid \lambda_j)p(\lambda_j \mid \alpha_j, \beta_j)$ over λ_j where $p(x_j \mid \lambda_j)$ is the Poisson, (11), and $p(\lambda_j \mid \alpha_j, \beta_j)$ is gamma distributed, (12).

Consequently, the probability of document d is

$$
\begin{aligned}
&p(d \mid \alpha_c, \beta_c) \\
&= \prod_{j=1}^{|V|} p\left(x_j \mid \alpha_{cj}, \beta_{cj}\right) \\
&= \prod_{j=1}^{|V|} \int_{\lambda_{cj}} p\left(x_j \mid \lambda_{cj}\right) p\left(\lambda_{cj} \mid \alpha_{cj}, \beta_{cj}\right) d\lambda_{cj} \\
&= \prod_{j=1}^{|V|} \left\{ \frac{\Gamma\left(\alpha_{cj} + x_j\right)}{x_j! \, \Gamma\left(\alpha_{cj}\right)} \left(\frac{\beta_{cj}}{\beta_{cj} + 1}\right)^{\alpha_{cj}} \left(\frac{1}{\beta_{cj} + 1}\right)^{x_j} \right\},
\end{aligned}
\tag{13}
$$

where the parameters are replaced with class-specific ones. In the last expression of (13), we can see that each term of the products becomes a mass function of the negative binomial distribution when α_{cj} is an integer value [6]. The classifier computes the class-specific probability $p(c \mid d) \propto p(c)p(d \mid \alpha_c, \beta_c)$, and the document d is assigned to the most probable class.

3.2. Normalization of Document Length. To satisfy the conditions for using the gamma-Poisson description, documents must be normalized in length. Although several methods for normalizing document vectors have been proposed [12, 14, 15], we choose the simplest one that normalize a resulting vector in terms of L_1. The conversion of the jth component in a count-valued document vector is expressed as

$$
x_j^{\text{new}} = \frac{x_j N}{\sum_{j=1}^{v} x_j},
\tag{14}
$$

which gives the predefined fixed length of the normalized document as N. The normalization factor in the L_1 sense is $1/\sum_{j=1}^{v} x_j$ as seen in (14); in our experience, this factor leads to better classification performance than the common L_2 sense normalization with a factor $1/\sqrt{\sum_{j=1}^{v} x_j^2}$. This is because, in generative modeling of text, the document length of L_1 sense (i.e., total word count of a document) is considered to be the number of trials in which the selection of a considered word corresponds to a success. We set $N = 100$ for all documents because it allows intuitive understanding of the composition of normalized count vectors.

The normalization using (14) with $N = 100$ converts an integer-valued document vector into a real-valued one. This means that x_j in (13) changes from integer to real but it is not necessary to take into account the effects of this change when (13) is used in the classifier; the factorial $x_j!$ in (13) does not depend on class c, and we can safely omit $x_j!$ from the calculation of class-specific probability $p(c \mid d)$. Thus, the real-valued x_j does not cause any further difficulties in the evaluation of (13).

3.3. Estimation of Parameters. To compute the class-specific probability $p(c \mid d) \propto p(c)p(d \mid \alpha_c, \beta_c)$, we must use sets of parameters α_{cj} and β_{cj} ($j = 1 \cdots |V|$) which are estimated for each specified class c from D_c (the set of training documents belonging to the class c). We use two different methods for the estimation: a rational approximation [16] and an iterative method [17].

The rational approximation estimates the parameters α_{cj} and β_{cj} through a set of equations:

$$\overline{x}_j = \frac{1}{|D_c|} \sum_{i=1}^{|D_c|} x_{ij}, \tag{15}$$

$$\widetilde{x}_j = \left(\prod_{i=1}^{|D_c|} x_{ij} \right)^{1/|D_c|}, \tag{16}$$

$$M_j = \ln\left(\frac{\overline{x}_j}{\widetilde{x}_j} \right), \tag{17}$$

$$\widehat{\alpha}_{cj} = \begin{cases} \dfrac{0.5000876 + 0.1648852M_j - 0.0544274M_j^2}{M_j} \\ \qquad\qquad\qquad (0 < M_j \le 0.5772) \\ \dfrac{8.898919 + 9.059950M_j + 0.9775373M_j^2}{M_j \left(17.79728 + 11.968477M_j + M_j^2 \right)} \\ \qquad\qquad\qquad (0.5772 < M_j \le 17) \\ \dfrac{1}{M_j} \qquad\qquad\qquad (17 < M_j), \end{cases} \tag{18}$$

$$\widehat{\beta}_{cj} = \frac{\widehat{\alpha}_{cj}}{\overline{x}_j}, \tag{19}$$

where x_{ij} is the count of jth word in ith document and $|D_c|$ is the number of documents belonging to the considered class.

The iterative method provides an update formula for α_{cj} as

$$\frac{1}{\alpha_{cj}^{\mathrm{new}}} = \frac{1}{\alpha_{cj}} + \frac{\ln \widetilde{x}_j - \ln \overline{x}_j + \ln \alpha_{cj} - \Psi\left(\alpha_{cj}\right)}{\alpha_{cj}^2 \left(1/\alpha_{cj} - \Psi'\left(\alpha_{cj}\right) \right)}, \tag{20}$$

where $\Psi(\cdot)$ and $\Psi'(\cdot)$ are the digamma and trigamma functions, respectively, and $\overline{x}_j$ and $\widetilde{x}_j$ are the same as in the rational approximation. The estimator for β_{cj} is still defined as $\widehat{\beta}_{cj} = \widehat{\alpha}_{cj}/\overline{x}_j$. In the iteration, we use

$$\alpha_{cj0} = \frac{0.5}{\ln \overline{x}_j - \ln \widetilde{x}_j} \tag{21}$$

as an initial value of α_{cj} [17] and apply a convergence criterion $|\alpha_{cj}^{\mathrm{new}} - \alpha_{cj}| \le 1.0 \times 10^{-5}$.

The resultant classification performance of each method in estimating parameters will be compared in the experimental section.

4. Experimental

To investigate the behavior of the proposed gamma-Poisson model described in the previous section, we perform experiments on automatic text categorization. In the experiments, the performance of a classifier using gamma-Poisson modeling is compared with the performance of other classifiers that also use probabilistic modeling but with different distributions. As mentioned above, the models selected for the comparison are the multinomial, the Dirichlet-multinomial, and the beta-binomial. In our experiments, the support vector machine (SVM) is also used as a standard discriminative classifier because previous comparative studies on classifiers [14, 18] have consistently shown that SVM is the state of the art in terms of classification accuracy.

4.1. Data Set. For our experiments, we use four different datasets that are chosen to represent a wide spectrum of text classification tasks.

The first one is the 20 Newsgroups dataset which was originally collected with a netnews-filtering system [19] and contains approximately 20,000 documents being partitioned (nearly) evenly across 20 different UseNet newsgroups. We use the 20news-18828 version (original data set is available from http://kdd.ics.uci.edu/databases/20newsgroups/20newsgroups.data.html. 20News-18828 is available from http://people.csail.mit.edu/jrennie/20Newsgroups/) from which cross-posts have been removed to give a total of 18,828 documents. Consequently, 20 Newsgroups is a single labeled dataset with approximately even class distribution, and the task is to apply one of the 20 possible labels to each test document. We build an initial vocabulary from all words left after stop word, punctuation, and number token removals. Capital letters are transformed to lowercase letters and no stemming algorithm is applied. Here, words are defined as alphabetical strings enclosed by whitespace. The size of the initial vocabulary is 103,135 words.

The second dataset is the Reuters-21578 data collection (data set is available from: http://kdd.ics.ics.uci.edu/databases/reuters21578/), which contains documents that appeared on the Reuters newswire in 1987 and were manually classified by personnel from Reuters Ltd. For applications in which enough numbers of training and test documents are required, the top 10 categories (the 10 categories with the highest number of positive training examples in the ModApte split) are usually used [2]. However, since we want to use a single labeled dataset as stated in Section 2.1, we make a slight modification to the usual top 10 categories; specifically, we eliminate all documents with more than one topic (category); in this way, two categories among the top 10 are excluded. We use documents in the resultant 8 categories as our dataset. Consequently, the task is applying one of the 8 possible labels to each of test documents. In contrast to the 20 Newsgroups, the class distribution of this dataset is quite imbalanced; the largest topic category "earn" has 3,923 documents while the smallest "grain" has only 51 documents. The preprocessing used to build an initial vocabulary is the same as for the 20 Newsgroups, and the resulting vocabulary has 22,793 words.

The third test collection is the Industry Sector dataset which is a collection of corporate web pages organized into hierarchical categories based on what a company produces or does. Although it has a hierarchy with three levels of depth, we do not take the hierarchy into account and use a flattened version of the dataset. This dataset contains a total of 9,555 documents divided into 104 categories. (We obtained the dataset from http://www.cs.umass.edu/mccallum/code-data.html. Because it was found that one of the original 105 categories was empty, the remaining 104 categories having documents were used in our experiments.) We use all 9,555 documents in our experiments without removing the multilabeled documents because the fraction of multilabeled documents is very small and the effect of these documents is negligible (only 15 documents out of 9,555 belong to two classes; thus, they cannot affect our results considerably). The largest and smallest categories have 105 and 27 documents, respectively, and the average number of documents per category is 91.9. For this dataset, we remove HTML tags by skipping all characters between "<" and ">", and we did not use a stop list. The resulting vocabulary has 64,680 words.

The fourth test collection is the TechTC-100 dataset which is a collection of web pages taken from the web directory of the Open Directory Project (ODP) (the TechTC-100 dataset is available from http://techtc.cs.technion.ac.il/techtc100/). Because this test collection was generated from the web directory in a fully automated manner [20], it is noisier than the other three test collections; for example, textual advertisements included in the web pages can be noise that affects the classification accuracy. The original TechTC-100 dataset contains 100 datasets, each of which consists of positive and negative documents that define a binary classification task, and these positive and negative documents are chosen from the pairs of the ODP categories. Although there are 100 different combinations of positive and negative categories in the datasets, we only use positive documents because positive documents for each class are sufficient to define a multiclass classification problem. We found that 40 distinct positive categories in the 100 pairs of positive and negative categories, and therefore the task becomes applying one of the 40 possible labels to each of test documents. We did not apply the preprocessing steps to this test collection because it is supplied in a preprocessed plain text format. This collection has a vocabulary of 103,003 words.

For all four datasets, we use 10-fold cross-validation to make maximal use of the data and to allow comparison with the previous work by Allison [9]. Ten obtained values of performance are averaged to give the final result.

4.2. Vector Creation. To investigate the effect of vocabulary size on classification performance, we use a simple feature selection method based on the collection term frequency as follows. First, we count the collection term frequency, CF, which is the total frequency of each word throughout the entire dataset. Second, we select all words that satisfy CF $\geq N_0$ where N_0 is a predefined integer. The feature selection by CF is one of the simplest methods, but is sufficient for the task at hand, namely, comparing different classifiers at each vocabulary size. The resultant vocabulary sizes after feature selection are summarized in Table 1.

Two different types of document vectors, namely, count-valued and normalized, are used to represent each document. A count-valued document vector is constructed from document term frequency (number of occurrences of a considered word in a document) for each word, and then each component in the vector is converted by use of (14) to give the normalized vector. The count-valued document vectors are supplied to the classifiers with multinomial, Dirichlet-multinomial, and beta-binomial modeling as training and test data. The normalized document vectors are supplied to the classifier with gamma-Poisson modeling that inherently requires the normalization. For SVM, we use both types of document vectors and find that the normalized vectors give better classification performance. We will thus show the performance of SVM with only normalized vectors.

4.3. Algorithm and Complexity. The algorithm of our classifier using gamma-Poisson modeling is shown in Algorithm 1 for the training and test phases. In the training phase, the classifier estimates the values of parameters $\hat{\alpha}_{cj}$ and $\hat{\beta}_{cj}$ for each class, from given training vectors; in the test phase, the classifier assigns the most probable label to a given test vector. As seen from the pseudocode in Algorithm 1, the time complexity of our classifier at the training phase with rational approximation of parameters is $O(|D||V|)$ where D and V denote the set of all training documents and the vocabulary (the set of all terms satisfying CF $\geq N_0$ in a corpus), while the complexity at the test phase is given by $O(|C||V|)$. The classifiers using multinomial and beta-binomial modeling also have the same complexity, $O(|D||V|)$ and $O(|C||V|)$, for the training and test phases, respectively, because they basically have the same code structure in our implementations and the differences are only in the equations for calculating parameters and estimating class-specific probabilities.

TABLE 1: Vocabulary size obtained by feature selection with CF.

Feature selection	20 Newsgroups	Reuters-21578	Industry Sector	TechTC-100
Initial vocabulary	103,135	22,792	64,680	103,003
CF $\geq$ 2	63,285	13,809	38,107	55,250
CF $\geq$ 5	34,152	7,268	21,681	29,070
CF $\geq$ 10	21,845	4,455	14,767	18,946
CF $\geq$ 20	13,792	2,626	9,885	12,254
CF $\geq$ 50	7,166	1,224	5,722	6,593
CF $\geq$ 100	4,056	689	3,580	3,937
CF $\geq$ 200	2,091	345	2,057	2,249
CF $\geq$ 500	693	110	854	936
CF $\geq$ 1000	230	36	420	432
CF $\geq$ 2000	57	18	159	195

```
gamma-Poisson classifier for training phase
01   for each c ∈ C
02      for each t ∈ V
03         for each d_c ∈ D_c
04            x_t ← count tokens of term t in d_c
05            x̄_t ← x̄_t + x_t
06            x̃_t ← x̃_t + log(x_t)
07         end for(d_c)
08         x̄_t ← x̄_t / |D_c|
09         x̃_t ← x̃_t / |D_c|
10         M_t ← log(x̄_t) − x̃_t
11         α_{c,t} ← rational Approximation(M_t)
12         β_{c,t} ← α_{c,t}/x̃_t
13      end for(t)
14   end for(c)
gamma-Poisson classifier for test phase
01   for each c ∈ C
02      score[c] ← log p(c) + log p(d | α_c, β_c)
03   end for(c)
04   return argmax_{c∈C} score[c]
```

ALGORITHM 1: Algorithm of classifier using gamma-Poisson modeling. In the training phase, the procedure of learning over D (entire training documents) is given, while in the test phase, the procedure to classify one test document d is described. D_c is the set of training documents belonging to a class c and d_c is a document vector in D_c. Note that $\sum_c |D_c| = |D|$, and thus the time complexity of the training phase is estimated as $O(|D||V|)$. For the test phase, the complexity is found to be $O(|C||V|)$ because $\log p(d | \alpha_c, \beta_c)$ in line 02 of the pseudo code is calculated through the entire summation over $|V|$ (see (13)).

On the other hand, the classifier using Dirichlet-multinomial modeling and using gamma-Poisson modeling *with iterative approximation* ((20)) has complexity given by $O(|D||V|n_{it})$ at the training phase, where n_{it} is the number of iteration cycles required for the convergence of the parameters. This is usually larger than $O(|D||V|)$ since n_{it} is typically of the order of ten and Dirichlet-multinomial modeling is therefore expensive in terms of computation time, as will be confirmed later.

Note that the time complexities described here ($O(|D||V|)$ or $O(|D||V|n_{it})$ for the training phase and $O(|C||V|)$ for the test phase) are all linearly dependent on the vocabulary size $|V|$. This linear dependence will be confirmed empirically

through comparisons of the practical computation times in the next section.

4.4. Implementation Issues. Except SVM, all the classifiers are implemented in the Java programming language. Supplementary information is as follows.

(i) In the learning phase of the classifier utilizing the Dirichlet-multinomial model, initial values of α_{cj} in the iterative evaluation with (9) are set to $\alpha_{cj} = 0.5$ for all j. When an estimated value of α_{cj} is equal to zero, which occurs when the corresponding jth term failed to appear in all the training documents in considered class D_c, we replace the value with $\alpha_{cj} = 1.0 \times 10^{-20}$. This smoothing is similar to the method used by Madsen et al. [7].

(ii) For the classifier with the beta-binomial model, the estimated α_{cj} also becomes zero when the corresponding jth term fails to appear at the estimation using the method of moments. As proposed by Allison [9], to prevent any α_{cj} from being zero, we supplement actual training documents with a pseudo-document in which every word occurs once.

(iii) For the classifier with the gamma-Poisson model, if x_{ij} in (15) and (16) is zero, then we replace the value with $x_{ij} = 0.001$ to prevent the geometrical means, $\tilde{x}_j$ defined by (16), from being zero (we preliminarily tried four values of x_{ij} for the replacement, namely, $x_{ij} = 0.1, 0.01, 0.001, 0.0001$, and obtained the best performance when $x_{ij} = 0.001$). Further, if the arithmetic mean given by (15) and the geometric mean given by (16) are equal, which happens when the corresponding jth term fails to appear for all i (in all the training documents), we set $M_j = 0.001$ in (18).

(iv) To compute several special functions, namely, the gamma function in (8) and (13), the beta function in (10), and the digamma and the trigamma functions in (20), components offered by the Apache Commons Mathematics Library (the library is available from http://commons.apache.org/proper/commons-math/) are used.

(v) For the SVM classifier, we use SVM^{multiclass} which is one of the popular implementations (the implementation is available from http://svmlight.joachims.org/svm_multiclass.html). of the multi-class support vector machine In the training phase of SVM, the trade-off parameter between training error and margin, c, is set to 5,000 to obtain high accuracy. For all other parameters, we use default values.

(vi) The experiments are conducted on a PC with a Phenom II X4 3.4 GHz processor and 8 GB of RAM.

(vii) A pilot implementation of the gamma-Poisson classifier using the C programming language is about 2.5 times faster than that using the Java. One should bear in mind this difference when comparing absolute computation times of our classifier with those of SVM, because the SVM classifier is implemented in C and the computation times of our classifier shown in the next section are those using the Java implementation.

5. Results

In this study, we use the simplest measure of classification performance, that is, accuracy, which is simply defined as a ratio of the total number of correct decisions to the total number of test documents in the dataset used. Note that for a single labeled dataset and a single labeled classification scheme as in this work, the microaveraged precision and

TABLE 2: Classification accuracy on the 20 Newsgroups dataset with two different methods for estimating parameters for the gamma-Poisson distribution. Values are shown as accuracy $\pm\sigma$ where σ is the standard deviation calculated through 10-fold cross-validation.

Feature selection	Accuracy	
	Rational approximation	Iterative method
Initial vocabulary	0.9148 ± 0.0066	0.9146 ± 0.0062
CF ≥ 5	0.9132 ± 0.0057	0.9133 ± 0.0058
CF ≥ 10	0.9084 ± 0.0072	0.9081 ± 0.0073
CF ≥ 20	0.9002 ± 0.0068	0.9005 ± 0.0063
CF ≥ 50	0.8775 ± 0.0079	0.8773 ± 0.0081
CF ≥ 100	0.8533 ± 0.0095	0.8532 ± 0.0094

recall are equivalent and hence equal to the *F1* measure [23], which we termed here "accuracy".

5.1. Parameter Estimation for Gamma-Poisson Modeling. We begin by considering the validity of the parameter estimation methods for gamma-Poisson modeling that were described in Section 3.3. As seen in Table 2, the accuracy values obtained for the two estimation methods are almost equivalent, indicating that the precision of the rational approximation and the convergence of the iterative method are both sufficient. From this result, it is confirmed that both methods are valid for estimating parameters, although in terms of computational speed, the rational approximation is superior to the iterative method. We will show the results only for the rational approximation in the next section.

5.2. Performance Comparison in Text Classification Tasks for 20 Newsgroups and Reuters-21578

5.2.1. Classification Accuracy. The main purposes of this work are to demonstrate the gamma-Poisson model as a new tool for text modeling and to show the extent to which it can be appropriately used in text classification tasks. In this sense, the performance comparison between the classifier using the gamma-Poisson model and those using other models are our primary result in this work. Figure 1 shows the performance comparison of various classifiers in the text classification task for the 20 Newsgroups dataset, and Figure 2 shows the same for the Reuters-21578 data collection. The exact vocabulary sizes at each data point in these figures are given in Table 1. In Figure 1, the best performance is seen for SVM, but the classifiers using the beta-binomial and gamma-Poisson models are almost equivalent and are highly competitive with SVM; they are inferior to SVM only in the range of limited vocabulary size below 20,000 words. The classifiers using the multinomial and the Dirichlet-multinomial models are apparently worse than the other three classifiers in terms of classification accuracy.

In Figure 2, SVM is again the best performer. An important difference between Figures 1 and 2 is that the classifier with the gamma-Poisson is superior to that with the beta-binomial in Figure 2, whereas they are almost equivalent

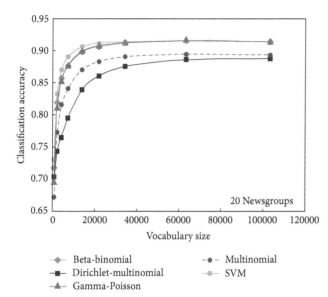

FIGURE 1: Performance of various classifiers for 20 Newsgroups dataset.

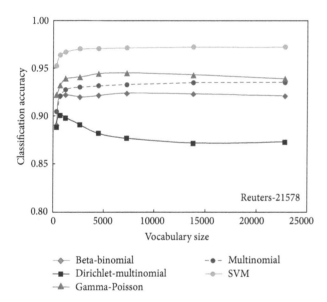

FIGURE 2: Performance of various classifiers for Reuters-21578 dataset.

in Figure 1. Another point is that the multinomial classifier performs better than the beta-binomial in Figure 2 but it was worse in Figure 1. The classifiers with the Dirichlet-multinomial exhibit the worst performance in both cases.

5.2.2. Computation Time.
Figures 3 and 4, respectively, show comparisons of computation times for various classifiers in the tasks for the 20-Newsgroups and Reuters-21578 datasets. Note that the computation time of each classifier is defined here as the sum of the training time and the test time; the former is the time needed in order to estimate parameters

from training vectors while the latter is the time needed to assign the most probable labels to test vectors. From the requirement of 10-fold cross-validation, the ratio of the numbers of training to test vectors is $9:1$ and the sum of these gives the total number of documents in a considered corpus. Measured 10 values of computation time through 10-fold cross validation are averaged and used as a final result in these figures. In Figures 3(a) and 4(a) the horizontal and the vertical axes are represented in linear scales while they are shown logarithmically in Figures 3(b) and 4(b) in order to show the lower vocabulary region clearly.

In Figures 3 and 4 the computation times of all the classifiers except SVM show almost linear dependence on the vocabulary size which is consistent with the time complexities of these classifiers described in Section 4.3. Clearly, SVM is very fast except in the limited vocabulary region. The classifier using beta-binomial modeling is slower than that using the gamma-Poisson because the method of moments used in the training phase of the beta-binomial classifier is time consuming compared with the rational approximation used in the gamma-Poisson classifier. The Dirichlet-multinomial classifier is the slowest because of the iterative procedures for estimating parameters.

5.3. Performance Comparison in Text Classification Tasks for Industry Sector Dataset.
Figures 5 and 6 show the classification accuracy and the computation time, respectively, in text classification for the Industry Sector dataset. As clearly seen in these figures, SVM is still the best performer in terms of the classification accuracy; however it is the worst in terms of the computation time. (We first used the binary version of SVM[multiclass] for Windows and found that the SVM[multiclass] suffers of memory errors when it is adapted to the Industry Sector and the TechTC-100 datasets. To avoid the error, we then used the SVM[multiclass] on Linux which was compiled with GCC. The results of SVM shown in this study were those obtained on Linux. The reason for the error is probably due to not enough heap memory available for the SVM[multiclass] on Windows.) The worst computation time of SVM indicates that this dataset has fundamentally different, undesirable characteristics for SVM. As will be discussed in the next section, the slow computation time of SVM is attributable to this dataset being not linearly separable because of its noisy nature. For the Industry Sector dataset, a reasonable and well-balanced choice of classier is found to be the gamma-Poisson because it achieves the second best accuracy and requires moderate computation time.

5.4. Performance Comparison in Text Classification Tasks for TechTC-100.
Figures 7 and 8 show the results of classification accuracy and those of computation time, respectively, at the task on the TechTC-100 dataset. The results are very similar to those seen in the Industry Sector dataset; that is, SVM wins in terms of the classification accuracy but losses in terms of the computation time. Note that the computation time of gamma-Poisson, which gives the second best classification accuracy as in the case of the Industry Sector dataset, is about ten times faster than that of SVM.

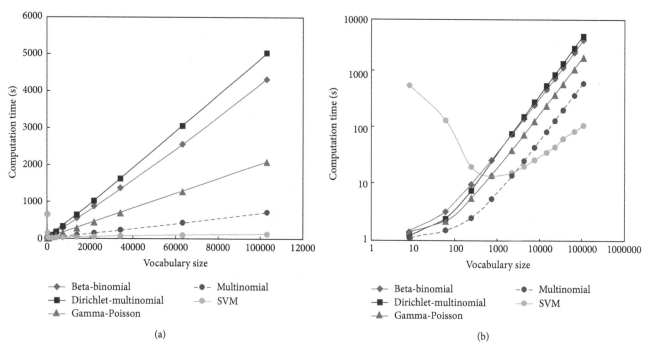

FIGURE 3: Computation time of various classifiers for 20 Newsgroups dataset.

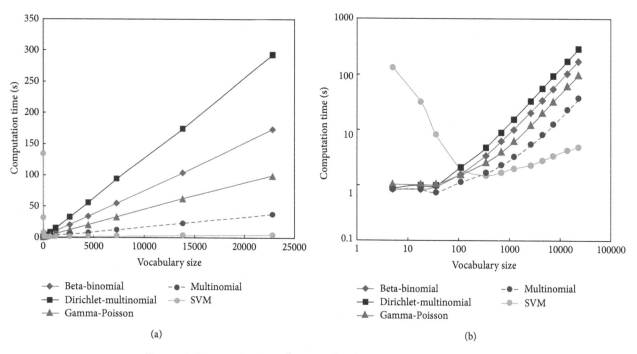

FIGURE 4: Computation time of various classifiers for Reuters-21578 dataset.

6. Discussion

6.1. Performance of the Probabilistic Classifiers. As seen in the previous section, the overall trend in classification performance for the five tested classifiers can be summarized as follows:

$$SVM \geq gamma\text{-}Poisson \geq beta\text{-}binomial$$
$$\geq Multinomial > Dirichlet\text{-}Multinomial, \tag{22}$$

where the symbols ">" and "≥" should be read as "better than" and "better than or equivalent to", respectively. Among the results, we first consider why the gamma-Poisson and the beta-binomial are superior to the Dirichlet-multinomial. The point is that these three classifiers perform differently; nevertheless, they have similar structures in terms of hierarchical text modeling with utilizing conjugate priors. This result probably arises from a difference in the properties of the conjugate priors used. As mentioned earlier, we cannot

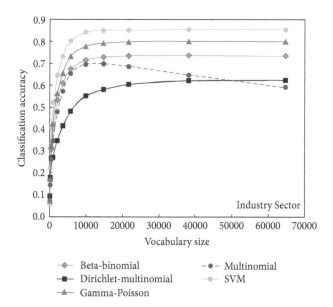

FIGURE 5: Classification performance of various classifiers for the Industry Sector dataset.

specify means and variances separately in the Dirichlet distribution while separate specification is possible for the beta distribution. Note that separate specification is also possible in the case of the gamma distribution; under the notations used in (12), the mean and variance of the gamma distribution are expressed as

$$E\left[\lambda_j\right] = \frac{\alpha_j}{\beta_j}, \qquad V\left[\lambda_j\right] = \frac{\alpha_j}{\beta_j^2}, \qquad (23)$$

and hence

$$\alpha_j = \frac{\left(E\left[\lambda_j\right]\right)^2}{V\left[\lambda_j\right]}, \qquad \beta_j = \frac{E\left[\lambda_j\right]}{V\left[\lambda_j\right]}. \qquad (24)$$

Equations (23) and (24) give us the separate specification which guarantees a more flexible description of word occurrence in gamma-Poisson modeling compared with the description in Dirichlet-multinomial modeling. Thus, the origin of superiority of the beta-binomial and the gamma-Poisson over the Dirichlet-multinomial can be attributed to their flexibility to describe various patterns of word distribution.

We next consider the reason that the gamma-Poisson gives somewhat better performance than the beta-binomial. As described in any textbook on probability distribution, the binomial can be approximated by the Poisson when the number of trials goes to infinity and the expected number of successes remains fixed. It is therefore reasonable to expect that the gamma-Poisson is almost equivalent to the beta-binomial but never exceeds it. Our expectation, however, is betrayed as seen in Figures 2, 5, and 7. A possible interpretation of this result is that the better performance of the gamma-Poisson model is attributable to the normalization of document vectors. In the beta-binomial model, each

term occurrence is treated as being equally important in the estimation of parameters with the method of moments and in the classification of test documents. However, in vectors normalized in the L_1 sense, the event of a word occurrence has remarkably different weight according to the original document length, and in our experiments these normalized vectors are only used for the gamma-Poisson and the SVM classifiers as training and test vectors. In the vector normalization, the word occurrence in a short document is converted to be more heavily weighted than that in a long document. The conversion in this manner is reasonable and considered to bring about the better performance because short documents usually have fewer unnecessary terms that are irrelevant to the topic, and the ratio of informative terms that represent a concept of the topic is higher than in long documents. From this aspect of the vector normalization, further discussion of a condition for improving accuracy is possible. If each document has almost the same length, then the normalization does not change the weight of word occurrences and thus does not contribute to the improvement of accuracy. Therefore, the normalization of document vectors can be effective in the situation where the distribution of document length is scattered in a considered dataset.

To confirm this, we introduce a measure that quantifies how many terms are used in a document vector. The measure we tentatively use here is a ratio of nonzero components defined as

(ratio of nonzero components)

$$= \frac{\text{\# nonzero components in the document vector}}{\text{\# all components comprising the document vector}}. \qquad (25)$$

For this ratio, we expect that when the distribution of the ratio becomes broader, the difference in accuracy between the gamma-Poisson and the beta-binomial will become increasingly evident. Figure 9 shows the distributions of the ratio of nonzero components for the four used datasets; the x-axis represents the ratio and the y-axis is the total number of documents which have that ratio of nonzero components. Statistic summaries of these four distributions are given in Table 3. In the table, we also give the values of

$$\Delta = \frac{P_{\text{GP}} - P_{\text{BB}}}{P_{\text{BB}}}, \qquad (26)$$

where P_{GP} is the classification accuracy of the gamma-Poisson classifier at the full vocabulary size and P_{BB} is that of the beta-binomial classifier. Since Δ represents the difference in performance in percent between the gamma-Poisson and the beta-binomial, we can test our hypothesis on the vector normalization described above by examining the correlation between Δ and other statistic measures. As confirmed from the values of interquartile range (IQR) and standard deviation (SD) in Table 3 and also as intuitively seen in Figure 9, 20 Newsgroups has the sharpest distribution, and it consistently has the smallest Δ. The ratio is more broadly distributed in the Reuters-21578 and TechTC-100 datasets, and Δ thus takes larger values. These results indicate that

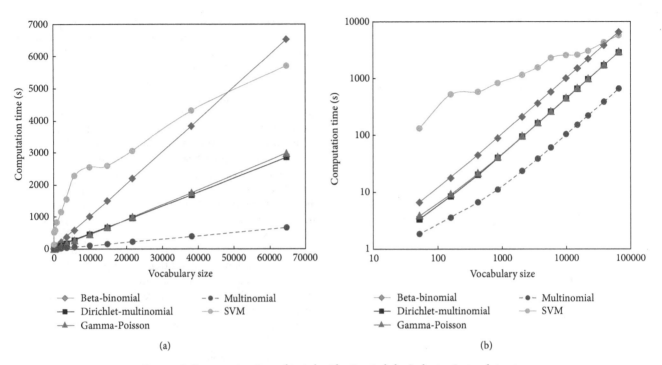

FIGURE 6: Computation time of text classification task for Industry Sector dataset.

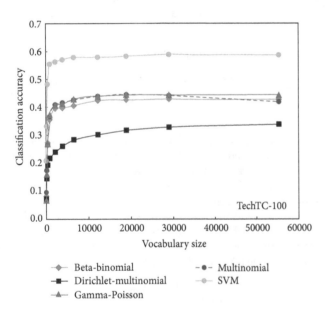

FIGURE 7: Performance of various classifiers for TechTC-100 dataset.

there is a positive correlation between Δ and the broadness of distribution, which supports our hypothesis regarding vector normalization. In comparison, the Industry Sector seems to have an unusually large value of Δ in relation to its IQR and SD values. However, this can be explained by the portion of very short documents being the largest in this dataset, which can be clearly seen in Figure 9. Since the improvement of accuracy with the vector normalization is more effective in short documents, the largest Δ for the Industry Sector dataset is consistent with our hypothesis. The superiority of the gamma-Poisson over the beta-binomial

observed for the Reuters-21578, Industry Sector, and TechTC-100 datasets is therefore explained, at least partially, in terms of the effectiveness of the vector normalization.

Table 4 lists our best classification results for 20 Newsgroups using all the words in the initial vocabulary. In the table, data obtained by other authors are also shown for comparison.

As shown in the table, our results agree reasonably well with those by the other authors. A detailed comparison is given below.

(i) Our result for the Dirichlet-multinomial is similar to that reported by Madsen et al. [7], whereas the same model was found to perform worse in the study of Allison [9]. This disagreement is attributed to the difference in the estimation of parameters; the iterative methods used in [7] and in this work give, in general, a better estimation than the method of moments used by Allison [9].

(ii) Our result for the beta-binomial is similar to the result reported by Allison [9]. This is because we made efforts to ensure maximal comparability with the work of Allison [9] for fair comparison.

(iii) The difference among the three results for SVM probably arises from the difference of term weighting methods to create document vectors and from the difference in the parameter settings of SVM. For document vectors, we use normalized vectors in the L_1 sense while more sophisticated term frequency-inverse document frequency (TF-IDF) was used by Kibriya et al. [22]. All parameters were set to be their default values in the study by Allison [9], whereas we used a large value of c to obtain higher accuracy.

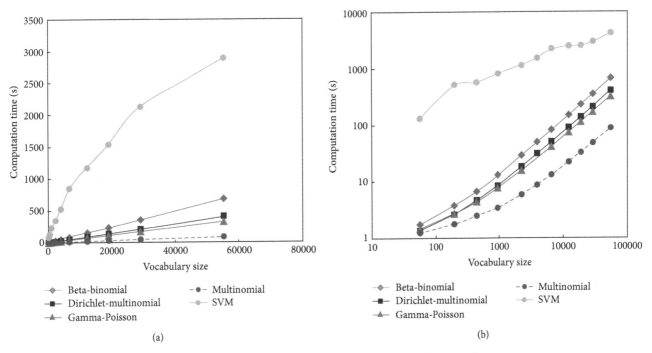

FIGURE 8: Computation time of text classification task for TechTC-100 dataset.

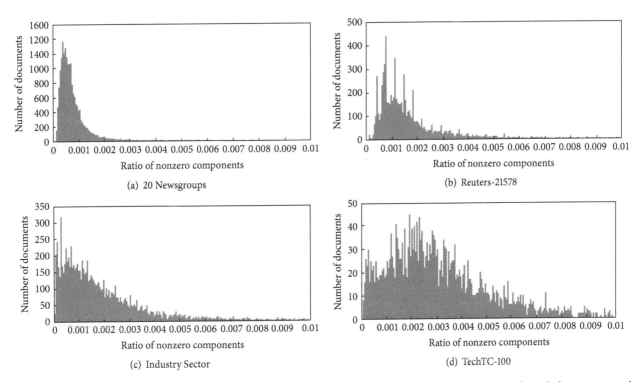

FIGURE 9: Distribution of the ratio of nonzero components for the four datasets used here. In all cases, t-he initial vocabularies were used to create document vectors.

(iv) The result of the multinomial in this work is almost identical to the result reported by Joachims [21], while Allison [9] and Madsen et al. [7] reported much worse values. The origin of this difference might be attributable to the differences in preprocessing (stop word removal and stemming) and vocabulary size. Although we obtained relatively high classification accuracy for the multinomial in this work, it is clear that the gamma-Poisson outperforms the multinomial by some margin.

TABLE 3: Statistical summary of the distribution of nonzero components for the four datasets used here. IQR and SD mean inter quartile range and standard deviation, respectively.

Dataset	Δ (%)	Median	Mean	IQR	SD
20 Newsgroups	0.05	0.00054	0.00077	0.0005	0.0011
Reuters-21578	1.97	0.00123	0.00167	0.0012	0.0015
Industry Sector	9.04	0.00135	0.00206	0.0019	0.0026
TechTC-100	3.70	0.00276	0.00352	0.0027	0.0037

6.2. Comparison of Gamma-Poisson Classifier and SVM.
Although the proposed classifier using gamma-Poisson modeling fails to outperform the SVM classifier as seen in the previous section, we believe that it is still useful for the following two reasons.

(i) The computation time of SVM can be intolerably deteriorated as in Figures 6 and 8, for the Industry Sector and the TechTC-100 datasets, respectively, while the gamma-Poisson classifier offers the second best classification performance with moderate computation times even for these two cases.

(ii) The gamma-Poisson classifier can be conveniently used for a wide range of practical systems in which continuous incremental learning tasks are required.

In the following, we first try to explain the origin of the slow computation times of SVM for the Industry Sector and the TechTC-100 datasets and then describe the effective incremental learning of the gamma-Poisson classifier which is suitable in practical systems.

6.2.1. Slow Computation Time of SVM for Noisy Dataset.
In general, the problem is linearly separable for SVM if each term in the vocabulary is almost peculiar to one of the all possible categories and, in this case, the SVM can be easily trained within a short time. Contrary, if many terms (a large portion of the vocabulary) tend to disperse over at least several categories with some finite probabilities, the linear separability decreases and the SVM suffers a long computation time to find an optimum hyperplane. For SVM, a dataset is regarded as noisy if the latter case occurs while the computation times of all the other probabilistic classifiers are not affected by the noisy nature because optimization procedures are not included in these classifiers. Concerning the origin of the noisy nature for the Industry Sector and the TechTC-100 datasets, we can consider following reasons.

(i) These datasets are generated from web pages. As mentioned earlier, the textual advertisements included in the web pages can make term distributions noisy because the same kind of advertisements tend to appear across multiple categories.

(ii) The numbers of classes, 104 for the Industry Sector and 40 for the TechTC-100, are much larger than those of the other two datasets. This causes the noisy nature because the similar concepts (almost similar topic) are nearly equally distributed among several adjacent

categories when the categorization has been made in a fine-grained manner for a dataset with a large number of classes.

Figure 10 depicts the noisy nature of the Industry Sector and the TechTC-100 datasets. To obtain the figure, the following procedures were applied.

(1) All the terms in the vocabulary were sorted by the collection term frequency, CF, which is the total frequency of each word throughout the entire dataset.

(2) 2,000 top terms were chosen based on the CF values.

(3) A probability $P(C_{\text{top}})$ defined by

$$P\left(C_{\text{top}}\right)$$

$$= \frac{\text{frequency of the term in the most relevant category}}{\text{collection term frequency, CF}}$$

(27)

was calculated for each of the top 2,000 terms. $P(C_{\text{top}})$ is regarded as the simple probability estimation for the occurrence of a considered term in the most relevant category. Note that, for example, if the considered term has $P(C_{\text{top}})$ less than 20%, then the term is distributed over at least 6 categories.

(4) The top 2,000 terms were sorted by the value of $P(C_{\text{top}})$ and plotted as in Figure 10 where the x-axis shows the respective rank of $P(C_{\text{top}})$ and the y-axis the value of $P(C_{\text{top}})$.

In the figure, we tentatively show the number of terms with $P(C_{\text{top}})$ that is larger than 20%. The result indicates that about three-quarters of the top 2,000 terms are distributed over at least 6 categories for the Industry Sector and the TechTC-100 datasets. Therefore, these two datasets are noisy for SVM in the sense that we have described above compared with the other two datasets.

The performance of SVM for "noisy" data might be improved by using other kernels instead of using linear kernel which is utilized in this study; however, selection of a new kernel and the optimization of kernel parameters are newly introduced as additional tasks in this case. Furthermore, the fast computation time of SVM for a linearly separable dataset as demonstrated in Figures 3 and 4 cannot be expected with other kernels (the SVM[multiclass] is optimized for the linear kernel so that the runtime can be scaled linearly with the number of training examples by use of a cutting-plane algorithm). By contrast, the performance of the gamma-Poisson classifier is stable even in the case of noisy datasets with moderate computation times.

6.2.2. Effective Incremental Learning of the Gamma-Poisson Classifier.
As mentioned above, the gamma-Poisson classifier can be used for a wide array of practical systems in which continuous incremental learning tasks are required. Typical examples are spam-filtering and adaptive news-alert systems.

TABLE 4: Classification results for the 20 Newsgroups dataset. For our results, we show the data obtained with all the words in the initial vocabulary.

Model	Present work	Allison [9]	Madsen et al. [7]	Clinchant and Gaussier [8]	Joachims [21]	Kibriya et al. [22]
Multinomial	0.8934 ± 0.0069	0.8566 ± 0.0050	0.853 ± 0.004	0.875	0.896	0.8836
Dirichlet-multinomial	0.8877 ± 0.0046	0.8503 ± 0.0051	0.890 ± 0.005	0.878		
beta-binomial	0.9143 ± 0.0049	0.9165 ± 0.0040				
gamma-Poisson	0.9148 ± 0.0066					
SVM	0.9144 ± 0.0060	0.8880 ± 0.0045				0.9352

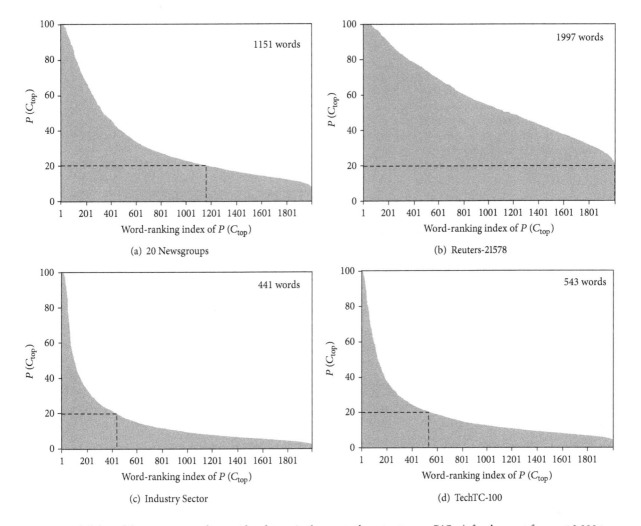

(a) 20 Newsgroups

(b) Reuters-21578

(c) Industry Sector

(d) TechTC-100

FIGURE 10: Probability of the occurrence of a considered term in the most relevant category, $P(C_{top})$, for the most frequent 2,000 terms.

In these systems, a small number of new training documents are continuously provided and the retraining of the classifier with the new training documents is routinely needed. In such an environment, the proposed classifier is more appropriate for practical systems rather than other complex learning models including SVM because our classifier ensures effective incremental learning.

To show the effectiveness, we consider a situation in which one new training document belonging to a class c with a document vector $d'_c = (x'_1, x'_2, \ldots, x'_{|V|})$ is supplied to our classifier. In this case, the set of training vectors becomes the union of original training vectors $D_c = \{d_{ci}\}$ ($1 \leq i \leq |D_c|$) and one newly supplied vector d'_c. The retraining of the classifier corresponds to estimating a new set of parameters

$\{\widehat{\alpha}'_{cj}\}$ and $\{\widehat{\beta}'_{cj}\}$ $(1 \le j \le |V|)$ from the $|D_c|+1$ training vectors. Referring to definitions of $\overline{x}_j$ and $\widetilde{x}_j$ ((15) and (16)), we can easily verify that the new values, $\overline{x}'_j$ and $\widetilde{x}'_j$ for $|D_c|+1$ training vectors, can be expressed in terms of the original $\overline{x}_j$ and $\widetilde{x}_j$ as

$$
\begin{aligned}
\overline{x}'_j &\equiv \frac{1}{|D_c|+1} \sum_{i=1}^{|D_c|+1} x_{ij} \\
&= \frac{1}{|D_c|+1} \left(|D_c| \, \overline{x}_j + x'_j \right), \\
\ln \widetilde{x}'_j &\equiv \ln \left(\prod_{i=1}^{|D_c|+1} x_{ij} \right)^{1/(|D_c|+1)} \\
&= \frac{1}{|D_c|+1} \left(|D_c| \ln \widetilde{x}_j + \ln x'_j \right).
\end{aligned}
\tag{28}
$$

The last expressions in (28) indicate that we can directly update the values of $\overline{x}_j$ and $\widetilde{x}_j$ from their original values. Because we can use these last expressions for the updates, and because the summation and the product over all training documents seen in the first expressions of (28) are actually unnecessary; the time complexity of retraining for all terms in the vocabulary using the combination of (28), (17), (18) and (19) is estimated to be only $O(|V|)$. This is a clear advantage of gamma-Poisson modeling for incremental learning for the following reasons.

(i) The time complexity of retraining the classifier using beta-binomial modeling in the same situation is given as $O(|V||D_c|)$ because it uses the method of moments for the estimation of parameters. The complexity is much higher than the case of gamma-Poisson modeling.

(ii) The time complexity for retraining the classifier using multinomial modeling is $O(|V|)$, exactly the same as in the case of gamma-Poisson modeling. (If the total counts for each term over original training vectors are stored in the classifier, then the counts are simply updated by adding the corresponding counts in the newly provided training vector and the new set of parameters $\{\widehat{\theta}_{cj}\}$ is immediately obtained by using (4) with these updated counts. This procedure results in complexity of $O(|V|)$.) However, from the comparison of overall performance described above, gamma-Poisson modeling is preferable over multinomial modeling since the former shows better performance.

(iii) In the case of SVM, it has been clarified that the support vectors, which can be regarded as summarized information of original training vectors, are sufficient for incremental learning [24]. Along the line of this framework, the new set of training vectors becomes the union of support vectors obtained from original training vectors and one newly provided training vector; we can thus retrain SVM with this new training set for incremental learning. The time for training an SVM is dominated by the time for solving the underlying quadratic programming, and

so the theoretical and empirical complexity varies depending on the method used to solve it. Although the number of support vectors is much smaller than $|D|$, the time for doing quadratic optimization is considered to be much slower than simply counting terms [25] as is done in multinomial and gamma-Poisson modeling.

The last expressions in (28) also imply that storing the set of all training vectors is needless for the incremental learning because only the values of $\{\overline{x}_j\}$ and $\{\widetilde{x}_j\}$ are sufficient for the update. This indicates that the gamma-Poisson classifier is suitable for incremental learning in terms of not only time complexity but also space complexity.

7. Conclusions and Future Work

In this paper, we have proposed a novel classifier in which the gamma-Poisson distribution is utilized as a new tool for text modeling. The gamma-Poisson was introduced in order to improve the insufficient description of word occurrences from the original Poisson distribution. The framework of gamma-Poisson modeling of texts and the construction of a classifier using the framework were demonstrated with practical techniques for parameter estimation and vector normalization. The efficiency of the proposed classifier was examined through experiments on automatic text categorization of the 20 Newsgroups, Reuters-21578, Industry Sector, and TechTC-100 datasets. For comparison, classifiers using three other distributions, namely, multinomial, Dirichlet-multinomial and beta-binomial distributions, were also applied to the same datasets, and in addition we also used SVM as a standard discriminative classifier with state-of-the-art classification accuracy. From the results, it was found that the proposed classifier with the gamma-Poisson model shows classification performance comparable with that of SVM. The origin of the superiority of the proposed gamma-Poisson modeling was discussed in terms of its flexibility in describing various patterns of word distributions and the effectiveness of vector normalization. We also showed that the proposed classifier is most suitable for applications in which continuous incremental learning tasks are required.

At present, the analysis of classification performance for the various classifiers remains unsatisfactory because the results are interpreted only qualitatively. We consider that further quantitative discussion is possible through analysis of the decision functions of the classifiers. An investigation along the line of such quantitative analysis is reserved for future research.

Acknowledgment

The authors would like to acknowledge Dr. Yusuke Higuchi for useful discussion and illuminating suggestions.

References

[1] K. Church and W. A. Gale, "Inverse Document Frequency (IDF): a measure of deviations from poisson," in *Proceedings of the 3rd Workshop on Very Large Corpora*, pp. 121–130, 1995.

[2] H. Ogura, H. Amano, and M. Kondo, "Feature selection with a measure of deviations from Poisson in text categorization," *Expert Systems with Applications*, vol. 36, no. 3, pp. 6826–6832, 2009.

[3] H. Ogura, H. Amano, and M. Kondo, "Distinctive characteristics of a metric using deviations from Poisson for feature selection," *Expert Systems with Applications*, vol. 37, no. 3, pp. 2273–2281, 2010.

[4] H. Ogura, H. Amano, and M. Kondo, "Comparison of metrics for feature selection in imbalanced text classification," *Expert Systems with Applications*, vol. 38, no. 5, pp. 4978–4989, 2011.

[5] K. Church and W. A. Gale, "Poisson mixtures," *Natural Language Engineering*, vol. 1, pp. 163–190, 1995.

[6] A. Gelman, B. Carlin, S. Stern, and B. Rubin, *Bayesian Data Analysis (Texts in Statistical Science)*, Chapman and Hall/CRC, 2nd edition, 2003.

[7] R. E. Madsen, D. Kauchak, and C. Elkan, "Modeling word burstiness using the Dirichlet distribution," in *Proceedings of the 22nd International Conference on Machine Learning (ICML '05)*, pp. 545–552, August 2005.

[8] S. Clinchant and E. Gaussier, "The BNB distribution for text modeling," in *Proceedings of the Advances in Information Retrieval. 30th European Conference on IR Research*, pp. 150–161, 2008.

[9] B. Allison, "An improved hierarchical Bayesian Model of Language for document classification," in *Proceedings of the 22nd International Conference on Computational Linguistics*, pp. 25–32, 2008.

[10] S. Eyheramendy, D. Lewis, and D. Madigan, "On the naive bayes model for text categorization," in *Proceedings of the 9th International Workshop on Artificial Intelligence and Statistics*, pp. 332–339, 2003.

[11] T. Mitchell, *Machine Learning*, McGraw Hill, 1997.

[12] S. Kim, K. Han, H. Rim, and H. Myaeng, "Some effective techniques for naive Bayes text classification," *IEEE Transactions on Knowledge and Data Engineering*, vol. 18, pp. 1457–1466, 2006.

[13] T. Minka, "Estimating a Dirichlet distribution," 2003, http://research.microsoft.com/en-us/um/people/minka/papers/dirichlet/.

[14] T. Joachims, *Learning to Classify Text Using Support Vector Machines [Ph.D. thesis]*, Kluwer, 2002.

[15] J. Grim, J. Novovičová, and P. Somol, "Structural Poisson mixtures for classification of documents," in *Proceedings of the 19th International Conference on Pattern Recognition (ICPR '08)*, pp. 1–4, December 2008.

[16] A. Greenwood and D. Durand, "Aids for fitting the Gamma distribution by Maximum Likelihood," *Technometrics*, vol. 2, p. 55, 1960.

[17] T. Minka, "Estimating a Gamma distribution," 2002, http://research.microsoft.com/en-us/um/people/minka/papers/.

[18] J. D. M. Rennie, L. Shih, J. Teevan, and D. Karger, "Tackling the poor assumptions of naive bayes text classifiers," in *Proceedings of the 20th International Conference on Machine Learning*, pp. 616–623, August 2003.

[19] K. Lang, "NewsWeeder: learning to filter netnews," in *Proceedings of the 12th International Machine Learning Conference*, pp. 331–339, Morgan Kaufmann, 1995.

[20] D. Davidov, E. Gabrilovich, and S. Markovitch, "Parameterized generation of labeled datasets for text categorization based on a hierarchical directory," in *Proceedings of Sheffield SIGIR 27th Annual International ACM SIGIR Conference on Research and Development in Information Retrieval*, pp. 250–257, July 2004.

[21] T. Joachims, "A probabilistic analysis of the Rocchio algorithm with TF-IDF for text categorization," in *Proceedings of the 40th International Conference on Machine Learning*, pp. 143–151, 1997.

[22] A. M. Kibriya, E. Frank, B. Pfahringer, and G. Holmes, "Multinomial naive bayes for text categorization revisited," in *Proceedings of the 17th Australian Joint Conference on Artificial Intelligence*, pp. 488–499, 2005.

[23] N. Slonim, G. Bejerano, S. Fine, and N. Tishby, "Discriminative feature selection via multiclass variable memory Markov model," *Eurasip Journal on Applied Signal Processing*, vol. 2003, no. 2, pp. 93–102, 2003.

[24] N. A. Syed, H. Liu, and K. K. Suang, "Incremental learning with support vector machines," in *Proceedings of the Workshop on Support Vector Machines at the International Joint Conference on Artificial Intelligence*, pp. 317–321, 1999.

[25] C. Manning, P. Raghavan, and H. Schutze, *Introduction to Information Retrieval*, Cambridge University Press, 2008.

14

Bag-of-Words Representation in Image Annotation: A Review

Chih-Fong Tsai

Department of Information Management, National Central University, Jhongli 32001, Taiwan

Correspondence should be addressed to Chih-Fong Tsai, cftsai@mgt.ncu.edu.tw

Academic Editors: F. Camastra, J. A. Hernandez, P. Kokol, J. Wang, and S. Zhu

Content-based image retrieval (CBIR) systems require users to query images by their low-level visual content; this not only makes it hard for users to formulate queries, but also can lead to unsatisfied retrieval results. To this end, image annotation was proposed. The aim of image annotation is to automatically assign keywords to images, so image retrieval users are able to query images by keywords. Image annotation can be regarded as the image classification problem: that images are represented by some low-level features and some supervised learning techniques are used to learn the mapping between low-level features and high-level concepts (i.e., class labels). One of the most widely used feature representation methods is bag-of-words (BoW). This paper reviews related works based on the issues of improving and/or applying BoW for image annotation. Moreover, many recent works (from 2006 to 2012) are compared in terms of the methodology of BoW feature generation and experimental design. In addition, several different issues in using BoW are discussed, and some important issues for future research are discussed.

1. Introduction

Advances in computer and multimedia technologies allow for the production of digital images and large repositories for image storage with little cost. This has led to the rapid increase in the size of image collections, including digital libraries, medical imaging, art and museum, journalism, advertising and home photo archives, and so forth. As a result, it is necessary to design image retrieval systems which can operate on a large scale. The main goal is to create, manage, and query image databases in an efficient and effective, that is, accurate manner.

Content-based image retrieval (CBIR), which was proposed in the early 1990s, is a technique to automatically index images by extracting their (low-level) visual features, such as color, texture, and shape, and the retrieval of images is based solely upon the indexed image features [1–3]. Therefore, it is hypothesized that relevant images can be retrieved by calculating the similarity between the low-level image contents through browsing, navigation, query-by-example, and so forth. Typically, images are represented as points in a high dimensional feature space. Then, a metric is used to measure similarity or dissimilarity between images on this space. Thus, images close to the query are similar to the query and retrieved. Although CBIR introduced automated image

feature extraction and indexation, it does not overcome the so-called semantic gap described below.

The semantic gap is the gap between the extracted and indexed low-level features by computers and the high-level concepts (or semantics) of user's queries. That is, the automated CBIR systems cannot be readily matched to the users' requests. The notation of similarity in the user's mind is typically based on high-level abstractions, such as activities, entities/objects, events, or some evoked emotions, among others. Therefore, retrieval by similarity using low-level features like color or shape will not be very effective. In other words, human similarity judgments do not obey the requirements of the similarity metric used in CBIR systems. In addition, general users usually find it difficult to search or query images by using color, texture, and/or shape features directly. They usually prefer textual or keyword-based queries, since they are easier and more intuitive for representing their information needs [4–6]. However, it is very challenging to make computers capable of understanding or extracting high-level concepts from images as humans do.

Consequently, the semantic gap problem has been approached by automatic image annotation. In automatic image annotation, computers are able to learn which low-level features correspond to which high-level concepts.

Specifically, the aim of image annotation is to make the computers extract meanings from the low-level features by a learning process based on a given set of training data which includes pairs of low-level features and their corresponding concepts. Then, the computers can assign the learned keywords to images automatically. For the review of image annotation, please refer to Tsai and Hung [7], Hanbury [8], and Zhang et al. [9].

Image annotation can be defined as the process of automatically assigning keywords to images. It can be regarded as an automatic classification of images by labeling images into one of a number of predefined classes or categories, where classes have assigned keywords or labels which can describe the conceptual content of images in that class. Therefore, the image annotation problem can be thought of as image classification or categorization.

More specifically, image classification can be divided into object categorization [10] and scene classification. For example, object categorization focuses on classifying images into "concrete" categories, such as "agate", "car", "dog", and so on. On the other hand, scene classification can be regarded as abstract keyword based image annotation [11, 12], where scene categories are such as "harbor", "building", and "sunset", which can be regarded as an assemblage of multiple physical or entity objects as a single entity. The difference between object recognition/categorization and scene classification was defined by Quelhas et al. [13].

However, image annotation performance is heavily dependent on image feature representation. Recently, the bag-of-words (BoW) or bag-of-visual-words model, a well-known and popular feature representation method for document representation in information retrieval, was first applied to the field of image and video retrieval by Sivic and Zisserman [14]. Moreover, BoW has generally shown promising performance for image annotation and retrieval tasks [15–22].

The BoW feature is usually based on tokenizing keypoint-based features, for example, scale-invariant feature transform (SIFT) [23], to generate a visual-word vocabulary (or codebook). Then, the visual-word vector of an image contains the presence or absence information of each visual word in the image, for example, the number of keypoints in the corresponding cluster, that is, visual word.

Since 2003, BoW has been used extensively in image annotation, but there has not as yet been any comprehensive review of this topic. Therefore, the aim of this paper is to review the work of using BoW for image annotation from 2006 to 2012.

The rest of this paper is organized as follows. Section 2 describes the process of extracting the BoW feature for image representation and annotation. Section 3 discusses some important extension studies of BoW, including the improvement of BoW per se and its application to other related research problems. Section 4 provides some comparisons of related work in terms of the methodology of constructing the BoW feature, including the detection method, the clustering algorithm, the number of visual words, and so forth and the experimental set up including the datasets used, the number

of object or scene categories, and so forth. Finally, Section 5 concludes the paper.

2. Bag-of-Words Representation

The bag-of-words (BoW) methodology was first proposed in the text retrieval domain problem for text document analysis, and it was further adapted for computer vision applications [24]. For image analysis, a visual analogue of a word is used in the BoW model, which is based on the vector quantization process by clustering low-level visual features of local regions or points, such as color, texture, and so forth.

To extract the BoW feature from images involves the following steps: (i) automatically detect regions/points of interest, (ii) compute local descriptors over those regions/points, (iii) quantize the descriptors into words to form the visual vocabulary, and (iv) find the occurrences in the image of each specific word in the vocabulary for constructing the BoW feature (or a histogram of word frequencies) [24]. Figure 1 describes these four steps to extract the BoW feature from images.

The BoW model can be defined as follows. Given a training dataset D containing n images represented by $D = d_1, d_2, \ldots,$ and d_n, where d is the extracted visual features, a specific unsupervised learning algorithm, such as k-means, is used to group D based on a fixed number of visual words W (or categories) represented by $W = w_1, w_2, \ldots,$ and w_v, where V is the cluster number. Then, we can summarize the data in a $V \times N$ cooccurrence table of counts $N_{ij} = n(w_i, d_j)$, where $n(w_i, d_j)$ denotes how often the word w_i occurred in an image d_i.

2.1. Interest Point Detection. The first step of the BoW methodology is to detect local interest regions or points. For feature extraction of interest points (or keypoints), they are computed at predefined locations and scales. Several well-known region detectors that have been described in the literature are discussed below [25, 26].

(i) Harris-Laplace regions are detected by the scale-adapted Harris function and selected in scale-space by the Laplacian-of-Gaussian operator. Harris-Laplace detects corner-like structures.

(ii) DoG regions are localized at local scale-space maxima of the difference-of-Gaussian. This detector is suitable for finding blob-like structures. In addition, the DoG point detector has previously been shown to perform well, and it is also faster and more compact (less feature points per image) than other detectors.

(iii) Hessian-Laplace regions are localized in space at the local maxima of the Hessian determinant and in scale at the local maxima of the Laplacian-of-Gaussian.

(iv) Salient regions are detected in scale-space at local maxima of the entropy. The entropy of pixel intensity histograms is measured for circular regions of various sizes at each image position.

(v) Maximally stable extremal regions (MSERs) are components of connected pixels in a thresholded image.

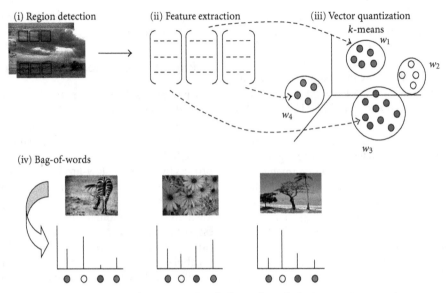

FIGURE 1: Four steps for constructing the bag-of-words for image representation.

A watershed-like segmentation algorithm is applied to image intensities and segment boundaries which are stable over a wide range of thresholds that define the region.

In Mikolajczyk et al. [27], they compare six types of well-known detectors, which are detectors based on affine normalization around Harris and Hessian points, MSER, an edge-based region detector, a detector based on intensity extrema, and a detector of salient regions. They conclude that the Hessian-Affine detector performs best.

On the other hand, according to Hörster and Lienhart [21], interest points can be detected by the sparse or dense approach. For sparse features, interest points are detected at local extremas in the difference of a Gaussian pyramid [23]. A position and scale are automatically assigned to each point and thus the extracted regions are invariant to these properties. For dense features, on the other hand, interest points are defined at evenly sampled grid points. Feature vectors are then computed based on three different neighborhood sizes, that is, at different scales, around each interest point.

Some authors believe that a very precise segmentation of an image is not required for the scene classification problem [28], and some studies have shown that coarse segmentation is very suitable for scene recognition. In particular, Bosch et al. [29] compare four dense descriptors with the widely used sparse descriptor (i.e., the Harris detector) [14, 15] and show that the best results are obtained with the dense descriptors. This is because there is more information on scene images, and intuitively a dense image description is necessary to capture uniform regions such as sky, calm water, or road surface in many natural scenes. Similarly, Jurie and Triggs [30] show that the sampling of many patches on a regular dense grid (or a fixed number of patches) outperforms the use of interest points. In addition, Fei-Fei and Perona [31],

and Bosch et al. [29] show that dense descriptors outperform the sparse ones.

2.2. Local Descriptors. In most studies, some single local descriptors are extracted, in which the Scale Invariant Feature Transform (SIFT) descriptor is the most widely extracted [23]. It combines a scale invariant region detector and a descriptor based on the gradient distribution in the detected regions. The descriptor is represented by a 3D histogram of gradient locations and orientations. The dimensionality of the SIFT descriptor is 128.

In order to reduce the dimensionality of the SIFT descriptor, which is usually 128 dimensions per keypoint, principal component analysis (PCA) can be used for increasing image retrieval accuracy and faster matching [32]. Specifically, Uijlings et al. [33] show that retrieval performance can be increased by using PCA for the removal of redundancy in the dimensions.

SIFT was found to work best [13, 25, 34, 35]. Specifically, Mikolajczyk and Schmid [34] compared 10 different descriptors extracted by the Harris-Affine detector, which are SIFT, gradient location and orientation histograms (GLOH) (i.e., an extension of SIFT), shape context, PCA-SIFT, spin images, steerable filters, differential invariants, complex filters, moment invariants, and cross-correlation of sampled pixel values. They show that the SIFT-based descriptors perform best.

In addition, Quelhas et al. [13] confirm in practice that DoG + SIFT constitutes a reasonable choice. Very few consider the extraction of different descriptors. For example, Li et al. [36] combine or fuse the SIFT descriptor and the concatenation of block and blob based HSV histogram and local binary patterns to generate the BoW.

2.3. Visual Word Generation/Vector Quantization. When the keypoints are detected and their features are extracted, such as with the SIFT descriptor, the final step of extracting the BoW feature from images is based on vector quantization. In general, the k-means clustering algorithm is used for this task, and the number of visual words generated is based on the number of clusters (i.e., k). Jiang et al. [17] conducted a comprehensive study on the representation choices of BoW, including vocabulary size, weighting scheme, such as binary, term frequency (TF) and term frequency-inverse document frequency (TF-IDF), stop word removal, feature selection, and so forth for video and image annotation.

To generate visual words, many studies focus on capturing spatial information in order to improve the limitations of the conventional BoW model, such as Yang et al. [37], Zhang et al. [38], Chen et al. [39], S. Kim and D. Kim [40], Lu and Ip [41], Lu and Ip [42], Uijlings et al. [43], Cao and Fei-Fei [44], Philbin et al. [45], Wu et al. [46], Agarwal and Triggs [47], Lazebnik et al. [48], Marszałek and Schmid [49], and Monay et al. [50], in which spatial pyramid matching introduced by Lazebnik et al. [48] has been widely compared as one of the baselines.

However, Van de Sande et al. [51] have shown that the severe drawback of the bag-of-words model is its high computational cost in the quantization step. In other words, the most expensive part in a state-of-the-art setup of the bag-of-words model is the vector quantization step, that is, finding the closest cluster for each data point in the k-means algorithm.

Uijlings et al. [33] compare k-means and random forests for the word assignment task in terms of computational efficiency. By using different descriptors with different grid sizes, random forests are significantly faster than k-means. In addition, using random forests to generate BoW can provide a slightly better Mean Average Precision (MAP) than k-means does. They also recommend two BoW pipelines when the focuses are on accuracy and speed, respectively.

In their seminal work, Philbin et al. [45], the approximate k-means, hierarchical k-means, and (exact) k-means are compared in terms of the precision performance and computational cost, where approximate k-means works best. (See Section 4.3 for further discussion).

Chum et al. [52] observe that feature detection and quantization are noisy processes and this can result in variation in the particular visual words that appear in different images of the same object, leading to missed results.

2.4. Learning Models.
After the BoW feature is extracted from images, it is entered into a classifier for training or testing. Besides constructing the discriminative models as classifiers for image annotation, some Bayesian text models by Latent Semantic Analysis [53], such as probabilistic Latent Semantic Analysis (pLSA) [54] and Latent Dirichlet Analysis (LDA) [55] can be adapted to model object and scene categories.

2.4.1. Discriminative Models.
The construction of discriminative models for image annotation is based on the supervised machine learning principle for pattern recognition. Supervised learning can be thought as learning by examples

or learning with a teacher [56]. The teacher has knowledge of the environment which is represented by a set of input-output examples. In order to classify unknown patterns, a certain number of training samples are available for each class, and they are used to train the classifier [57].

The learning task is to compute a classifier or model $\hat{f}$ that approximates the mapping between the input-output examples and correctly labels the training set with some level of accuracy. This can be called the *training* or *model generation* stage. After the model $\hat{f}$ is generated or trained, it is able to classify an unknown instance, into one of the learned class labels in the training set. More specifically, the classifier calculates the similarity of all trained classes and assigns the unlabeled instance to the class with the highest similarity measure. More specifically, the most widely developed classifier is based on support vector machines (SVM) [58].

2.4.2. Generative Models.
In text analysis, pLSA and LDA are used to discover topics in a document using the BoW document representation. For image annotation, documents and discovered topics are thought of as images and object categories, respectively. Therefore, an image containing instances of several objects is modeled as a mixture of topics. This topic distribution over the images is used to classify an image as belonging to a certain scene. For example, if an image contains "water with waves", "sky with clouds", and "sand", it will be classified into the "coast" scene class [24].

Following the previous definition of BoW, in pLSA there is a latent variable model for cooccurrence data which associates an unobserved class variable $z \in Z = z_1, ..., z_Z$ with each observation. A joint probability model $P(w, d)$ over $V \times N$ is defined by the mixture:

$$P(w \mid d) = \sum_{z \in Z} P(w \mid z) P(z \mid d), \qquad (1)$$

where $P(w \mid z)$ are the topic specific distributions and each image is modeled as a mixture of topics, $P(z \mid d)$.

On the other hand, LDA treats the multinomial weights $P(z \mid d)$ over topics as latent random variables. In particular, the pLSA model is extended by sampling those weights from a Dirichlet distribution. This extension allows the model to assign probabilities to data outside the training corpus and uses fewer parameters, which can reduce the overfitting problem.

The goal of LDA is to maximize the following likelihood:

$$P(w \mid \phi, \alpha, \beta) = \int \sum_z P(w \mid z, \phi) P(z \mid \theta) P(\theta \mid \alpha) P(\phi \mid \beta) d\theta, \qquad (2)$$

where θ and ϕ are multinomial parameters over the topics and words, respectively, and $P(\theta \mid \alpha)$ and $P(\phi \mid \beta)$ are Dirichlet distributions parameterized by the hyperparameters α and β.

Bosch et al. [24] compare BoW + pLSA with different semantic modeling approaches, such as the traditional global based feature representation, block-based feature representation [59] with the k-nearest neighbor classifier. They show that BoW + pLSA performs best. Specifically, the HIS histogram + cooccurrence matrices + edge direction histogram are used as the image descriptors.

However, it is interesting that Lu and Ip [41] and Quelhas et al. [60] show that pLSA does not perform better than BoW + SVM over the Corel dataset, where the former uses blocked based HSV and Gabor texture features and the latter uses keypoint based SIFT features.

3. Extensions of BoW

This section reviews the literature regarding using BoW for some related problems. They are divided into five categories, namely, feature representation, vector quantization, visual vocabulary construction, image segmentation, and others.

3.1. Feature Representation. Since the annotation accuracy is heavily dependent on feature representation, using different region/point descriptors and/or the BoW feature representation will provide different levels of discriminative power for annotation. For example, Mikolajczyk and Schmid [34] compare 10 different local descriptors for object recognition. Jiang et al. [17] examine the classification accuracy of the BoW features using different numbers of visual words and different weighting schemes.

Due to the drawbacks that vector quantization may reduce the discriminative power of images and the BoW methodology ignores geometric relationships among visual words, Zhong et al. [61] present a novel scheme where SIFT features are bundled into local groups. These bundled features are repeatable and are much more discriminative than an individual SIFT feature. In other words, a bundled feature provides a flexible representation that allows us to partially match two groups of SIFT features.

On the other hand, since the image feature generally carries mixed information of the entire image which may contain multiple objects and background, the annotation accuracy can be degraded by such noisy (or diluted) feature representations. Chen et al. [62] propose a novel feature representation, pseudo-objects. It is based on a subset of proximate feature points with its own feature vector to represent a local area to approximate candidate objects in images.

Gehler and Nowozin [63] focus on feature combination, which is to combine multiple complementary features based on different aspects such as shape, color, or texture. They study several models that aim at learning the correct weighting of different features from training data. They provide insight into when combination methods can be expected to work and how the benefit of complementary features can be exploited most efficiently.

Qin and Yung [64] use localized maximum-margin learning to fuse different types of features during the BoW modeling. Particularly, the region of interest is described by a linear combination of the dominant feature and other features extracted from each patch at different scales, respectively. Then, dominant feature clustering is performed to create contextual visual words, and each image in the training set is evaluated against the codebook using the localized

maximum-margin learning method to fuse other features, in order to select a list of contextual visual words that best represents the patches of the image.

As there is a relation between the composition of a photograph and its subject, similar subjects are typically photographed in a similar style. Van Gemert [65] exploits the assumption that images within a category share a similar style, such as colorfulness, lighting, depth of field, viewpoints and saliency. They use the photographic style for category-level image classification. In particular, where the spatial pyramid groups features spatially [48], they focus on more general feature grouping, including these photographic style attributes.

In Rasiwasia and Vasconcelos [66], they introduce an intermediate space, based on a low dimensional semantic "theme" image representation, which is learned with weak supervision from casual image annotations. Each theme induces a probability density on the space of low-level features, and images are represented as vectors of posterior theme probabilities.

3.2. Vector Quantization. In order to reduce the quantization noise, Jégou et al. [67] construct short codes using quantization. The goal is to estimate distances using vector-to-centroid distances, that is, the query vector is not quantized, codes are assigned to the database vectors only. In other words, the feature space is decomposed into a Cartesian product of low-dimensional subspaces, and then each subspace is quantized separately. In particular, a vector is represented by a short code composed of its subspace quantization indices.

As abrupt quantization into discrete bins does cause some aliasing, Agarwal and Triggs [47] focus on soft vector quantization, that is, softly voting into the cluster centers that lie close to the patch, for example, with Gaussian weights. They show that diagonal-covariance Gaussian mixtures fitted using expectation-maximization performs better than hard vector quantization.

Similarly, Fernando et al. [68] propose a supervised learning algorithm based on a Gaussian mixture model, which not only generalizes the k-means by allowing "soft assignments", but also exploits supervised information to improve the discriminative power of the clusters. In their approach, an EM-based approach is used to optimize a convex combination of two criteria, in which the first one is unsupervised and based on the likelihood of the training data, and the second is supervised and takes into account the purity of the clusters.

On the other hand, Wu et al. [69] propose a Semantics-Preserving Bag-of-Words (SPBoW) model, which considers the distance between the semantically identical features as a measurement of the semantic gap and tries to learn a codebook by minimizing this semantic gap. That is, the codebook generation task is formulated as a distance metric learning problem. In addition, one visual feature can be assigned to multiple visual words in different object categories.

In de Campos et al. [70], images are modeled as orderless sets of weighted visual features where each visual feature is associated with a weight factor that may inform re its relevance. In this approach, visual saliency maps are used to determine the relevance weight of a feature.

Zheng et al. [71] argue that for the BoW model used in information retrieval and document categorization, the textual word possesses semantics itself and the documents are well-structured data regulated by grammar, linguistic, and lexicon rules. However, there appears to be no well-defined rules in the visual word composition of images. For instance, the objects of the same class might have arbitrarily different shapes and visual appearances, while objects of different classes might share similar local appearances. To this end, a higher-level visual representation, visual synset for object recognition is presented. First, an intermediate visual descriptor, delta visual phrase, is constructed from a frequently co-occurring visual word-set with similar spatial context. Second, the delta visual phrases are clustered into a visual synset based their probabilistic "semantics", that is, class probability distribution.

Besides reducing the vector quantization noise, another severe drawback of the BoW model is its high computational cost. To address this problem, Moosmann et al. [72] introduce extremely randomized clustering forests based on ensembles of randomly created clustering trees and show that more accurate results can be obtained as well as much faster training and testing.

Recently, Van de Sande et al. [51] proposed two algorithms to combine GPU hardware and a parallel programming model to accelerate the quantization and classification components of the visual categorization architecture.

On the other hand, Hare et al. [73] show the intensity inversion characteristics of the SIFT descriptor and local interest region detectors can be exploited to decrease the time it takes to create vocabularies of visual terms. In particular, they show that clustering inverted and noninverted (or minimum and maximum) features separate results in the same retrieval performance when compared to the clustering of all the features as a single set (with the same overall vocabulary size).

3.3. Visual Vocabulary Construction.

Since related studies, such as Jegou et al. [74], Marszałek and Schmid [49], Sivic and Zisserman [14], and Winn et al. [75], have shown that the commonly generated visual words are still not as expressive as text words, in Zhang et al. [76], images are represented as visual documents composed of repeatable and distinctive visual elements, which are comparable to text words. They propose descriptive visual words (DVWs) and descriptive visual phrases (DVPs) as the visual correspondences to text words and phrases, where visual phrases refer to the frequently co-occurring visual word pairs.

Gavves et al. [77] focus on identifying pairs of independent, distant words—the visual synonyms—that are likely to host image patches of similar visual reality. Specifically, landmark images are considered, where the image geometry guides the detection of synonym pairs. Image geometry is used to find those image features that lie in a nearly identical physical location, yet are assigned to different words of the visual vocabulary.

On the other hand, López-Sastre et al. [78] present a novel method for constructing a visual vocabulary that takes into account the class labels of images. It consists of two stages: Cluster Precision Maximisation (CPM) and Adaptive Refinement. In the first stage, a Reciprocal Nearest Neighbours (RNN) clustering algorithm is guided towards class representative visual words by maximizing a new cluster precision criterion. Next, an adaptive threshold refinement scheme is proposed with the aim of increasing vocabulary compactness, while at the same time improving the recognition rate and further increasing the representativeness of the visual words for category-level object recognition. In other words, this is a correlation clustering based approach, which works as a kind of metaclustering and optimizes the cut-off threshold for each cluster separately.

Constructing visual codebook ensembles is another approach to improve image annotation accuracy. In Luo et al. [18], three methods for constructing visual codebook ensembles are presented. The first one is based on diverse individual visual codebooks by randomly choosing interesting points. The second one uses a random subtraining image dataset with random interesting points. The third one directly utilizes different patch information for constructing an ensemble with high diversity. Consequently, different types of image presentations are obtained. Then, a classification ensemble is learned by the different expression datasets from the same training set.

Bae and Juang [79] apply the idea of linguistic parsing to generate the BoW feature for image annotation. That is, images are represented by a number of variable-size patches by a multidimensional incremental parsing algorithm. Then, the occurrence pattern of these parsed visual patches is fed into the LSA framework.

Since one major challenge in object categorization is to find class models that are "invariant" enough to incorporate naturally-occurring intraclass variations and yet "discriminative" enough to distinguish between different classes, Winn et al. [75] proposed a supervised learning algorithm, which automatically finds such models. In particular, it classifies a region according to the proportions of different visual words. The specific visual words and the typical proportions in each object are learned from a segmented training set.

Kesorn and Poslad [80] propose a framework to enhance the visual word quality. First of all, visual words from representative keypoints are constructed by reducing similar keypoints. Second, domain specific noninformative visual words are detected, which are useless for representing the content of visual data but which can degrade the categorization capability. A noninformative visual word is defined as having a high document frequency and a small statistical association with all the concepts in the image collection. Third, the vector space model of visual words is restructured with respect to a structural ontology model in order to solve visual synonym and polysemy problems.

Tirlly et al. [81] present a new image representation called visual sentences that allows us to "read" visual words in a certain order, as in the case of text. Particularly, simple spatial relations between visual words are considered. In addition, pLSA is used to eliminate the noisiest visual words.

3.4. Image Segmentation. Effective image segmentation can be an important factor affecting the BoW feature generation. Uijlings et al. [43] study the role of context in the BoW approach. They observe that using the precise localization of object patches based on image segmentation is likely to yield a better performance than the dense sampling strategy, which sample patches of $8 * 8$ pixels at every 4th pixel.

Besides point detection, an image can be segmented into several or a fixed number of regions or blocks. However, very few compared the effect of image segmentation on generating the BoW feature. In Cheng and Wang [82], 20–50 regions per image are segmented, and each region is represented by a HSV histogram and cooccurrence texture features. By using contextual Bayesian networks to model spatial relationship between local regions and integrating multiattributes to infer high-level semantics of an image, this approach performs better and is comparable with a number of works using SIFT descriptors and pLSA for image annotation.

Similarly, Wu et al. [46] extract a texture histogram from the $8 * 8$ blocks/patches per image based on their proposed visual language modeling method utilizing the spatial correlation of visual words. This representation is compared with the BoW model including pLSA and LDA using the SIFT descriptor. They show that neither image segmentation nor interest point detection is used in the visual language modeling method, which makes the method not only very efficient, but also very effective over the Caltech 7 dataset.

In addition to using the BoW feature for image annotation, Larlus et al. [83] combine BoW with random fields and some generative models, such as a Dirichlet processes for more effective object segmentation.

3.5. Others

3.5.1. BoW Applications. Although the BoW model has been extensively studied for general object and scene categorization, it has also been considered in some domain specific applications, such as human action recognition [84], facial expression recognition [85], medical images [86], robot, sport image analysis [80], 3D image retrieval and classification [87, 88], image quality assessment [89], and so forth.

3.5.2. Describing Objects/Scenes for Recognition. Farhadi et al. [90] propose shifting the goal of recognition from naming to describing. That is, they focus on describing objects by their attributes, which is not only to name familiar objects, but also to report unusual aspects of a familiar object, such as "spotty dog", not just "dog", and to say something about unfamiliar objects, such as "hairy and four-legged", not just "unknown".

On the other hand, Sudderth et al. [91] develop hierarchical, probabilistic models for objects, the parts composing them, and the visual scenes surrounding them. These models share information between object categories in three distinct ways. First, parts define distributions over a common low-level feature vocabulary. Second, objects are defined using a common set of parts. Finally, object appearance information is shared between the many scenes in which that object is found.

3.5.3. Query Expansion. Chum et al. [52] adopt the BoW architecture with spatial information for query expansion, which has proven successful in achieving high precision at low recall. On the other hand, Philbin et al. [92] quantize a keypoint to the k-nearest visual words as a form of query expansion.

3.5.4. Similarity Measure. Based on the BoW feature representation, Jegou et al. [74] introduce a contextual dissimilarity measure (CDM), which is iteratively obtained by regularizing the average distance of each point to its neighborhood. In addition, CDM is learned in an unsupervised manner, which does not need to learn the distance measure from a set of training images.

3.5.5. Large Scale Image Databases. Since the aim of image annotation is to support very large scale keyword-based image search, such as web image retrieval, it is very critical to assess existing approaches over some large scale dataset(s). Chum et al. [52], Hörster and Lienhart [21], and Lienhart and Slaney [93] used datasets composed of 100000 to 250000 images belonging to 12 categories, which were downloaded from Flickr.

Moreover, Philbin et al. [45] use over 1000000 images from Flickr for experiments and Zhang et al. [94] use about 370000 images collected from Google belonging to 1506 object or scene categories.

On the other hand, Torralba and Efros [95] study some bias issues of object recognition datasets. They provide some suggestions for creating a new and high quality dataset to minimize the selection bias, capture bias, and negative set bias. Furthermore, they claim that in the state of today's datasets there are virtually no studies demonstrating cross-dataset generalization, for example, training on ImageNet, while testing on PASCAL VOC. This could be considered as an additional experimental setup for future works.

3.5.6. Integration of Feature Selection and/or (Spatial) Feature Extraction. Although modeling the spatial relationship between visual words can improve the recognition performance, the spatial features are expensive to compute. Liu et al. [96] propose a method that simultaneously performs feature selection and (spatial) feature extraction based on higher-order spatial features for speed and storage improvements.

For the dimensionality reduction purpose, Elfiky et al. [97] present a novel framework for obtaining a compact pyramid representation. In particular, the divisive information theoretic feature clustering (DITC) algorithm is used to create a compact pyramid representation.

Bosch et al. [98] investigate whether dimensionality reduction using a latent generative model is beneficial for the task of weakly supervised scene classification. In their approach, latent "topics" using pLSA are first of all discovered, and a generative model is then applied to the BoW representation for each image.

In contrast to reducing the dimensionality of the feature representation, selecting more discriminative features (e.g., SIFT descriptors) from a given set of training images has been considered. Shang and Xiao [99] introduce a pairwise image matching scheme to select the discriminative features. Specifically, the feature weights are updated by the labeled information from the training set. As a result, the selected features corresponding to the foreground content of the images can highlight the information category of the images.

3.5.7. Integration of Segmentation, Classification, and/or Retrieval. Simultaneously learning object/scene category models and performing segmentation on the detected objects were studied in Cao and Fei-Fei [44]. They propose a spatially coherent latent topic model (Spatial-LTM), which represents an image containing objects in a hierarchical way by over-segmented image regions of homogeneous appearances and the salient image patches within the regions. It can provide a unified representation for spatially coherent BoW topic models and can simultaneously segment and classify objects.

On the other hand, Tong et al. [100] propose a statistical framework for large-scale near duplicate image retrieval which unifies the step of generating a BoW representation and the step of image retrieval. In this approach, each image is represented by a kernel density function, and the similarity between the query image and a database image is then estimated as the query likelihood.

Shotton et al. [101] utilize semantic texton forests, which are ensembles of decision trees that act directly on image pixels, where the nodes in the trees provide an implicit hierarchical clustering into semantic textons and an explicit local classification estimate. In addition, the bag of semantic textons combines a histogram of semantic textons over an image region with a region prior category distribution, and the bag of semantic textons is computed over the whole image for categorization and over local rectangular regions for segmentation.

3.5.8. Discriminative Learning Models. Romberg et al. [102] extend the standard single-layer pLSA to multiple layers, where the multiple layers handle multiple modalities and a hierarchy of abstractions. In particular, the multilayer multimodal pLSA (mm-pLSA) model is based on a two leaf-pLSAs and a single top-level pLSA node merging the two leaf-pLSAs. In addition, SIFT features and image annotations (tags) as well as the combination of SIFT and HOG features are considered as two pairs of different modalities.

3.5.9. Novel Category Discovery. In their study, Lee and Grauman [103] discover new categories by knowing some categories. That is, previously learned categories are used to discover their familiarity in unsegmented, unlabeled images. In their approach, two variants of a novel object-graph descriptor to encode 2D and 3D spatial layout of object-level cooccurrence patterns relative to an unfamiliar region, and they are used to model the interaction between an image's known and unknown objects for detecting new visual categories.

3.5.10. Interest Point Detection. Since interest point detection is an important step for extracting the BoW feature, Stottinger et al. [104] propose color interest points for sparse image representation. Particularly, light-invariant interest points are introduced to reduce the sensitivity to varying imaging conditions. Color statistics based on occurrence probability lead to color boosted points, which are obtained through saliency-based feature selection.

4. Comparisons of Related Work

This section compares related work in terms of the ways the BoW feature and experimental setup are structured. These comparisons allow us to figure out the most suitable interest point detector(s), clustering algorithm(s), and so forth used to extract the BoW feature from images. In addition, we are able to realize the most widely used dataset(s) and experimental settings for image annotation by BoW.

4.1. Methodology of BoW Feature Generation. Table 1 compares related work for the methodology of extracting the BoW feature. Note that we leave a blank if the information in our comparisons is not clearly described in these related works.

From Table 1 we can observe that the most widely used interest point detector for generating the BoW feature is DoG, and the second and third most popular detectors are Harris-Laplace and Hessian-Laplace, respectively. Besides extracting sparse BoW features, many related studies have focused on dense BoW features.

On the other hand, several studies used some region segmentation algorithms, such as NCuts [116] and Mean-shift [117], to segment an image into several regions to represent keypoints.

For the local feature descriptor to describe interest points, most studies used a 128 dimensional SIFT feature, in which some considered using PCA to reduce the dimensionality of SIFT, but some "fuse" the color feature and SIFT resulting in longer dimensional features than SIFT. Except for extracting SIFT related features, some studies considered conventional color and texture features to represent local regions or points.

About vector quantization, we can see that k-means is the most widely used clustering algorithm to generate the codebook or visual vocabularies. However, in order to solve the limitations of k-means, for example, clustering accuracy and computational cost, some studies used hierarchical k-means, approximate k-means, accelerated k-means, and so forth.

For the number of visual words, related works have considered various amounts of clusters during vector quantization. This may be because the datasets used in these works are different. In Jiang et al. [17], different numbers of visual words were studied, and their results show that 1000 is a reasonable choice. Some related studies also used similar numbers of visual words to generate their BoW features.

On the other hand, the most and second most widely used weighting schemes are TF and TF-IDF. This is consistent with Jiang et al. [17], who concluded that these two weighting schemes perform better than the other weighting schemes.

Finally, SVM is no doubt the most popular classification technique as the learning model for image annotation. In particular, one of the most widely used kernel functions for

TABLE 1: Comparisons of interest point detection, visual words generation, and learning models.

Work	Region/point detection	Local descriptor	Clustering algorithm	No. of visual words	Weighting scheme	Learning model
2012						
de Campos et al. [70]	DoG	SIFT				Logistic regression
Elfiky et al. [97]	Harris-Laplace	SIFT/HSV color + SIFT	k-means			SVM
Fernando et al. [68]	Harris-Laplace	PCA-SIFT/SIFT/SURF[1]	k-means	2000		SVM
Gavves et al. [77]		SIFT/SURF		200000		
Kesorn and Poslad [80]	DoG	SIFT	SLAC[2]		Binary/TF/TF-IDF	Naïve bayes/SVM-linear/SVM-RBF
Lee and Grauman [103]	NCuts[3]	Texton histogram	k-means	400		SVM
Qin and Yung [64]		Color SIFT	k-means			SVM-linear/SVM-poly/SVM-RBF
Romberg et al. [102]		SIFT	k-means			mm-pLSA[4]
Shang and Xiao [99]		SIFT	k-means	1000		SVM
Stottinger et al. [104]	Harris-Laplace	RGB Harris with Laplacian scale selection	k-means	4000		SVM
Tong et al. [100]	Harris-Laplace	SIFT	AKM[5]			
2011						
Hare et al. [73]	DoG/MSER	SIFT	AKM	1000–100000	IDF	
López-Sastre et al. [78]	Hessian-Laplace	SIFT	CPM and Adaptive Refinement	3818		SVM
Luo et al. [18]	DoG	SIFT	k-means	500	TF	SVM
Van Gemert [65]	Harris and Hessian-Laplace	SIFT	k-means	2000		
Yang et al. [37]		SIFT	k-means	1000		SVM
Zhang et al. [76]	DoG	SIFT	HKM[6]	32357	TF-IDF	
Zhang et al. [38]	DoG	SIFT	HKM	32400	TF-IDF	
2010						
Bae and Juang [79]	Dense sampling			171329		
Chen et al. [62]	Hessian-Laplace	SIFT	GMM-BIC[7]	3500	TF	
Cheng and Wang [82]	Mean-shift[8]	HSV color histogram and co-occurrence matrix				SVM
Ding et al. [105]	DoG	PCA-SIFT	k-means	2000		SVM
Jégou et al. [22]	Hessian-Laplace	SIFT	k-means	200000	TF-IDF	
Jiang et al. [17]	DoG	SIFT	k-means	500–10000	Binary/TF/TF-IDF/soft-weighting	SVM
Li and Godil [87]	DoG	SIFT	k-means	500/700/800	TF	pLSA
Qin and Yung [106]		PCA-SIFT	Accelerated k-means	32/128/2048/4096		SVM
Tirilly et al. [107]	Hessian-Laplace	SIFT	HKM	6556 to 117151		
Uijlings et al. [33]		PCA-SIFT	k-means/random forest	4096		SVM
Wu et al. [69]		SIFT	k-means	2500–4500		Naïve Bayes/SVM

TABLE 1: Continued.

Work	Region/point detection	Local descriptor	Clustering algorithm	No. of visual words	Weighting scheme	Learning model
2009						
Chen et al. [39]	DoG	SIFT	k-means	1000	Spatial weighting	
Lu and Ip [41]	Dense sampling	HSV color + Gabor txture	k-means	100/200		SVM
Lu and Ip [42]	Dense sampling	HSV color + Gabor txture	k-means	100/200		LLP[9]/GLP[10]/ SVM
S. Kim and D. Kim [40]	Dense sampling	SIFT/SURF	k-means	500/1500/3000	TF	pLSA/SVM
Uijlings et al. [43]	Dense sampling	SIFT	k-means	4096		SVM
Xiang et al. [108]	NCuts	36 region features[11]				MRFA[12]
Zhang et al. [94]		SIFT	HKM	32357	TF-IDF	
2008						
Bosch et al. [98]	Harris-Laplace	Color SIFT	k-means	1500		k-NN/SVM
Liu et al. [96]	Harris-Laplace	SIFT	k-means	1000		SVM-linear
Marszałek and Schmid [109]	Harris-Laplace	SIFT	k-means	8000		SVM
Rasiwasia and Vasconcelos [66]		DCT[13] coefficients				Hierarchical Dirichlet models/SVM
Tirilly et al. [81]		SIFT	HKM	6556/61687	TF-IDF	SVM
Van de Sande et al. [110]	Harris-Laplace	Color SIFT	k-means	4000		SVM
Zheng et al. [71]	DoG + Hessian-Laplace	SIFT + Spin[14]	k-means	1010		SVM
2007						
Bosch et al. [24]	Dense sampling	HSV color + co-occurrence + edge	k-means	700		pLSA
Chum et al. [52]	Hessian-Laplace	SIFT	k-means		TF-IDF	
Gökalp and Aksoy [28]	Dense sampling	HSV color	k-means			Bayesian classifier
Hörster and Lienhart [21]	DoG/dense sampling	Color SIFT	k-means			LDA
Jegou et al. [74]		SIFT	k-means	30000		
Li and Fei-Fei [111]	Dense sampling	SIFT	k-means	300	TF	LDA
Lienhart and Slaney [93]		SIFT	k-means		TF	pLSA
Philbin et al. [45]	Hessian-Laplace	SIFT	AKM	1 M		
Quelhas et al. [13]	DoG	SIFT	k-means	1000		SVM/pLSA
Wu et al. [46]	Dense sampling	Texture histogram				Unigram/ bigram/trigram models
Junsong et al. [112]	DoG	PCA-SIFT	k-means	160/500		
2006						
Agarwal and Triggs [47]	Dense sampling	SIFT	EM[15]			LDA/SVM
Bosch et al. [29]	Dense sampling	Color SIFT	k-means	1500		k-NN/pLSA
Lazebnik et al. [48]	Dense sampling	SIFT	k-means	200/400		SVM
Marszałek and Schmid [49]	Harris-Laplace	SIFT	k-means	1000	TF	SVM

TABLE 1: Continued.

Work	Region/point detection	Local descriptor	Clustering algorithm	No. of visual words	Weighting scheme	Learning model
Monay et al. [50]	DoG	SIFT	k-means	1000	TF	pLSA
Moosmann et al. [72]	Dense sampling/DoG	HSV color + wavelet/SIFT	Extremely randomized trees			SVM
Perronnin et al. [113]	DoG	PCA-SIFT		1024		SVM-linear

[1] Speeded up robust features [114].
[2] Search ant and labor ant clustering algorithm [115].
[3] Normalized cuts [116].
[4] Multilayer modality pLSA.
[5] Approximate k-means.
[6] Hierarchical k-means.
[7] Gaussian mixture model with Bayesian information criterion.
[8] Mean shift region segmentation algorithm [117].
[9] Local label propagation on the k-NN graph.
[10] Global label propagation on the complete graph.
[11] Region color and standard deviation, region average orientation energy (12 filters), region size, location, convexity, first moment, and ratio of region area to boundary length squared [118].
[12] Multiple Markov random fields.
[13] Discrete cosine transform.
[14] A rotation-invariant two-dimensional histogram of intensities within an image region [71].
[15] Expectation maximization.

constructing the SVM classifier is the Gaussian radial basis function. However, some other SVM classifiers, such as linear SVM and SVM with a polynomial kernel have also been considered in the literature.

4.2. Experimental Design.

Table 2 compares related work for the experimental design. That is, the chosen dataset(s) and baseline(s) are examined.

According to Table 2, most studies considered more than one single dataset for their experiments, and many of them contained object and scene categories. This is very important for image annotation that the annotated keywords should be broadened for users to perform keyword-based queries for image retrieval.

Specifically, the PASCAL, Caltech, and Corel datasets are the three most widely used benchmarks for image classification. However, the datasets used in most studies usually contain a small number of categories and images, except for the studies focusing on retrieval rather than classification. That is, similar based queries are used to retrieve relevant images instead of training a learning model to classify unknown images into one specific category.

For the chosen baselines, most studies compared BoW and/or spatial pyramid matching based BoW since their aims were to propose novel approaches to improve these two feature representations. Specifically, Lazebnik et al. [48] proposed spatial pyramid matching based BoW as the most popular baseline.

Besides improving the feature representation per se, some studies focused on improving the performance of LDA and/or pLSA discriminative learning models. Another popular baseline is that of Fei-Fei and Perona [31], who proposed a Bayesian hierarchical model to represent each region as part of a "theme."

4.3. Discussion.

The above comparisons indicate several issues that were not examined in the literature. Since the local features can be represented using object-based regions by region segmentation [143, 144] or point-based regions by point detection (c.f. Section 2.1), regarding the BoW feature based on tokenizing, it is unknown which local feature is more appropriate for large scale image annotation (For large scale image annotation, this means that the number of annotated keywords is certainly large and their meanings are very broad, containing object and scene concepts.)

In addition, the local feature descriptor is the key component to the success of better image annotation; it is a fact that the number of visual words (i.e., clusters) is another factor affecting image annotation performance. Although Jiang et al. [17] conducted a comprehensive study of using various amounts of visual words, they only used one dataset, that is, TRECVID, containing 20 concepts. Therefore, one important issue is to provide the guidelines for determining the number of visual words over different kinds of image datasets having different image contents.

The learning techniques can be divided into generative and discriminative models, but there are very few studies which assess their annotation performance over different kinds of image datasets which is necessary in order to fully understand the value of these two kinds of learning models. On the other hand, a combination of generative and discriminative learning techniques [145] or hybrid models are considered for the image annotation task.

For the experimental setup, the target of most studies was not image retrieval. In other words, the performance evaluation was usually for small scale problems based on datasets containing a small number of categories, say 10. However, image retrieval users will not be satisfied with a system providing only 10 keyword-based queries to search relevant

TABLE 2: Comparisons of datasets used and annotation performance.

Work	Categories		Dataset	No. of categories	No. of images	Baseline
	Scene	Object				
2012						
de Campos et al. [70]		v	PASCAL'07/'08[16]	20	9292	
Elfiky et al. [97]	v	v	Sport event/15 scene/butterflies[17]/ PASCAL'07/'09	15/20	6000/21000/ 2000/160k/ 4194k	Spatial pyramid
Fernando et al. [68]		v	PASCAL'06/ Caltech 10[18]	10/10/11	5304/3044	BoW
Gavves et al. [77]	v		Oxford 5k[19]	11	5062	
Kesorn and Poslad [80]	v		Olympic organization website + Google images	8	16000	pLSA
Lee and Grauman [103]	v	v	MSRC-v0[20]/-v2/ PASCAL'08/ Corel/Gould'09	21/20/7/14	3457/591/1023/ 100/715	LDA
Qin and Yung [64]	v		SCENE-8/-15	8/15	2688/4485	BoW
Romberg et al. [102]	v	v	Flickr-10M	>300	10080251	pLSA
Shang and Xiao [99]		v	Caltech 256/ MSRC	20/20		BoW
Stottinger et al. [104]			PASCAL'07	20	9963	
Tong et al. [100]	v	v	Tattoo dataset /Oxford/Flickr		101745/5062/ 1002805	RS[21]/HKM/AKM
2011						
Hare et al. [73]	v	v	UK Bench/MIR Flickr-25000[22]			BoW
López-Sastre et al. [78]		v	Caltech 101	10	890	Mikolajczyk et al. [25]; Stark and Schiele [119]
Luo et al. [18]		v	Caltech 4/Graz-02[23]	5/2	400/200	Li and Perona [31]; Moosmann et al. [72]
Van Gemert [65]	v	v	Corel/PASCAL'09	20	2000/7054	BoW/spatial pyramid
Yang et al. [37]		v	PASCAL'08	20	8445	Divvala et al. [120]; Zhong et al. [109]
Zhang et al. [76]	v	v	Google images/ Caltech 101and256	15	376500	BoW
Zhang et al. [38]	v	v	ImageNet[24]	15 queries	1.5 million	Nister and Stewenius [121]; Zhong et al. [61]
2010						
Bae and Juang [79]	v		Corel	15	20000	LSA
Chen et al. [62]		v	Oxford buildings/ Flickr 1k	11 (55 queries)/7 (56 queries)	5062/11282	Sivic and Zisserman [14]; Philbin et al. [45]; Lazebnik et al. [48]
Cheng and Wang [82]	v		6-scene dataset	6	700	Vogel and Schiele [122]; Bosch et al. [98]; Quelhas et al. [13]; Boutell et al. [123]
Ding et al. [105]	v		TRECVID'06[25]	20	61901	Binary/TF/TF-IDF weighting
Jégou et al. [22]	v	v	Holidays[26]/Oxford 5k/U. of Kentucky object recognition[27]	500/11 (55 queries)	1491/5062/6376	BoW by HE[28]/

TABLE 2: Continued.

Work	Categories		Dataset	No. of categories	No. of images	Baseline
	Scene	Object				
Jiang et al. [17]		v	TRECVID'06	20	79484	
Li and Godli [87]	v	v	Corel	50	5000	Duygulu et al. [118]; Jeon et al. [124]; Lavrenko et al. [125]; Monay and Gatica-Perez, 2007 [126]
Qin and Yung [106]	v	v		8/13/15	2688/3759/ 4485	Siagian and Itti [127, 128]; Bosch et al. [29]; Li and Perona [31]; Quelhas et al. [60]; Lazebnik et al. [48]
Tirilly et al. [107]	v	v	U. of Kentucky object recognition/Oxford 5k/ Caltech 6 & 101	300/55/200 queries	10200/5062/ 8197	TF-IDF weighting
Uijlings et al. [33]		v	PASCAL'07/ TRECVID'05/ Caltech 101	20/101/15	9963/12914/4485	BoW
Wu et al. [69]		v	LabelMe[29]/ PASCAL'06	495/10		BoW; Bar-Hillel et al. [129]; Davis et al. [130]; Goldberger et al. [131]; Perronnin et al. [113]; Weinberger et al. [132]
2009						
Chen et al. [39]	v		LabelMe	8 (448 queries)	2689	Yang et al. [133]
Lu and Ip (a) [41]	v		LabelMe + Web images	3	1239	k-NN; LDA
Lu and Ip (b) [42]	v	v	Corel/histological images	10/5	1000	pLSA/SVM
S. Kim and D. Kim [40]	v	v	Corel/histological images	10/5	1000	LLP/GLP/SVM/pLSA
Uijlings et al. [43]		v	PASCAL'07	20	9963	BoW
Xiang et al. [108]		v	Corel/TRECVID'05	50/39	5000	Feng et al. [134]
Zhang et al. [94]	v	v	Google images/ Corel/Caltech 101 and 256	1506 queries/ 50/15	376500/500/ 2250	BoW
2008						
Bosch et al. [98]	v		6-/8-/13-/15-scene	6/8/13/15	2688/702	BoW
Liu et al. [96]	v		PASCAL'06/Caltech 4/MSRC-v2	20/5/15		Savarese et al. [135]
Marszalek and Schmid [109]	v	v	Caltech 256	256		Lazebnik et al.[48]; Zhang et al. [35]
Rasiwasia and Vasconcelos [66]	v		15-natural scene/ Corel	15/50		Bosch et al. [29]; Lazebnik et al. [48]; Li and Perona [31]; Liu and Shah [136]
Tirilly et al. [81]		v	Caltech 6 and 101	6/101	5435/8697	SVM
Van de Sande et al. [110]	v	v	PASCAL'07/ TRECVID'05	20		
Zheng et al. [71]		v	Caltech 101/ PASCAL'05	12/4		BoW

TABLE 2: Continued.

Work	Categories		Dataset	No. of categories	No. of images	Baseline
	Scene	Object				
2007						
Bosch et al. [24]	v		Corel	6	700	Global and block-based features + k-NN; Vogel and Schiele [122]
Chum et al. [52]	v	v	Oxford + Flickr		104844	BoW
Gökalp and Aksoy [28]	v		LabelMe	7	1050	Bag of individual regions/ bag of region pairs
Hörster and Lienhart [21]	v		Flickr	12 (60 queries)	246348	BoW/color based BoW
Jegou et al. [74]	v	v	Object recognition benchmark[30]		10200	Object recognition benchmark
Li and Fei-Fei [111]	v		8 events	8	240	LDA
Lienhart and Slaney [93]	v		Flickr	12 (60 queries)	253460	LSA
Philbin et al. [45]	v	v	Oxford 5 k/Flickr 1 and 2	11/145 and 450 tags	5062/99782/ 1040801	BoW
Quelhas et al. [13]	v		Corel + Web images	5	6680/3805/ 9457/6364	BoW; Vailaya et al. [137]
Wu et al. [46]	v	v	Caltech 7/Corel	8/6	600	LDA/pLSA
Yuan et al. [112]		v	Caltech 101	2	558	BoW
2006						
Agarwal and Triggs [47]		v	Caltech 7 + Graz/ KTH-TIPS[31]/ Cal-IPNP[32]	4/10/2	1337/810/360	LDA
Bosch et al. [29]	v		6-/8-/13-scene	6/8/13	2688/702/1071	BoW
Lazebnik et al. [48]	v	v	15-scene/Caltech 101/Graz	15/101/2		Zhang et al. [138]; Opelt et al. [139]
Marszalek and Schmid [49]		v	PASCAL'05			Wang et al. [20]
Monay et al. [50]	v		Corel	4	6600	
Moosmann et al. [72]		v	Graz-02/ PASCAL'05	3/4		BoW
Perronnin et al. [113]	v	v	Corel	10	1000	BoW; Farquhar et al. [140]; Deselaers et al. [141]

[16] http://pascallin.ecs.soton.ac.uk/challenges/VOC/.
[17] http://www.comp.leeds.ac.uk/scs6jwks/dataset/leedsbutterfly/.
[18] http://www.vision.caltech.edu/Image_Datasets/Caltech101/.
[19] http://www.robots.ox.ac.uk/~vgg/data/oxbuildings/.
[20] http://www.cs.utexas.edu/~grauman/research/datasets.html.
[21] Random seed [142].
[22] http://press.liacs.nl/mirflickr/.
[23] http://lear.inrialpes.fr/people/marszalek/data/ig02/.
[24] http://www.image-net.org/.
[25] http://www-nlpir.nist.gov/projects/tv2006/tv2006.html.
[26] http://lear.inrialpes.fr/~jegou/data.php.
[27] http://vis.uky.edu/.
[28] Hamming embedding.
[29] http://labelme.csail.mit.edu/.
[30] http://vis.uky.edu/%7Estewe/ukbench/.
[31] http://www.nada.kth.se/cvap/databases/kth-tips/.
[32] http://crl.ucsd.edu/.

images. Some benchmarks are much more suitable for larger scale image annotation, such as the Large Scale Visual Recognition Challenge 2012 (ILSVRC2012) by ImageNet (http://www.image-net.org/challenges/LSVRC/2012/index) and Photo Annotation and Retrieval 2012 by ImageCLEF (http://www.imageclef.org/2012/photo). In particular, the ImageNet dataset contains over 10000 categories and 10000000 labeled images and ImageCLEF uses a subset of the MIRFLICKR collection (http://press.liacs.nl/mirflickr/), which contains 25 thousand images and 94 concepts.

However, it is also possible that some smaller scale datasets composed of a relatively small number of images and/or categories can be combined into larger datasets. For example, the combination of Caltech 256 and Corel could be regarded as a benchmark that is more close to the real world problem.

5. Conclusion

In this paper, a number of recent related works using BoW for image annotation are reviewed. We can observe that this topic has been extensively studied recently. For example, there are many issues for improving the discriminative power of BoW feature representations by such techniques as image segmentation, vector quantization, and visual vocabulary construction. In addition, there are other directions for integrating the BoW feature for different applications, such as face detection, medical image analysis, 3D image retrieval, and so forth.

From comparisons of related work, we can find the most widely used methodology to extract the BoW feature which can be regarded as a baseline for future research. That is, DoG is used as the kepoint detector and each keypoint is represented by the SIFT feature. The vector quantization step is based on the k-means clustering algorithm with 1000 visual words. However, the number of visual words (i.e., the k values) is dependent on the dataset used. Finally, the weighting scheme can be either TF or TF-IDF.

On the other hand, for the dataset issue in the experimental design, which can affect the contribution and final conclusion, the PASCAL, Caltech, and/or Corel datasets can be used as the initial study.

According to the comparative results, there are some future research directions. First, the local feature descriptor for vector quantization usually by point-based SIFT feature can be compared with other descriptors, such as a region-based feature or a combination of different features. Second, a guideline for determining the number of visual words over what kind of datasets should be provided. The third issue is to assess the performance of generative and discriminative learning models over different kinds of datasets, such as different dataset sizes and different image contents, for example, a single object per image and multiple objects per image. Finally, it is worth examining the scalability of BoW feature representation for large scale image annotation.

References

[1] A. W. M. Smeulders, M. Worring, S. Santini, A. Gupta, and R. Jain, "Content-based image retrieval at the end of the early years," *IEEE Transactions on Pattern Analysis and Machine Intelligence*, vol. 22, no. 12, pp. 1349–1380, 2000.

[2] M. L. Kherfi, D. Ziou, and A. Bernardi, "Image retrieval from the World Wide Web: issues, techniques, and systems," *ACM Computing Surveys*, vol. 36, no. 1, pp. 35–67, 2004.

[3] R. Datta, D. Joshi, J. Li, and J. Z. Wang, "Image retrieval: ideas, influences, and trends of the new age," *ACM Computing Surveys*, vol. 40, no. 2, article 5, 2008.

[4] Y. Choi and E. M. Rasmussen, "Users' relevance criteria in image retrieval in American history," *Information Processing and Management*, vol. 38, no. 5, pp. 695–726, 2002.

[5] M. Markkula, M. Tico, B. Sepponen, K. Nirkkonen, and E. Sormunen, "A test collection for the evaluation of content-based image retrieval algorithms—a user and task-based approach," *Information Retrieval*, vol. 4, no. 3-4, pp. 275–293, 2001.

[6] A. Goodrum and A. Spink, "Image searching on the Excite Web search engine," *Information Processing and Management*, vol. 37, no. 2, pp. 295–311, 2001.

[7] C. F. Tsai and C. Hung, "Automatically annotating images with keywords: a review of image annotation systems," *Recent Patents on Computer Science*, vol. 1, no. 1, pp. 55–68, 2008.

[8] A. Hanbury, "A survey of methods for image annotation," *Journal of Visual Languages and Computing*, vol. 19, no. 5, pp. 617–627, 2008.

[9] D. Zhang, M. M. Islam, and G. Lu, "A review on automatic image annotation techniques," *Pattern Recognition*, vol. 45, pp. 346–362, 2011.

[10] A. Pinz, "Object categorization," *Foundations and Trends in Computer Graphics and Vision*, vol. 1, no. 4, pp. 255–353, 2006.

[11] C. F. Tsai, K. Mcgarry, and J. Tait, "CLAIRE: a modular support vector image indexing and classification system," *ACM Transactions on Information Systems*, vol. 24, no. 3, pp. 353–379, 2006.

[12] W.-C. Lin, M. Oakes, J. Tait, and C.-F. Tsai, "Improving image annotation via useful representative feature selection," *Cognitive Processing*, vol. 10, no. 3, pp. 233–242, 2009.

[13] P. Quelhas, F. Monay, J. M. Odobez, D. Gatica-Perez, and T. Tuytelaars, "A thousand words in a scene," *IEEE Transactions on Pattern Analysis and Machine Intelligence*, vol. 29, no. 9, pp. 1575–1589, 2007.

[14] J. Sivic and A. Zisserman, "Video google: a text retrieval approach to object matching in videos," in *Proceedings of the 9th IEEE International Conference on Computer Vision (ICCV '03)*, pp. 1470–1477, October 2003.

[15] J. Sivic, B. C. Russell, A. A. Efros, A. Zisserman, and W. T. Freeman, "Discovering objects and their location in images," in *Proceedings of the 10th IEEE International Conference on Computer Vision (ICCV '05)*, pp. 370–377, October 2005.

[16] R. Fergus, L. Fei-Fei, P. Perona, and A. Zisserman, "Learning object categories from Google's image search," in *Proceedings of the 10th IEEE International Conference on Computer Vision (ICCV '05)*, pp. 1816–1823, October 2005.

[17] Y. G. Jiang, J. Yang, C. W. Ngo, and A. G. Hauptmann, "Representations of keypoint-based semantic concept detection: a comprehensive study," *IEEE Transactions on Multimedia*, vol. 12, no. 1, pp. 42–53, 2010.

[18] H. L. Luo, H. Wei, and L. L. Lai, "Creating efficient visual codebook ensembles for object categorization," *IEEE Transactions on Systems, Man, and Cybernetics Part A*, vol. 41, no. 2, pp. 238–253, 2010.

[19] J. Fan, Y. Gao, and H. Luo, "Multi-level annotation of natural scenes using dominant image components and semantic

concepts," in *Proceedings of the 12th ACM International Conference on Multimedia (MM '04)*, pp. 540–547, October 2004.

[20] G. Wang, Y. Zhang, and L. Fei-Fei, "Using dependent regions for object categorization in a generative framework," in *Proceedings of the IEEE Computer Society Conference on Computer Vision and Pattern Recognition (CVPR '06)*, pp. 1597–1604, June 2006.

[21] E. Hörster and R. Lienhart, "Fusing local image descriptors for large-scale image retrieval," in *Proceedings of the IEEE Computer Society Conference on Computer Vision and Pattern Recognition (CVPR '07)*, pp. 1–8, June 2007.

[22] H. Jégou, M. Douze, and C. Schmid, "Improving bag-of-features for large scale image search," *International Journal of Computer Vision*, vol. 87, no. 3, pp. 316–336, 2010.

[23] D. G. Lowe, "Distinctive image features from scale-invariant keypoints," *International Journal of Computer Vision*, vol. 60, no. 2, pp. 91–110, 2004.

[24] A. Bosch, X. Muñoz, and R. Martí, "Which is the best way to organize/classify images by content?" *Image and Vision Computing*, vol. 25, no. 6, pp. 778–791, 2007.

[25] K. Mikolajczyk, B. Leibe, and B. Schiele, "Local features for object class recognition," in *Proceedings of the 10th IEEE International Conference on Computer Vision (ICCV '05)*, pp. 1792–1799, October 2005.

[26] T. Tuytelaars and K. Mikolajczyk, "Local invariant feature detectors: a survey," *Foundations and Trends in Computer Graphics and Vision*, vol. 3, no. 3, pp. 177–280, 2007.

[27] K. Mikolajczyk, T. Tuytelaars, C. Schmid et al., "A comparison of affine region detectors," *International Journal of Computer Vision*, vol. 65, no. 1-2, pp. 43–72, 2005.

[28] D. Gökalp and S. Aksoy, "Scene classification using bag-of-regions representations," in *Proceedings of the IEEE Computer Society Conference on Computer Vision and Pattern Recognition (CVPR '07)*, pp. 1–8, June 2007.

[29] A. Bosch, A. Zisserman, and X. Munoz, "Scene classification via pLSA," in *European Conference on Computer Vision*, pp. 517–530, 2006.

[30] F. Jurie and B. Triggs, "Creating efficient codebooks for visual recognition," in *Proceedings of the 10th IEEE International Conference on Computer Vision (ICCV '05)*, pp. 604–610, October 2005.

[31] L. Fei-Fei and P. Perona, "A bayesian hierarchical model for learning natural scene categories," in *Proceedings of the 6th IEEE Computer Society Conference on Computer Vision and Pattern Recognition (CVPR '05)*, pp. 524–531, June 2005.

[32] Y. Ke and R. Sukthankar, "PCA-SIFT: a more distinctive representation for local image descriptors," in *Proceedings of the IEEE Computer Society Conference on Computer Vision and Pattern Recognition (CVPR '04)*, pp. 506–513, July 2004.

[33] J. R. R. Uijlings, A. W. M. Smeulders, and R. J. H. Scha, "Real-time visual concept classification," *IEEE Transactions on Multimedia*, vol. 12, no. 7, pp. 665–681, 2010.

[34] K. Mikolajczyk and C. Schmid, "A performance evaluation of local descriptors," *IEEE Transactions on Pattern Analysis and Machine Intelligence*, vol. 27, no. 10, pp. 1615–1630, 2005.

[35] J. Zhang, M. Marszałek, S. Lazebnik, and C. Schmid, "Local features and kernels for classification of texture and object categories: a comprehensive study," *International Journal of Computer Vision*, vol. 73, no. 2, pp. 213–238, 2007.

[36] Z. Li, Z. Shi, X. Liu, Z. Li, and Z. Shi, "Fusing semantic aspects for image annotation and retrieval," *Journal of Visual Communication and Image Representation*, vol. 21, no. 8, pp. 798–805, 2010.

[37] L. Yang, N. Zheng, and J. Yang, "A unified context assessing model for object categorization," *Computer Vision and Image Understanding*, vol. 115, no. 3, pp. 310–322, 2011.

[38] S. Zhang, Q. Tian, G. Hua et al., "Modeling spatial and semantic cues for large-scale near-duplicated image retrieval," *Computer Vision and Image Understanding*, vol. 115, no. 3, pp. 403–414, 2011.

[39] X. Chen, X. Hu, and X. Shen, "Spatial weighting for bag-or-visual-words and its application in content-based image retrieval," in *Pacific-Asia Conference on Knowledge Discovery and Data Mining*, pp. 867–874, 2009.

[40] S. Kim and D. Kim, "Scene classification using pLSA with visterm spatial location," in *Proceedings of the 1st ACM International Workshop on Interactive Multimedia for Consumer Electronics (IMCE '09)*, pp. 57–66, October 2009.

[41] Z. Lu and H. H. S. Ip, "Image categorization with spatial mismatch kernels," in *Proceedings of the IEEE Computer Society Conference on Computer Vision and Pattern Recognition (CVPR '09)*, pp. 397–404, June 2009.

[42] Z. Lu and H. H. S. Ip, "Image categorization by learning with context and consistency," in *Proceedings of the IEEE Computer Society Conference on Computer Vision and Pattern Recognition (CVPR '09)*, pp. 2719–2726, June 2009.

[43] J. R. R. Uijlings, A. W. M. Smeulders, and R. J. H. Scha, "What is the spatial extent of an object?" in *Proceedings of the IEEE Computer Society Conference on Computer Vision and Pattern Recognition (CVPR '09)*, pp. 770–777, June 2009.

[44] L. Cao and L. Fei-Fei, "Spatially coherent latent topic model for concurrent segmentation and classification of objects and scenes," in *Proceedings of the IEEE 11th International Conference on Computer Vision (ICCV '07)*, pp. 1–8, October 2007.

[45] J. Philbin, O. Chum, M. Isard, J. Sivic, and A. Zisserman, "Object retrieval with large vocabularies and fast spatial matching," in *Proceedings of the IEEE Computer Society Conference on Computer Vision and Pattern Recognition (CVPR '07)*, pp. 1–8, June 2007.

[46] L. Wu, M. Li, Z. Li, W. Y. Ma, and N. Yu, "Visual language modeling for image classification," in *Proceedings of the 9th ACM SIG Multimedia International Workshop on Multimedia Information Retrieval (MIR '07)*, pp. 115–124, September 2007.

[47] A. Agarwal and B. Triggs, "Hyperfeatures—multilevel local coding for visual recognition," in *Conference on Computer Vision*, pp. 30–43, 2006.

[48] S. Lazebnik, C. Schmid, and J. Ponce, "Beyond bags of features: spatial pyramid matching for recognizing natural scene categories," in *Proceedings of the IEEE Computer Society Conference on Computer Vision and Pattern Recognition (CVPR '06)*, pp. 2169–2178, June 2006.

[49] M. Marszałek and C. Schmid, "Spatial weighting for bag-of-features," in *Proceedings of the IEEE Computer Society Conference on Computer Vision and Pattern Recognition (CVPR '06)*, pp. 2118–2125, June 2006.

[50] F. Monay, P. Quelhas, J. M. Odobez, and D. Gatica-Perez, "Integrating co-occurrence and spatial contexts on patch-based scene segmentation," in *Proceedings of the Conference on Computer Vision and Pattern Recognition (CVPR '06)*, pp. 14–21, June 2006.

[51] K. E. A. Van De Sande, T. Gevers, and C. G. M. Snoek, "Empowering visual categorization with the GPU," *IEEE Transactions on Multimedia*, vol. 13, no. 1, pp. 60–70, 2011.

[52] O. Chum, J. Philbin, J. Sivic, M. Isard, and A. Zisserman, "Total recall: automatic query expansion with a generative

feature model for object retrieval," in *Proceedings of the IEEE 11th International Conference on Computer Vision (ICCV '07)*, pp. 1–8, October 2007.

[53] S. Deerwester, S. T. Dumais, G. W. Furnas, T. K. Landauer, and R. Harshman, "Indexing by latent semantic analysis," *Journal for the American Society for InFormation Science*, vol. 41, no. 6, pp. 391–407, 1990.

[54] T. Hofmann, "Unsupervised learning by probabilistic latent semantic analysis," *Machine Learning*, vol. 42, no. 1-2, pp. 177–196, 2001.

[55] D. M. Blei, A. Y. Ng, and M. I. Jordan, "Latent Dirichlet allocation," *Journal of Machine Learning Research*, vol. 3, no. 4-5, pp. 993–1022, 2003.

[56] T. Mitchell, *Machine Learning*, McGraw-Hill, New York, NY, USA, 1997.

[57] S. Haykin, *Neural Networks: A Comprehensive Foundation*, Prentice Hall, Upper Saddle River, NJ, USA, 2nd edition, 1999.

[58] V. Vapnik, *Statistical Learning Theory*, John Wiley & Sons, New York, NY, USA, 1998.

[59] M. Summer and R. W. Picard, "Indoor-outdoor image classification," *IEEE International Workshop on Content-Based Access of Image and Video Databases*, pp. 42–50, 1998.

[60] P. Quelhas, F. Monay, J. M. Odobez, D. Gatica-Perez, T. Tuytelaars, and L. Van Gool, "Modeling scenes with local descriptors and latent aspects," in *Proceedings of the 10th IEEE International Conference on Computer Vision (ICCV '05)*, pp. 883–890, October 2005.

[61] W. Zhong, K. Qifa, M. Isard, and S. Jian, "Bundling features for large scale partial-duplicate web image search," in *Proceedings of the IEEE Computer Society Conference on Computer Vision and Pattern Recognition (CVPR '09)*, pp. 25–32, June 2009.

[62] K. T. Chen, K. H. Lin, Y. H. Kuo, Y. L. Wu, and W. H. Hsu, "Boosting image object retrieval and indexing by automatically discovered pseudo-objects," *Journal of Visual Communication and Image Representation*, vol. 21, no. 8, pp. 815–825, 2010.

[63] P. Gehler and S. Nowozin, "On feature combination for multiclass object classification," in *Proceedings of the IEEE International Conference on Computer Vision (ICCV '09)*, pp. 221–228, 2009.

[64] J. Qin and N. H. Yung, "Feature fusion within local region using localized maximum-margin learning for scene categorization," *Pattern Recognition*, vol. 45, pp. 1671–1683, 2012.

[65] J. C. Van Gemert, "Exploiting photographic style for category-level image classification by generalizing the spatial pyramid," in *Proceedings of the 1st ACM International Conference on Multimedia Retrieval (ICMR '11)*, pp. 1–8, April 2011.

[66] N. Rasiwasia and N. Vasconcelos, "Scene classification with low-dimensional semantic spaces and weak supervision," in *Proceedings of the 26th IEEE Conference on Computer Vision and Pattern Recognition (CVPR '08)*, pp. 1–8, June 2008.

[67] H. Jégou, M. Douze, and C. Schmid, "Product quantization for nearest neighbor search," *IEEE Transactions on Pattern Analysis and Machine Intelligence*, vol. 33, no. 1, pp. 117–128, 2011.

[68] B. Fernando, E. Fromont, D. Muselet, and M. Sebban, "Supervised learning of Gaussian mixture models for visual vocabulary generation," *Pattern Recognition*, vol. 45, pp. 897–907, 2011.

[69] L. Wu, S. C. H. Hoi, and N. Yu, "Semantics-preserving bag-of-words models and applications," *IEEE Transactions on Image Processing*, vol. 19, no. 7, pp. 1908–1920, 2010.

[70] T. de Campos, G. Csurka, and F. Perronnin, "Images as sets of locally weighted features," *Computer Vision and Image Understanding*, vol. 116, pp. 68–85, 2012.

[71] Y. T. Zheng, M. Zhao, S. Y. Neo, T. S. Chua, and Q. Tian, "Visual synset: towards a higher-level visual representation," in *Proceedings of the 26th IEEE Conference on Computer Vision and Pattern Recognition (CVPR '08)*, pp. 1–8, June 2008.

[72] F. Moosmann, B. Triggs, and F. Jurie, "Fast discriminative visual codebooks using randomized clustering forests," in *International Conference on Neural Information Processing Systems*, pp. 985–992, 2006.

[73] J. S. Hare, S. Samangooei, and P. H. Lewis, "Efficient clustering and quantisation of SIFT features: exploiting characteristics of the SIFT descriptor and interest region detectors under image inversion," in *Proceedings of the 1st ACM International Conference on Multimedia Retrieval (ICMR '11)*, pp. 1–8, April 2011.

[74] H. Jegou, H. Harzallah, and C. Schmid, "A contextual dissimilarity measure for accurate and efficient image search," in *Proceedings of the IEEE Computer Society Conference on Computer Vision and Pattern Recognition (CVPR '07)*, pp. 1–8, June 2007.

[75] J. Winn, A. Criminisi, and T. Minka, "Object categorization by learned universal visual dictionary," in *Proceedings of the 10th IEEE International Conference on Computer Vision (ICCV '05)*, pp. 1800–1807, October 2005.

[76] S. Zhang, Q. Tian, G. Hua, Q. Huang, and W. Guo, "Generating descriptive visual words and visual phrases for large-scale image applications," *IEEE Transactions on Image Processing*, vol. 20, no. 9, pp. 2664–2677, 2011.

[77] E. Gavves, C. G. M. Snoek, and A. W. Smeulders, "Visual synonyms for landmark image retrieval," *Computer Vision and Image Understanding*, vol. 116, pp. 238–249, 2012.

[78] R. J. López-Sastre, T. Tuytelaars, F. J. Acevedo-Rodríguez, and S. Maldonado-Bascón, "Towards a more discriminative and semantic visual vocabulary," *Computer Vision and Image Understanding*, vol. 115, no. 3, pp. 415–425, 2011.

[79] S. H. Bae and B. H. Juang, "IPSILON: incremental parsing for semantic indexing of latent concepts," *IEEE Transactions on Image Processing*, vol. 19, no. 7, pp. 1933–1947, 2010.

[80] K. Kesorn and S. Poslad, "An enhanced bag-of-visual words vector space model to represent visual content in athletics images," *IEEE Transactions on Multimedia*, vol. 14, no. 1, pp. 211–222, 2012.

[81] P. Tirilly, V. Claveau, and P. Gros, "Language modeling for bag-of-visual words image categorization," in *Proceedings of the International Conference on Image and Video Retrieval (CIVR '08)*, pp. 249–258, July 2008.

[82] H. Cheng and R. Wang, "Semantic modeling of natural scenes based on contextual Bayesian networks," *Pattern Recognition*, vol. 43, no. 12, pp. 4042–4054, 2010.

[83] D. Larlus, J. Verbeek, and F. Jurie, "Category level object segmentation by combining bag-of-words models with dirichlet processes and random fields," *International Journal of Computer Vision*, vol. 88, no. 2, pp. 238–253, 2010.

[84] Y. Wang and G. Mori, "Human action recognition by semilatent topic models," *IEEE Transactions on Pattern Analysis and Machine Intelligence*, vol. 31, no. 10, pp. 1762–1774, 2009.

[85] B. Fasel, F. Monay, and D. Gatica-Perez, "Latent semantic analysis of facial action codes for automatic facial expression

recognition," in *Proceedings of the 6th ACM SIGMM International Workshop on Multimedia Information Retrieval (MIR '04)*, pp. 181–188, October 2004.

[86] J. Wang, Y. Li, Y. Zhang et al., "Bag-of-features based medical image retrieval via multiple assignment and visual words weighting," *IEEE Transactions on Medial Imaging*, vol. 30, no. 11, pp. 1996–2011, 2011.

[87] X. Li and A. Godil, "Investigating the bag-of-words method for 3D shape retrieval," *EURASIP Journal on Advances in Signal Processing*, vol. 2010, Article ID 108130, 2010.

[88] R. Toldo, U. Castellani, and A. Fusiello, "A bag of words approach for 3D object categorization," in *International Conference on Computer Vision/Computer Graphics Collaboration Techniques*, pp. 116–127, 2009.

[89] P. Ye and D. Doermann, "No-reference image quality assessment using visual codebooks," *IEEE Transactions on Image Processing*, vol. 21, no. 7, pp. 3129–3138, 2012.

[90] A. Farhadi, I. Endres, D. Hoiem, and D. Forsyth, "Describing objects by their attributes," in *Proceedings of the IEEE Computer Society Conference on Computer Vision and Pattern Recognition (CVPR '09)*, pp. 1778–1785, June 2009.

[91] E. B. Sudderth, A. Torralba, W. T. Freeman, and A. S. Willsky, "Describing visual scenes using transformed objects and parts," *International Journal of Computer Vision*, vol. 77, no. 1–3, pp. 291–330, 2008.

[92] J. Philbin, O. Chum, M. Isard, J. Sivic, and A. Zisserman, "Lost in quantization: improving particular object retrieval in large scale image databases," in *Proceedings of the 26th IEEE Conference on Computer Vision and Pattern Recognition (CVPR '08)*, pp. 1–8, June 2008.

[93] R. Lienhart and M. Slaney, "PLSA on large scale image databases," in *Proceedings of the IEEE International Conference on Acoustics, Speech and Signal Processing (ICASSP '07)*, pp. IV1217–IV1220, April 2007.

[94] S. Zhang, Q. Tian, G. Hua, Q. Huang, and S. Li, "Descriptive visual words and visual phrases for image applications," in *Proceedings of the 17th ACM International Conference on Multimedia (MM '09)*, pp. 75–84, October 2009.

[95] A. Torralba and A. A. Efros, "Unbiased look at dataset bias," in *Proceedings of the IEEE International Conference on Computer Vision and Pattern Recognition (CVPR '11)*, pp. 1521–1528, 2011.

[96] D. Liu, G. Hua, P. Viola, and T. Chen, "Integrated feature selection and higher-order spatial feature extraction for object categorization," in *Proceedings of the 26th IEEE Conference on Computer Vision and Pattern Recognition (CVPR '08)*, pp. 1–8, June 2008.

[97] N. M. Elfiky, F. S. Khan, J. van de Weijer, and J. Gonzalez, "Discriminative compact pyramids for object and scene recognition," *Pattern Recognition*, vol. 45, pp. 1627–1636, 2012.

[98] A. Bosch, A. Zisserman, and X. Muñoz, "Scene classification using a hybrid generative/discriminative approach," *IEEE Transactions on Pattern Analysis and Machine Intelligence*, vol. 30, no. 4, pp. 712–727, 2008.

[99] L. Shang and B. Xiao, "Discriminative features for image classification and retrieval," *Pattern Recognition Letters*, vol. 33, pp. 744–751, 2012.

[100] W. Tong, F. Li, R. Jin, and A. Jain, "Large-scale near-duplicate image retrieval by kernel density estimation," *International Journal of Multimedia Information Retrieval*, vol. 1, pp. 45–58, 2012.

[101] J. Shotton, M. Johnson, and R. Cipolla, "Semantic texton forests for image categorization and segmentation," in *Proceedings of the 26th IEEE Conference on Computer Vision and Pattern Recognition (CVPR '08)*, pp. 1–8, June 2008.

[102] S. Romberg, R. Lienhart, and E. Horster, "Multimodal image retrieval: fusing modalities with multilayer multimodal pLSA," *International Journal of Multimedia Information Retrieval*, vol. 1, no. 1, pp. 31–44, 2012.

[103] Y. J. Lee and K. Grauman, "Object-graphs for context-aware visual category discovery," *IEEE Transactions on Pattern Analysis and Machine Intelligence*, vol. 34, no. 2, pp. 346–358, 2012.

[104] J. Stottinger, A. Hanbury, N. Sebe, and T. Gevers, "Sparse color interest points for image retrieval and object categorization," *IEEE Transactions on Image Processing*, vol. 21, no. 5, pp. 2681–2692, 2012.

[105] G. Ding, J. Wang, and K. Qin, "A visual word weighting scheme based on emerging itemsets for video annotation," *Information Processing Letters*, vol. 110, no. 16, pp. 692–696, 2010.

[106] J. Qin and N. H. C. Yung, "Scene categorization via contextual visual words," *Pattern Recognition*, vol. 43, no. 5, pp. 1874–1888, 2010.

[107] P. Tirilly, V. Claveau, and P. Gros, "Distances and weighting schemes for bag of visual words image retrieval," in *Proceedings of the ACM SIGMM International Conference on Multimedia Information Retrieval (MIR '10)*, pp. 323–332, March 2010.

[108] Y. Xiang, X. Zhou, T. S. Chua, and C. W. Ngo, "A revisit of generative model for automatic image annotation using markov random fields," in *Proceedings of the IEEE Computer Society Conference on Computer Vision and Pattern Recognition (CVPR '09)*, pp. 1153–1160, June 2009.

[109] M. Marszalek and C. Schmid, "Constructing category hierarchies for visual recognition," in *European Conference on Computer Vision*, pp. 479–491, 2008.

[110] K. E. A. Van De Sande, T. Gevers, and C. G. M. Snoek, "A comparison of color features for visual concept classification," in *Proceedings of the International Conference on Image and Video Retrieval (CIVR '08)*, pp. 141–150, July 2008.

[111] L. J. Li and L. Fei-Fei, "What, where and who? Classifying events by scene and object recognition," in *Proceedings of the IEEE 11th International Conference on Computer Vision (ICCV '07)*, pp. 1–8, October 2007.

[112] Y. Junsong, W. Ying, and Y. Ming, "Discovery of collocation patterns: from visual words to visual phrases," in *Proceedings of the IEEE Computer Society Conference on Computer Vision and Pattern Recognition (CVPR '07)*, pp. 1–8, June 2007.

[113] F. Perronnin, C. Dance, G. Csurka, and M. Bressan, "Adapted vocabularies for generic visual categorization," in *European Conference on Computer Vision*, pp. 464–475, 2006.

[114] H. Bay, A. Ess, T. Tuytelaars, and L. Van Gool, "Speeded-Up Robust Features (SURF)," *Computer Vision and Image Understanding*, vol. 110, no. 3, pp. 346–359, 2008.

[115] H. Lee, G. Shim, Y. B. Kim, J. Park, and J. Kim, "A search ant and labor ant algorithm for clustering data," in *International Conference on Ant Colony Optimization and Swarm Intelligence*, pp. 500–501, 2006.

[116] J. Shi and J. Malik, "Normalized cuts and image segmentation," *IEEE Transactions on Pattern Analysis and Machine Intelligence*, vol. 22, no. 8, pp. 888–905, 2000.

[117] D. Comaniciu and P. Meer, "Mean shift: a robust approach toward feature space analysis," *IEEE Transactions on Pattern Analysis and Machine Intelligence*, vol. 24, no. 5, pp. 603–619, 2002.

[118] P. Duygulu, K. Barnard, J. F. G. de Freitas, and D. A. Forsyth, "Object recognition as machine translation: learning a lexicon for a fixed image vocabulary," in *European Conference on Computer Vision*, pp. 97–112, 2002.

[119] M. Stark and B. Schiele, "How good are local features for classes of geometric objects," in *Proceedings of the IEEE 11th International Conference on Computer Vision (ICCV '07)*, pp. 1–8, October 2007.

[120] S. K. Divvala, D. Hoiem, J. H. Hays, A. A. Efros, and M. Hebert, "An empirical study of context in object detection," in *Proceedings of the IEEE Computer Society Conference on Computer Vision and Pattern Recognition (CVPR '09)*, pp. 1271–1278, June 2009.

[121] D. Nister and H. Stewenius, "Scalable recognition with vocabulary tree," in *IEEE International Conference on Computer Vision and Pattern Recognition (CVPR '06)*, pp. 1470–1477, 2006.

[122] J. Vogel and B. Schiele, "Semantic modeling of natural scenes for content-based image retrieval," *International Journal of Computer Vision*, vol. 72, no. 2, pp. 133–157, 2007.

[123] M. R. Boutell, J. Luo, and C. M. Brown, "Scene parsing using region-based generative models," *IEEE Transactions on Multimedia*, vol. 9, no. 1, pp. 136–146, 2007.

[124] J. Jeon, V. Lavrenko, and R. Manmatha, "Automatic image annotation and retrieval using cross-media relevance models," in *ACM SIGIR Conference on Research and Development in Information Retrieval*, pp. 119–126, 2003.

[125] V. Lavrenko, R. Manmatha, and J. Jeon, "A model for learning the semantics of pictures," in *International Conference on Neural Information Processing Systems*, pp. 553–560, 2003.

[126] F. Monay and D. Gatica-Perez, "Modeling semantic aspects for cross-media image indexing," *IEEE Transactions on Pattern Analysis and Machine Intelligence*, vol. 29, no. 10, pp. 1802–1817, 2007.

[127] C. Siagian and L. Itti, "Gist: a mobile robotics application of context-based vision in outdoor environment," in *IEEE International Conference on Computer Vision and Pattern Recognition (CVPR '05)*, pp. 1063–1069, 2005.

[128] C. Siagian and L. Itti, "Rapid biologically-inspired scene classification using features shared with visual attention," *IEEE Transactions on Pattern Analysis and Machine Intelligence*, vol. 29, no. 2, pp. 300–312, 2007.

[129] A. Bar-Hillel, T. Hertz, N. Shental, and D. Weinshall, "Learning distance functions using equivalence relations," in *Proceedings of the 20th International Conference on Machine Learning*, pp. 11–18, August 2003.

[130] J. V. Davis, B. Kulis, P. Jain, S. Sra, and I. S. Dhillon, "Information-theoretic metric learning," in *Proceedings of the 24th International Conference on Machine Learning (ICML '07)*, pp. 209–216, June 2007.

[131] J. Goldberger, S. Roweis, G. Hinton, and R. Salakhutdinov, "Neighborhood component analysis," in *International Conference on Neural Information Processing Systems*, pp. 513–520, 2004.

[132] K. Weinberger, J. Blitzer, and L. Saul, "Distance metric learning for large margin nearest neighbor classification," in *International Conference on Neural Information Processing Systems*, pp. 1473–1480, 2006.

[133] J. Yang, Y. G. Jiang, A. G. Hauptmann, and C. W. Ngo, "Evaluating bag-of-visual-words representations in scene classification," in *Proceedings of the 9th ACM SIG Multimedia International Workshop on Multimedia Information Retrieval (MIR '07)*, pp. 197–206, September 2007.

[134] S. L. Feng, R. Manmatha, and V. Lavrenko, "Multiple Bernoulli relevance models for image and video annotation," in *Proceedings of the IEEE Computer Society Conference on Computer Vision and Pattern Recognition (CVPR '04)*, pp. 1002–1009, July 2004.

[135] S. Savarese, J. Winn, and A. Criminisi, "Discriminative object class models of appearance and shape by correlatons," in *Proceedings of the IEEE Computer Society Conference on Computer Vision and Pattern Recognition (CVPR '06)*, pp. 2033–2040, June 2006.

[136] J. Liu and M. Shah, "Scene modeling using co-clustering," in *Proceedings of the IEEE 11th International Conference on Computer Vision (ICCV '07)*, pp. 1–8, October 2007.

[137] A. Vailaya, M. A. T. Figueiredo, A. K. Jain, and H. J. Zhang, "Image classification for content-based indexing," *IEEE Transactions on Image Processing*, vol. 10, no. 1, pp. 117–130, 2001.

[138] J. Zhang, M. Marszalek, S. Lazebnik, and C. Schmid, "Local features and kernels for classification of texture and object categories: an in-depth study," Tech. Rep. RR-5737, INRIA Rhône-Alpes, 2005.

[139] A. Opelt, M. Fussenegger, A. Pinz, and P. Auer, "Weak hypotheses and boosting for generic object detection and recognition," in *European Conference on Computer Vision*, pp. 71–84, 2004.

[140] J. Farquhar, S. Szedmak, H. Meng, and J. Shawe-Taylor, "Improving "bag-of-keypoints" image categorication," Tech. Rep., University of Southampton, 2005.

[141] T. Deselaers, D. Keysets, and H. Ney, "Classification error rate for quantitative evaluation of content-based image retrieval systems," in *Proceedings of the 17th International Conference on Pattern Recognition (ICPR '04)*, pp. 505–508, August 2004.

[142] F. Li, W. Tong, R. Jin, A. K. Jain, and J. E. Lee, "An efficient key point quantization algorithm for large scale image retrieval," in *Proceedings of the 1st ACM Workshop on Large-Scale Multimedia Retrieval and Mining (LS-MMRM '09)*, pp. 89–96, October 2009.

[143] A. K. Bhogal, N. Singla, and M. Kaur, "Comparison of algorithms for segmentation of complex scene images," *International Journal of Advanced Engineering Sciences and Technologies*, vol. 8, no. 2, pp. 306–310, 2011.

[144] H. Zhang, J. E. Fritts, and S. A. Goldman, "Image segmentation evaluation: a survey of unsupervised methods," *Computer Vision and Image Understanding*, vol. 110, no. 2, pp. 260–280, 2008.

[145] A. Perina, M. Cristani, U. Castellani, V. Murino, and N. Jojic, "Free energy score spaces: using generative information in discriminative classifiers," *IEEE Transactions on Pattern Analysis and Machine Intelligence*, vol. 34, no. 7, pp. 1249–1262, 2012.

Permissions

The contributors of this book come from diverse backgrounds, making this book a truly international effort. This book will bring forth new frontiers with its revolutionizing research information and detailed analysis of the nascent developments around the world.

We would like to thank all the contributing authors for lending their expertise to make the book truly unique. They have played a crucial role in the development of this book. Without their invaluable contributions this book wouldn't have been possible. They have made vital efforts to compile up to date information on the varied aspects of this subject to make this book a valuable addition to the collection of many professionals and students.

This book was conceptualized with the vision of imparting up-to-date information and advanced data in this field. To ensure the same, a matchless editorial board was set up. Every individual on the board went through rigorous rounds of assessment to prove their worth. After which they invested a large part of their time researching and compiling the most relevant data for our readers. Conferences and sessions were held from time to time between the editorial board and the contributing authors to present the data in the most comprehensible form. The editorial team has worked tirelessly to provide valuable and valid information to help people across the globe.

Every chapter published in this book has been scrutinized by our experts. Their significance has been extensively debated. The topics covered herein carry significant findings which will fuel the growth of the discipline. They may even be implemented as practical applications or may be referred to as a beginning point for another development. Chapters in this book were first published by Hindawi Publishing Corporation; hereby published with permission under the Creative Commons Attribution License or equivalent.

The editorial board has been involved in producing this book since its inception. They have spent rigorous hours researching and exploring the diverse topics which have resulted in the successful publishing of this book. They have passed on their knowledge of decades through this book. To expedite this challenging task, the publisher supported the team at every step. A small team of assistant editors was also appointed to further simplify the editing procedure and attain best results for the readers.

Our editorial team has been hand-picked from every corner of the world. Their multi-ethnicity adds dynamic inputs to the discussions which result in innovative outcomes. These outcomes are then further discussed with the researchers and contributors who give their valuable feedback and opinion regarding the same. The feedback is then collaborated with the researches and they are edited in a comprehensive manner to aid the understanding of the subject.

Apart from the editorial board, the designing team has also invested a significant amount of their time in understanding the subject and creating the most relevant covers. They scrutinized every image to scout for the most suitable representation of the subject and create an appropriate cover for the book.

The publishing team has been involved in this book since its early stages. They were actively engaged in every process, be it collecting the data, connecting with the contributors or procuring relevant information. The team has been an ardent support to the editorial, designing and production team. Their endless efforts to recruit the best for this project, has resulted in the accomplishment of this book. They are a veteran in the field of academics and their pool of knowledge is as vast as their experience in printing. Their expertise and guidance has proved useful at every step. Their uncompromising quality standards have made this book an exceptional effort. Their encouragement from time to time has been an inspiration for everyone.

The publisher and the editorial board hope that this book will prove to be a valuable piece of knowledge for researchers, students, practitioners and scholars across the globe.

List of Contributors

A. WiliNski, A. Bera, W. Nowicki and P. BBaszyNski
West Pomeranian University of Technology, Zołnierska 49, 71-210 Szczecin, Poland

Md. Rabiul Islam
Department of Computer Science & Engineering, Rajshahi University of Engineering & Technology, Rajshahi 6204, Bangladesh

Md. Abdus Sobhan
School of Engineering & Computer Science, Independent University, Dhaka 1229, Bangladesh

Hongxing Yao
Institute of System Engineering, Faculty of Science, Jiangsu University, 301 Xuefu, Zhenjiang 212013, China
College of Finance and Economics, Jiangsu University, 301 Xuefu, Zhenjiang 212013, China

Mary Opokua Ansong
Institute of System Engineering, Faculty of Science, Jiangsu University, 301 Xuefu, Zhenjiang 212013, China
Department of Computer Science, School of Applied Science, Kumasi Polytechnic, P.O. Box 854, Kumasi, Ghana

Jun Steed Huang
Computer Science and Technology, School of Computer Science & Telecommunication, Jiangsu University, 301 Xuefu, Zhenjiang 212013, China

Binu Thomas
Department of BCA, Marian College, Kuttikkanam, Kerala, India

G. Raju
Department of Information Technology, Kannur University, Kannur, Kerala, India

Mobyen Uddin Ahmed, Hadi Banaee and Amy Loutfi
Center for Applied Autonomous Sensor Systems, Orebro University, 701 82 Orebro, Sweden

Kefaya Qaddoum, E. L. Hines and D. D. Iliescu
School of Engineering, University of Warwick, Coventry CV4 7AL, UK

Antti Evesti and Eila Ovaska
VTT Technical Research Centre of Finland, Kaitovayla 1, 90571Oulu, Finland

Joseph J. LaViola Jr.
Department of EECS, University of Central Florida, Orlando, FL 32816, USA

K. Latha
Department of Instrumentation Engineering, Anna University, M.I.T Campus, Chennai 600 044, India

V. Rajinikanth and P. M. Surekha
Department of Electronics and Instrumentation Engineering, St. Joseph's College of Engineering, Chennai 600 119, India

Johannes Svante Spurkeland, Andreas Schmidt Jensen and Jørgen Villadsen
Algorithms, Logic and Graphs Section, Department of Applied Mathematics and Computer Science, Technical University of Denmark, Matematiktorvet, Building 303B, 2800 Kongens Lyngby, Denmark

Markus Schatten
University of Zagreb, Faculty of Organization and Informatics, Pavlinska 2, 42000 Varazdin, Croatia

Mostafa Ekhtiari
Department of Industrial Management, Management and Accounting, Shahid Beheshti University, Tehran, Iran

Shahab Poursafary
Department of Industrial Engineering, Mazandaran University of Science and Technology, Babol, Iran

Hiroshi Ogura, Hiromi Amano and Masato Kondo
Department of Information Science, Faculty of Arts and Sciences, Showa University, 4562 Kamiyoshida, Fujiyoshida City, Yamanashi 403-0005, Japan

Chih-Fong Tsai
Department of Information Management, National Central University, Jhongli 32001, Taiwan

Printed in the USA
CPSIA information can be obtained
at www.ICGtesting.com
JSHW051444221024
72173JS00006B/1579

9 781632 400086